CUTTING LOOSE

CUTTING LOOSE: Making the Transition From Employee to Entrepreneur

THOMAS A. EASTON
RALPH W. CONANT

PROBUS PUBLISHING COMPANY
Chicago, Illinois

© Thomas A. Easton and Ralph W. Conant, 1985

ALL RIGHTS RESERVED. No part of this publication may be reproduced, stored in a retrieval system, or transmitted, in any form or by any means, electronic, mechanical, photocopying, recording, or otherwise, without the prior written permission of the publisher and the copyright holder.

This publication is designed to provide accurate and authoritative information in regard to the subject matter covered. It is sold with the understanding that the publisher is not engaged in rendering legal, accounting or other professional service. If legal advice or other expert assistance is required, the services of a competent professional person should be sought.

FROM A DECLARATION OF PRINCIPLES JOINTLY ADOPTED BY A COMMITTEE OF THE AMERICAN BAR ASSOCIATION AND A COMMITTEE OF PUBLISHERS.

Library of Congress Cataloging-in-Publication Data

Easton, Thomas A.
　　Cutting loose.

　　Bibliography: p.
　　Includes index.
　　1. New business enterprises.　2. Entrepreneur.
I. Conant, Ralph Wendall, 1926–　　. II. Title.
HD62.5.E38 1985　　658.4'2　　85-17040
ISBN 0-917253-14-0

Library of Congress Catalog Card No. 85–17040

Printed in the United States of America

1　2　3　4　5　6　7　8　9　0

The literature of entrepreneurship answers a host of questions asked by would-be entrepreneurs:

—What are entrepreneurs?
—What sorts of people become entrepreneurs?
—How can you plan, set up, and run your own business?
—How can you find the money you need?

and so on. But the focus is always on *being* an entrepreneur. One issue the literature largely avoids is how people *become* entrepreneurs, and especially how they move from being employees to being entrepreneurs, as many do.

We resolved to do something to fill in this void. That is the purpose of this book. Our focus is on the transition from employee to entrepreneur, although we do pay some attention to the common questions. After a brief look at the role of entrepreneurs in society, we examine how they develop the wish to set up their own businesses, where they find their ideas, and how they plan and finance their ventures. We look at the ethical demands of cutting loose from employers, the problems of getting along with partners, investors, employees, friends, and family, and the setbacks and surprises that inevitably await the entrepreneur. We consider the growing pains that accompany the successful business, and finally, we discuss the hindsightful lessons entrepreneurs express when they say how they might have done things differently.

We have based this book on our own entrepreneurial experiences, on the available literature, and—most importantly—on interviews with a number of entrepreneurs. We conducted these interviews first by mail, sending the entrepreneurs the questionnaire reproduced in the Appendix; this had the advantage of allowing our subjects to respond at leisure and at whatever length they preferred, as well as to document their requests for anonymity (if any). When we wanted more detail than they provided, we followed up with telephone interviews; in a few cases we met face to face.

We did not try to seek a random sample of entrepreneurs. Instead, we recruited personal acquaintances and people mentioned in the various business magazines. Our aim was to collect material from established entrepreneurs and new-borns, from the wildly successful and the utter failures, from the large and the small. We wanted a broad range of cases to guide and support our thinking, and in this we believe we succeeded. In the process of researching and writing this book, we learned a great deal. We believe that what we learned is worth sharing with all those people who, though they are now employees, dream of becoming entrepreneurs. In these pages are the urges and plans, the pitfalls and successes, the curses and blessings, of many people who have cut loose, who have made the transition from employee to entrepreneur. We hope that their experiences will prove both illuminating and helpful.

For their help, we wish to thank J. W. Anderson, "Ralph Brown," Katie Crane, "Winston Cross," Larry Gleeson, Ellen Green, Patricia C. Heffernan, Judith Kaplan, Gregory I. Kravitt, Thomas Lisle, Ronald MacCrae, Howard Mordue, "John North," Mike and Carol Resnick, Sandra Sakurai, Ronald Slatin, Samuel J. Wallace, and William Wernsing.

Their comments have been invaluable, as has been the editorial assistance of J. Michael Jeffers. Infelicities, errors, and misunderstandings undoubtedly remain, but they are our own responsibility; we hope they are few.

We also wish to thank all readers of this book who feel moved to send us their own experiences. Use the copy of the questionnaire in Appendix I as your guide, and mail your accounts to the publisher, who will forward them to us for use in future projects, perhaps including a second edition of this book. Your comments on the book itself are welcome.

Thomas A. Easton
Ralph W. Conant

CONTENTS

Contents**xi**

CHAPTER 1

The Prometheus Factor: Entrepreneurs & Prosperity

According to myth, Prometheus and his brother Epimetheus were assigned by the gods the task of creating the human species and of giving humans and all other animals the abilities necessary for their survival. Prometheus molded humans from mud, giving them an upright stature so they could look to the stars.

His brother so freely handed out to the beasts claws, wings, speed, and cunning that when he got around to the humans he had none of these weapons of survival left to give them. Therefore Prometheus, with the aid of Minerva, the goddess of wisdom, lighted a torch from the chariot of the sun and brought humanity the gift of fire. This, according to Thomas Bulfinch's *The Age of Fable* (1942), made possible not only survival but the arts, science, technology, commerce, and with these prosperity.

Thus, Prometheus was the first entrepreneur. Breaking the bonds of his divine environment, he cut loose to create humanity and to nurture his creation. He built our kind. He gifted us with the means to prosperity as every entrepreneur since has done.

The Promethean myth speaks also of individuals who improve their personal tools or invent new crafts for their own use alone. It refers also to inventors, scientists, and artists, creators all. It refers most of all to those who tell the world about their creations and spread the fruits of their creativity.

Today the vanguard of entrepreneurs are those who build new

businesses on new products and new techniques and make those products widely available. However, many new businesses bring old products and techniques to new or ill-served markets—either way we can truly say that Prometheus is the predecessor of all entrepreneurs.

THE ENTREPRENEURIAL IMPACT

Not everyone wishes to be an entrepreneur, for not everyone has the dream of independence. Of those who have the dream, not everyone will ever fulfill it, for it takes courage to cut loose from the security of a job and run the risk of failure. But enough people do take the leap to account for much of the innovation that energizes the national economy. This effect is so strong that the literature on entrepreneurs credits the economic dominance of the Western world to the power of entrepreneurship. Kirzner (1979, 1983), for example, says that the entrepreneur is the reason why capitalism works. The entrepreneur brings together initiative, knowledge, materials, labor, and capital to produce goods and services from computers to garbage removal. The entrepreneur sees new markets for old products, new products for old markets, inefficiencies that can be corrected and exploited, more effective marketing methods, and so forth.

The entrepreneur's secret is his or her ability to spot the opportunity to make a buck. The end result is increased supply and variety of products, more jobs, more wages, more profit, more investment capital, and an expanding Gross National Product.

Virtually every business in the United States today was founded by an entrepreneur. These entrepreneurs were people who had an idea for a service or product. The entrepreneur is usually someone who has tired of working for others or is exasperated with the inefficiencies and inertia of an employer. The entrepreneur is one who has seen an opportunity and traded the security of a regular pay check and well-defined schedule for the satisfaction of setting up and running an independent operation.

That operation might be a workshop, a retail or wholesale business, a publishing house, an energy-related business, a consultancy, a manufacturing operation. Some entrepreneurs are service-oriented, writing and selling computer software or newsletters. Some are product-oriented, turning new technologies into novel devices. Some are writers, artists, craftspersons, and so on. In each group, some aim high, dreaming of the world of big business. Others want no more than to be independent and to earn enough money to support themselves and their families.

Entrepreneurs come from every walk of life. They come from business, academia, industry, government, and the professions. They come from every social class. The successful ones make it by hard work, perseverance, good judgment and timing, some luck, and talent. The successful ones create the personal wealth, the employment opportunities, and the consumer choices that mark the economies and political systems of the free-market nations of the world.

Unfortunately, many people do have a poor opinion of entrepreneurs. This has been true ever since the days of Adam Smith, famous for his "invisible hand" theory of economics. George Gilder (1984) quotes Smith as saying:

"In spite of their natural selfishness and rapacity, though they mean only their own conveniency, though the sole end which they propose from the labors of all the thousands they employ, be the ratification of their own vain and insatiable desires . . . they are led by an invisible hand . . . and without intending it, without knowing it, advance the interest of society."

Gilder considers the entrepreneur the main hero of our time, disagreeing strongly with those modern economists and politicians who see this individual only as someone to be exploited with punitive taxes and beaten down with laws intended to protect society from his "depredations." It is true that entrepreneurs are motivated by the prospect of personal gain, but that is neither sin nor crime. Profit-seeking entrepreneurs perform wonders for the economy, and the 1980s are seeing the birth of the Age of the Entrepreneur in the U.S. and abroad.

ENTREPRENEURS IN AMERICA

It is instructive to look at some statistics on American entrepreneurialism. The U.S. Department of Labor's Bureau of Labor Statistics (BLS) reports that in 1983 just over 600,000 new businesses incorporated. One-third are corporate fictions intended to facilitate mergers, or are short lived. Yet the total is still impressive compared with 186,000 in 1963 and 330,000 in 1973.

A useful measure of "real" new businesses, according to Russell (1984), is the Dunn & Bradstreet index of business starts. This index counts the number of new businesses on which banks, suppliers, and other potential creditors have made credit inquiries. The 1983 count was 100,868, up eleven percent from the previous year.

Over the years, such figures add up. The Internal Revenue Service tells us that in 1982, 3.1 million companies filed corporate income tax returns, 85 percent more than in 1970. The Small Business Administration reports that in 1982 there were 3.9 million businesses that employed fewer than twenty people, up 31 percent from 1976.

Those small businesses were established by individual entrepreneurs, and they account for many of the nation's entrepreneurs. The actual count of individual entrepreneurs is hard to know. Some entrepreneurs start more than one business and many people who otherwise fit within the entrepreneurial rubric, such as artists, writers, and craftsmen, never start formal businesses at all.

We may get a better count if we look at the total number of self-employed people in the country, a category that includes not only people who run their own businesses but also writers, artists, contract workers, and consultants. All these self-employed people resemble entrepreneurs in their craving for independence. The IRS counted them at 9.6 million in 1981 (not including persons in agriculture), up 7 percent from 1980 and 66 percent from 1970. The BLS says there were 7.58 million self-employed in 1983; the discrepancy seems to exist because the BLS does not count those who have incorporated their own businesses.

The number of self-employed—whichever figures we use—tells us that roughly a tenth of the American labor force share the entrepreneural spirit enough to seek actively their independence from an employer. Many more (who knows how many?) yearn for independence. Some lack the courage to cut loose from their employers. Some merely await their opportunity; they will cut loose when they find the right idea, the funds, or the partner they need.

How many entrepreneurs will make a success of the businesses they start? Most will fail and return to being employees. Some who fail the first time will try again as they are able to rebuild their funds and find renewed courage. A few will succeed at the first try, but how many?

Several studies that address this question have been summarized by Arnold C. Cooper (1982). In one study, the U.S. Department of Commerce looked at the performance of 6,294,000 firms of all kinds founded between 1947 and 1954. Twenty-three percent of these firms faded or sold out within six months. Another 23 percent died within a year. Only 29 percent survived intact past the 4.5 year mark.

A 1977 study of 250 new firms in and around Palo Alto, California, turned up less discouraging numbers. These firms were engaged in high-technology areas of business (such as electronics). Only five percent failed or sold out within the first three years. Twenty-four percent ceased operating within seven years. Another 29 percent ceased operations within ten years.

It seems that entrepreneurs who bet their shirts on technology— which often means new products for health, defense, communications, and information markets—have the best prospects for survival and success. But only about three percent of 1983's new firms were based in technology. The more numerous retail, service, and manufacturing startups face greater odds: one-third to one-half of all such firms do not survive their first five years. Precise figures are not well established, and Karl Vesper (1983) stresses that many published figures appear to overestimate the failure rate. Nevertheless, it is clear that the failure rate of new businesses is high.

It is fortunate for the nation that entrepreneurs are optimists. Vesper (1983) notes various studies that credit small businesses of less than 50 employees with providing three out of four new jobs. Peter Drucker (1984) tells us that between 1970 and 1980, small and new businesses provided most of the American economy's 20 million new jobs. Before 1970, three-quarters of all new jobs came from big business and government. By contrast, in the 1980's, Fortune 500 firms (the nation's largest) lost about three million jobs, while newer businesses (those under ten years old) created over 750,000 jobs and hired more than a million employees. Drucker adds that less than a third of all these jobs are in high-tech areas and that entrepreneurship is booming not only in the United States but in Europe as well.

According to Allen Kennedy (*Inc.*, 1984), the pattern of job creation will continue to emphasize small business and entrepreneurs. Kennedy was trained as a nuclear physicist at MIT, became a consultant with McKinsey & Co., and in 1982 set up as a software development entrepreneur. Also in 1982, he and Terrence Deal published the influential book *Corporate Cultures*. His background gives him a unique view of the business world, and his words seem well worth attending.

Kennedy cites the enormous growth in new business formations as evidence that Americans are more willing than ever to face and accept risks, and this willingness is one essential hallmark of the entrepreneur. This growth of the entrepreneurial attitude is fostered by the increase in personal income and two-earner families. In short, more people have the personal capital to invest in their own business. There is also a readier supply of venture capital from investors, although at the time of this writing venture money, as a whole, has become more selective about the new enterprise it chooses to invest in. Another stimulant to entrepreneurship is the availability of new tools that make efficient management and organization easy. Economical personal computers are a prime example of labor saving, business-organizing tools.

Kennedy notes that there are also changes afoot in the world of big business. Large companies such as Hewlett-Packard are recognizing that a way to maximize morale, motivation, productivity, and performance is to subdivide their operations into units of 50 to 100 employees, often directed by "internal entrepreneurs," to take advantage of their employees' entrepreneurial energies. Kennedy expects that many large companies will subdivide in the future, perhaps to the point where virtually all workers will have the opportunity to be entrepreneurs, independently or with larger organizations.

The trend is not an entirely new one. Moses Shapiro (1983) observes that companies have used franchises, spin-offs, and new ventures at least since the 1950s to create semi-autonomous organizations. Some of the big corporations have used the "profit center" concept to put entrepreneurs to work within their own structures and "Big Business Small Investment Companies" to provide venture capital in encouraging entrepreneurs. He also notes that such sources of funds are not usually available to new businesses until after the start-up phase proves their viability.

Thus, as always, individual entrepreneurs must initially depend on their own resources and those of friends and relatives. Frequently, only after they have demonstrated the success of their projects do venture capitalists and other outside sources of funds come into the picture.

Demonstrating success means proving that the new technology works, that the market they are targeting wants their product, and that they have the staying power and management skill to make their enterprise into a profitable concern. Enough entrepreneurs succeed to account for the statistics and make the 1980s truly the Age of the Entrepreneur.

THE ENTREPRENEURIAL NATURE

Alan Kennedy predicts that a time will come when everyone or nearly everyone can be an entrepreneur. It may be that the world will benefit from a vast increase in the number of independent, creative, problem-solving business people. It may be that technology will continue to encourage the fragmentation of big businesses. It may be that start-up capital, management expertise, and business opportunities will be available in ample quantities, and that there will be few obstacles to entrepreneurship.

But not everyone wants to be or is qualified to be an entrepreneur. Most businesses are founded by former employees, but by no means are all employees inclined to start up their own businesses. Shapiro (1983) makes the point that entrepreneurs do not make good employees. They are typically dissatisfied with routine, frustrated by the constraints of supervision, frustrated by management's unwillingness to listen to their innovative ideas, and frustrated by the lack of freedom to be creative on their own terms. Venture capitalist A. David Silver (1982) quotes Burt McMurtry, a high-tech start-up investment specialist, as saying that one entrepreneur's former boss complained that while he liked what he accomplished on the job, he nearly drove the boss crazy, would not take no for an answer, and had no grasp of corporate politics.

Most employees fit into the corporate structure much more easily than the latent entrepreneur. Most employees work well as members of teams, accept supervision and constraints, and value the regularity and security of working for others. Entrepreneurs often *have* to work on teams, but they prefer to play leading roles. Deaver Brown (1980) says that all of the entrepreneurs he has known are natural leaders. Shapiro (1983) credits entrepreneurs with "a unique vision of the future and a driving persistence to achieve that vision." The vision precludes the "accomodation and compromise of large social systems." Indeed, Shapiro continues, "The entrepreneur is not daunted by the fact that no one else agrees with him . . . he seems to thrive on demonstrating that he is right and 'they' are all wrong." Such features, Shapiro notes, are what make it difficult to encourage and use the entrepreneurial attitude within their own structures, although a few large companies seem to have managed the trick. Entrepreneurs who lack the initiative or opportunity to leave their employers often turn to office politics and empire building—marking off their territory within the company—often to the detriment of the company.

Successful entrepreneurs are decisive, self-motivated people who tolerate, and even thrive on, risk and uncertainty. They maintain personal control of all aspects of their operations. They are "generalists" who do not often seek the help of employees or consultants. Not seeking help and advice is why the failure rate among entrepreneurial personalities is so high.

Shapiro (1983) believes that most entrepreneurs seek power and status, although some studies have concluded otherwise. Collins and Moore (1970), in a Michigan State University study of 150 successful light-manufacturing entrepreneurs, suggest that instead of seeking power, entrepreneurs are expressing a fundamental need to escape the authority of others. They saw the male entrepreneur as having unresolved fears of his father which make him uncomfortable working under any authority figures or within any organization that belongs to someone else. Jobs do not last long. Eventually, the entrepreneurial personality sets up his own business as a symbolic solution to his Oedipal problem, making the business the equivalent of his mother that enables him to prove his masculinity. Yet he grows increasingly anxious as his business succeeds. He must (subconsciously) cause his own failure. He can then repeat his success by starting a new business or by bringing the first one back from the brink.

Collins and Moore called this entrepreneurial career pattern (which they insisted is typical) a ride on a roller coaster. In fact, many entrepreneurs do fail at least once before they succeed. An alternative explanation preferred by business consultants is that the entrepreneurial personality thrives on risk and uncertainty and thereby avoids the safer path of experienced advice. He or she is almost always going to fail once or twice (or several times) before acquiring the personal knowledge, skills, and experience that bring success. In short, some people have to learn the hard way.

Theories of entrepreneurial behavior are valuable only insofar as they encourage further probing by researchers into actual cases that reveal patterns of failure as well as success. We do well to bear in mind that cases of failure are at least as instructive as cases of success.

THE MOMENT OF TRANSITION

Whatever their motivations, there comes a time when aspiring entrepreneurs cease dreaming and actually become entrepreneurs. This is the moment of transition. This is the day when you cut loose. You are on your own. You are your own boss. You are free of the demands of your employer. You are independent at last! The dream becomes reality. *This moment and its aftermath are the topic of this book.*

Various surveys have reported that undergraduate and MBA students overwhelmingly say that they hope one day to run their own businesses. Most have little idea of the realities involved, but they know they want a crack at the satisfactions and rewards of making it on their own. Most will remain employees all their lives. In the past, very few have actually tried to make it on their own, and even fewer have succeeded as entrepreneurs.

Despite past trends to the contrary, more and more people with the inclination to be entrepreneurs are taking the leap. The "very few" are becoming the "many" and in the rapidly changing conditions of the American economy, the "many" may become "most." The increasing availability of capital and technology is giving strong encouragement to energetic, imaginative people to "go for it." Current national leadership is in no small way cheering on the entrepreneur.

There is help for those who want to become entrepreneurs. There are seminars and workshops, some run by the Small Business Administration and others run by for-profit entrepreneurs. There are courses in entrepreneurial behavior in some business schools around the country. There is talk of adapting European government programs to encourage American entrepreneurialism (Friedman, 1984). Programs that allow the unemployed to use their unemployment or other benefits to set up small businesses have led directly to some 63,000 new businesses in Great Britain and France, and similar programs might work here. In the U.S., using welfare benefits for business investment is illegal!

However, such aids may not be of much help to people who lack experience in management. Silver (1982) emphasizes that the successful entrepreneur must know how to choose key people and keep the company on the track laid down by the business plan. (No entrepreneur should begin operations without a carefully drawn business plan; indeed no competent venture capitalist will consider an investment that lacks one. More on the business plan later in this book.)

Many studies confirm that successful entrepreneurs have had previous successful experience in business. Some go out on their own when they feel their careers have reached a plateau or the satisfaction of advancement in the company has evaporated. This is the point, says Levinson (1983) when many executives look for second careers. They may shift from one business or industry to another. They may become professors or consultants or a combination of both. They may go back to school to study law or medicine or theology. They may become artists. Or they may cut loose and start their own companies.

Levinson cautions that no experienced executive should make so drastic a change without a thorough evaluation of what he or she wants from life. An evaluation means careful consideration of personal, family, and cultural values of the experiences that yield the most satisfaction, pleasure, pride, and fulfillment of personal ideals. Levinson also warns that whether the decision to build a second career is wise or not, the executive can expect a year (or two) of depression—feelings of loss, ambivalence, and fear of failure. Self-esteem in this period may be very much at stake. It is no easy time.

Through it all, a successful change, however drastic, can be invigorating and of lasting value. You might even make it as big as Ray Kroch, who founded the MacDonalds franchises at the age of fifty after a relatively undistinguished career in sales.

Levinson notes that one reason for a career shift may be that as the executive ages, he or she may begin to find the pace of the job exhausting. The pace of the entrepreneur may be even faster, but the satisfactions of personal creativity may make the pace enjoyable. This is to say that age may not be the real cause of personal and professional weariness. Boredom and frustration may be the enemy that takes years off the productive life of a talented person.

Boredom and frustration are what Collins and Moore sum up in the phrase "role deterioration," a condition that can develop so gradually over so many years as to go unnoticed and unheeded. The victims tend to blame themselves or to wait out retirement, thus wasting years of unused productive talent and energy. The entrepreneurial types among these victims experience acute frustration to the point of desperation. They grow too frustrated with the conditions of their professional lives to continue in the old patterns. They make the tough, sometimes traumatic decision to cut loose. The precipitating events may be any one or some combination of the following:

—*Blocked mobility* occurs when a promotion or raise fails to come through despite full devotion to an employer's interests and despite excellent performance. Many persons in this situation respond with resignation, sticking with a dead-end job until retirement. Some look for a new job. Those who are cast in the entrepreneurial mold take more decisive steps: they quit to start their own businesses, where their pay and rank will depend solely on their own efforts.

—*Losing out.* Some people achieve high position in a company, only to see the owners or backers sell out to a larger company that brings in its own management. Or the owner might jump a family member into the presidency. Or partners might pressure one member into surrendering power. Again, entrepreneurial types are likely to answer by creating new roles that put them in charge of their destinies. They set up their own companies.

—*Doubt and disgust* can be stimuli to entrepreneurialism. Some people become entrepreneurs when they become convinced that their employers do not know how to do things right or pay too little attention to the demands of the business. Similarly, many writers pen their first novels when they come to feel that they can do a better job than the author of whatever book they have just pitched across the room.

—*Unemployment*. Some people react to the loss of a job or to the unavailability of a suitable one by inventing one for themselves. Many men returned from World War II to find jobs scarce; those offered jobs often found that they did not match their career expectations or life goals. Often, their response was to start their own business, and the years after the war saw a great many business start-ups.

—*Lack of appreciation*. Collins and Moore cite case histories of several men whose employers rejected or stole their ideas or failed to credit their contribution to the business. To get their due, they too turned entrepreneur.

Collins and Moore, and the colleagues who helped their study, collected their data twenty years ago. The 100 businesses they studied were all founded between 1945 and 1958. Their results have proved to be sound and of value today.

However, it is now the 1980s, the Age of the Entrepreneur. New businesses are being formed at a fast pace, faster than ever before in our history. And the pace is increasing. New entrepreneurs are on the average in their mid-thirties (Russell, 1984). Do the same precipitating factors drive them to become entrepreneurs? Accounts of entrepreneurs in the various business magazines suggest that to some extent the drives are the same. The craving for independence is the classic motive. But additional ones have also come into play. They are wealth and self-realization. Some veteran observers will say that these "new" factors are really not new at all but only more pronounced or more talked about among the latest generation of Promethians.

In part, the current emphasis on wealth and self-realization may stem from the rapid social change of the past quarter century. The revolutions of the 1960s produced the "Me" generation of the 1970s, a generation that is maturing and focussing on the practicalities of making a living. This generation is a remarkably self-oriented one, reenforced by the widely popularized humanistic psychologies that stress self-development and the practical expression of creativity.

This generation is finding expression in goals of economic afflu-ence and in the parallel and supportive goal of governmental conservatism. If their leader could not be a Gary Hart (who looked and talked like one of them) then they would settle for Ronald Reagan who had brought in the era of prosperity that made possible their personal aspirations. Not all of the so called "Yuppies" are entrepreneurs, but most young entrepreneurs are indeed Yuppies. Success is their goal and increasing numbers of them are finding that success in entrepreneurial activities.

The goal of the questionaire survey on which this book is largely based is in part to learn more about the factors that in today's world propel people into entrepreneurial activities. Most of our respondents and their businesses are a whole generation younger than those studied by Collins and Moore, and we are interested in their experiences and motives in making the transition from employee to entrepreneur. We are also interested in the problems they encountered during and after their transitions.

ENCOURAGING ENTREPRENEURIALISM

Entrepreneurs are valuable assets to any society. They enhance productivity, innovation, and growth in personal and national wealth. It is they who solve pressing problems, small and large, and move a society into the future. Entrepreneurs provide jobs for growing populations and for those who are displaced by technological change.

Vesper (1983) has analyzed the ways in which new businesses appear. He notes, as others have, the many positive and negative factors that impel entrepreneurs to strike out on their own. Once impelled, entrepreneurs face a number of obstacles, including the difficulties of obtaining licenses and protecting patents, dealing with legal constraints and regulations, and possibly facing the negative attitudes that some people hold toward entrepreneurs.

Other obstacles can be the lack of a viable business concept, market knowledge, essential technical skills (including business know-how), and capital. The aspiring entrepreneur who holds a high-paying job and generous perquisites and benefits may be the prisoner held by golden handcuffs. Time pressures and other distractions may leave little time for planning a new enterprise.

Each of these barriers is surmountable—with some help. Vesper lists what he calls "environmental helps": successful role models, educational courses and seminars, books and articles on how to be an entrepreneur, experienced advisors, sources of seed capital, suppliers who extend credit and technical advice, competent manpower, and market contacts.

One especially valuable help is the local incubator company. These are companies that hire capable, ambitious people, experience periodic crises, have relatively few employees, and encourage the entrepreneurial attitude. Some are organized according to products rather than functions. Some are not companies at all, but universities such as MIT and Texas A&M. The end result is a continual series of employee departures to generate new firms. One example of an incubator company is Fairchild Semiconductor, founded in 1957. Its offspring have amounted to at least 35 new companies.

Another kind of incubator is the venture capital outfit that actively trains the entrepreneurs it funds. The venture capital firm of Kleiner, Perkins and Company once brought James Treybig into its office and exposed him for a year to entrepreneurs' business plans. When he had learned enough about how to launch a new enterprise, he set up the Tandem Computer Corporation.

Catalyst Technologies was set up by Nolan Bushnell from the wealth he acquired from Atari, which he also founded. Catalyst offers space, secretarial, legal, and financial services, and entrepreneurial advice to several high-tech start-ups at a time (Mamis, 1983). As soon as each entrepreneur has his or her product developed and selling, he leaves the Catalyst nest to make room for another. Catalyst's firstborn is Androbot, a maker of domestic robots, although it—and some of Bushnell's related enterprises—are facing some serious difficulties (Coll, 1984).

Institutions such as Catalyst Technologies can provide many of Vesper's "environmental helps" in an extremely nurturing environment. Yet such institutions are rare. They are in fact so rare that Vesper (1983) ignores them completely when he assembles recommendations for how the federal government might encourage entrepreneurs to set up new businesses and thereby aid national innovation, productivity, and employment.

CONCLUSION

It is this book's purpose to examine the transitions entrepreneurs have made from being employees to being their own people, from dependence to independence. We are not seeking the entrepreneurial personality. Nor are we seeking explicitly a list of barriers to entrepreneurship and of ways to overcome those barriers. Yet inevitably, an entrepreneurial personality will emerge as we look at the problems which entrepreneurs have faced and overcome—or to which they have succumbed. We will also see numerous ways in which entrepreneurs have been blocked or hampered, and therefore as many ways in which the entrepreneurial transition could be aided by either government or private enterprise.

The most important function of this book will emerge from its distillation of the experiences of a broad variety of entrepreneurs. Because it synthesizes successes and failures in many areas, it will serve as a kind of role model for people who dream of becoming entrepreneurs. It will demonstrate that entrepreneurship is possible and that, while entrepreneurs face problems in plenty, those problems can be surmounted.

PART I

Cutting Loose

Some entrepreneurs are entrepreneurs from the very starts of their careers. They graduate from high school or college or graduate school and immediately set up their own businesses. They may do so on a very small scale, opening a local bookstore, gift shop, or the like. They may start with something more ambitious, perhaps manufacturing and selling some invention of their own, or a family craft item, perhaps buying a fast-food franchise, perhaps even taking over an existing business. They may find the money they need in family wealth, or they may be able to promote it from others. Whatever, they are never employees, and they never go through the "cutting loose" process that is the basic theme of this book.

Most entrepreneurs do cut loose. They spend years of their lives as employees, and eventually they decide to seek their personal independence and freedom as entrepreneurs. In the next five chapters, we discuss how they do this. What makes them decide that entrepreneurship is an attractive option? Where do they get the ideas for their businesses? How do they—and how should they—plan their enterprises? Where do they find the money they need? And finally, how do they set up their businesses in an honorable, ethical way?

The answers to these questions are varied, and they do not always agree with the conventional wisdom offered by business advisors in books and magazine articles. Each entrepreneur finds his or her own path to success. Along the way, many learn the value of the conventional wisdom. However, many also learn that the conventional wisdom is by no means the only way to make a business work.

CHAPTER 2

The Entrepreneurial Itch

Throughout this book, we will use the experiences of entrepreneurs (the respondents to our questionaire) to link theory with practice. We draw upon the literature of entrepreneurship to summarize what business advisors, scholars, journalists, and entrepreneurs have had to say about business planning, sources of capital, ethical problems, and on-the-job and personal problems. We then interweave these lessons from the literature with the insights and experiences of our respondents. The result is a practical guide for readers who are tempted to cut loose from a job—or from job seeking—to take the plunge as an entrepreneur in an independent business.

That temptation—the itch to become an entrepreneur—is what defines the readers of this book. Cutting loose is an aspect of entrepreneurialism about which very little is known—except by those who have tried it.

Constructing a consistent theory as to why some people are driven to leave one company to start or purchase one of their own would, inevitably, take us beyond the scope and intentions of this book. Individual motivations for making the break, needless to say, vary widely.

This has not, however, kept researchers from trying to construct theories of entrepreneurial motivations. Looking back at the 1960s, Collins and Moore (1970) believed that "role deterioration" was the driving force behind the entrepreneur.

Role deterioration, as we noted in Chapter 1, means anything that interferes with a business person's perceptions of what he or she is or can be as an employee. An expected raise or promotion can fail to materialize. Changes in company ownership or management can erase prospects or positions. Doubts about a superior's competence or ethics can cause a desire for change. Loss of a job or persistent unemployment can force independence.

Any of these deterioration factors can bring on feelings of frustration, boredom, and despair. Many people respond by "toughing it out," resigning themselves to years of unhappiness until retirement. Others respond more actively by getting out and creating their own businesses. These are the entrepreneurs.

Not all entrepreneurs find their destiny from unhappy beginnings. Some are impelled by dreams of wealth and independence which they believe can only be had by founding a business. Others seek the freedom to develop their talents to the utmost, as only entrepreneurs can, or to pursue their own destinies without the restraints of an employer's plans, practices, policies, and politics. Occasionally an entrepreneur is nudged into the calling by a parent or friend who wants a partner or a successor.

If you do not find yourself among these sources for the entrepreneurial urge, does that mean that you should not try to be a entrepreneur? No. The list Collins and Moore offer also recognizes people who are literally brought up to be entrepreneurs because one or both of their parents were entrepreneurs. The entrepreneur who was raised by one probably assumes that being an entrepreneur is a natural way to make it in the world.

Some entrepreneurs seize upon the opportunities of the time. Roger Michaud is president of American Stabilis, Inc., of Lewiston, Maine (Ledoux, 1983). When he and a friend were law students at Georgetown University, the two of them designed an innovative heating device. More than a decade later, the company he founded to market the device now sells several dozen energy-conserving products. Why did Michaud give up the law to become an entrepreneur? Because, he says, he was turned on by the creative process of developing and finding a market for a product he had invented himself. Now he has developed other products in the same line and he is "having fun."

Jean Yates founded Yates Ventures to service users of the computer operating system Unix. For her, cutting loose was a chance to meet a need in the industry and to make some money. Her annual revenues were running at $4 million by the time she sold out. As we will see in Chapter 3, recognition of an opportunity is how many entrepreneurs hit upon the ideas for their businesses.

Still another source of entrepreneurial impetus is the wish to keep control of an idea one has developed. Witness the growing biotechnology industry. University researchers have developed the techniques of genetic engineering, cell fusion, hybridomas, and more, all holding potential for great impacts on medical and agricultural practice—and hence for enormous profits from products such as hormones and vaccines.

The excitement in this field began in the early 1970s, when molecular biologists first learned how to take functional genes from one living thing and plant them in others. At the time, they were talking of "recombining" the genes—the DNA—of distinct organisms. They soon realized that their "recombinant DNA" techniques—genetic engineering—promised the ability to give living things new or modified characteristics, or to correct faulty ones.

They saw the possibility of transplanting the gene for a scarce substance, such as human growth hormone (essential for treating dwarfism), from a human body into bacteria. The bacteria could then be grown in vast quantities and the hormone harvested in plenty. The result would be greatly increased supplies of essential drugs at prices more people could afford, and precisely this is already happening.

One of the molecular biologists who helped develop the techniques of genetic engineering is Herbert Boyer of Stanford University. In 1976, he and venture capitalist Robert Swanson put up $500 apiece to found Genentech, the first and still the leader of the genetic engineering companies. Boyer's motivation was surely in part the dream of wealth, but he could have obtained the wealth by licensing his ideas to other companies. He founded a genetic engineering company because he also wanted to be a creative participant in the field he had helped to pioneer.

There are similar stories in many other fields in recent years, especially in computer hardware and software, in electronics, and in mechanical engineering. A researcher or tinkerer comes to believe that he or she has a marketable product. Some readers of this book may be among them. You decide the time is approaching to set up your own company. Perhaps you have sounded out one or two companies in a preliminary effort to sell your product design. The reaction you have gotten is not encouraging, or you are bothered by a nagging feeling that you could make a fortune by going on your own with the product. So you decide to set up a new company—your company.

Why? Is it that you want to retain control of the product you have worked so hard at developing? Is it the dream of wealth that urges you on? It is the attraction of freedom and independence? Perhaps it is because no one seems to want your idea and you are certain of its potential. You just can't let it slip into oblivion.

For the person who has worked upon an idea and has become convinced of its value and marketability, the entrepreneurial route may seem the only viable way to go. There may be no role deterioration or job dissatisfaction involved. There may be no negative "push factors" involved. There may be only a felt urgency to carry a creative effort into the productive phase—and to reap profits from a good idea. Perhaps as much to the point is the American legend of the independent individual who seizes the opportunity to join the ranks of the nation's folk heroes.

There are other factors as well that create entrepreneurs. Among them is education. Some entrepreneurs find that only in founding a business do they use to full effect what they have learned in school and on the job.

Another factor is the desire to base one's living as totally as possible on one's own creative powers. This is the essence of the urge to be independent.

Luck can also play a role in the making of the entrepreneur, for some people fall into entrepreneurship when someone brings them an offer of an idea or funding they had not sought. Occasionally, an employer says, "We need a supplier. Here's the capital. Here's the contract. Want to do it?"

Most entrepreneurs are motivated not by one, but by several factors. By our examples throughout the book, we seek to illustrate not types of entrepreneurs so much as combinations of types. You will discover parts of yourself in most of the examples we offer. These examples are real people whom we have come to know through our explorations with them of their motivations and their problems, their successes as well as their failures. You will find in their motivations and experiences frustrations, hunger, idealism, ambition, logic, the elusive search for happiness and security. We can be certain that the ones among our respondents who cite only one or two reasons for their enterprise have others not mentioned, perhaps hidden even from themselves. Entrepreneurialism is like every other activity of human life—mixed and contradictory emotions, multiple motivations, and a complex and sometimes confused set of reasons are more likely than not to govern people's actions.

If you have reached the point of seriously considering going into business for yourself, one of the most valuable things you can do is to invest some time in sorting out your particular set of reasons and motives. Emotional stability and self-awareness could become your greatest assets and guarantees of success.

Let us now turn to the entrepreneurs who responded to our survey and hear from them why they became entrepreneurs. Their responses are illuminating, for they demonstrate our point that almost any reason can serve as a plausible excuse for cutting loose. We reserve one of our subjects (John North) for later, for his story needs to be told with a minimum of interruption.

CASE HISTORIES

Patricia C. Heffernan of Heffernan & Associates in Killington, Vermont, is the very model of a successful entrepreneur in that she thought through her business idea and plan before she took the plunge and made projected profits the first month and the first year of her new operation. Yet in fourteen years of professional work in industry and education, she had not given any serious consideration to becoming an entrepreneur until shortly before she actually made the decision. Unlike many entrepreneurs before they make the break, Pat said that she had loved her job and its predecessors. But she feared that, sooner or later, the challenges would be gone and she would become bored and boring.

By the time she began thinking about setting up her own business, she knew what she was good at. She also knew what she wanted out of going it alone: variety, challenge, continued mental growth, control, impact, independence, travel, and a decent financial return. She wanted to stay in Vermont too, and, she said, there were no positions of this kind for a woman in her part of the state. She felt she had to start her own business to get what she wanted in her work, and in 1982 she did just that.

Her expertise is in business efficiency. Hence, Heffernan & Associates offers management consulting services that help businesses to improve performance. The firm's services include manual and automated systems analysis, equipment (including computer) and software evaluation, business planning, interim project management, and personnel selection and training.

Samuel J. Wallace of Xodex Enterprises, Ltd., in Oakland, California, is an example of role deterioration leading to a decision to set up a new business. In the early 1970s, Wallace acquired an MBA in marketing and finance at Columbia University. During the next eight years, he worked as a brand manager for Procter and Gamble, Best Foods, and Clorox. He reports that evaluations of his performance by superiors consistently centered around "jumping the gun," being over-aggressive and "somewhat pushy." It became apparent to him that "sooner or later, corporate protocol would be my death knell."

Wallace had tasted independence during graduate school in handling direct sales for such firms as Amway. During his eight years as an employee of large corporations, he discovered that his "greatest excitement came from new products activity." In his words, "New product marketing came to be the grand idea." The grand idea was what impelled him to establish Xodex, a consulting firm that provided market research, advertising, and promotion.

Today, Samuel Wallace counts himself as one of the fortunate few who mustered the courage to cut loose from the frustrations of corporate niceties to sail his own boat on his own course by his own rules.

William (Bill) Wernsing of Williams Laboratories in Ithaca, New York, illustrates a different kind of role deterioration. After Wernsing obtained his electrical engineering degree from MIT, he spent ten years with General Electric in Ithaca, working as an electronic development project manager.

In 1963, GE announced the impending closing of the Ithaca plant. Wernsing, not wanting to move his family, decided "to cut the umbilical and start out on my own." He had no entrepreneurial experience, but he had long thought that it would be "kind of neat to have your own business and be your own boss." He adds, "If you have an idea (which I get lots of), [it is good] to be able to pursue it and not have somebody say, 'No, that's not within our business charter' or 'Yeah it's great, but we can't do it now' and so forth.''

Despite the secret dream to be on his own, Wernsing says that he was happy at GE. He says that he probably would have stayed on indefinitely if the company had not closed the plant. But GE did close the plant, and instead of making the move to another plant, Wernsing founded Williams Laboratories to market the products he would develop. Wernsing has also used the company as the base for his services as a consultant and contract engineer.

Judith Kaplan of Action Packets, Inc., in Ocala, Florida, started out in the business world as a stockbroker and insurance sales person. Then, she and her husband began to sell "first day covers" to stamp collectors. That business was slow in the summer and, to fill in, Kaplan started putting together packets of space-related stamps for planetarium gift shops.

Kaplan branched out when she discovered a demand for similar items in other gift shops. Now her firm, Action Packets, Inc., distributes more than 3000 items to museum, zoo, botanical, and planetarium gift shops, to NASA facilities, and even to aerospace companies. Her husband runs a separate company for stamps alone.

Why did Judith Kaplan become an entrepreneur? She was involved in the early days of the New York chapter of the National Organization for Women. At that time, she says, she was feeling strongly the lack of effective roles for women, especially in the business world. Eventually, she decided to become a business woman whom other women could emulate.

Today, Kaplan frequently speaks to civic and women's groups, offering herself as proof that ''women can do whatever they set out to do if they are persistent, hardworking, and driven to succeed.'' Kaplan reports that she also felt ''a strong urge to achieve and create . . . to leave something behind'' when she is done. Kaplan's success is measured by Action Packets' position as number 92 on *Inc*. magazine's 1983 list of America's 500 fastest growing private companies.

Gregory I. Kravitt of The North American Group, Ltd., in Chicago, Illinois, was an honors student in college and graduate school. He worked for a year for a public relations and advertising agency in an executive training program learning marketing analysis first hand, a kind of professional internship. Then he joined one of the nation's major banks in Chicago (Continental Illinois) and learned about loans, business valuation and development, and investment.

Ambitious to make it on his own, just five years out of graduate school, Kravitt teamed up with a partner to organize The North American Group, Ltd., and several specialized subsidiaries. The conglomerate provides a variety of venture capital, investment banking, mortgage banking, publishing, and real estate services.

The water was deep, but Kravitt knew he could swim. He was also possessed of a driving creative urge, a strong desire for the freedom to apply his own ideas and skills, and a need for a sense of "joy and fulfillment" in his work. He also wanted the financial rewards and security of a successful venture.

Kravitt said he liked his job at the bank, but grew tired of "being at the mercy of the decisions of a large corporation. He was sometimes frustrated at the lack of flexibility, and toward the end of his time with the bank he began to sense what he called "the peaking of my learning curve." He was ready for a serious challenge. His North American Group proved to be a formidable one, as we will see in later chapters.

Winston Cross of Cross Books in New York City is the pseudonym for one of our respondents who requested anonymity. Cross came to our attention in 1984 shortly after he cut loose from the large publishing firm in which he had been employed for several years. His aim was to set up a new publishing company to serve a carefully defined segment of the professional market. His books would be tailored to a specific consumer market and would deal with topics of high current interest.

Why did Cross want to take the plunge? The publishing business is known to offer high risk with little expectation of returns on investment in less than five years of start-up. Cross says he was dissatisfied with what he considered to be the "bureaucratic, sometimes illogical workings of a large corporation . . . decisions made for reasons unrelated to good business judgment." He declined to give specific examples, but said that the situation "became increasingly frustrating."

Cross also saw "a significant opportunity in the marketplace" for the type of books he wanted to publish: good quality professional books, "presented and marketed with care and ingenuity." He called such a product "a rare combination in the professional book marketplace.'' He told us that he had identified this opportunity while working for his corporate employer, but ''the dissatisfaction precipitated the break.'' In other words, he could have pursued his idea from within the corporation but preferred to try it on his own. Careful planning and persistence allowed him to make the break on a sound basis, and so far, less than two years later, he is doing well.

Mike Resnick, of Cincinnati, Ohio, is today a well-known science fiction writer. In the late 1960s and early 1970s, he was churning out sleazy paperbacks under pseudonyms and ghost-writing tabloids. He reports that he ''got fed up with turning out more than a million words a year of high-paying drivel.'' Despite the income his writing generated, he also felt at the mercy of a small number of publishers whose own futures were constantly in doubt. The kind of writing Resnick was doing never produced the long-term royalties well-established, serious authors can expect.

Resnick is now a serious writer, but getting there was a struggle. In the year after he broke with hack writing, he made $3800. He knew at that point that he had the choice of returning to his frustrating past or finding another source of income. For Resnick, after years of being his own boss, that new source of income would have to be from some entrepreneurial venture. ''Having been on my own for more than a decade, I had no desire to go back and work for someone else. So I cast around for some entrepreneurial way to make a buck.''

Resnick and Thomas Lisle, our next subject, deliberately minimized the prospects of failure. Both men took over failing businesses that they felt confident they could turn around. In Resnick's case, the business was the Briarwood Pet Motel, which Resnick and his wife Carol turned into ''one of the largest luxury cat and dog boarding and grooming establishments in the country.''

Why a pet motel? We save the answer to this question for Chapter 3. For the moment, we note only that the answer reveals much about why Resnick could see security rather than risk in an entrepreneurial venture—and in independence. This paradox is found to a greater or lesser degree in most entrepreneurs. An understanding of the paradox and its resolution is essential to understanding how entrepreneurs maximize their chances for success.

For Thomas Lisle, now of Oconto, Wisconsin, the entrepreneurial life was a natural outgrowth—perhaps a culmination—of his career. After thirteen years with the Eaton Corporation as a lawyer and mechanical engineer, Lisle was feeling that his career had hit a plateau. At Eaton, he was mainly an acquisitions specialist, manager, and planner. "Having completed what I call a full cycle of tasks," he reports, "I decided I was both knowledgeable and experienced sufficiently to make a reasonably sizable acquisition of my own. Having participated in several hundred million dollars' worth of acquisitions and divestitures, I was reasonably well-versed in acquisition analysis, both from an opportunity as well as a financial standpoint."

Lisle, an analytically minded person, insists that he became an entrepreneur because "it was the next logical step." He finds it difficult to explain why the step was logical for him. Actually, many executives reach a similar stage in their careers without concluding to strike out on their own.

Lisle did not establish a new company. Instead, he found a troubled firm that he was able to acquire in a leveraged buy-out deal (see Chapter 5). The enterprise, Cruisers, Inc., is now a successful manufacturer of pleasure boats.

J. W. Anderson of ShowAmerica in Elmhurst, Illinois, cut loose in 1969 from a 15 year career as a public relations executive. He had earned a degree in ornamental horticulture, tried his hand at operating his own small business, failed, and taken a sales job with the Johnson Wax Company. He managed the Johnson Wax Pavillion at the New York World's Fair in the mid-1960s. Later, he spent two years with Wilding Film Productions and two more as director of marketing services for Keebler Company.

During his last few years in corporate work, Anderson founded and operated the United States Festivals Association which put on an annual awards competition for the commercial film industry. By the time he left Keebler, he was earning $25,000 a year from the Festival Association and had the base upon which to go on his own.

Soon after leaving Keebler, he founded ShowAmerica, specializing in remotely controlled robots for display at trade shows, sales meetings, grand openings, and other events where attractions and crowd-pleasing entertainment were required. Anderson's robots were among the first used extensively for commercial display and advertising.

Anderson was a successful corporate executive who gave up a secure and lucrative income to become an entrepreneur. Why did he do it? He says he had never felt that he fit the "corporate mold." He had his own way of doing things, his own goals and objectives, and he did not work well within corporate constraints and policies. Eventually, he says, it became clear to him that the only way he could reach self-satisfaction in a career was to strike out on his own. "I am a highly creative individual, and I wasn't finding the creative opportunities I wanted in a structured and sometimes stifling corporate life."

Anderson was well prepared for the entrepreneurial step when he finally took it. IIc gavc up the corporate income but he had already built a good second income from the Festival. In addition he had thought through and carefully planned the ShowAmerica enterprise. Anderson was a risk-taker, but like so many successful entrepreneurs, he was a cautious risk-taker. He knew what he was doing and how to do it when he made his move.

On a Friday in 1982, Katie Crane left the bankrupt advertising agency where she had been employed for several years. On the following Monday, she started Crane Marketing Communications in White River Junction, Vermont. Before the failed agency, she had worked ten years for large corporations in public relations and communications. She had always had good relations with the people she worked for and with, and so "charging ahead" into her own business seemed to her to be exactly right for her to do.

Katie says that she had known for a long time that she was "an entrepreneurial type," and that what confirmed it for her was when she went to work for a small advertising company after six years with a large company. "I loved the environment of the small business and threw myself into the responsibilities as if I were part owner . . . So in the back of my mind, I had always had the urge to go out on my own."

The opportunity came for Katie unexpectedly. "I was literally cut loose from a company that was rapidly slipping into bankruptcy . . . I was vice president and the owner/boss and I made a deal . . . I would be the first laid off because I wanted an excuse to start up on my own anyway and someone had to go." She cleaned out her desk over the weekend and started on Monday with two writing assignments.

Would she have cut loose from the vice presidency of a succesful agency? It is hard for her to say for sure, but the urge had been there for a long time, and so she believes it was just a matter of time and the right circumstances.

Ellen Green of Allied Systems Design, Inc., in Bangor, Maine, made the break early in her career. After three and a half years in a public sector job in health education, she felt ready to establish herself as a private "health systems" consultant. By the time she incorporated as Allied Systems Design in 1982, she had two projects ready to offer clients. Now she designs packages and inserts for beauty and health care products, and she is developing a health newsletter for teenagers.

She was prompted to make the break by "creative urges" and because she felt she "had reached the limit on variety" in the public sector job. She had noted in the latter job "what materials were not out there" and that is when she began developing her first products, using her "networking skills."

Ellen's early months in her own firm were encouraging. "I never knew how well known I was before being on my own." Her reputation in the field made a big difference in attracting the first few contracts.

Sandy Sakurai's experience in cutting loose was like Katie Crane's. The counseling firm that employed her closed its Baltimore office and the event presented Sandy with the choice of moving or commuting to Washington, D.C., 50 miles away, or setting up a service of her own. For Sandy the only serious issues were the practical problems of choosing a location and attracting clients. Deciding to work out of her home, she found her first clients among past clients of the firm she had left who, like herself, could not commute to D.C.

Sandy had other choices. She could have looked for another counseling job in the Baltimore area. But, she reasoned, she had spent three years as a counselor in a large, international career counseling firm and had developed a style of her own and a feel for which type of clients she was most successful with. "I was convinced of the worth of the process and my ability to deliver the service with a unique style and effectiveness."

She also had reservations about how the company's program was sold to clients, the high "up-front" fee, and the small portion that went to the counselors. These reservations were "heightened by severe economic difficulties at the corporate level and my perception that the company had lost its soul."

In her decision to go on her own with her Career Counseling Service in Baltimore, Maryland, she asked herself several questions: "What gives me joy? How do I need to grow?" Her answers were that counseling was a source of joy. "Nothing is so thrilling as the 'finger-tip' communication that sometimes takes place in counseling.'' As to the question of personal growth, ''As a 50s woman and a shy person, I have always had an overriding concern for pleasing others . . . and always assuming that others knew better than I . . . at 49, I have come to trust myself and my intuition. . . . But to really make the break, I had to have no master, supervisor, leader. . . . The time had come. . . . The path was clear.''

Ronald MacCrae started RAM Inc. as an Atlanta, Georgia, computer consulting service in 1979 when he saw a need of users of computer equipment and software that was not being met. His training in computer science had assured him of a secure career in the industry, and for several years he worked for large corporations. But he soon discovered that he valued creativity above routine applications of his skill and knowledge, and he began to consider going into business for himself.

When the company for which he worked wanted to move him, he declined. That decision led to the incorporation of RAM Inc.

Ronald Slatin of Medimicro Systems, Inc., in Tucson, Arizona, is one of a host of entrepreneurs who maintains a full-time university position. In Slatin's case, he and several colleagues developed a computer software program to assist hospitals and diagnostic clinics to analyze and interpret tests on patients who suffer from pulmonary problems. His academic base is the pulmonary function laboratory of the University of Arizona's Health Service Center.

Slatin and his colleagues developed their pulmonary function interpretation program under the auspices of the laboratory, and with the permission of appropriate University authorities, they organized Medimicro Systems, Inc., to produce and market the program. They have assigned the actual marketing task to a Braintree, Massachusetts, firm which handles such products for hospitals.

Slatin does not yet think of himself as a full-fledged entrepreneur, since his company so far has developed only the one product. From our standpoint, he is an early-stage entrepreneur still hatching in the incubator of the University. His experience is valuable as an illustration of some of the common problems entrepreneurs must solve if their enterprise is to mature.

Ralph Brown of Integrity Products in Popham Falls, Maine, was enjoying life as a firetower watchman on Mt. Blue in rural Maine when his aging parents prevailed upon him to take over a small toy manufacturing business they had begun eight years before. Ralph was forty years old and "much plagued with back problems, knee problems, low wages, and winter joblessness." He agreed on condition that he move the business from a Boston suburb to his town in Maine and take on a partner experienced in machine maintenance. Moreover, he had worked with his parents in the business during one previous winter and both enjoyed some of the comforts of relative financial security and acquired a deep respect for the "truly beautiful, valid, useful, positive, unique, and stable playthings product—created, manufactured, and marketed with integrity. . . . From all this, and with very limited goals, I took courage and accepted the challenge. . . . From that moment on, moving the whole factory to an abandoned garage in Popham Falls, Maine—all in one 45' trailer truck—I dedicated heart and soul to entrepreneurship . . . the date—November 7, 1968." In the ensuing years, Ralph has built a $57,000 a year business into one that grosses over $3 million annually and is still growing. In 1984, Integrity Products moved into a modern new, custom-built factory building on land carved out of the woods near Ralph's rustic home.

Larry Gleeson is the entrepreneur behind Maine Hydro-Electric Development Corp., headquartered in Belfast, Maine. Ever since 1977, he has been setting up hydroelectric generating facilities at small dams in the Northeast. His office sits next to his first project, which generates about 100 kilowatts using a dam that once powered a small mill. He gains his revenues by selling power to the local utility, not by transmitting it to consumers or by acting as a consultant.

Before 1977, Larry was a "systems planning administrator" with Sun Oil in Philadelphia. He felt very fortunate, he says, in his position, for he had interesting assignments and got the credit and visibility he deserved. However, he did bridle a bit at having to do things someone else's way. He wanted "more than just a salary stake" in the results of his labors. He wanted to be able to "put extra time in for long-term benefit," and he wanted to pursue some of his own ideas.

Larry's urge to be an entrepreneur thus came from several of the wellsprings we have discussed—not role deterioration, but the wish for independence, the need for self-determination, the drive to own what he produced. His chance came when, with the energy crisis of the early 1970s, he saw an opportunity to cut loose, as we will see in Chapter 3.

Entrepreneurs are entrepreneurs for a host of reasons. They wish to set up their businesses because they desire freedom, wealth, creativity, and even status as a role model. They are pragmatic, eclectic, even idealistic. They are anything but predictable.

However, saying why entrepreneurs want to be entrepreneurs tells only a very small part of the story. No one *is* an entrepreneur simply because he or she wants to be one. Much, much more is necessary, and the first of many essentials is some idea of what the entrepreneur's personal enterprise will be. We therefore now turn to the subject of where our entrepreneurial subjects got the ideas for their businesses. Later we will address the details of how they turned their ideas into reality.

CHAPTER 3

Searching For Business Ideas

The generation of new and commercially viable ideas is not, for most entrepreneurs, a formal process of the type found in business creativity seminars. We will gain little insight into how ideas are born by assuming there is a systematic, or for that matter, mystical process through which the *great idea* is deduced or conjured.

Entrepreneurs find the ideas for their businesses in their daily experiences, in newspapers and magazines and books, in dreams. Entrepreneurs even borrow ideas from each other. Most entrepreneurs have more ideas than they can ever turn into profitable items or working businesses.

THE NOVELTY FACTOR

Do new businesses have to be based on new ideas? No, they do not have to be, and they usually are not. Of course, a new business must have some new feature, something that distinguishes it from competitors, something different that gives it an identity and a chance of success.

The new feature can be new management. Thomas Lisle took over Cruisers, Inc., and Mike and Carol Resnick took over the Briarwood Pet Motel. These two businesses remained essentially the same in the product and services they offered, but were successfully reconstituted as new businesses under new managers.

The new feature can be location or market area. Is someone selling hot tubs in California? Then try peddling them in New England. The location factor is the key to all the franchise operations in the country, from fast food to photo-copying to car dealers. It is what Tom Fatjo is now doing with fitness centers (Waters, 1984). It is what anyone can do with a business that appeals to large markets and works best operating from local centers.

The new feature can be a change in market targeting, going from local to national (or vice versa), moving from the youth market to the homeowners market, and so on. A new entrepreneur may choose to work with a different image (and hence an altered market). Consider how MacDonalds has upgraded the fast-food restaurant business from the greasy-spoon image to squeaky-clean, fast service in attractive surroundings. Consider Bonanza's "classier" decor and salad bars that attracted an "upscale" market that could pay higher prices for a cheap steak.

The new feature can be lower prices, better quality, faster shipping, or longer warranties. It can be as complex as a new product, as when Apple Computer offered the first desk-top personal computer and priced it within reach of a mass market. The Apple personal computer changed the image of an entire industry and inspired a horde of imitators.

The new feature can be a change in scale. Tom Fatjo showed how a change in scale works when he acquired scores of garbage disposal companies and forged them into Browning-Ferris Industries. The Justice Department also showed how this works when it forced the fragmentation of AT&T and created the conditions in which dozens of small communications companies could compete.

Further, a new business can try to fill a need that existing companies do not fully satisfy. That is precisely what Judith Kaplan and Action Packets did when they began to provide museum gift shops with a convenient source of souvenirs. It is what Samuel Wallace did when he began providing market research and related services in the Oakland, California, area. It is what our publisher respondent did when it moved to supply targeted books for a professional market.

The new feature of a new business is often linked to external conditions. The new feature is new by comparison to the products and markets of existing companies. In some cases, however, the newness of the product or service is less important to the entrepreneur than finding a new role, as did Bill Wernsing when General Electric closed the plant in which he worked.

WHERE DO THE NEW IDEAS COME FROM?

So far in this chapter, we have looked only at the various kinds of new business ideas. We will now consider where entrepreneurs find their ideas—new or adapted. The remaining pages of this chapter will be devoted to covering, one by one, the entrepreneurs (our respondents) who have told us where they found their ideas.

We will see two principal sources for business ideas. First, many entrepreneurs draw their ideas from the same source that gave them the urge to become entrepreneurs. Second, many more find their ideas in long-standing interests, in hobbies and other sidelines. Very few entrepreneurs dive headlong into a business in which no previous interest can be traced.

Patricia C. Heffernan of Heffernan & Associates, Killington, Vermont, zeroed in on her business idea "by process of elimination." She had always been a consultant, she says, even among her friends who relied on her to give them advice about everything from a new car purchase to choice vacation spots. At her job, she was "really an in-house consultant, a trouble shooter, and a problem solver." When any question or problem came up, her approach was to read up on it, get information, analyze it, and figure out the optimal solution. "I am a developer of solutions, a natural researcher."

Her idea was to offer for hire through an independent consulting firm what she was good at doing. Before she started her company, she lined up a year's worth of work and wrote her idea into a business plan.

Samuel J. Wallace of Xodex Enterprises, Ltd., Oakland, California, left corporate marketing because he could not tolerate corporate protocol when it interfered with his entrepreneurial ideas and instincts. His experience and training were in marketing and so were his natural talents. When he cut loose from his corporate job, his idea—his "grand idea," as he likes to call it—was to invest his professional identity and experience in a marketing-oriented consulting business. The firm he created was Xodex.

For Bill Wernsing of Williams Laboratories, Ithaca, New York, the idea for his business sprang from his reasons for becoming an entrepreneur. As an electrical engineer, he had managed development projects for General Electric until GE closed its Ithaca plant. In the aftermath of the closing, Wernsing had no great difficulty making the transition to independent inventor and developer of electrical devices. Thus, for Wernsing the problem was finding not a single business idea, but rather a string of product ideas to sustain a business.

Wernsing is fortunate in that he has always had plenty of ideas of his own, and other people bring ideas to him. When he first cut loose from GE, he wanted to develop a radio receiver built into a fireman's helmet for rapid, no-hands communications. He also wanted to develop a sonar device for pleasure craft. In both cases, he could see a need for the products, and as an entrepreneur he wished to meet those needs. The catch was that both ideas proved to require far too much development work for a one-man shop in 1964. This obstacle did not end his entrepreneurial efforts for the simple reason that NASA offered him a subcontract. Thus, for the first few years on his own, Wernsing designed and built rocket payloads for NASA and the Air Force. He also worked as a consultant to GE.

After several years, Wernsing was in a position to develop his own product ideas. One was an oil seal analyzer for the automotive industry. Another, the one that put him on easy street, was a device that turned an electric typewriter into a computer printer. He is now developing a device to check the quality of computer cables.

Judith Kaplan of Action Packets, Inc., Ocala, Florida, provides us with an example of a sideline that turned into a profitable business. Recall from Chapter 2 that Kaplan was still selling stocks and life insurance when she and her husband began selling stamps out of their basement. Their main item, first day covers, "were bought and sold by the one." To increase volume and fill in the slow summer season, the couple began to package space stamps for local planetariums. The business grew from that modest, unplanned beginning.

Gregory I. Kravitt's idea for The North American Group evolved from his work in loans and business development at the Illinois Continental Bank. He says that the potential for an independent venture capital company "was evaluated subjectively based on my gut feeling of what I thought I could do with the help of a capable partner." In Kravitt's case, the idea for the company was nothing new nor was the service he would provide. Kravitt's idea was that he could do more, be more creative, and make more money as an independent. So he found a suitable partner and set up his conglomerate.

Winston Cross of Cross Books, New York City, like so many other entrepreneurs who strike out on their own from a job in a big corporation, got his idea on the job. In his work at a major publishing house, he thought he saw a market among professionals for specific kinds of books, provided they were imaginatively packaged and promoted. Seeing little likelihood of support for the idea from his employer, he decided to pursue it on his own. His confidence in the idea was reenforced by the good results he was having with ideas he was able to apply in the company for which he worked.

Mike and Carol Resnick of Briarwood Pet Motel, Cincinnati, Ohio, demonstrate how a hobby can provide the interests and background to build a successful business. Mike tells us that the two had been "successful breeders and exhibitors of show collies in the late 1960s and early 1970s, and one day it occurred to Carol that if the pair of us could care for some 25 collies a day and still have time left over for other pursuits," there might be money to be made in caring for other people's animals.

"We didn't know much about the business, but we did know dogs, and we knew that we were a) smart and agressive, b) willing to work long hours, and c) willing to be innovative." Mike Resnick continued, "When we began totalling up the figures, we realized that only a huge kennel could generate the kind of profits we were seeking." Mike added that "neither of us had ever owned a business, and when we saw some of the people who had become successful, we decided that it wasn't all that much of a handicap."

Thomas Lisle of Cruisers, Inc., Oconto, Wisconsin, decided to find a company he could buy at a bargain price, buy it out, and make it a financial success. His business idea was to own his own company, to be an entrepreneur, to make money. He had learned how to handle acquisitions in his previous job, and he could see that there was money to be made for one who knew how to pick a bargain and how to make the best of the company's assets in the deal. In the two years he spent developing his plans and searching for a suitable take-over candidate, he found only one—Cruisers, Inc.—that met his criteria. He went with it and managed the buy-out.

J. W. Anderson of ShowAmerica, Elmhurst, Illinois, cannot pinpoint when he got the ideas that support his enterprises. "I don't remember reaching any one time when the ideas came to me . . . it was more of a mellowing and maturing evolvement." At Wilding, the world's largest producer of industrial films, Anderson was frustrated by the "faddishness of current film festivals." He felt the festivals then occurring did not serve all of the producers of industrial films. So he set out to create a festival that would serve the industry and would be well received by the industry. The result of that idea is the annual U.S. Industrial Film Festival. When that enterprise got to the point it paid him a living wage, he cut loose and added a second festival for TV and radio commercials, and in due time developed the show robots of ShowAmerica.

Katie Crane of Crane Marketing Communications, White River Junction, Vermont, did not really get an idea for her business. She simply decided she was ready to go it alone when the agency for which she worked began to slip into oblivion. In her own words, "I never thought about any other kind of activity. . . . I had been doing fundamentally the same job for 13 years and it's all I knew how to do. . . . I didn't have any doubts about my ability to sell my skills—but I never sat down and did all the planning that I probably should have. . . . I just charged!"

Ellen Green of Allied Systems Design, Inc., Bangor, Maine, worked for several years in the public sector. During that experience, she noticed a considerable gap in the materials that were available for health education. Now she feels she is meeting a demand that is evidenced by the call for her services after having been in business for only a year (since 1984). She has projected goals for a three year initial planning period.

Sandy Sakurai, career counselor, Baltimore, Maryland, also got her idea for an independent counseling business from the needs she saw in her previous job with a large career counseling firm. Her idea was to provide a less expensive counseling service on a more personal basis by keeping overhead to a minimum. She demonstrated her idea to several clients of her former employer who could not make the commute to a new office location fifty miles away. Sandy has been able to offer similar services for a substantially lower fee. One reason is that she works in her home, and another is that she does not have nonprofessional support staff or promotional costs.

She honed her idea by looking at services that were available in the Baltimore area and reviewing the needs of the educational and economic group that had been her target group when employed.

Ron MacRae of RAM, Inc., Atlanta, Georgia, says he got his business idea from his education in computer science. He says, "I recognized a need among the users of computer equipment and software that was not being met."

Ron Slatin of Medimicro Systems, Inc. and the University of Arizona, Tucson, got his idea for his pulmonary function interpretation program from his observation that small hospitals "frequently lack the medical expertise to evaluate specialized medical tests." Originally his program was developed to be an integral part of an outreach program that let small hospitals share time on the University of Arizona's Health Center minicomputer. When this idea worked in Tucson, Slatin and his colleagues decided to try to market the program nationally through a new for-profit company—Medimicro Systems, Inc.

Ralph Brown of Integrity Products, Popham Falls, Maine, had no idea of becoming an entrepreneur when his parents asked him to take over the family toy business. He calls the opportunity "pure luck." His parents had begun Integrity Products eight years earlier. "As they crossed into their seventies, they felt compelled to retire and were very insistent that I should take over the business. . . . Had the business been large I most assuredly would have refused it from recognition of both my inexperience and disinclination. . . . As it was, the smallness of the business helped me to overcome anxiety. . . . While I then, in truth, had no dream whatever of great expansion, my parents offered me guidelines for solvency (which I have followed to this day)."

Long before Larry Gleeson of Maine Hydro-Electric Development Corp. set up his company, he had been interested in water power. He tells us that he had viewed it as a hobby, though, not as a business, and there are some very large differences between the two approaches. Running a small hydroelectric generator in the backyard is not at all the same as running one for profit. However, when in the early 1970s the price of oil began to soar, Larry began to think that it would be very good to find a form of energy whose source, or raw material, was not subject to wild price fluctuations. As the cost of oil continued to skyrocket, he says, hydroelectric power began to seem increasingly attractive, and he began to look at ways of turning his hobby into a business. His background as a planner helped, for he was well versed in improving an operation's profitability. He had more help from a cousin he calls a financial expert, as well as from other acquaintances and his eventual business partners and associates. Together, they evaluated the idea very carefully. By 1977, he was ready to cut loose.

EVALUATING THE BUSINESS IDEA

For the entrepreneur, finding business ideas is not really much of a problem. Most people have a hobby, a sideline, a skill or training that can be turned into a profitable enterprise. There is not necessarily a need for high technology, nor for huge amounts of money, nor for enormous potential markets. Businesses come in all sizes, and almost anything can be the basis of one.

Anything? Consider the "Moose Birds" that appeared under Christmas trees in 1984. They were a pair of small tan ovoids glued to a wooden plaque and painted to resemble owls. They were made from moose droppings, dried and varnished. Some entrepreneurial craftsman had found a way to sell manure for hundreds of dollars a pound!

Yet businesses may never really get off the ground; or, if they do, they fail after a short period. The cause may be traceable to poor management—faulty planning or budgeting, inadequate funding, bad marketing. But it can happen that the business idea does not appeal to potential investors (including banks) or the product does not appeal to buyers.

Once you hit on a business idea or product, your first move before approaching potential partners or investors is to evaluate the idea or product. You may need the help of a business advisor or product specialist. The most important question is: Will the product or service sell? Does it have a sufficient potential market to justify the investment required to make it available? If the answer is a clear affirmative, you will find the capital to get the business started and off the ground. Any problems you encounter after the business is up and running can be charged to faulty management.

The evaluation process can take many forms. For Thomas Lisle, evaluation was an intuitive process, developed from years of analytic experience and confidence in his own judgment and abilities. Experience was also the key for the Resnicks, who counted on their background as dog breeders, their intelligence, and their energy to evaluate the efficacy of their business idea. Samuel Wallace checked to see how much competition there was in his area for a marketing consultant and called on potential customers to test their interest in his proposed enterprise.

Some entrepreneurs do even less to evaluate their business idea. Judith Kaplan reports that she did no formal evaluation of her business idea until the enterprise was well underway. In a sense, there never was a "business idea"; Kaplan's one-product sideline expanded until she came to recognize that she had a real business going. What happened with Kaplan is what happens with businesses that "just grow." Like Kaplan, the entrepreneurs who run them keep fine-tuning product choices, marketing methods, and management methods in response to and in anticipation of demand. You may ask, "Is that an okay way to develop a business?" And we can only respond, "If it works, why not?" But do not start out by deliberately not planning and evaluating. That wouldn't make sense.

For Bill Wernsing, evaluation of products was more important than evaluation of the business. He had defined himself as an independent inventor. What he had to decide was the value of working on a particular device. Could he develop it before he and his family starved to death? Would anyone want it once it was ready for the market?

Wernsing learned the hard way. One of his first efforts was the sonar device for pleasure craft. He knew that the device was needed. In his own words: "Having been on pleasure crafts like that where its need is often great—traveling at night in a canal . . . and not having anything inexpensive available—it looked like a good product not by any market survey but just a gut feeling." In the end, the problem was not the lack of a market survey but, again in Wernsing's own words: "I really did not analyze very well how big a project it was going to be." The time and resources required to develop that early product idea proved to be beyond the limited capacities of the fledgling enterprise. Fortunately for Wernsing, the first NASA contract saved him from the consequences of a major miscalculation.

From Wernsing's experience with the pleasure craft sonar device, we learn that an effective product evaluation should be aimed at weeding out any idea that cannot be efficiently developed and marketed either by the entrepreneur's company or by a competent distributor.

How does one evaluate a business idea? For Wernsing, the key was experience. For the Resnicks, the key was self-examination. For Wallace, the key was market research. Many entrepreneurs talk to potential customers, perform market testing, and study demographics in order to estimate market size and receptivity. They look for signs of a need for product, quality, or price that they can meet over any other competitor. If the signs are favorable, they feel confident. If the signs are not favorable, they seek a new product or market.

There are entrepreneurs who are so confident of their intuition and experience that they put their product on the market without any justifying research. Many such entrepreneurs fail. A few succeed if they have the right product that happens to hit the right market at the right time. Consider the Moose Birds. We do not know who makes them. We do not know what market research the entrepreneur did, if any. We suspect that particular entrepreneur was satisfied that the idea was both unique and humorous enough for a one-time success.

In such cases, the initial marketing is a legitimate form of test marketing. The product flies or it does not. If the business is a single-product enterprise, then the business flies so long as the product flies. Thus, reliance on intuition to judge saleability may be appropriate for businesses such as novelty makers that can put out dozens of product items and shut off or increase production to match whatever demand does develop.

The intuitive approach can also work for businesses that rely on catalogue sales. Judith Kaplan reports that she listens to her gift shop customers and tries to give them what they want. She also offers many items in her catalog which she must later drop for lack of demand. This approach to marketing is an aspect of the fine-tuning that she talks about.

Intuition is not for businesses that must stake all on a single roll of the dice. The entrepreneur who decides, intuitively, that the world will buy a new kind of luxury car—as did John DeLorean—is making a date with disaster. Careful, thorough, preferably professionally guided evaluation must back up any major investments in design, equipment, material, and people. Evaluation should be considered avoidable only when the investment is trivial.

SECURITY VS. RISK

By now, the paradox we noted in Chapter 2 should be clear. When we introduced the Resnicks, we remarked that they seemed unusual in that they saw as a source of security what others might consider a risk. The resolution to this paradox lies in their sense of confidence in their own abilities.

Most entrepreneurs accept some risk when they start their businesses. They do not expect to strike it rich immediately. If they are entrepreneurs because they are looking for wealth or security, they expect to achieve these goals over the long term, after considerable growth and much hard work. Yet the Resnicks sought security from the start, in the short run. They could do so because of their past experience with a hobby and because their personal abilities did give them confidence in the soundness of their undertaking.

Was their confidence justified? By their second year in business, they had brought the Briarwood Pet Motel into the black, and they had already begun to have time for other pursuits. When we interviewed them in 1984, they reported that most of the responsibilities of the business were left to a hired manager.

Confidence plays a similar role for most entrepreneurs. Lisle, Wernsing, Wallace, and the others all show that confidence is a necessary factor in the effort required to turn a business idea into a successful business. An aspect of confidence is the expectation of success, an ingredient we found to be present in all our respondents. The expectation of success, realistic or not, reduces the entrepreneur's perception of risk. The result is that most of the entrepreneurs we interviewed seemed to expect an early profit and seemed to be unaware of—or dismissing of—any serious risk.

This observation raises the classic question about entrepreneurs: Are they risk-takers? Probably most entrepreneurs are risk-takers— from the standpoint of those who watch them in action. But are they risk-takers from their own viewpoint? The ones we interviewed regarded their initiatives as sound and carefully thought through, not very risky at all. This is especially clear in Bill Wernsing's case, for he tells us that though people called him gutsy, he himself didn't feel that way at all. He knew himself and his abilities, like the Resnicks, like all the others, and he was sure he could make it on his own.

CHAPTER 4

The Business Plan: The Essential Dream

Exciting business ideas. Dreams of profit, wealth, and freedom. These are the beginnings of the entrepreneurial urge. But success in bringing the dream to reality requires hard-headed thinking and a plan—a business plan.

A sound business plan is the starting point of serious entrepreneurship. Without one, the aspiring entrepreneur is unlikely to find financial backing from friends and relatives, much less from commercial sources of capital such as banks and venture capitalists. Without a good plan, the would-be entrepreneur is well advised not to risk even personal resources.

The benefits of a good business plan far exceed its value as a money-raising tool. With a good business plan, the entrepreneur can demonstrate the feasibility of a business idea and spell out the steps toward profitability. It also shows resource allocation, and it contains an analysis of the risks involved. A workable business plan gives everyone concerned, including the entrepreneur, the confidence to go forward with the proposed enterprise.

What is a business plan and what can it accomplish? Basically, the business plan describes how a promising idea can be turned into a profitable operation. The business plan specifies in clear and precise detail the requirements for equipment, space, information processing, production workers, sales people, and managers. It specifies the cost and function of each item of equipment and each category of personnel.

The business plan also describes the management organization, including the role of the board of directors, the functions and responsibilities of senior management, and the distribution of responsibilities to line managers and specialists. The plan provides a detailed description of the proposed product(s), and a documented analysis of the expected market.

The business plan identifies sources and prices of raw materials and other supplies. It documents prospective markets and projected sales. It describes a sales and servicing organization and methods for expanding or reducing that organization as demand changes. It spells out a philosophy and approach to public and customer relations.

A crucial aspect of the business plan is a projection of anticipated income and expenses. This part of the plan must provide an accurate appraisal of near-term cash flow as well as a supportable estimate of the date of initial profitability. As we will see in Chapter 5, this appraisal should take the form of month by month estimates of receipts and expenditures up to and beyond the point when the income will exceed the outgo.

Besides providing key financial ratios ("financial touchstones"), the business plan must reveal exactly how much money the entrepreneur will have to spend before the business begins to pay for itself. This information and its supporting data become the basis for determining the extent of the investment required to bring the business into operation. What the entrepreneur does not have in investable funds and other resources must be obtained in loans, from outside investors, venture capitalists or other financing sources.

FROM DREAMS TO PLANS

In business, plans turn dreams into goals and define the steps to success. The entrepreneur who has a serious business idea will diligently acquire all available knowledge and information that bears upon the subject. He or she will read, listen, and experiment.

Larry Gleeson began the planning of his hydroelectric venture by talking to the utilities to whom he hoped to sell the electricity he wanted to generate. He thus learned the prices he could expect and the kinds of deals he would have to strike. He also talked to representatives of environmental groups, such as the Sierra Club and state fisheries agencies, frankly seeking obstacles to his plans to bring old dams back into productive use. He pored over studies of water flow and dam operation dating back to the late 1800s, as well as more recent studies from the Army Corps of Engineers. He talked to financial people and to manufacturers of the equipment he would need. In the end, he was able to prepare a business plan that included expense and income forecasts for his first ten years. These forecasts, he says, proved only as accurate as his initial assumptions. He notes that very soon after he began his business, interest rates rose dramatically, and half to two-thirds of his revenue was going to fixed costs, largely debt service.

A crucial part of Larry's planning was the first hydroelectric site he developed. It was too small, he says, for a real commercial operation, but it was small enough to get working quickly. The dam was intact, the mill that had been using it had burned down recently, the water turbine was there, and the right to use the river's water flow came with the property. It was a $30,000 project, not a million-dollar one, and it gave him the chance to test his ideas on a relatively small scale, much as John North (see Chapter 8) says he should have done. The experience bolstered his own confidence, improved his planning, and led directly to later, larger projects.

What must entrepreneurs learn? Except for the product-related details, every business founder—manufacturers, retailers, even lawyers and physicians—needs to know certain basics: how to rent office space; how to buy supplies, insurance, equipment; how to market the product or service; how to keep track of receipts and expenditures; how to hire help; how to schedule time. One of the main reasons new businesses fail is that inexperienced entrepreneurs fail to anticipate expenses by overlooking one or more of the obvious essentials. This is, in fact, one of the most common reasons for the failure of new ventures.

A cause of failure that is closely related to unanticipated expenses is unanticipated losses. A good business plan will include a contingency plan to cover "worst case" projections of revenues. The remedy for early losses is capital and the remedy for losses that go beyond the expected period of negative cash flow is more capital. The lesson here is to develop a plan that calls for maximum capitalization, not minimum. Several of our respondents cited undercapitilization as one of their initial mistakes.

Lacking a plan, or lacking one that has had the benefit of expert review, inexperienced entrepreneurs may spend too large a proportion of their money on production people and machinery and go under for lack of a competent bookkeeper, market analyst, or sales manager.

Lacking a plan, entrepreneurs can fail by neglecting to develop all aspects of the business in proper relation to any planned objectives. They may concentrate on product development and fail to identify or to evaluate their market. They may take for granted quality control only to find out too late that products or services fall short of customer expectations. They may ignore financial controls until serious cash flow problems force bankruptcy. They may fail to provide adequate product orientation and training for the sales staff. They may waste resources on new equipment when used equipment would have served the purpose. They may hire personnel too soon or too late or hire key people who are not committed or competent.

There is a lot to learn about going into business, but the most important lesson is about planning: the importance of writing out a plan; what to put into it; how to fit the pieces together; and how to make it work.

One of our respondents, Samuel Wallace, underlined this point. When he and his partners founded Xodex Enterprises, they made several fundamental errors. They failed to estimate accurately the size of the Oakland-area market for their market research, advertising, and promotion firm; they seriously underestimated the amount of money they would need for expenses in the period before they became profitable; and Wallace's partners proved unable to perform as the firm needed. Today the partners are no longer with the firm, and Wallace is struggling to recover from the earlier difficulties. Wallace himself attributes his troubles to his tendency to be too aggressive, too pushy, a "gun-jumper."

Many of our subjects believe that the most important part of planning is marketing. Wallace is only one of many who emphasize the importance of marketing, both in the planning process and in subsequent performance.

Bill Wernsing of Williams Laboratories in Ithaca, New York, reports that he began as a total greenhorn in the marketing area and that, while he still is no marketing expert, he is convinced that "one's success lies very strongly in the marketing area.'' Mike Resnick, who with his wife bought out the money-losing Briarwood Pet Motel in Cincinnati, turned it around largely by improving its appeal to customers and by adding services and redirecting its advertising.

Still others among our subjects—and among the experts—believe that the planning process is most valuable for raising money, restraining unwarranted enthusiasm, or meeting contingencies. Thomas Lisle of Cruisers, Inc., speaks for planning as an experienced acquisitions manager. He had quit after many years as a lawyer and acquisitions specialist with the Eaton Corporation to take over the troubled Cruisers. For him, ''Having been a 'strategic planner' as a profession, planning came as a second nature. . . . The planning process I used in developing my acquisition objective was to assess my strengths and weaknesses as an executive. . . . Having developed most of my skills in a large organization and as manager of a larger organization, it was further clear that a small company demanding product specialty skills was not appropriate. . . . Having bought and sold companies through several previous business cycles, I realized the opportune time to buy was in the depth of a recession. . . . The pricing and terms would be most attractive at that time assuming you could get the financing and develop a specific business plan that would carry you through the recession. . . . At the time [I left Eaton], I had spent the previous 24 months developing the plan and doing preliminary acquisitions screening. . . . [Cruisers] met the planning criteria. . . . In addition to the strategic plan of what type of business to enter and how to enter the business, there was also a requirement to develop specific business plans for potential acquisitions . . . this was done in each instance.''

FORMAL BUSINESS PLANS

For Lisle, formal business planning is so much a part of standard operating procedure that he never thinks of avoiding the process. Many entrepreneurs, perhaps most, find planning very easy to put off or ignore. Katie Crane just charged ahead with her new business with no thought of drawing up a plan. In fact, many entrepreneurs prepare formal business plans only when they decide to seek capital from prospective investors who demand them. Few outside investors are interested in new, untested enterprises, for they can be precarious. Businesses that have established themselves as serious—even though small—contenders in the market place can be attractive to venture capitalists, who trade their funds for partial ownership.

Venture capitalists are risk-takers, but the successful ones are careful risk-takers. They always try to minimize their risk, and one way is to require detailed plans from entrepreneurs who solicit their support. Often, interested venture capitalists will themselves assist in developing the business plan in exchange for "intelligence equity"— a piece of the action. Yet having a plan is no guarantee that venture capitalists will make the investment. One in a hundred business plans that are reviewed by venture capitalists ever accomplish their purpose.

From the standpoint of the venture capitalist, commercial banker, or outside investor, a good business plan is a valuable sign of the entrepreneur's serious intent. A good plan demonstrates an investment of time and energy in study, thought, and analysis that signal the entrepreneur's potential for success.

The formal business plan can be used not only to attract business capital, but also to persuade suppliers that the new business is worth credit. Short-term credit extended to a new business is itself a form of investment in the new venture.

Formal business plans can serve to restrain impetuous or poorly timed actions of the overly enthusiastic entrepreneur. Many inexperienced entrepreneurs are so tempted by early success or so impressed by their own "brilliant ideas" that they rush headlong into the market with all the products they can dream up. Lacking a sound analysis of the company's capacity to follow through with quality products and of the markets to be served, they then find disaster crowding out success. Venture capitalists value most the entrepreneur who knows how to follow through with one marketable product before going on to another (Welsh and White, 1983). A well-designed business plan defines the product and the market and continually cautions the entrepreneur against temptations to over-extend. Of course, no plan can speak out on its own; the entrepreneur and others charged with the company's direction must be resolved to heed the plan with reasonable discipline.

The business plan of Win Cross's publishing firm specified "ink-on-paper" books for its first years. Later, once the books program is well established, it will consider other information products and services.

Over-extension is an all-too-common problem among entrepreneurs. Androbot, Inc., one of the companies nurtured in Nolan Bushnell's Catalyst Technologies incubator, ran into serious trouble when it over-reached its engineering design and marketing capabilities in attempting development (from scratch) of too many types of home robots whose purposes (and therefore markets) were as yet ill-defined with respect to marketplace and function. Spectacular earlier successes colored the judgment and caution of Bushnell himself and that of a group of competent associates. Androbot's reorganization plan calls for producing just one of the models and getting it right (Coll, 1984).

Finally, formal business plans give entrepreneurs a convenient yardstick for appraising their progress. The plan lists milestones—dates for moving into the office, getting the production line up and operating, selling the first units, "going public," and so on. The business plan allows the entrepreneur to see when and where something goes wrong, to anticipate and prevent chain reaction effects, and above all to adjust the plan to meet realities inside the fledgling company and in the marketplace.

For any business, circumstances can change abruptly and dramatically. For new ventures, where sources of materials, manufacturing, advertising or sales are initially limited, a sudden and dramatic change can prove devastating—unless, of course, this possibility has been anticipated in the business plan. In such circumstances, the business plan can provide the entrepreneur with guidelines to quickly resolve the problems that can attend a predictable change in circumstances. Whatever the solution, it should be anticipated in the formal business plan. In the end, the business must above all anticipate every possible problem that could compromise success, it must include contingency plans that address each of the problems, and it must anticipate investors' questions. If the plan meets each of these three tests, it is probably a good plan.

We will explore several actual experiences when we discuss how our survey subjects have used planning in their new businesses. Before we come to these specifics, we will outline the characteristics and content of a business plan. We list some of the many books on business planning in the bibliography. One of the best is *The Entrepreneur's Master Planning Guide* by John A. Welsh and Jerry F. White (Prentice-Hall: Englewood Cliffs, NJ, 1983). An excellent do-it-yourself business planning book is *How to Raise Capital: Preparing and Presenting the Business Plan* by Gregory I. Kravitt et al. (Dow Jones-Irwin: Homewood, IL., 1984).

OUTLINES FOR A BUSINESS PLAN

Formal business plans can range from ten or so pages in length to one hundred or more pages. A complex new enterprise whose capital requirements run into many millions of dollars can take several hundred pages to describe its plans with supporting data. The length depends to some extent on the size and complexity of the proposed business. But the more concise the plan, the more likely it is to be read by prospective investors, suppliers, and customers. The formal business plan should provide all necessary detail in the briefest possible form. Conciseness gives the impression of clear and careful thinking, while also making the business plan more accessible and digestible to the investor.

There is no standard format for a business plan. One expert recommends fourteen sections and eleven appendices for a manufacturing company example (White, 1976) (see Exhibit 4-1).

Kravitt and colleagues suggest eleven topics plus a series of appendices and exhibits keyed to specified topics (Kravitt et al., 1984) (see Exhibit 4-2.)

These lists may seem too elaborate for many entrepreneurs who are starting new and small businesses. Certainly, an adequate business plan can be written that follows a briefer and simpler sequence. Welsh and White (1983) recognize this need of the smaller entrepreneur when they list only six areas that should be covered in a formal business plan:

1. The product (description and production)
2. The target market (who and where are the customers?)
3. The competition (who satisfies these customers now, and how?)

EXHIBIT 4-1:   The White (1976) Planning Outline.

 1. Executive summary
 2. Tables of contents, illustrations, tables, and graphs
 3. Brief background and history
 4. Product/service description
 5. Market description
 6. Competition
 7. Marketing strategies
 8. Manufacturing plans
 9. Quality control
10. Financial plans
11. Money-leveraging strategies
12. Ownership distribution
13. Organization chart and descriptions of founders and key employees
14. Founders' stock incentives
15. Appendices—product/service details
            —research and development plans
            —manufacturing details
            —marketing details
            —financial budgets and projections
            —administrative goals and company milestones
            —organization and personnel
            —management methods
            —list of assumptions
            —summary of potential problem areas
            —parallel case histories
            —letters of intent from customers and distributors

   4. Marketing (how will the business find and reach its customers?)
   5. Management (who will run the company, and how?)
   6. Finances (profit and net worth projections; getting capital)

   A plan that covers all six areas suggested by Welsh and White
will also cover most of the ground in the longer lists suggested by
Richard M. White and Kravitt et al. The reason is that any business
plan must consider certain essential elements, namely, product, market and marketing, competition, management, and money.
   What Kravitt and colleagues do in their very useful volume is to
present the reader with a series of questions that cover every imagi-
nable entrepreneurial situation. The questions are arranged under the

EXHIBIT 4-2:   The Kravitt et al. (1984) Planning Outline.

 1. Background
 2. Management
 3. Ownership
 4. Employees
 5. Investment criteria
 6. Markets and competition
 7. Customers and suppliers
 8. Production and operations
 9. Government regulation
10. Financial data
11. Strategic planning
12. Appendices—Supporting documentation for: general and legal background; management organization chart and letters of recommendation; market surveys; feasibility studies; contracts, purchase orders, and letters of intent; suppliers' contracts, production flow chart; regulatory licenses and approvals; financial analyses; projected income statements; appraisals, leases, and loan documents; past financial and income statements and tax returns; accounts receivable and payable; pension, profit-sharing, and stock bonus plans; principals' financial statements and resumes; stock offering memoranda; lists of sales representatives, distributors, and wholesalers; current price lists, catalogs, and other promotional material; news clippings; credit reports; competitors' annual reports; etc.

eleven topics of the business plan. You are invited to read each question and decide whether it is relevant to your business. If it is, you answer it as fully as you feel necessary. If you come to a question that is not relevant, you explain to yourself why it is not relevant, and then you pass on to the next question. Kravitt leaves nothing out and nothing to guesswork or interpolation. When you have answered or not answered all of his questions, you have the draft of your business plan.

If you have been conscientious and honest, your plan will be as complete as it would have been had some business plan consultant prepared it for you. We recommend that you try the Kravitt format in your efforts to write a business plan. At the very least you will be in an improved position to judge the work of the experts you may eventually hire to do the job for you.

Another excellent way to approach writing a business plan is outlined by Thurston (1983). He advocates beginning with a statement of goals that lays out the nature of the business, its strengths

EXHIBIT 4-3:   Simplified PERT Chart.

Activities		**Steps (Months or Quarters)**		
product	1. prototype	2. test	3. cost estimates	4. begin
production				
equipment	. . .	. . .	. . .	. . .
plant	. . .	. . .	. . .	. . .
administration	1. hire engineer	2. hire accountant	3. hire sec'y, bookkeeper	4. hire workers
production				
administration	. . .			
finance	. . .			
marketing	. . .			

and priorities, potential problem areas, and numbers and dates for financial and other milestones. A Thurston plan then incorporates subplans, that is, separate plans for distinct areas—marketing, sales, production, new product development, personnel, organization, budgets, finance, and controls.

The value of the Thurston approach is that each distinct area is recognized as having its own path of development with its own milestones. For example, the development of marketing flows from a description of the product and its advantages over those of competitors, to an analysis of the target market and ways of reaching it, to pricing and the effects of changes in the market.

A personnel plan may outline a hiring sequence: product developers first, followed by managers and marketers. The personnel plan should also deal with the need to maintain morale and motivation, the need to find replacements, and the need to train new employees. This plan may also deal with management methods as they bear upon personnel.

A systematic method of summarizing your business plan is the commonly used PERT chart. PERT stands for "program evaluation and research tool," which is planning jargon for a diagram showing the sequence and interrelationships of the main components of your business plan. The value of including a PERT chart in the summary section of your plan will be immediately apparent to you if you take a few minutes to study the sample PERT chart in Exhibit 4-3. (We use another version in Chapter 5). Even this simplified PERT chart illustrates how complicated business planning can be and therefore how important it can be to spell out all the details of the tasks of founding a business. Once you have sold your backers on your business idea, you will find the PERT chart a very convenient guide in your own management work and a handy reference for people who are working with you (see Silver, 1982).

Welsh and White (1983) recommend writing a business plan with investors in mind as the primary audience. This means emphasizing the attractiveness of the investment, focussing on the appeal and profitability of the product, projecting future changes in product management, ownership, and growth, and showing how and why the business will avoid trouble.

It is important that the entrepreneur not succumb to the temptation to paint too rosy a picture. You must give the impression in your plan that you are a hard-headed realist, for you will be addressing tough-minded people who review dozens of business plans every week. Experienced investors and commercial bankers are natural-born pessimists who are hard to fool. They are aware of the statistics on business failures and of the myriad ways a business can fail. They will invest in the entrepreneur who has laid out in the business plan all of the conceivable problems and specific ways of dealing with them.

The entrepreneur who demonstrates a willingness to recognize all of the problems and pitfalls of a new venture is likely to produce a very attractive business plan. That same plan will prove to be invaluable in the management of the business, especially in the critical stages leading up to the first profits. What the plan does for the business is to keep everyone concerned mindful of schedules and goals. Used effectively, the plan is an *aide-memoire* for details of production, budget, and market—the three crucial elements of a successful business. The good business plan brings the whole business into focus as no other instrument can.

Irene Smith, one who learned the hard way, founded The Business Center in New York City in 1977 and wrote a book about the experience called *Diary of a Small Business*. In the closing chapter, aptly titled "If I Had It To Do Over Again . . . And Knew What I Know Now," she writes, "If I were planning this business today, I would find a competent, entrepreneurial accountant to help me put together a formal business plan." Only well into her experience did she learn that "I myself don't like to plan. . . . I like to have plans to follow, but I find the discipline of planning extremely difficult and time-consuming. . . . Nevertheless, the bigger my business gets, the more useful I find this exercise, and I am working very hard to become more disciplined about doing it.''

FLYING BY THE SEAT OF THE PANTS AND OTHER NIGHTMARES

Most new entrepreneurs ignore formal business planning in favor of flying by the seat of the pants. Most new entrepreneurs fail the first time around. Most entrepreneurs who have tried to start a business and failed are more deliberate about planning the second time around. The most experienced and consistently successful entrepreneurs always do careful planning as a basis for a new enterprise.

The typical new entrepreneur will come up with a business idea, scrape up enough money to begin operation, and then wing it on a day-to-day basis. They usually do not anticipate trouble except in occasional bad dreams, and they make decisions only as issues arise. They run on instinct and intuition. They are extremely vulnerable to economic shifts, changes in customer tastes or needs, and the maneuvers of more experienced competitors.

The sad fate of large numbers of well-intentioned, seat-of-the-pants, new entrepreneurs teaches the hard lesson that planning is the more promising route to take. Many of our survey subjects have come to the same conclusion, some of them only after long and frustrating periods of intuitive management.

Bill Wernsing never prepared a formal or informal business plan, and he too can bear witness to the problems that produces. Cutting loose despite the responsibility of raising a family with no assured income, he says, ''was a little bit scary,'' but he had his wife's support. Thereafter, he found that the lack of planning—and of knowledge of what to plan for—led to several failures of anticipation, especially of how long it can take to develop a product and get it on the market.

Judith Kaplan, of Action Packets, Inc., in Ocala, Florida, prepared her first business plan when she decided to take her company public in 1984. She first tried a professional writer of business plans, but that did not satisfy her (outside planners rarely suit entrepreneurs, because they know too little of the business and they sometimes push their own ideas rather than eliciting the entrepreneur's ideas). She then tackled the job herself and found it to be "a terrific learning experience. . . . Very eye-opening." She told us that writing the business plan helped her to conceptualize the company and to clarify her vision "of where we were and where we could go." Most of our respondents found conceptualization a powerful tool, one that allowed them to quickly imagine alternatives as well as enabling them to criticize creatively what they were presently doing.

Judith Kaplan had not been totally innocent of planning when she approached the task. She told us that she and her staff always had weekly (or as needed) meetings to review "past accomplishments, current projects, current problems, and future opportunities." She did little research but instead spent time selling and listening to customers. "Living in New York was a plus in that trade shows enabled us to find and purchase items that our customers were looking for." These remarks reveal that Judith Kaplan did pay attention to many of the key elements of the formal business plan; yet she was definitely a reactive, seat-of-the-pants manager.

It was a need for space that prompted her to move to Florida. The additional space let the business expand until it needed the sums of money only a public offering could—and eventually did—supply.

Katie Crane, sole proprietor of Crane Marketing Communications in White River Junction, Vermont, is an example of an entrepreneur who has not developed a formal plan for her business. Crane Marketing Communications is a one-person operation. Ms. Crane's objective is to keep busy and prosperous as a marketing consultant and public relations writer. She began with no more than the thought, "I'll try this for three months . . . and I'll see where I am then."

Soon she had to figure what minimum monthly billings she wanted, how to define her services, and how to charge and to bill. Initial success gave Ms. Crane the option of growth, but she decided against an expansion because she did not want the responsibility of managing employees.

Mike and Carol Resnick show a very different kind of winging it. They focussed on identifying things to avoid by talking to hundreds of other dog breeders and kennel operators. They found that "most breeders set their sights too low." They took up commercial kennel space with their own animals, continually left their businesses in charge of unqualified assistants. . . .'' Most kennel operators were unwilling to talk with them, but they toured many, ''gathered ideas and learning by observation of what *not* to do.'' Among their major observations was that ''most kennels, being primarily cash businesses, illegally skim so much money off the top that banks refuse to make loans based on their tax returns. (That wasn't the case with the one we eventually bought; it was losing so much money that the owner didn't have to lie.)''

The Resnicks have never prepared a formal business plan, but they have achieved many of the same results by arming themselves against disaster in this way. They have also ''planned'' by adopting innovative practices—including special relationships with veterinarians—that strengthened their business over the years.

TO INC. OR NOT TO INC.

The question of incorporating is largely a technical and legal one. Basically, the decision comes down to the need or lack of need for personal protection from law suits and other claims against the business. There are also other considerations.

We mentioned that some experts believe a business plan should include a discussion of how ownership of the enterprise should be set up. In most cases, this issue must be addressed from the start, for many businesses are set up by teams of partners, each of whom puts in money and expects a share of future profits. Win Cross is an example. His publishing firm was organized by four partners. They could have chosen to form a partnership. The major disadvantage is that the partners are individually and personally liable for any business debts. They chose to incorporate because that legal arrangement restricts liabilities to the assets of the business. Another advantage is that they can, if they choose, sell stock to finance growth.

Pat Heffernan decided not to incorporate since she found that the individual proprietor of a corporation may be vulnerable to legal actions under certain circumstances. She does not want her company to be subject to corporate taxes. However, she recalculates her taxes annually to determine what advantages there might be in an incorporation.

Ellen Green incorporated as Allied Systems Design, Inc., to ''be established officially" and to be in a position to "enter financial agreements as a business, not as a liable individual."

What is important for the new entrepreneur in making the decision whether to incorporate is to give careful and informed consideration to the question. This is a place to consult an experienced business attorney or a professional business planner.

One of us did consulting for many years under the informal arrangement of Conant Associates. People were hired for each project as needed. There were no partners, only professional colleagues who had other full-time jobs. A major contract with a large public utility to work out a federally required environmental impact statement for a nuclear power generating station caused Conant to incorporate. The reason? Anything could go wrong in the highly complex world of federal regulation and especially in the extremely sensitive arena of nuclear power.

Partnership arrangements may be safe for those businesses that are unlikely to be exposed to significant liability. However, partnerships are most often established, and in most states required by law, where there is significant exposure to personal liability such as in medical, legal and accounting practices. Even in professional corporations, direct liability is still assumed by the individual professionals in the firm.

There are no set fees associated with establishing a partnership, and fees for professional corporations are established by each state.

Limited partnerships are for investors who want profit but not a role in running the business. Limited partners are liable only to the extent of their investment in the business. Research and development partnerships allow a group of investors to contract with an entrepreneur to develop a product. Thus R&D partnerships are less for the business than an arrangement of legal convenience for the backers. They also serve as a tax shelter because at the research and development stage, a business is usually operating at a loss.

There are several types of corporations from which a new entrepreneur may choose depending on the nature and objectives of the business. The standard corporation referred to above is the most common. Its great advantages are limited liability and ease of financial growth (sale of stock). Its main disadvantage may be double taxation—once on the profits of the business and again on the money received by the shareholders (money paid as salary to owner–managers is a business expense and is taxed only once).

The "Subchapter S" provision of the federal tax code allows corporations with fewer than ten shareholders to avoid double taxation. Profits of Subchapter S corporations are taxed only after they have been distributed to shareholders.

Most entrepreneurial businesses are neither corporations nor formal partnerships. They are sole proprietorships, and they are treated by the U.S. Internal Revenue Service as identical with their proprietors. That is, they pay personal income tax rates, but they pay only once. They enjoy no limitations on liability, but they have the advantage of freedom from the legal and regulatory paperwork required of corporations.

Mike and Carol Resnick represent another advantage of the sole proprietorship. When they took over the business, they chose not to incorporate "because we had to sign the mortgage note personally— and since we were personally on the hook if the business failed, we saw no reason to incorporate and pay double taxes."

Yet Mike, a busy and successful writer, did face the possibility of libel suits. They therefore put the business in Carol's name. Wearing his other hat, Mike was then liable only for his personal assets, and the business was just as safe as if it had been incorporated.

Sole proprietorship may be the most convenient and flexible arrangement for one-person operations that are not likely to go bankrupt or to be sued. Certainly, the sole proprietorship allows a business to end operations simply by doing so. By the same token, it is easy to convert a sole proprietorship to a partnership or corporation when circumstances require a more formal legal entity.

Katie Crane finds the sole proprietorship ideal for her purposes. "My financial advisor suggests it," she says, "and I trust her." The sole proprietorship is also the usual arrangement for all small shopowners, truckers, physicians, lawyers, home contractors, artists, and writers. Those, like physicians, who must worry about liability may spend large sums for liability insurance as an alternative to incorporation.

CHAPTER 5

Seed Money

Itch, idea, and plan. All are essential to the birth of any business. So is money. No matter how intense the itch, hot the idea, or persuasive the business plan, no business gets off the ground without economic nourishment.

Think of it. The entrepreneur has to survive until the new business starts to generate enough income to pay for the necessities: office space, furnishings, equipment, telephone, letterhead, business cards, paper clips, insurance, a lawyer, and an accountant. Also personnel: secretaries, bookkeepers, production workers, and a sales force.

The entrepreneur rarely has to pay for everything at once, but there is always a long list of expenses before there is much return. As an entrepreneur, you will probably start your business in a hole, and the hole keeps getting deeper until that happy day when sales reach the point where they are bringing more in than is going out. Among our respondents, only Pat Heffernan reports making a profit in the first month.

If you don't like the word "hole," call it a deficit, or an investment in the future. But the deficit does look like a hole in a graph of any new company's cash flow (Exhibit 5-1).

As we pointed out in Chapter 4, an essential part of business planning is to estimate as closely as possible the greatest depth the hole is likely to reach before profits begin to fill it. The depth of

Exhibit 5-1. Typical Cash-flow Projection.

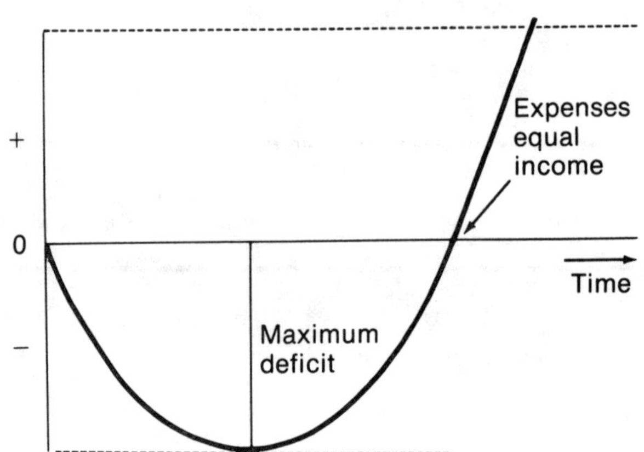

"negative cash flow" varies—a one-person secretarial service may need no more than a few thousands of dollars to set up and survive until payments start coming in. A nationally circulated magazine may require several million dollars before subscriptions and advertising begin to put money back in the bank.

Accurate forecasts of negative cash flow are essential to effective planning, for they dictate the entrepreneur's search for start-up or seed money. The entrepreneur who needs only a few thousands of dollars may be able to meet that need out of his or her personal resources. But the entrepreneur who needs millions faces a hopeless task without convincing cash-flow projections for the launching phase of the business.

Most new businesses need, not millions, but tens or hundreds of thousands of dollars, and there are sources of start-up capital in these ranges that can be tapped. Before we discuss these sources and how our subjects have used them, we should say a little about how to forecast a business's initial expenses.

FORECASTING THE START-UP DEFICIT

Forecasting the start-up deficit means listing *all* foreseeable expenses. It is usually wise to include in the forecast a contingency item for unforeseeable expenses, a cushion for unexpected jolts.

Adding a 15-20 percent margin for expenses is a good rule of thumb. The cash-flow forecast (we might as well call it by its right name) should be laid out on a month-by-month basis and revised monthly to provide a series of deadlines for meeting cash needs. So long as the cash-flow or deficit plan is explicit and in writing, the entrepreneur may not have to have all of the start-up funds at the beginning of operations. Funding sources should be identified and tentative commitments made, but prudence and economy may suggest that cash be available before actual bills come due.

The most useful forecasts also show the timing of projected income, revealing to the entrepreneur and to backers when and to what extent sales will meet (and surpass) expenses.

Let us see how the cash-flow forecast works in a fictitious example. Entrepreneur Hiram Parker has invented a useful household device he calls a diddley-whocker. It can be made with one 6" × 3" × 1" piece of polished hardwood, one screw, one 4" × 1" strip of spring steel, two drops of glue, and a 1" ball of lamb's wool. Parker has the prototype in hand to slow suppliers and chain-store buyers, and he has done enough research to be sure that he can manufacture diddley-whockers for $1.50 apiece and sell them wholesale for $5.50. So he quits a $40,000-a-year position as an investment counselor to set up his business. First, however, he lists the expenses he expects to incur before he will turn a profit, as shown in Exhibit 5-2.

It would not be hard to plug in some actual figures for Hiram Parker's first four months. You might try some estimates as an exercise in cash-flow projections, as though Parker's business were yours.

Business expenses vary from region to region around the country and from year to year. In Hiram Parker's case, costs of $10,000 could easily be run up in his first month; $20,000 in his second; $30,000 in his third and again in his fourth, and so on in later months. Parker could spend at least $90,000 in the first four months before he receives payment for his first shipment to a chain-store customer.

The chances are the first shipment is small, because the customer wants to see how the product moves in a few of its stores before committing to a larger order. That first payment may be no more than $5000. Month five may be a little better, with $10,000 coming in. Month six may bring $20,000, but by then Parker is running a deficit of $115,000. If orders come in at a quickening pace, month seven

EXHIBIT 5-2: Expense and "Milestone" Forecast for Parker's Diddley-Whockers.

Month 1
  own salary ($40,000/12 = $3,333)
  office deposit & rent
  phone deposit & rent
  other utilities
  supplies (business cards, stationery)
  insurance (medical, property, liability)
  travel (to visit suppliers & customers)
  legal fees
  accountant's fees
  state franchise tax

Month 2   MILESTONE 1: first order received
  own salary
  office rent
  phone and utility bills
  supplies, insurance, and travel
  secretary, salary and fringes (FICA, medical, unemployment insurance)
  factory rent
  manufacturing equipment, down payments
  legal fees
  accountant's fees

Month 3   MILESTONE 2: first production & shipment
  office and factory rent
  phone and utility bills
  supplies, insurance, and travel
  secretary
  equipment payments
  production workers, salary, etc.
  raw materials
  shipping costs

Month 4   MILESTONE 3: first customer payment
  own salary
  office and factory rent
  phone and utility bills
  supplies, insurance, and travel
  equipment payments
  payroll and materials
  shipping costs

Exhibit 5-3.   Parker's Diddley-Whockers, Cash-flow Projection.

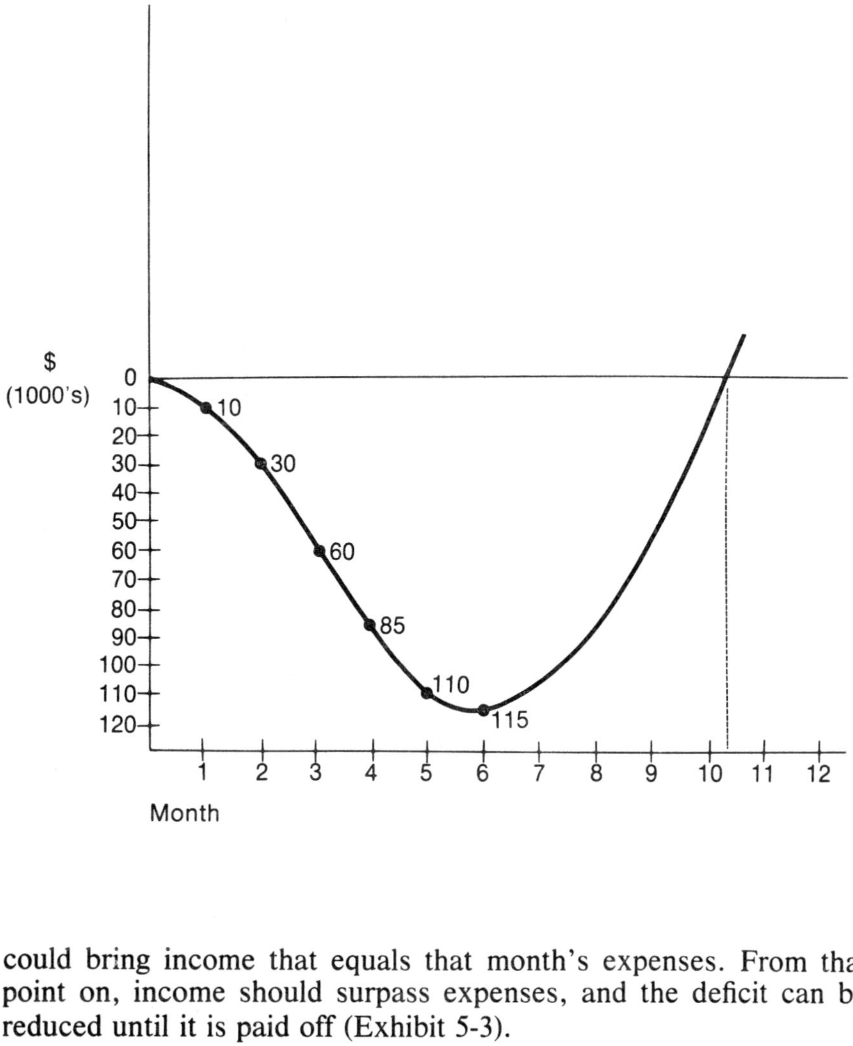

could bring income that equals that month's expenses. From that point on, income should surpass expenses, and the deficit can be reduced until it is paid off (Exhibit 5-3).

As we have described Hiram Parker's situation, he needed $115,000 in start-up money to get the diddley-whocker business moving. But we did make several optimistic assumptions—that Parker gets a firm order as early as month 2; that he is able to fill it in month 3; that he gets paid in month 4; and that orders and payments both increase rapidly. Failing any of them, the cash-flow projections based upon them must be stretched out in time.

Every entrepreneur soon learns that assumptions can be and usually are so unreliable that they require constant monitoring and revision. Orders come later than expected and grow more slowly. Payments are delayed. At the same time, suppliers and other creditors insist upon receiving their money promptly. It is for this reason that we emphasize the important of contingency budgeting; some advisors (Baty, 1981) recommend that any entrepreneur add ten to fifteen percent to initial deficit estimates to cover contingencies.

Entrepreneurs who do not hedge their projections run into trouble. When Samuel Wallace and his partners started up Xodex Enterpreises, Ltd., as a marketing consulting firm, they expected to be able to operate with $80,000–$120,000, but they "knew" they could operate with less. Hence, they tried to get by with the $65,000–$75,000 they were able to raise, expecting that amount of funds "would be sufficient for the first year." Wallace later observed, "We were mistaken . . . the $120,000 figure would have been more realistic. . . . The $65,000–$75,000 generated, minus the cost of equipment, meant that seed capital for operations was only $40,000, limiting our ability to pay adequate salaries to do the job. . . . The expenses we failed to foresee were the costs of early-on equipment and advertising, as well as travel and entertainment expenses for sales reps. . . . To accomodate the variance in our projection versus what was needed, we cut back salaries to a small retainer plus commission and provided no reembursement of expenses during the first year. . . . This is not the way to start a new business operation."

Thomas Lisle was more fortunate when he took over Cruisers. He tells us that, "Insofar as specific expense forecasting goes, our overall plan turned out to be quite conservative. . . . While we did not anticipate every expense, we forecast more expenses than we in fact experienced. . . . Where we erred in our forecasts was the severity of the recession [of the early 1980s]. . . . We assumed in May, when we made the acquisition, that we were pretty close to the bottom of the recession in the boating business. . . . Other problems encountered were lightning striking the warehouse and manufacturing facility just at the time the business was taking off. . . . This taxed both our personal and financial resources."

Pat Heffernan was faced with the problem of having underestimated the rapidity with which her business took off, and so her cash flow problem stemmed from the need to enlarge support staff before she had planned to do so.

SHARING COSTS

A careful study of Exhibit 5-2 shows that our fictitious Hiram Parker has been cautious in his plans to spend money. He has delayed many expenditures. In month one, for instance, he focussed on setting up an office and on finding suppliers and customers. He did not hire a secretary, rent factory space, or buy manufacturing equipment until month two. He did not engage production workers until month three, when he had to begin filling the first orders.

In this phased approach to setting up the business, Parker used a version of "critical path" or PERT planning (see Silver, 1982). This is a useful way to control start-up costs; it is based on the idea that once many expenditures are begun, they recur from month to month. Therefore, they should be delayed until they are necessary.

Yet Parker has been careless in some ways. Instead of renting an office right away, he might have worked out of his home for a month or two. (Many of our respondents have done precisely this.) Then, when he got around to renting factory space, he could have set up the office at the factory.

Instead of hiring a secretary, he might have used a secretarial service, paying only for needed time and materials. Instead of buying new manufacturing equipment, office furniture, and so on, he might have bought used, as did Sandy Sakurai. Instead of buying a word processor, he might have settled for a typewriter. Instead of setting up his own factory, he might have subcontracted the production of his diddley-whockers.

All of these measures might have cut projected costs considerably, and all of them are frequently recommended by business advisors. Note, in the first line of Exhibit 5-2, that Parker expects to pay himself the same salary he had been receiving in his previous job. Instead, he might have arrived at a salary by adjusting his personal and family expenses to an acceptable minimum for the launching phase of the new business. Usually, investors look favorably upon entrepreneurs who demonstrate their serious intent by personal sacrifices through the deficit phase.

Taking all of these measures together, Hiram Parker might have reduced the projected initial deficit to perhaps $50,000. Adding a contingency of 15 percent, Parker's up-front cash requirements might have come in at around $57,500, half of the $115,000 reflected in Exhibit 5-3.

Some other examples of initial cost savings include shared office and production space, do-it-yourself painting and carpentry, using the equipment of other businesses at night and on weekends, using part-time secretaries, bookkeepers, accountants, engineers, technical writers, etc., using commission agents instead of full-time sales people, getting free publicity through news releases and articles to trade publications and local press, and piggy-back purchasing with an established company for the advantage of quantity discounts.

Many new businesses are wholesale, retail, and service providers. But every one of them faces the same problems as manufacturers in estimating and minimizing start-up expenses. Every new entrepreneur in every kind of business has to know as nearly as possible how much of a deficit they face, and how much money they must find.

It is worth noting that some attempts to shave costs do not work well. Bob Praegitzer (Solomon, 1984) was a successful logger who shifted to making electronic circuit boards. His Praegitzer Industries in Dallas, Oregon, is today a growing concern, but money is a problem. In 1981, he borrowed $800,000 from a local bank to build a plant. In 1983, he decided to refinance the mortgage, but the bank wanted to impose a $50,000 prepayment penalty on the old loan. He stopped payment on the old loan, figuring that when the bank notified him of imminent foreclosure, he could pay off and avoid the penalty. However, the bank foreclosed without notice, and a second bank, learning of his attempt to avoid the penalty at the first bank, declined to issue Praegitzer an industrial bond for which he had applied.

FINDING SEED MONEY

The entrepreneur's next problem is finding the money he or she needs to set up in business. The first place any entrepreneur usually must look is in his or her own pocket. The sources might be savings and investments; cash value of insurance policies; equity in the home; an expensive automobile; salary from a full-time job during the planning period.

Must the aspiring entrepreneur pledge everything to the dream? Not always, but you should be prepared to do so. Given the willingness to pledge your all, you may find that it is not necessary. Gordon

Baty (1981) cites the case of a Massachusetts man who was preparing to set up as a specialty food packager. He had prepared a careful business plan and expense forecast and totted up all his personal assets. Then he showed his employer, a food broker, his plans. The employer, himself an entrepreneur, was impressed both by his employee's willingness to put everything at risk and by the quality of his employee's planning. He believed he was looking at a good investment opportunity and volunteered the seed money in return for minority ownership. As a result, the employee was able to keep three-quarters of his savings, avoided a second mortgage, and kept his income up to par. The new partners both made considerable gains from the enterprise.

Most entrepreneurs are not so lucky and must follow through on their willingness to commit every available personal asset to their new enterprise. Bill Wernsing, of Williams Laboratories, didn't need vast sums of money to set up as an independent inventor, but he did go through his savings, just surviving while he struggled toward his first income. He also needed money to buy parts for his product models, and when savings ran out, he had to borrow on his house. People called him gutsy, he says, "when I just took the bull by the horns and plunged ahead," but "it didn't seem to be quite that gutsy. . . . What the heck, I started out ten years ago with nothing, I can start at nothing again and make it somehow. . . . I had my education and so forth."

Wernsing illustrates a basic aspect of the entrepreneurial personality. So do Mike and Carol Resnick, who raised the down payment on their Briarwood Pet Motel by selling their "luxury home on Chicago's North Shore for more than twice what we paid for it a few years earlier." Ronald MacCrae financed his RAM, Inc., computer company by taking out a second mortgage on *his* house.

Larry Gleeson, of Maine Hydro-Electric Development Corp., found his start-up money in both usual and unusual sources. Family loans, savings, the proceeds from selling his house, all helped. But his business was such that it opened doors many entrepreneurs never see. The Department of Energy, says Larry, was "as curious as we were" about whether small hydroelectric development projects would really work, and it made cost-sharing arrangements available. Manufacturers of equipment such as turbines and electrical controls were interested in developing new markets for their products and saw

Larry's projects as demonstration opportunities; they helped by letting him defer payments. In addition, since in some ways Larry's hydroelectric activities were not new, but a revival of ancient practices, there was some old equipment available cheap; we have already mentioned the turbine that came with his first site.

The money raised (and saved) in all these ways would have been enough if "hardware" expenses were all Larry had to worry about. He notes that he did fail to foresee how high would grow the costs of legal help and of obtaining the necessary permits and licenses. This failure was aggravated because as he sought his licenses, various groups became aware of how hydroelectric development would affect their special interests. Their participation in hearings increased both the time and the paperwork necessary, and hence the expense.

What options are available for those entrepreneurs who lack substantial personal resources? Most entrepreneurs do in fact find that they need far more funds than they can easily lay hands on. Where do they turn?

They begin with relatives. Uncle Arthur and Aunt Emma may have spent careers in law or medicine or business and amassed small—or large—fortunes. They may be willing to help a trusted nephew with a good business idea. Help may be available from parents or grandparents, brothers or sisters, or in-laws. It may be possible to tap friends and associates. Every one of these people will expect—and deserve—to receive some equity (ownership) in the new business. The problem you face is to make deals that attract the needed funds without giving up control of the enterprise. Judith Kaplan, of Action Packets, raised some of the money she needed with a bank credit line, but that was not enough. She parted with a small portion of her equity when she sold shares in the business to friends, family members, and associates.

In most cases, personal assets and the investments of family members, friends, and associates do not entirely meet the needs of the business. Where does the entrepreneur turn next? Many business advisers suggest approaching local bankers, lawyers, and accountants. They may have personal funds for investment; they will almost certainly know of other locals who are on the lookout for investment opportunities or tax shelters.

"Locals" is the key word here. Local people looking for promising business investments are often inclined to keep their funds in businesses close to home. Some take a measure of satisfaction in supporting local employment, local minorities, and the local economy. Local may mean town, county, state, or region.

PRIVATE OFFERINGS AND VENTURE CAPITAL

Private offerings include offering equity to friends, family, and wealthy locals. They are "private" offerings because they do not involve "going public."

Private offerings can also be an important source of venture capital. As such, however, they are not true seed money, for venture capitalists are universally shy of most start-ups. The venture capitalists usually want to put their funds in companies that have made it over the first hurdles and are on the verge of making their breakthrough to big markets. The venture capitalists are in the game to help small companies become larger, not as a rule to assist untried newcomers.

There are exceptions. Venture capital companies will on rare occasion, and for sound reasons, get behind a start-up and aid in its birth. Some venture capitalists actually seek and create such occasions. For example, Kleiner, Perkins and Company, a venture capital firm that specializes in advanced technology, once brought James Treybig into its offices for a year. The idea was for Treybig to design a product and learn by observation all he could about writing business plans and setting up a new business. When he was ready, Kleiner, Perkins backed him, and Tandem Computers was born. In 1984, the company was number 3 on *Venture* magazine's list of the 100 largest entrepreneurial companies founded in the last decade, "The Fast-Track 100."

We see the essence of the private offering when a new business in the advanced stages of development convinces individual investors to provide funds in return for partial ownership. These investors may be the same people who kicked in for the start-up. The investors may be entrepreneurs themselves who have confidence in their ability to evaluate a new business. Sometimes they draw in their friends to form an investment syndicate. The aim in syndication may be potentially major capital gains or the tax benefits of participating in a "Subchapter S" corporation. They are often willing, even eager, to get involved in the business's operations as advisers or as members of the board of directors.

One type of investor who is important to some entrepreneurs is the entrepreneur who has made it big and wants to use his or her new-found wealth to back other entrepreneurs (Mamis, 1984). Mamis describes Charles Ying, one of the founders of Atex, Inc., a maker of text-processing computer equipment. He backed David Chung, who had no more than a design for an improved way to send data from computer to computer. Ying supplied Chung with the money to develop a prototype, even though Chung had no business plan, no product, and no defined market. Today, Chung Telecommunications, Inc., is a success.

Individuals like Ying are adventure capitalists. They supply the seed money where the risk is greatest. The adventure capitalists have appeared in recent years most often in high technology areas, where the potential rewards have sometimes proven to be enormous. They do not ordinarily work alone. Mamis reports that "the network" is a word-of-mouth informal system of investors who occasionally take adventure-capital flyers and who help each other when a flight is struggling to get off the ground. For Chung, Ying brought in Richard Black, who both invested and helped design Chung's marketing strategy. Ying also set up a Small Business Administration-licensed minority small business investment corporation in Seattle.

Ying himself says that supporting certain new entrepreneurs is "good for everybody . . . nobody loses . . . first the entrepreneurs win . . . then I win—and the U.S. is maybe a little bit closer to Japan. . . . That's why I'm doing what I'm doing instead of sitting on a beach in Maui."

Ying is only one of the 20–30 "Silicon Valley" rich who form Summerhill Partners, a group that seeks and invests in high-tech entrepreneurial opportunities. It was Summerhill who backed Steven Kirsch in turning his improved "mouse" (a hand-held device that controls a computer display by sliding around a desktop) into a company. Kirsch provides another example of the adventure capitalists going with an entrepreneur who had no business plan, no financial projections, no market projections, and none of the other data required by more conventional investors. Summerhill provided Kirsch with an initial $50,000 and three board members, while individual partners on their own kicked in another $250,000.

Private investors are often more willing to consider smaller businesses than usually attract the large venture capital corporations. One reason the private investor is attracted to smaller businesses is the opportunity to buy more equity. Also smaller companies usually are looking for funds in the amounts likely to be available from private investors as compared to large venture capitalists.

New businesses may also find equity capital from large, institutional investors, but Baty (1981) cautions that private investors are likely to be less averse to risk than institutional investors.

The institutional investors include not only the venture capital companies, but also closed-end investment funds, which put money into young firms. Once into a company, institutions are likely to be willing to add to their investment when the company needs more funds. The institutional investors can also be more patient than other investors about waiting for the payoff.

Equity capital is available from insurance companies, university endowments, and pension funds, but such sources treat venture capital as a minor portion of their investment portfolios. Since the funds they manage must not be seriously depleted, they are obliged to stick largely to "prudent" investments.

Baty (1981) points out that business itself is a growing source of venture capital. Large corporations like Exxon, Time, and Santa Fe have found considerable profit in buying equity in new businesses. However, such investors are understandably more interested in their own corporate health than in the health of the businesses in which they invest. Their investment in many cases is a way of getting creative, energetic people (captive entrepreneurs, as it were) to work on new products. In other cases, the equity investment is a way of buying into key suppliers and customers, of neutralizing competition, or of developing new divisions.

Large corporations may invest because they genuinely believe in the new company's potential, or because they hope to share in some of the glamour of the high-tech industry. In most cases, their expectations are more concrete. Several corporations that have backed the early biotechnology firms or provided funds for university departments of biotechnology have said that they hope to develop a relationship that will give them a window on the development of profitable new technologies. The university departments they support are sources of trained researchers and places where their own researchers can obtain advanced, up-to-date training. The new companies in which they buy equity can give them exclusive rights to new technological developments.

Industry can be a very good source of seed money, and with the money can come valuable help in management, marketing, and production. There can be beneficial arrangements that place the new entrepreneur in the enviable position of preferred supplier or customer. But with the help and preferential treatment comes the inevitable price tag—in addition to the equity position of the investor. Industrial investors may want to keep their young protegees private by vetoing—in the initial funding agreement or later—any inclination to take the new company public. They may prevent the company from selling to the investor's competitors. They may forbid obtaining supplies or raw materials from other sources, even when other sources may be cheaper. They may impose charges for "consultation" (as may some venture capital companies). They may dictate the terms of any future attempt to acquire a new investor.

Some entrepreneurs feel that if they should accept major funding from large corporations, they would end up as employees. Yet industrial funding can work, provided the investing company is one that values the entrepreneur's independence as an advantage and an asset to both parties.

The respect for independence, as well as for the entrepreneur's desire to profit from his or her enterprise, is one of the keys to what Gifford Pinchot III (1985) calls "intrapreneuring," a topic of the next chapter. Ralph Brown would never have thought to call it that, but when he tried to encourage his executives and even his employees to be independently creative, he was trying to foster "intrapreneurship." His efforts did not take very well and so, he laments, "after sixteen years the industrial community spirit I conceived does not exist."

LOANS

So far, we have discussed seed money sources that cost the entrepreneur equity in his or her enterprise. Loans are less desirable for, since they must be repaid, they constitute a drain on a new business's future resources. Yet the entrepreneur may find that the available equity market is not sufficient to meet the needs of the business. Borrowed seed money may be the remaining alternative.

This means approaching bankers as professionals rather than as private investors. Borrowing means grim reality, for banks are notoriously reluctant to make seed loans to unproven businesses. You very nearly have to show that you do not need the loan to get one. They demand collateral, accounts receivable, a distinguished track record—in short anything and everything that reduces their risk to zero. Banks that do make seed money loans will ask for the entrepreneur's personal signature on the note, thus removing the protection of the corporation in the event of bankruptcy.

Some banks are associated with small business investment companies (SBICs) designed especially to work with small businesses, including new starts. Others are linked to the Small Business Administration (SBA) and can take advantage of federal loan guarantee programs. We will have more to say about the SBA below.

Other sources of loans include state, regional, and local development agencies, both public and quasi-public, that stand ready to support any enterprise that looks as though it will make a contribution to the local economy and employment. There are also credit unions and, for import-export businesses, export banks that offer attractive credit to encourage trade.

It is often possible to negotiate extended credit terms from the suppliers of equipment and raw materials and to talk customers into advance or progress payments (in some industries, such arrangements are the norm). Suppliers of capital equipment may be the kindest, as Larry Gleeson found. They will usually bend over backward to make it easy for a new business to buy their goods through leasing contracts or conditional sales agreements (wherein the seller retains title until the equipment is paid for). These suppliers can make these deals because capital equipment keeps its value and serves as its own collateral.

Suppliers of nondurable and consumable goods want payment in full as soon as possible, but they will usually give 30 days without a penalty and up to an additional 60 days with interest.

THE SMALL BUSINESS ADMINISTRATION

The Small Business Administration, set up in the early 1950s to help small businesses (defined as having less than 500 employees) become established, runs four major programs. The financial assistance program is of primary interest here, but entrepreneurs should also be familiar with the assistance the SBA can provide in management training and counseling (much of it through free and low-cost pamphlets), securing government contracts, and advocacy (Hershey, 1984). The SBA also sponsors SCORE, the Service Corps of Retired Executives, whose unpaid volunteers apply their experience and knowledge from successful business careers, often as entrepreneurs, to help new businesses organize and improve their operations. Sandy Sakurai reports that she attended a two-day seminar by SCORE to learn "the basics of setup" when she was organizing her career counseling service.

The SBA was originally designed to make loans to businesses that could not get credit "on reasonable terms" from some other source, but also to make only loans for which the odds on repayment were reasonably good. Richman (1984) notes that "the two main conditions were frequently contradictory, and thus the SBA was born schizophrenic" and in one of its personalities "saw itself as a welfare agency."

SBA's dual role has led to a host of horror stories. Richman cites the 1974 case of Elizabeth Taylor (not the actress), who applied to SBA for $86,900 to start a restaurant. SBA said no, on the grounds that Taylor would not have enough cash to run the restaurant. Then, SBA turned around and lent Taylor $36,700, which was just enough to open the restaurant, but not enough to keep it going. Taylor wound up losing her savings, her home, and her health.

Richman also describes the 1978 case of the Stutts, who tried to borrow $50,000 to purchase inventory for their appliance store. SBA refused the loan on the grounds that repayment was unlikely. The Stutts borrowed the funds from another source and five years later, in 1983, made fifth place on *Inc.* magazine's annual list of the nation's fastest growing businesses.

In the Taylor case, SBA failed as a welfare agency; in the Stutts case, SBA failed as a banker. But these may not be its worst problems. According to Burlingame (1983), SBA seems to have its greatest difficulties in recognizing the promise of businesses in new technologies. In the case of Frank Jones' Imre Corporation, set up to make and sell a medical device that holds promise for helping the bodies of cancer patients to fight cancers, Imre had the device, the seed capital, the people, and even the advance orders to support the case for an SBA loan. But SBA's Seattle office refused the loan, not once but several times. Imre came back again and again with additional information and documentation requested by SBA. In the end, Imre found the seed money from venture capitalists, but at the expense of "a significant portion of ownership."

Some SBA loans are direct, involving transfer of government funds to entrepreneurs. Others are indirect, relying on government guarantees of up to 90 percent of loans made by commercial banks. Direct loans were the most common in the 1950s and 1960s. Since the late 1960s, the guarantees have been predominant. In 1980, for example, SBA guaranteed $1.7 billion in loans; another $100 million only were in direct loans. The guarantees are involved in about 13 percent of all small business loans and as much as 40 percent of all long-term small business credit. Thus, despite the horror stories, SBA has long been and remains an important source of funds for small business.

LEVERAGED BUY-OUTS

One source of capital is never available to entrepreneurs who are starting from scratch, and that is the capital that comes to a firm in a so-called leveraged buy-out. The reason is simple: a leveraged buy-out is a method of taking over a company, and the capital the entrepreneur uses for the take-over comes from leveraging the company's own assets. The entrepreneur who engineers the leveraged buy-out may be an individual, a group of employees or investors, or perhaps one or more officers of a subsidiary. The entrepreneur puts up a relatively small amount of cash and then uses the target company's assets—land, buildings, equipment, accounts receivable—as collateral for a large bank loan. The loan will be repaid out of the company's earnings.

The leveraged buy-out has become possible in recent years with changes in Federal Reserve regulations that allow investment bankers to arrange funding for purchase of stock in public companies. Leveraged buy-outs have helped encourage a trend among conglomerates to sell subsidiary companies. They may in the future facilitate the trend toward decentralization in American business. In addition, leveraged buy-outs help public companies go private (Waters, 1983a) and let company founders "cash out" when they lose interest or wish to do other things.

Waters (1983b) describes the case of Universal Electric Company of Owosso, Michigan, a subsidiary of Inco, Ltd., of Toronto. When in 1980 Inco decided to get rid of Universal Electric, UE's management found out about leveraged buy-outs. With some good advice, they collectively put up $250,000 of their own funds toward the $45 million purchase price, thus gaining among them a 25 percent ownership in the firm for which they had been working as employees. To ease tax problems, a leveraged buy-out specialist helped them merge with a second company that was running at a loss. By the end of 1983, UE was doing $80 million in annual sales, was employing 2000 people, and had paid off $9 million of its $34 million debt. Performance went sharply up, according to UE president Bill Lawson, because its senior managers "have all got a piece of the action."

Among our subjects, only Thomas Lisle became an entrepreneur by using the leveraged buy-out, in his case to take over Cruisers, Inc., a maker of pleasure boats. He reports that, "funding was a problem in many of the potential acquisitions I viewed. . . . In the case of the Cruisers opportunity, the seller would provide the financing." He arranged a bank line of credit for operating capital, but "the essence of our forecast was to liquidate assets of the operation to provide operating capital in conjunction with bank financing. . . . As it turned out, we were able to liquidate assets and generate more capital than was necessary; consequently the bank line of credit was not required."

Thus the range of seed money sources goes from the personal bank account all the way to the complex arrangements of the leveraged buy-out. As an entrepreneur with a business idea and the determination to see it through to a profitable business, you will probably do what you must to get the start-up money. If your personal savings won't do it, you are likely to think next of a loan on your house or other assets. Next come investors among family and friends. If you have an exceptionally promising idea or product, you may attract venture or even adventure capital, or you may "go public" with a stock offering. The point is that some, perhaps all, of these options may be open to you, and they should be examined thoroughly in light of your needs and the scope of the operation you are planning.

CHAPTER 6

Setting Up Under Cover: Ethics in Limbo

This chapter is about ethics and old-fashioned honesty. There are no grey areas between honesty and dishonesty—only rationalizations. It is not right to spend time owed the employer writing a business plan or phoning prospective customers and suppliers. It compounds the wrong to call on the employer's own customers, suppliers, and contacts in hopes of wooing them away on the employer's time.

It is just as wrong to use the employer's office supplies or postage meter for promoting a private entrepreneurial scheme, although some employees regard such use as a normal company "perk." It is no better to talk up the prospective new business to coworkers in order to offer them ground-floor opportunities as partners or employees.

The entrepreneur is on sound ethical grounds only when spending his or her own money for supplies and raw materials and machine time, for copies and postage and telephone bills, when doing everything that needs doing on his or her own time, when finding contacts, customers, partners, and employees, all without taking advantage of his or her employer.

Not surprisingly, many entrepreneurs do not set out entirely clean. They may be cautious about walking out with furniture, but they pay less attention to the ethics of "trivial" borrowings. Samuel Wallace and his Xodex partners saw the ethical problems in their own case, but they largely ignored them. Wallace reports that, "There were some obvious problems since we were required to make a number of copies of proposals and documents we thought would be needed and this therefore required doing these after hours, more often during the day. . . . However, even when such borrowings were evident to the employer, we tended to be pretty arrogant and aggressive about it, since there is no loyalty to these corporations at the point when the decision has been made to leave. . . . Further, I particularly worked for an individual who was in the process of leaving the firm as well, and this minimized the degree to which my activities would be seen directly by higher management."

On the larger scale, many new businesses wind up staffed by the entrepreneur's former coworkers and dealing with the entrepreneur's former employer's suppliers, contacts, and customers. How can this be? Can new businesses appear without dishonest entrepreneurs?

This question is important. Every employer who has been around awhile knows that the pirates exist and most do not hesitate to prosecute or sue when wronged. Every entrepreneur wants to avoid early legal troubles and, when possible, to remain on reasonably good terms with a former employer. For one thing, the entrepreneur might fail and need the old job back. Or the former employer might turn out to be a valuable friend and advisor, possibly an investor.

Contrast Pat Heffernan's and Ellen Green's attitudes to Samuel Wallace's when they left their respective employers to become entrepreneurs. Pat Heffernan told us that she was "very careful not to use any of the facilities or resources" of her employer. She said that she had witnessed such abuses and "felt quite strongly" that she should avoid them. She avoided doing any of her preparatory work at the office, doing it evenings and on weekends. She takes pleasure in the fact that her former employer is now a client.

Ellen Green also "didn't take anything that wasn't mine (except my wastebasket which was used instead of a box to take out my office accoutrements). . . . My employer was supportive because he was going to get the benefits of new and better materials for his staff."

Sandy Sakurai took both the knowledge of her employer's client procedures and some of the clients with her when she left to set up her own career counseling service. She explains, "Most of what Bernard Haldane Associates knows is in published books available to the public. . . . The clients I invited to continue with me I did not charge—they had already paid an upfront/in full fee to B.H.A. . . . I did it for good will and contacts." She also pointed out that her former employer was no longer operating in Maryland and so she was not competing.

Larry Gleeson accomplished many of the necessary tasks involved in setting up his Maine Hydro-Electric Development Corporation while still employed by Sun Oil in Philadelphia. He did his planning, found suppliers and customers, located and dealt for dam sites, and even incorporated before he actually cut loose. However, he did it all "with Sun's knowledge and consent. They allowed me to do it as long as it was on my own time and on my own expense." Sun was not actively helpful, but neither was it obstructive, and Larry was careful to avoid conflicts of interest, accomplishing much of what he needed to do on vacation time. When he did cut loose, he was ready to begin construction on his first powerhouse.

THE WATCHFUL EMPLOYER

Thievery is thievery, whether it involves furniture or paper clips or time. Many employers protect themselves with security systems of one sort or another. They use inventory and check-out systems to monitor supplies, electronic keys or sign-in sheets or operators to control use of copiers and other office machinery, and restricted access or watchmen to control use of production equipment.

Yet most employers worry less about supplies and equipment than they do about theft of ideas and people. That is why employers or their legal advisers insist upon agreements with key employees that preclude post-employment competition and guard against loss of trade secrets. Such agreements often make employee inventions the property of the employer.

Invention agreements are commonly used for technicians, engineers, and scientists, the people who are most likely to come up with an idea on the job that they could later use as the basis of a new business. But not all such ideas are of interest to the employer, who may foresee too long or too expensive a period of development, or too small an immediate market. Inventors are sometimes years or decades ahead of the market with their creativity.

Some employers are prepared to give or license the rights to an invention to the employee-inventor. Some are not, and in most cases, it falls to the employee-inventor to clarify the matter at the time an employer-employee invention agreement is signed. We strongly advise caution on the part of the employee-inventor in signing any such agreement. If you are an idea person who is likely to come up with a timely and valuable new product, your best course in considering an employer-initiated inventor contract is to consult an attorney who had had specific experience with such contracts.

You and your attorney should go over the proposed contract and the invention-assignment forms both at the point of accepting employment and again at the point when you begin to think about setting up a new business that is to be based upon an invention that you developed during your employment. It is especially important to be clear about the contract status of an invention you develop on your own time at home or in your private shop. Some invention-assignment agreements are phrased to cover all employee creations, whether they are produced at the company or at home. The more liberal ones apply only to ideas developed at work.

It is important that any invention-assignment contract be absolutely clear on this point and that you take steps to stay within the agreement. For example, if the agreement allows you to retain possession of inventions developed at home on your own time, with your own resources, then you should keep a diary and other careful records that document the circumstances and resources pertaining to development of the invention.

Nondisclosure statements may be required of all company employees. These statements are legal contracts and, upon close examination, they may go so far as to forbid setting up a competing business. They will certainly forbid taking customer lists to a competing company, or using proprietary information such as product designs, production techniques, and business and marketing plans.

Noncompetition agreements usually focus more narrowly (see Spanner, 1985). They are standard in modern employee contracts, and their goal, in simplest terms, is to prevent employees from opening a duplicate shop after learning the business. The noncompetition agreement tries to guard against the damaging action of an employee who deliberately builds a network of loyal customers who stay with the employee when he or she sets up a competing company.

Some noncompetition agreements define competition very narrowly. Others impose restrictions so broad that they are legally unenforceable. The courts have consistently held that the former employer cannot prevent a person from using his or her field of expertise.

Noncompetition agreements can be tricky legal ground for the uninitiated, and so again the soundest course is to review any such agreements with an attorney who has had specific experience with them. If you are an employee who has already signed a noncompetition agreement, and you are thinking seriously of setting up a new business that will be directly in competition with your employer, it is all the more necessary that you go over the agreement with an experienced attorney. The reason we urge experienced legal advice is that it may prove very difficult to avoid the appearance of breach of contract.

For example, an entrepreneur's new business may make a product that does the same thing as the former employer's product, except that the new product may be more reliable, more flexible, or less expensive. The former employer's customers flock to the new product, and the entrepreneur is hauled into court.

Was the ex-employee, now entrepreneur, competing unfairly? Did he or she steal the customers from the former employer? Or would the same have happened if someone else had developed the improved product? Could someone else have developed the improved product without experience in the plaintiff's company? These are the kinds of questions you may have to face in a court of law if you fail to get good legal advice a) before you sign a noncompetition agreement, or b) before you venture out to set up a competing business based on a product similar to one your employer makes.

Baty (1981) cautions that lawsuits can have a chilling effect on potential investors in new businesses. No one wants to back a new business that might lose all its resources because a court finds that it is using stolen information, infringing on patents, violating trade secrets, or competing unfairly with a former employer. No one wants to back a firm that is facing even the nuisance lawsuits of a jealous or paranoid former employer. The only sound defense against the latter—and against unintentionally harming a fair-minded former employer—is scrupulously ethical behaviour. Do what you know is right from start to finish even down to the smallest details. Guard against your own rationalizations of the supposed grey areas of conduct. Buy your own paper clips.

THE ETHICAL ENTREPRENEUR

Time and time again our subjects have reported careful attention to ethics. Win Cross's New York publishing firm was created when one of the principals decided to cut loose from his publisher employer. He planned to produce similar books, but not the same books and not for quite the same market. More of a problem than the intended product was finding partners. The partners he chose were colleagues and executives in the firm of the former employer, but he did not approach them with offers until after he had resigned from his job.

A publisher needs authors. This publisher made some of his early book contracts with authors who had previously dealt with the former employer, but he did not contact the authors about his new firm until after he had left his old job and set up his company. His editorial partner did the author recruiting for the new firm, but only after leaving his job with the former employer. The authors who had published with the former employer were invited to submit new manuscripts that had not been on the agenda of the former employer. Many of the authors who signed with the new firm had not had previous connections with the former employer.

In the publishing world, as in every line of business, unethical competitive behavior is common to the point of being taken for granted. In the publishing world, editors build personal relationships with authors and usually "take them along" when they move to another publisher or set up their own operation. Executives plot new ventures over lunch in the company dining room. Noncompetition agreements are not the norm in the publishing industry, although authors often sign contracts with clauses that oblige them to give the publisher first refusal rights to their next book.

Does the common practice of unethical behavior and therefore the common expectation of it lend it a certain justification? We argue that unethical behavior is disruptive and socially dysfunctional wherever it occurs. Business relationships (like all human relationships) require a stable set of expectations—commonly accepted rules of the game—to function smoothly.

PRODUCTS

The publishing industry has no real need of invention assignments, but other industries do. Bill Wernsing, president of Williams Laboratories in Ithaca, New York, reports that when he left General Electric in 1964, he was never troubled by the agreements that he had signed. He was going into business for himself largely because he had never had any difficulty thinking up new ideas; he felt no need to try to take any past inventions with him.

Here we see a common problem that faces technical entrepreneurs. They usually are forced by invention assignment contracts to leave past inventions behind when they leave a company and to rely upon their creativity to come up with new ideas. If they lack the confidence to do so, they probably stay put and could not be called entrepreneurial in the first place.

In some cases, an inventor can succeed in keeping an invention private, developing it in secret at home in the basement or converted garage. The invention becomes the foundation of a new enterprise. Innumerable entrepreneurs have begun this way, as the legends of American enterprise recount. Each entrepreneur must wrestle his or her own conscience over the ethical questions as they apply to his or her particular situation.

University researchers and technicians frequently come up with salable products. In such cases, the institution usually owns the patent rights. Sometimes, a government funding agency, foundation, or corporate sponsor owns the rights. Except in the last case, the researcher or technician can often gain the right to develop the product into a business by proposing a mutually advantageous arrangement, such as a royalty payment to the institution or foundation. The latter may eagerly go along with the proposal, especially if the inventor has a unique understanding of the product or process by which it is made. Another incentive for the institution may be the willingness of the inventor to remain on the staff of the institution while directing the operations of the new enterprise.

University spin-offs usually involve advanced technology, as with the computer industry, where both software and hardware are first worked out in campus laboratories. Ronald Slatin, of the University of Arizona, had no difficulty getting an okay from his employer to produce and market his pulmonary functions interpretation program because the University Health Center was already making it available to hospitals in the Tucson area and could only benefit from wider national use of the program.

In all such cases, the high-tech entrepreneur must negotiate the right to undertake his or her enterprise. Only the unethical entrepreneur tries to set up without a clear agreement covering the rights of an employer. The attempt to avoid such an agreement only leaves the way open for unwanted legal troubles.

Ethical entrepreneurs recognize the rights of those to whom they have ceded ownership of their ideas, and they strive to work out compromises. Licensing arrangements are only one of the possibilities, as we demonstrate in the discussion below on ways employers can be actively helpful to entrepreneurs.

CUSTOMERS

When it comes to customers, ethical entrepreneurs face some very fuzzy problems. Many have spent their careers working for one company or in one industry. When they go out on their own, because they know the industry and the people in it, the chances are that they will know beforehand who their customers are likely to be. Yet it is not considered ethical when they leave the old job to take with them a list of their employer's customers.

There are ways out of this seeming dilemma. The entrepreneur can start by offering the former employer's customers a product or service that the former employer does not offer. In that case, no ethical issue is raised when the entrepreneur takes along the former employer's customer list. The employer may even be willing to give a friend and former employee the list to help him or her get off to a good start. The former employer may think that the entrepreneur's marketing efforts will somehow enhance the demand for the company's own products and services. This happy relationship will surely develop when the entrepreneur's product improves the capabilities of those of the former employer. Both Pat Heffernan and Ellen Green retained their respective former employers as customers when they left to set up their businesses. Pat Heffernan has been assisting the law school which she had served as associate dean to improve office procedures with computer equipment. Ellen Green developed two health education products which provided "new and better materials" for her former employer's staff.

Another way around the dilemma starts when the entrepreneur's market is seen by both parties as different from or not quite the same as that of the former employer. Also the entrepreneur may be interested in only a few of the former employer's customers. Or the entrepreneur's business idea may involve offering a similar product to a much broader market. In such cases, the entrepreneur may be able to get the former employer's entire customer list and use it as a starting point. The entrepreneur then builds on it the longer list he envisions as the broader market.

Entrepreneurs confront the customer dilemma head-on when they offer essentially the same product or service to all of the same customers served by the former employer. Perhaps the only differences are in price, quality, or service policies. The entrepreneur cannot then avoid the impression that he or she has made off with the former employer's customer list—even when the entrepreneur is guilty to no greater extent than to be blessed with a good memory or knowledge of where to look for customers.

Protection from lawsuits then rests on scrupulous and documented avoidance of any conflict of interest. The rule is straightforward: do not contact or approach an employer's customers until you have left the old job and set up the new company.

DOCUMENTS

The ethical entrepreneur should be as careful with marketing plans and business plans as with product ideas and customers. Legal and ethical guidelines aside, plans developed by a former employer are unlikely to be specifically applicable to the circumstances the new entrepreneur will face. Objectives will differ, not to mention style and personalities. At best, someone else's plan might be a useful template, but not the substance and content.

Be forewarned that a new enterprise requires a new and entirely original set of plans. The product, except in the unlikely case of an exact copy, will be different. The customers will be different or, if they are the same people, their needs for your different product will dictate a different planning approach. Surely the size and future growth pattern of the new enterprise will be all its own, although, of course, not without precedent. In a word, you should take care to tailor the business plan to reflect the specific objectives and needs of your new enterprise. Likewise, you should design a marketing plan especially suited to the new product. Your customer list, whatever its sources, should be tailored to the new product. Your advertising and media strategy should reflect your concept of what you want the company to be.

Any entrepreneur who tries to build a business on the dubious foundation of "borrowed" documents is almost certainly doomed to an early failure. The mismatch between the business for which borrowed documents were prepared and any new enterprise will almost always be too great to bridge.

Borrowed plans may be useful as templates or outlines, and they may be useful as instructional guides to provide insight into the value and function of planning in the business context. In fact, many business texts and courses are built around examples of actual business plans (for example, Welsh and White, 1983). Most such books and courses warn as we do against any attempt to lift model plans without expert adaption.

We should note that any business involves many other documents than business and marketing plans. These others include marketing research reports and consultant reports. In each case, the documents were prepared for a particular business, and the applicability to a new business would require careful—and expert—evaluation, not a task for a neophyte entrepreneur. Market reports may be adaptable, provided the product to be marketed is similar. In the long run, the new company is on the soundest ground when it uses reports that are prepared specifically for it. Why run the risks of hazardous shortcuts?

Some entrepreneurs may be tempted to use an employer's audited financial statements, tax returns, and the like. Again these documents are far too specific to the business for which they were prepared to be useful to anyone else. In addition, using them in any way except as models can lead to serious trouble. The Internal Revenue Service will react swiftly to fictitious figures on tax returns, and the Securities Exchange Commission is very strict about enforcing its regulations on financial statements.

SETTING UP UNDER COVER

Many, if not most, entrepreneurs set up their businesses while still employed. The obvious advantage of starting a business in this way is the shield it provides against the hazards of self-employment. The regular income continues, as do medical insurance and the employer's contribution to the FICA tax. There may be access to photocopiers, telephones, and other office equipment, preferably with the employer's permission. Countless employees have used their employer's office supplies, parts bins, and production equipment; some have even used these resources through an above-board arrangement with the employer.

One of the greatest advantages of setting up under cover may be travel arrangements on behalf of the employer. This is called piggyback travel. Any business traveller finds free time in distant cities, evenings, weekends, marking time waiting for an appointment or a plane, and certainly during lunch hours. Business people who are working on setting up their own business can legitimately use such spare hours to contact potential suppliers, customers, and backers. They can arrange valuable face-to-face luncheon meetings when at the home office. Some business advisers recommend that would-be entrepreneurs take full advantage of these times to do as much of the groundwork as possible before cutting loose.

The disadvantage to the entrepreneur is the scarcity of time available to lay the groundwork of an entirely new organization. Building a new enterprise in the cracks of daily business means building piecemeal, and perhaps in the process sacrificing some coherence. Building a business bit by bit calls for great patience and the ability to maintain one's dedication and self-confidence.

The disadvantage to the employer is that these spare-time activities, even when meticulously limited to spare time by the employee, may be a distraction from the work the employee is being paid to do. The employee cannot ordinarily focus entirely on the work at hand.

We caution employers and employees alike that psychic focus is a crucial aspect of any but the most routine jobs. If your mind is not on the work you are being paid to do, you cannot possibly give full value. Probably the employer should tolerate an employee setting up under cover of the business only when it clearly serves the interest of the business. For example, the employer is trying to cut back on the executive staff or research division by attrition, and the company has decided to help people to move on to other jobs. Or the employee-turned-entrepreneur is developing a business that could become a valuable customer or supplier.

Setting up under cover inevitably entails some conflict of interest. When this conflict becomes appreciable—when the entrepreneur is spending large amounts of effort on the new enterprise—the time has come to resign. Making the change at this point removes the employment shield, but it will avoid unwanted trouble on both sides.

Once you have taken this step, you are on your own financial resources. Now you are free—truly free—to approach former colleagues at the old job and recruit them as partners or employees. You are now free to contact past customers and invite their business. Your efforts from here on out in such matters are entirely within the bounds of business ethics.

Several of our subjects prepared or set up their businesses while still employed. One of these, Ron Slatin of Medimicro Systems, remains on the staff of the University of Arizona for the simple reason that his company has only one product that does not have a sufficient market to support a full-time operation. J. W. Anderson set up the U.S. Industrial Film Festival while employed at the Keebler Company. His employer did not object because his activities as chairman of the Festival were mainly once a year and spare time. On occasions when he had to cut into company time, his staff covered for him. Samuel Wallace did use company time and resources to set up Xodex under cover of a superior who was also leaving the firm. "There was no loyalty . . . at the point where a decision to leave had been made," he explained.

The others among our respondents worked on arrangements for their new businesses with full knowledge of their employers. Greg Kravitt's prospective partner was his boss at the bank where both of them were employed. The two of them had full discussions of plans and "Accordingly, any appearance of conflict was removed." Larry Gleeson had his employer's "knowledge and consent" and the stipulation that he do his own work with his own time and money.

Win Cross was careful not to let his work on his proposed new publishing company interfere with his work for his employer, never discussing or working "on the new venture during company time or on company premises." He reports that he did not "approach any company contacts . . . authors, suppliers, customers, etc. . . . until after the break was made.'' He also ''made sure that any and all documents relating to former employer were returned before making the break.''

Thomas Lisle reports that by the time he undertook the concentrated acquisitions effort, he and his employer ''had already agreed on a mutual parting of the ways.'' The company Lisle finally selected for acquisition was not competitive with any business of his former employer, so there were no conflicts. His relations with his former employer have left Lisle with ''a very useful contact.''

RESPONSIBLE TERMINATION

When you finally do resign to go into business for yourself, you continue to have certain responsibilities to your former employer. It is both wise and right to recognize and fulfill these responsibilities. On a practical level, your reputation is at stake as reflected in future letters of recommendation to support applications for credit and to support your efforts to attract investors. Your integrity and competence may be your most valuable long-term assets in your efforts at building your business. These character traits are always under scrutiny by the people for whom you work and with whom you deal as an entrepreneur. You should be careful to establish these assets in people's judgments of you right from the start of your new work. Don't burn your bridges. A clean and amicable break from the old job can make it easier to return should your new business not succeed.

Responsible termination means finishing whatever you have started or making sure that your replacement is thoroughly briefed. Any resigning employee, not just one who is starting a new business, should attend to the following guidelines:

—Wrap up current projects. This means completing reports and research work and helping to train a replacement for tasks that cannot be finished by the termination date. It means meeting near-term obligations such as the presentation of a marketing plan, or arrangments for a major sales meeting, or staying on the job until the pilot plant is on line. What cannot be finished should be left to people who have been well briefed on schedules, loose ends, and partially made arrangements.

—Help train the replacement. This means being around until the new man or woman has learned the ropes. It may mean recommending the promotion of a competent subordinate.

—Make sure that the departure leaves no monkey wrenches in the corporate machinery. This injunction covers the first two above, but it also means making sure that customers and suppliers are informed about any changes in lines of communication between them and the company; making sure that they know who the replacement is. It means making sure that some responsible person knows about an impending visit from OSHA or about the rumor of an impending coup in Mauritania, which supplies 95 percent of a crucial raw material.

A congenial separation can prove very helpful to the entrepreneur. Thomas Lisle tells us that when he began his concentrated acquisition effort for Cruisers, Inc., he and the Eaton Corporation "had already agreed on a mutual parting of the ways. . . . [Cruisers was not] competitive with any business of Eaton. . . . With respect to contacts and information, the Eaton source was and remains very useful. . . . This, however, is more of a personal nature, i.e., contacting former associates and getting direct information or opinions. . . . Since the parting was not acrimonious, I am able to continue to use these contacts extensively."

The unethical entrepreneur usually has numerous opportunities at the crucial time of departure to handicap the former employer for weeks, months, or even years. It is possible at this juncture for the villain entrepreneur to give the new enterprise a lasting advantage over the former employer. He or she need only leave chaos and confusion behind. Of course, such behavior can backfire in lawsuits, poor recommendations, and the like. The person who behaves badly when resigning can expect the word to spread in the industry, and perhaps to encounter difficulties obtaining credit from suppliers, attracting quality customers, and securing capital. Ethical behavior at the crucial stage of transition from employee to entrepreneur is as sound a long-term investment as you can make.

THE HELPFUL EMPLOYER

In Chapter 1 we mentioned Nolan Bushnell's Catalyst Technologies, whose business is to nurture new businesses until they are ready to make it on their own. Bushnell's operation is but one example of an "incubator organization." Other kinds of incubators exist as well. Some of the large venture capital companies deliberately train novice entrepreneurs to write effective business plans, and to make the business they have planned work. Some large corporations deliberately encourage their employees to start their own businesses, sometimes as subsidiaries, but often as totally independent operations. They may help by providing seed money and free or low-cost space, equipment, and/or machine time.

Entrepreneurs who work for such companies are lucky. Most do not. Yet some employers can be surprisingly helpful even if they do not have a deliberate policy of encouraging entrepreneurs within their ranks. Actively obstructive employers are by no means the rule on the American business scene.

Many business advisers (for example, Baty, 1981) urge employees who are planning to set up their own businesses to discuss their plans with their employer before resigning. One benefit of this step is that it promptly identifies obstructive employers. A greater benefit is that it reveals the helpful ones.

Disclosing plans gives the entrepreneur and his or her employer a chance to discuss possible problems of competition, customer lists, proprietary products, trade secrets, and patents. Some employers will respond with threats of lawsuits. Others will recognize the advantages of offering licenses, selling rights to the entrepreneur for stock or cash, or even contracting the entrepreneur to manufacture parts or products, or to provide a service.

Bill Wernsing left General Electric with the company's blessing, and a month after he left, GE hired him as a consultant. Later he was even invited to develop, under contract, a project for which he had written a proposal while an employee. (He turned the opportunity down because his payload work for NASA interfered.)

Ellen Green got her employer interested in her proposed venture, involved them in a project, and once she got set up, her former employer became a client. Pat Heffernan managed her situation in much the same way. She was very careful not to use the facilities or resources of her employer during the period of her preparations. She worked on plans evenings and weekends. Her former employer is also now a client.

As we mentioned in Chapter 5, employers can also offer to buy equity in the new enterprise, thus providing needed seed money. They may also decide that it is to their advantage to offer space or other facilities. They may offer to serve as marketers or distributors, or to produce the product the entrepreneur has designed. In exchange, they will expect some payoffs, in the form of licenses, design rights, or patent rights. In any case, if they offer help to the newly launched entrepreneur, then they qualify as incubator organizations.

There are also other possible results of the entrepreneur's decision to reveal plans to his or her employer. The very fact of the plans—of the expressed intention to give up secure employment in return for the risks and satisfactions of independence—demonstrates to the employer an initiative, energy, and determination in the employee-turned-entrepreneur that the employer may not have suspected. The employer may conclude that the prudent course is to try to persuade the entrepreneur to remain with the company in some more responsible, perhaps entrepreneurial capacity. The employer may offer a substantial pay raise or promotion. The employer may offer to create a new subsidiary or division for the newly discovered talent to run, perhaps offering to incorporate the entrepreneur's own business plan. Or the employer may offer to buy major equity in the new enterprise, thus providing actual venture capital. Such an offer sometimes includes an option to buy out the new business at a later date, or to make it a subsidiary of the employer's company.

Such arrangements are so common now that some observers are noting a trend among large companies to keep emerging entrepreneurs within the corporate structure. Employers have begun to recognize that the unusual energies of entrepreneurial types can pay off when appropriately encouraged by the employer. Many companies are experimenting with efforts at making "internal entrepreneuring" work to their benefit.

Internal entrepreneuring is already generating its own descriptive buzzwords. Gifford Pinchot III (1985) calls the phenomenon "intrapreneuring," hardly a word destined to capture the popular imagination. Pinchot argues that the innovations in large corporations have always come from internal entrepreneurs, meaning people who devote great energies to getting new ideas accepted and making them work. Yet, Pinchot observes, these people have usually had to "fight the system" to be heard. Now, he claims, corporate people are learning to encourage the entrepreneurs in their midst.

Encouraging the entrepreneurs requires substantial corporate flexibility in both procedures and goals. Corporate entrepreneurs work best when they are allowed, like independent entrepreneurs, to take responsibility for their whole show—planning, production, marketing, finance, and especially personnel. The employer must be willing to let his entrepreneurs go beyond narrowly defined responsibilities and, when they do, the employer must reward them appropriately—with a piece of the action, as the phrase goes.

The companies that take entrepreneurship within their ranks seriously are helpful to the entrepreneurs, but they are usually even more helpful to themselves. As Pinchot observes, "intrapreneurship pays."

Intrapreneurship and other forms of employer help are great for the entrepreneurial employee, but there is a price. The company allows you to carry out your dream. The company relieves you of most of the ethical concerns. The company offers you a shot at accomplishment and wealth. The company even offers you freedom. But not total freedom, or true independence.

It is true that total freedom may not be attainable in the uncertain game of entrepreneurship. Every entrepreneur needs help from someone—credit from suppliers, advance payment from customers, funds from investors—but nothing comes closer to real psychological freedom than being boss of your own company.

PART II

Personal Transitions

Once an entrepreneur has established his or her business—once he or she has developed the entrepreneurial itch, found the business idea, done the planning (or plunged ahead without any planning), raised the money, and resolved (or ignored) the ethical questions—there remain the personal problems: How to make professional and personal relationships work for the success of the business, how to handle surprises and setbacks, how to cope with success, and how to learn from past mistakes.

Some of these problems are virtually ignored in the business literature. Yet these are problems created by the fact of entrepreneurship, by the lack of a regular paycheck, by uncertainty and risk, by the need for unremitting hard work. Some are the difficulties of getting along with partners and employees, with investors and accountants and lawyers, with family members and friends, even with self.

Some of these problems arise from the fact of being in business for oneself. Others arise when the business encounters setbacks and surprises. Still others arise when a business succeeds. (Yes, there are problems of success, and they are not always pleasant ones, as we will see in Chapter 9.) The entrepreneur must be prepared to cope with them all to achieve and sustain success.

Finally, most entrepreneurs develop keen hindsight as a result of making it through the cutting loose stage and the various personal transitions. Looking back, many entrepreneurs realize that they might have done things differently. They have learned much in the school of hard knocks, and our last chapter will describe some of their conclusions.

CHAPTER 7

Getting Along

We all have to get along with the people around us. When we cross a friend or coworker, the consequences are usually manageable. At worst, a friend stays away for a week or a coworker becomes stiff and distant. The most serious interpersonal problems that most people have to worry about are difficulties with a boss or a spouse. Unresolved bad feelings in either relationship can end in disaster.

Entrepreneurs have many more opportunities for catastrophe. Where the rest of us pretty much build our lives around two main relationships, a marriage and a job, entrepreneurs of necessity build theirs around many. Practically every one is vital to the success of the enterprise. Entrepreneurs must get along with their partners, investors, employees, customers, suppliers, even their lawyers and accountants. The rare entrepreneur who has a happy marriage and a good home life is fundamentally well situated for productive relations in the business world.

This chapter discusses first the entrepreneur's professional relationships, then moves on to personal relationships with family, friends, and self. It considers the possible consequences of blurring the lines between personal and professional relationships, as in family businesses. We hope the reader will draw helpful lessons from this exceedingly difficult and hazardous area of entrepreneurship.

PROFESSIONAL RELATIONSHIPS

A professional relationship requires mutual trust and respect. It also requires that the people involved be able to work well together. For people to work well together, there must be mutual trust and respect, but the reverse may not hold, as we often see in businesses run by family members or close friends. Thus, it is important that good friends and relatives who are considering going into business together thoroughly discuss the conditions of their future planned working relationship. Doing a very detailed business plan together can be an effective test of the promise and potential of the relationship. Every entrepreneurial activity requires a suitable distribution of skills, congenial personalities, and matching or complementary attitudes toward work.

PARTNERS

Writing for *Inc.*, Robert Mamis (1984b) tells what happens when trust fails between partners. In one case, Blanchard and Simon founded a chemical company. Blanchard was a retail financial officer. Simon was a sales rep. They met, hit it off well, and decided to become entrepreneurs. For several years, they worked together profitably, each trusting the other's skills and goals. But they were very different kinds of people, and in time difficulties cropped up between them. Each of the two partners considered himself to be the more important one to the business, and each developed his own priorities. The clash was inevitable. In the end, these two unfortunate people fell to locking each other out of their offices and selling off company assets behind each other's backs. They wound up in receivership.

What causes rifts in partnerships? Self-importance? That is some of what brought Simon and Blanchard down. It nearly did in a boutique run by two women, one of whom insisted upon referring to the shop as "my business." Successful partners have to work consciously at treating each other with respect. Respect means honest recognition of each other's contributions.

The causes of rifts in partnerships are endless. Our purpose here is to give a few typical examples as a caution especially to the new entrepreneur who may wish to avoid problems that have proved fatal or near fatal to the battle-weary veterans who have gone before.

Differences in personality and temperament can set up damaging and unproductive confrontations between partners who actually share identical values and goals. This happens in marriages all the time. It is at least one of the causes in practically every troubled business partnership. Differences in personality and temperament can be especially harmful when they translate into very different lifestyles. Mamis points to the case of an engineering firm set up by three college chums. As the years passed, one of the partners married and became a dedicated, industrious worker. The second acquired the reputation of a womanizer inside and outside the firm. The third turned into a slob, albeit the firm's research and development genius and idea man. The resulting conflict led to a three-way split of the company.

This raises the question, do personality differences necessarily lead to trouble? No. Some venture capitalists actually avoid companies whose partners appear to be too much alike. They find more vigor, more creativity and innovation, in firms whose partners are different enough to stimulate each other. When does stimulation become irritation? The hazard comes when some of the people involved cannot cope with the differences, great or small.

Thomas Lisle, president of Cruisers, Inc., in Oconto, Wisconsin, reports that he acquired his firm with the aid of one partner, who had been president of the boat company when it was a division of the seller. How has the partnership worked? Lisle says that the two have worked together for several years (since 1981) without serious difficulties. He attributes their success to some luck and a lot of hard work.

Lisle describes the personal relationship between the two partners as reflecting the diverse but flexible personalities of two individuals who were brought together in the Cruisers enterprise. "We are mutually able to accomodate the other's idiosyncracies and to date have not allowed them to be an issues." Reading between the lines, it seems fair to observe that some of the hard work that went into building a successful company of Cruisers, Inc., also went into developing a productive personal relationship between the two partners.

Ralph Brown has had two partners in the sixteen years since taking over his parents' toy manufacturing business. The first one was chosen for his expertise in machinery maintenance. From Ralph's standpoint, it was a near-perfect functional match, but when it came to the commitment Ralph soon discovered was required to make a developing business work, the partner proved unwilling to depart from the forty-hour week arrangement they had both felt would be desirable for balance in their lives. So, after two years, Ralph's first partner sold his share of the business to a toy designer. By that time, Ralph felt more sure-footed in the business and more comfortable about hiring a machinery expert.

The second partner was also a good match for Ralph in that he was, in Ralph's own words, "an extremely talented and hardworking artist who made enormous contributions to the attractiveness, usefulness and promotion of our product line." This partnership lasted ten years. Unfortunately, cooperation between the two partners "was hampered from the beginning by his distant domicile and unwillingness to relocate to the factory area. . . . As the years passed, his weekly visits declined to monthly and ultimately annual visits as he withdrew into an 'ivory tower' for his new product and graphics designing. . . . Hours-long telephone calls were inadequate substitutes for . . . joint decision-making. . . . At a distance, he created a private and secret product domain which I as his partner had no share in, while he maintained a firm hand on my activities as sales partner. . . . We avoided a confrontation for a long time. . . . Ultimately our partnership foundered upon the question of how next to utilize our success. . . . He wanted to minimize expenditures and harvest the profits. . . . For my part, always cognizant of the grinding poverty around me, I wanted to reinvest all of the profits into spiralling growth to expand the company into a truly effective vehicle of employment for my area. . . . Five years ago I bought his interest and became sole owner."

A fairly common source of trouble between partners is differences in skills. Samuel Wallace, of Xodex Enterprises, Ltd., in Oakland, California, reports that a major difficulty in going into business with friends was the difference in skill levels between himself and the other partners. As Wallace assumed a strong leadership role and made demands for performance, "the friendships disintegrated pretty quickly." Wallace's situation was greatly complicated as the female partners outperformed a male partner in generating business for the company. Ellen Green found a related problem when she found herself doing both her work and her partner's. The partner is now a consultant. The two women still share an office, but now the pressure is off.

Another obvious source of trouble can come from unfriendly personal rivalries between or among partners. In the case of Xodex, Wallace's male partner initiated an affair with one of the female partners with the consequence that the partner's job performance suffered and Wallace asked him to leave the company.

Sound familiar? These kinds of situations are always damaging to the efficiency of any business; when they occur in a new or struggling enterprise, they can be fatal. The entrepreneur who sees personal rivalries developing in the organization needs to take prompt action to head them off before they become seriously disruptive. Wallace survived by getting rid of all of his partners. Perhaps these particular people were not good choices in the first place. If they had been competent and valuable to the business, some frank discussions about "ground rules," trust, and mutual respect might have led to the development of a mature and productive set of relationships among them.

Larry Gleeson of Maine Hydro-Electric Development Corp. reports that his favorite partner is his wife Cathy, who has played a large part in making his company work. He has other partners too, and he says that it is crucial to have people whose personalities and work styles complement—but do not compete with—your own. In some cases, problems can be visible with would-be partners, who expect that for their investment, they should receive an inordinate share of equity in the operation.

Trust is also clearly an issue. Larry recalls one would-be partner who studied his materials carefully and then went out to set up an imitative company. He now feels that he should ask partners and would-be partners to sign a confidentiality agreement, even though such agreements are both difficult and expensive to enforce.

The relationships between partners are different in every situation, and therefore no pat solutions can be offered or applied. What is always required is a thoughtful, objective analysis based upon careful exploration of the attitudes and actions of the people involved. Such an approach is best handled by what is known in the trade as a process consultant, that is, a psychological counselor who specializes in sorting out relationships among people in organizations. What? Another expense? In response, we suggest that the entrepreneur should first decide whether the people involved in a disruptive relationship are valuable enough to the organization to warrant the time and expense of consultation.

Baty (1981) observes that entrepreneurial teams can cause as many problems as they solve. Smaller teams, he says, are better than larger ones for, in larger teams, problems arise more easily. The problems come from differences in the ways people "handle pressure, their willingness to deal with ambiguity, their ethical standards, their sense of humor, and their innate intelligence." In addition, Baty notes, "personal or noncomplementary relationships" may dilute the value of a team. Thus, in potentially difficult situations (such as the launching phase of a new enterprise) it can be beneficial to have prospective members of the team (partners and employees both) evaluated for compatibility by psychological testing.

You may be asking yourself whether that isn't going a bit too far. Consider that half or more of all new enterprises fail and sometimes the entrepreneurs who start them fail more than once. Why? Because many entrepreneurs fail to recognize and deal with some of the most vexing problems they are up against, namely problems that have psychological roots. Our advice throughout this book is to try to anticipate problems before they arise or as they become apparent and to deal with them promptly and objectively. Usually, objectivity in personal and interpersonal problems requires professional help.

Yet, even with careful evaluation of prospective partners, there may be trouble. If the difficulty proves to be beyond reasonable agreement and if one of the parties to the dispute can be removed without serious damage to the enterprise, then a severance arrangement should be prompt and decisive. The anticipated costs of removal and replacement must be regarded as secondary to the ongoing operation. The costs in stock buy-backs, employment agency fees, even "outplacment" consulting fees are likely to be worth the trouble-free atmosphere that should result. A caution: waiting too long to find replacements can handicap a business for years to come.

INVESTORS

Investors share many characteristics within business partners. They own a piece of the action. They care. They may help with advice or contacts. They may *be* partners.

Investors who are not partners present their own unique problems of getting along. Mutual trust is as basic between entrepreneur and investor as it is between entrepreneur and partners. Lacking trust, an investor may try to pressure the entrepreneur into a premature sale to repay the investment, or to put off essential capital purchases or new product development.

The entrepreneur can go a long way toward getting along with investors by heading off problems before they arise. The entrepreneur has the initial responsibility for a carefully drawn business plan based upon a viable business idea. The entrepreneur's next responsibility is to find investors who make a firm commitment to the business plan and agree to support the entrepreneur in carrying out the plan. Clear, tightly drawn plans and unambiguous written agreements are the key to heading off problems with investors.

The choice of investors is as crucial as the form and content of plans and agreements. As entrepreneur, you must choose investors with whom you can work, and you must be open and honest with them right from the start. You must also pick investors who have the cash when you need it; Ellen Green didn't, but she says she has now learned "to be more specific with my requests and to keep better documentation."

The importance of a good fit between investor and entrepreneur runs both ways. Trust and confidence are as critical to one party as to the other. The investor must choose an entrepreneur who can be left alone to get on with the job. Most investors *want* to trust their entrepreneurs, and experienced investors go out of their way to select entrepreneurs whom they can trust to build the business without a lot of monitoring.

Once the entrepreneur has made a suitable choice of investors, getting along with them requires a few simple considerations. The entrepreneur must abide by whatever agreements have been made with the investors. In most cases, this means sticking to the business plan and reporting progress as well as any major problems that affect the plan. The entrepreneur should also keep investors informed through company newsletters and press releases. An occasional telephone call and luncheon help to maintain informal lines of communication.

One kind of investor who needs special care is the entrepreneur's banker. Baty (1981) recommends selecting a bank and banker only after thorough comparison of relevant services and of recommendations from other business people, accountants, and lawyers. Once the banker is selected, the entrepreneur should:

1. Keep the banker informed by putting the bank on the mailing list for press releases, customer newsletters, monthly operating statements, and annual audited statements.

2. Press the flesh. Meet your banker every few months for lunch or to review plans. Invite your banker to the plant.

3. Borrow, need it or not. Establish a record for business-like dealings.

4. Meet targets. There is nothing like a little sloppiness in meeting loan payments to cool a banker on a business relationship.

EMPLOYEES AND OTHER HIRELINGS

The entrepreneurial team consists not only of the entrepreneur, partner(s), and investors. It also includes lawyers, accountants, and full-time employees, most of whom receive their compensation in the form of salaries, retainers, or fees, but usually not in equity in the firm.

These people must be able to work together and also with the entrepreneurial partners. Here also, there must be mutual trust and respect, compatible personalities, and willingness to work hard toward initial company success. Wherever any of these factors is substantially lacking, the entrepreneur must be prepared (legally and psychologically) to replace people. The entrepreneur who cannot bear to fire people when necessary, or who cannot recognize trouble spots, will find the task of establishing a new enterprise an overwhelming one and is a prime candidate for failure. These are hard words, but they fit the tough world of successful entrepreneurship.

Lawyers, accountants, consultants, and other part-time and as-needed people are usually easier to deal with than full-time employees. The business is not so committed to them nor are they so dependent upon the business for their livelihood. They can be replaced simply by finding someone else the next time their services are needed. Although these professionals are easily replaced, they should be neither hired nor replaced without utmost attention to their place and function in the company. Rapid or abrupt turnover in any of these key functions, especially in the early stages of founding a new enterprise, can be extremely disruptive.

In choosing accountants, Baty (1981) advises picking only from the "Big Eight" public accounting firms, at least for firms with more than local ambitions. What is at stake is your new company's credibility with out-of-town investors, customers, and suppliers. Financial statements prepared by a reputable national firm simply raise fewer questions and doubts than do ones prepared by a local firm.

We recognize with Baty that local firms can be more economical and personalized and equally as competent as a "Big Eight" firm. The choice comes down to the specific needs of the individual entrepreneur, the special expertise of the accounting firms under consideration (as they bear upon the requirements of the entrepreneur), and the recommendations of interested bankers, lawyers, and consultants.

Lawyers are essential as legal and business advisers, as negotiators, as intermediaries with investors, and as defenders against suits. They too should be chosen according to specific need and recommendations. Never select a lawyer for a new business enterprise just because he or she is a friend or family counselor, and never at random from the Yellow Pages. We offer this seemingly gratuitous caution because inexperienced entrepreneurs often select lawyers by these dubious means.

Lawyers should be selected for their proven experience in the specific type of legal work your new company will need. In choosing lawyers, Baty (1981) recommends watching out for actual or potential conflicts of interest. Fees can make a difference in the selection. The price of a large, established law firm may cover far more in prestige and stand-by services than your company will ever need. You should find out who is likely to stand in for your attorney when he or she is not available. You should also look for a comfortable personality fit between you, your partners, and the candidate attorney. You certainly want a creative strategist and a tough negotiator with whom you can work effectively. To get what you want, you may have to do a lot of good comparative shopping before you settle on the law firm for your company.

Choosing a consultant is a very different and in some ways a more difficult task than choosing accountants and lawyers. The choice depends entirely on the job to be done or the problem to be solved. The key to hiring a consultant is the definition of the assignment. If you lack the expertise to solve a particular problem or the capability in the company to perform a needed task, then you need a consultant. How to find the right one and how to get your money's worth are two of the questions we answer in our book, *Using Consultants* (Easton & Conant, 1985). Our recommendations for entrepreneurs are summarized in our concluding chapter, "Getting Your Money's Worth."

Full-time employees are harder to deal with than partners, investors, or as-needed professionals. They can be replaced only by firing them or eliminating a job or position. Firing a person can be very hard on both parties.

Many employers cannot bring themselves to fire anyone, and so their organizations gradually fill up with deadwood and misfits. The result is inefficiency or failure. The result for a new enterprise can be fatal. In new companies, every job counts toward essential productivity, toward the day when income exceeds outgo. A few misfits or goof-offs can postpone or prevent early success.

Bill Wernsing finds it embarrassing to fire someone. Firing is especially hard when the employer is or becomes personally involved with the employees. Mike and Carol Resnick, of the Briarwood Pet Motel in Cincinnati, told us that "since the kennel business is by nature a very informal one, we tended at first to get too close to our employees: we helped those in school with their homework, listened to the married ones complain about their spouses, found ourselves learning more about their personal lives than we cared to know . . . as a result, we found that releasing an employee became an unbearable strain. . . ." The Resnicks finally hired a manager to handle the day to day operations, including hiring and firing employees. The manager thus acted as a buffer between them and the people who worked for Briarwood.

It is not always possible to anticipate and avoid situations that call for firing someone, but it is possible to minimize the incidence of those situations. The key is careful selection of personnel. The Resnicks early learned that the ideal kennel staffers were *not* strong, athletic young men, but women, both young and middle-aged, who were ''neater, more meticulous, gentler with the animals, and more courteous to the customers.''

The Resnicks got around the problem of finding competent, qualified people by doubling their salary scale, ''which gave us first crack at just about everyone in the city who wanted to work with animals.'' After that, it was a matter of careful selection.

Baty (1981) warns that the selection process often comes down to a choice between talent and experience. He recommends that the entrepreneur choose talent in hopes of getting with it energy, ambition, and ability to grow with the business.

It is also a fact that the entrepreneur can short-circuit talent, energy, and growth by failing to provide an environment that fosters creativity. The hallmark of a creative environment is open respect and encouragement for new ideas from the president to the people on the production line and out in the field. A creative environment is one that deliberately encourages entrepreneurial attitudes in everyone—and maintaining that atmosphere and those attitudes after the excitement of the start-up has faded.

Judith Kaplan, of Action Packets in Ocala, Florida, fosters creativity and identification with the business through discussion groups. Every other week, she has most of her employees at her home for pizza and talk, centering on such books as *Megatrends, In Search of Excellence,* and *A Whack on the Side of the Head.* The result, says Kaplan, is ''mind-expanding,'' and the spin-offs include improvements in shipping practices and interdepartmental coordination.

Getting along with employees requires support of their functions. There must be enough money for people to do their jobs. When there is not, as was the case with Samuel Wallace's Xodex Enterprises (which at one point could not reemburse sales reps' expenses), morale suffers, production and sales fall off, and the enterprise falters. With technical people such as engineers, other kinds of support—such as computers, machine tools, technicians, and clerical help—may be even more crucial than direct monetary support.

Support is also important when the time comes to fire someone. Yes, you should be prepared to ease an employee out of a job even when you are satisfied that your decision is well founded. There should be a termination interview, not just a pink slip. The entrepreneur as boss should explain in straightforward terms why the employee must go—incompetence, insufficient dedication to the job, habitual tardiness, delays, or a company need to reduce payroll. The explanation should be clear, firm, factual, and objective. Discrimination of any kind should be absent.

The employer should offer references that emphasize the positive qualities and potential of the employee, and help in finding a new job. The employer has a special obligation in the case of an unexpected reduction in force. An example of help is to inform the employee about another company that is hiring people, or recommending a job training program that might strengthen the employee's shortcomings.

One valuable consequence of going out of your way to offer support and help to an employee who is being discharged is the message of reassurance it sends to other employees. If you treat fired employees in a fair and helpful way, you are likely to gain the respect and loyalty of the employees who remain with the company.

Is support a one-way process? On the rocky and uncertain road to success as an entrepreneur, you will serve your own interest best by developing mutual loyalties between you and your employees. The value of strong mutual loyalties is evident in the experience of many successful entrepreneurs. One of the most dramatic examples is the story of how Fred Smith, founder of Federal Express, was bailed out of a financial hole when his employees pawned their watches to loan him urgently needed cash!

Among our subjects, the best tale comes from Thomas Lisle of Cruisers, Inc. Lisle tells us that when he acquired the company, "there were approximately 135 employees. The workforce was unionized, but though the issue of the union was not a serious problem at the time, survival of the company was the issue. . . . We used a very direct approach with the entire management and workforce. We held frequent meetings . . . advising employees of the risks and the opportunities . . . and emphasizing that the employees . . . had more than sufficient strength to bring the company to its knees. . . . We preached the shallow-pockets doctrine. . . . If we did not all pull together hard, there would be no company. . . . Since the company had been very close to being liquidated, we had a great deal of credibility.'' Today the company is out of trouble partly because Lisle was able to gain the support of his employees when their help was urgently needed. He gained their support by showing his respect for their positions, trusting their value, and recognizing their shared concerns.

Larry Gleeson also reports that with employees trust is essential. He notes that in his business, there is a lot of highly portable equipment, and theft *is* an occasional problem. He finds that he can't tolerate employees of whom he is suspicious, even when he can't prove they have stolen anything. In such cases, as well as in cases of incompetence, he feels obliged to fire employees. Usually, however, he eases them out, reducing their hours for awhile before shutting them out completely.

CUSTOMERS AND SUPPLIERS

Good relations with customers and suppliers are also essential to business success. With customers, good relations means such practical matters as quality control, on-time deliveries, and prompt attention to complaints. It also means keeping customers informed of changes in production or delivery schedules, and other developments that might affect their trade.

Good customer relations can mean extending generous credit terms to best customers and offering appropriate help to ones that are having temporary problems. Many businesses have found that such measures build loyalties and are protection against new competitors. The new entrepreneur often experiences this reality in efforts to attract customers away from competitors who got there first and established firm loyalties.

Good relations with suppliers is the other side of the coin. You are the customer, but you need the trust and good will of those whose products you buy. Again, the basis of good will rests on such practices as paying your bills on time and keeping suppliers informed of developments that might affect orders. Abrupt cancellations can be unavoidable, but you do well to avoid them, whenever possible, by anticipating them well in advance.

If the supplier runs into a cash flow problem or worse, you treat that supplier as a friend if you can pay some bills early or place orders that the supplier might be able to use in support of a loan. The result is a loyalty that could have tangible future value.

PERSONAL RELATIONSHIPS

The popular stereotype is that the entrepreneur's life revolves around his or her business to the exclusion of all else. This is true for a great many entrepreneurs, especially ones who are insecure and ones who do not have a satisfying personal life or marriage. It is also likely to be true of so-called workaholics and of people who suffer from obsessive–compulsive personalities.

There is a myth abroad that venture capitalists prefer divorced entrepreneurs. It is said that they believe that such people are free of compelling personal commitments, or that they have an extra drive that comes from needing to prove their worth to the spouse who rejected them.

The fact is that most entrepreneurs are not divorced. They have spouses, children, parents, brothers, sisters, and close friends. They do not, indeed should not, turn off the important relationships in their lives. Those who do run the risk of physical and mental illness. Most people do not function well in isolation.

Yet the entrepreneur's work can be a lonely pursuit. You often work alone, without the company of the colleagues who were there before you cut loose. You may have partners, but they probably function in different specialties, themselves involved in lonely work. You may have one partner or two, seldom more. The reality is that you have to work very hard a lot of the time, spending most of your waking hours on the business, especially in the early stages, and you actually do not have much left over for other interests, or people, even those who have always been close to you. The result is loneliness.

Gumpert and Boyd (1984) documented this condition among 450 small-business chief executive officers they surveyed. Their respondents complained of having no confidants with whom to discuss their concerns and no time for friends and family. These same people also displayed strong tendencies to being solitary. They were almost all "loners" by preference, most with a penchant for solitary hobbies. Many of them demonstrated a reluctance to admit difficulties. A common characteristic was an insistent optimism about their enterprise.

In an earlier study of the same 450 subjects, Boyd and Gumpert (1983) found a high frequency of stress-related ailments, from insomnia to back and heart trouble. One in ten had sought psychiatric counseling. The investigators attributed the stress among these entrepreneurs to a driving need to achieve, to anxieties over financial risk, to inadequacies of subordinates, to the loneliness of isolation.

Gumpert and Boyd (1984) recommend that entrepreneurs deliberately change their life style to beat the problems of loneliness. If you fit the Gumpert-Boyd profile, you should seriously consider restructuring your business to encourage increased interaction with others. You might try peer groups such as civic and professional societies, or lunch-together gangs of fellow entrepreneurs. Ellen Green deals with stress by exercising and by communicating "a lot about the good things happening and it helps to keep an eye that this too shall pass. . . . It helps to love my work and my family and friends."

Among our subjects, only two (both in new, one-person businesses located in their homes) mention loneliness as the major drawback to having their own businesses. Katie Crane works by herself in an office at home and farms out all of the clerical and support work she needs. "Working alone can be a disadvantage," she says, for "there's no one to turn to for ideas and opinions. . . . That can be tough." She deals with the problem in two ways. "Luckily, my husband has taken such an interest in the business that he often provides that [sounding board] service." The other solution for Katie lies in the business itself; writing is lonely, but the consulting side brings her into regular contact with the people she serves.

Sandy Sakurai also works at home, and her problem of loneliness derives primarily from not yet having a full schedule of clients. She also misses having colleagues around with whom to "talk shop."

Most of our subjects are more likely to say they have too few hours in the day to do their work. They typically mention that family and friends complain of being deprived of their companionship, but they do not seem deprived themselves. These are the loners who gain great satisfaction in their work and are not especially bothered by aloneness. Loners, in fact, seek aloneness.

One of our loners is Pat Heffernan, who is a natural-born researcher, a harvester and user of knowledge, and a solver of problems. Her preferred contact with people is to hear their problems and to provide solutions. When she hit on the idea of setting up her own consulting business, she read everything she could find on entrepreneurship and the more she read, the more the idea excited her. She craved the "independence, control, and impact" entrepreneurship would give her. She did not even consider partners or investors. "I wouldn't want to divide the independence," she told us. She wanted to do it alone, without help, without anyone else's involvement.

How does Pat handle the problem of reduced family time? She hints that her working life has always monopolized her time. Now she sets aside most weekends and does not permit business interruptions.

When Ralph Brown took over his business, he soon realized "that survival in commerce was going to demand an excruciating work-week for a very long time if the enterprise was going to prosper—or even survive. . . . Without a conscious decision to do so, I met the need—and 'married' the factory. . . . My wife of ten years, unwilling or unable to join me at the administration, in time became a factory widow. . . . We never succeeded in solving the needs of both the marriage and the factory. . . . After a dozen years, my wife left me and divorced me. . . . Having remarried, I zealously maximize alone-time with my wife, at the expense of socializing."

Entrepreneurs, including the loners, should try to follow Ralph's example and deliberately make time for family and friends. If your business has moved your interests too far away from those of former friends, you should find new ones. Try switching from solo hobbies and recreation to team, small group, or duo activities—handball, golf, tennis, family hikes, picnics, camping. Gumpert and Boyd tell us that "nonlonely" entrepreneurs outperform the lonely ones.

Our subjects report similar difficulties in their private lives. Mike Resnick told us that the big problem he and Carol had at the outset of their enterprise was "literally no leisure time." The worst of it was that they had no time for their own show dogs and had to give them up. They bought the pet motel to make enough money so that Mike would be free to write the kind of stuff he wanted to write. But for three years, from 1976 to 1979, Mike wrote almost nothing. "I simply didn't have the time," he told us.

Samuel Wallace of Xodex Enterprise, Ltd., reported a "diminishing of social activity and any leisure free time during the first three years." But, he adds, he had expected to work that hard and "saw no major problem in it." Once that initial period was over, Wallace was able to resume a "reasonable personal life."

Thomas Lisle calls his only serious problem the depletion of liquidity from his acquisition of Cruisers. That problem, he says, was more than offset by the pleasure derived from owning a business which deals in leisure and recreational products. "Most importantly," he told us, "I am doing something that I have wanted to do for many years and achieving a modest degree of success doing it . . . with job satisfaction comes better family life, health, etc." Lisle concedes that his busines at first demanded long hours, but his personal involvement has been declining to reasonable levels. This is because Cruisers had a competent management group in place when Lisle took over.

Bill Wernsing of Williams Laboratories also had money problems at the outset, reporting that "things were getting a little bit tense when we started to get income again." He adds that the first few months were a period of painful adjustment, working at home instead of in the GE plant, and having to adapt to interruptions by family distractions, personal errands, and the like. He found it hard to develop the personal discipline necessary for productivity.

After a time, he learned to appreciate the freedom he had traded for an 8-to-5 job. In a few months, he found himself working longer hours than he had at GE, but those hours were far more satisfying. What helped him reach that point was a personal commitment by Wernsing and his wife and their religious faith.

As for leisure time, Wernsing assures us that "with a small company . . . either there's so much work that you can't afford vacations, or there's a lull, and you feel obliged to be looking for business."

Larry Gleeson notes relatively few personal problems. His business does get more time than his past job, but he was always wrapped up in his work and the difference, he says, is that for the entrepreneur there are very few excuses for less than total dedication. One result is that because there is no one to whom to pass the buck, "you find yourself taking some [physical] risks." At the time of the interview, he had recently injured both his knee and his back; he noted that this happens every year. In addition, as we will see in Chapter 8, his business has proven controversial in the community, and he feels that this has cost him some potential friendships.

Vacations and time off seem to be a particular problem for very small businesses. Businesses that have more than two or three employees can usually function when the entrepreneur takes a few days off. Gumpert and Boyd (1984) advise that entrepreneurs should not allow the demands of the business to dominate completely their lives. If they do, they are likely to fall victim to the stress and loneliness that can work against the chances of real success.

Soon after Pat Heffernan went into business for herself, she found that her friends and family were having difficulty understanding the problems that she confronted. She considers herself to be a communicative person, and she says she tried to explain things to the people close to her without much success. Out of sheer exasperation, she says she would like to "find and send to friends and family a short book or videotape on how to get along with an entrepreneur." Pat's idea is that the family and friends of entrepreneurs each believe that their particular experience is unique." But, she insists, "the experience is not unique. . . . The patterns are similar. . . . I've heard many entrepreneurs, especially men, say they could never, for example, tell their spouse about a short-term cash-flow problem, because the immediate assumption is that you are losing your house or the kids won't be fed. . . . That places a tremendously stressful burden on the entrepreneur simply because the spouse is not aware of how common the problem is or how to judge how serious it is."

As Judith Kaplan got her business going, she found it hard to relax, hard to raise a family, and "always felt guilty." But she did manage to raise her family, and by her own account, her marriage has if anything been strengthened by the shared entrepreneurial venture. She did not reveal to us whether she has learned to relax or to throw off the feelings of guilt. She does say that she has found a great deal of help in studying business practices similar to her own that she had thought might be seen as too innovative, too much against the tide. She concludes with some satisfaction that she is not against the tide, merely ahead of the crowd.

BLURRING THE LINES

Gleeson, Kaplan, Wernsing, and the Resnicks demonstrate that involving members of the entrepreneur's family in the business can pay off. Mutual support is one of the important advantages; there is always someone there who knows the problems of the business and who cares about the entrepreneur. Another advantage is that time spent with the business is also time spent with members of the family who are involved. A spouse partner can result in heading off the kind of marriage conflict that results when one spouse plunges whole hog into an entrepreneurial venture leaving the other spouse out in the cold.

It is also a fact of life that family businesses can have their own major problems. Levinson (1971) notes that the entrepreneur's preoccupation with the business as an extension of self, for personal gratification and achievement, raises the possibility of rivalry among the involved family members. The classical rivalry between parent and offspring is one that occurs too frequently to be ignored or shrugged off. In this contest, the parent is reluctant to surrender control, and the children resent being kept in a subordinate position. Ralph Brown seems fortunate to have missed these problems in his buy-out of his supportive, encouraging parents.

Rivalry can also emerge between siblings who are going into business together. They can bring with them dominance relationships left over from childhood and family roles that can interfere with a realistic distribution of responsibilities based upon innate abilities, professional training, and experience.

Sibling rivalries can be exacerbated when the children inherit the family business and one has been brought up to expectations of assuming command. Levinson's example is the eldest son who, he says, is likely to impose harsh demands upon himself and his younger siblings. The younger brother buys into the game in endless striving to compensate for his subservient position by carving out a niche of his own in the company. Caught in a no-win situation, the younger sibling may finally have to leave the company and strike out on his own.

Rivalry between siblings can take a variety of other forms. The older one (male or female) can threaten parental dominance and be denied a role in the company because of it, while the younger child can gain parental favor and assume command by parental sanction. However the rivalry pattern works itself out, the business is affected, and unless objective standards are used to assign policy and managerial roles when the time comes for the senior generation to retire, then the future of the company is left to the capriciousness of fate and fortune.

We should add that there are many examples of successful family companies where the problem of succession has been handled with remarkable objectivity. In these cases, the good of the company was placed over the aspirations of individual family members. One well-known example is the John Deere Company (Broehl, 1984).

Similar problems can plague the interactions of other family members in a business. Members who depend on the business for income may try to dictate financial policy, for example, by blocking or attempting to block capital expenditures on plant and equipment in favor of dividend payments. Such conflicts can lead to lowered productivity and profitability and poor morale in management. Levinson (1971) suggests that the constructive solution to such damaging interference is to replace family management with hired professionals. The reorganization of a family business under professional management usually involves replacing family managers who could not resolve family conflicts.

What difficulties can be expected from bringing friends into the business? The answer is that psychological conflicts are less likely to occur than with family members. It is not that friends are free of such conflicts. It is just that people who have gotten along well as friends are likely also to get along as partners in a business.

Friends can run into conflict when the business encounters serious difficulties. Under such circumstances, friends can lose confidence in each other. As in any relationship, when friendship cools to enmity, work relationships can go from awkward to impossible. At that point, unless someone jumps ship, the business can suffer or fail. Samuel Wallace almost lost his business when trouble among the partners boiled over into personal difficulties.

Many entrepreneurs prefer to keep friendships separate from their businesses. They refrain from striking up close friendships with associates and employees, and some go to the length of keeping their friends away from their work place. Because the Resnicks had trouble firing people, due to mixing business relationships with personal ones, they have deliberately distanced themselves from their employees.

Other successful entrepreneurs do the opposite. They play golf, tennis, and poker with their partners, bankers, and accountants. How do they make it work? They have an ability to maintain a friendly relationship and at the same time keep the distance required by a business relationship. Some of our most successful political leaders have demonstrated this capacity and the valuable political currency it can generate. Examples that come readily to mind are Abraham Lincoln, who seldom shared his inner thoughts with anyone, and Franklin Roosevelt, whose happy-go-lucky exterior concealed the subtle mind of a master politician.

CHAPTER 8

Setbacks and Surprises

In Chapter 7, we showed that many of the entrepreneur's problems can arise from difficulties in getting along with people. They can be personal problems or business problems. They can involve spouses, friends, partners, employees, and backers. The problems, whatever their source, can become complex and frustrating when business and personal relationships overlap.

In this chapter, we focus on what can go wrong with your enterprise and how you can cope with problems that arise. When the setbacks and surprises arise out of problems in getting along with people, the discussion harks back to the problems dealt with in Chapter 7. It is more the rule than the exception that the setbacks and surprises of a new venture emerge from difficulties in human relationships and ineffective or dysfunctional ways of coping with such difficulties.

The setbacks and surprises we see in this chapter range from cash-flow problems to a warehouse fire to a business failure. The ways the entrepreneurs dealt with these problems include deliberate efforts to be innovative, enlisting employee support, religion, and flight.

Entrepreneurs often seem to fail before they succeed in setting up a thriving business. In the process, the lessons can be learned that eventually lead to success. In the first effort, the entrepreneur can learn about planning, marketing, idea evaluation (a most demanding task), and raising money. If the entrepreneur is willing to profit from the lessons of a failed first (or second or even third) attempt, the chances are good that he or she will make it sooner or later.

DISASTER AND FLIGHT

John North is the pseudonym we have given another of our respondents, this one to protect him from any damaging effects of publishing his story. At this writing, North is a very bitter, cynical fellow who feels betrayed by former partners. He is swamped by a mass of debts which he voluntarily assumed as a matter of conscience. The debts legally belong to his defunct corporation.

The story of North's setback began when he picked up the brochure of a new natural resources company that was selling franchises to offer land management by contract on an as-needed basis to private landowners in the forestry industry. The franchises were being distributed nationwide and management services to franchisees were coordinated from a central office in the West. North found the idea exciting and saw it as an opportunity to go into business for himself.

North had begun his working life as an employee and manager for a building supplies company. Later, he worked as a service manager for an automobile dealer. Eventually, he tried working for himself as a carpenter and builder. "I wanted to be in control of my own destiny," he explained. When that work proved to be less prosperous and satisfying than he expected, he went back to school to study natural resource management.

North earned a degree and landed a position with a large natural resources company. The recession of the early 1980s led to massive layoffs, and North lost his job. It was at that point that we find him studying the brochure in the university placement office.

As he stood there perusing the brochure, he found himself caught up in a vision of providing thousands of jobs and at the same time providing for a "stewardship of the land." He also saw himself making a lot of money.

As we will see, North was indulging in fantasy. The fact that North did not recognize his "vision" as a fantasy was the first step in his undoing. The second was his failure to check out the facts behind the sales pitch of the company's president. Two of North's former classmates had purchased franchises, the president told him. A telephone call to either of them would have revealed that neither of them had, as of that time, signed up. There were other exaggerations of fact and reality, but North was so anxious to join the company that he simply took the president's word for everything.

North borrowed money from his family and purchased a franchise. Almost at once, he was offered a vice presidency in charge of operations. At about the same time, he accepted a part-time position at the university where he had earned his degree. North's professional life seemed to be taking off at last. He was convinced that the franchise business was "too good to fail," and his enthusiasm attracted substantial support from some of his friends on the faculty.

The surprises came almost as soon as he joined the company. A flush of blinding enthusiasm had drawn him into the venture. He had committed himself emotionally and financially. He had used borrowed money to buy in. But the ink was hardly dry on his franchise when, as a new vice president, he discovered the faulty planning, unrealistic goals, a cash flow imbalance, and incompetence or lack of commitment in key personnel. He learned to his dismay that the firm had no accounts receivable, except payments due on franchises. Moreover, very little contract work was being lined up and billed. Worse still, there were large accounts payable and the franchises were not getting the managerial services they were supposed to receive.

In the next few weeks, North tried hard to repair the various deficiencies, including reorganizing the company, writing a business plan, budgeting expenses, and raising money. He even took on the presidency of the reorganized company and sold stock to friends, family, and anyone else he could interest.

But the job proved to be an impossible one. The former president, still with the company, arbitrarily used the new capital to pay off the debts of the original company. Hard-pressed competitors underbid his firm in contract after contract. The new company, bled white, simply could not function. "Basically, everything just decayed. . . . We reached a point of no motion. . . . Even when we tried to sell the idea to larger consulting companies, hoping to be paid to develop it, we failed."

As matters got worse, the original franchise holders disconnected themselves from the company. Things hit bottom when North stepped out of the house early one morning and the company car was gone. A call to the sheriff provided the answer: the car had been repossessed.

"Hitting bottom" is how North described his feelings at that moment. His next step was to write a letter to the investors, many of whom were family and friends, to tell them that he was giving up, that he had reached the end of his effectiveness, and that his health was in jeopardy. Then he borrowed some money from his father, packed his wife and infant son into his pickup truck and left town.

A few weeks later, after a much-needed "vacation," he returned to the university and got part of his old job back, but he could not easily face the people there who had invested in the failed venture. After several months he quit, borrowed more money, and "puttered." Then he took a job with his father-in-law and has been living with his "guilt" ever since.

In the end, all of the investors lost their money. North promised them repayment. He says he had the personal satisfaction of stopping the sales of additional franchises before the company folded.

Can we say that North benefitted from his setback? North concedes that he was "carried away by enthusiasm" for the idea the company was promoting. He now says that he should have insisted upon seeing a business plan (none existed) and that he should have checked on investors and holders of franchises. He says that one of the pursuasive factors was the alleged involvement of old friends in the company.

Only in the bitter aftermath did North judge the people in the company to be "lousy projectors and planners . . . Nice guys, but stupid, no imagination, brains, or discipline . . . just not managers."

Now he says, "A business has to be run with a calculator, through management by objectives . . . there is no room for affection . . . you have to keep friends, marriage, personal life separate from the business . . . you can't afford remorse."

But, he goes on to say, "I'm not like that . . . I went into the personal hurt part much too deeply . . . I couldn't absorb it all." In an afterthought, North commented, "It would have been a real good idea to get help from people who know how to evaluate people . . ." He also says, "I got a fantastic education out of that whole experience . . . the only thing I kick about is the cost of tuition."

John North's story underscores the imperative need for careful evaluation of the business idea behind a proposed enterprise, whether it is your idea or someone's who is trying to interest you in it. North's story also underscores the cruical importance of developing a realistic and detailed business plan that is both conscientiously followed by management and revised periodically as new conditions develop. North's experience teaches that, once underway, the business operation must be closely managed through a carefully drawn budget and strict expenditure controls.

North's unfortunate experience illustrates the value of honesty in relations with potential partners and investors, and the havoc that can result from dishonesty. It also demonstrates the necessity of screening prospective partners and key employees for their integrity and willingness to work hard. Prior friendships and vivid imaginations are not enough.

As for the question of whether John North benefitted from his setback, only another entrepreneurial venture will show what he learned from the experience. The lessons are there, and though they are bitter, they may be worth their weight in gold if applied to a new venture.

NEW TWISTS UNTANGLE OLD PROBLEMS

One of our favorite success stories is that of Mike and Carol Resnick, of the Briarwood Pet Motel in Cincinnati. They began the venture in a "setback" position, for when they bought Briarwood, it had been losing money. The first task was to turn the business around.

Mike tells us that he and Carol tried a number of innovations and promotions on the assumption that none of them could harm a failing business, and some might help. The turnaround began to show in the first six months.

The basic strategy the Resnicks decided upon was to turn the kennel into a luxury service. This strategy required considerable borrowing beyond that involved in the original acquisition. They chose the luxury route because of rapid attrition in the regular clientele of the kennel. They read the attrition as a falling off of the local market for an ordinary kennel. In shifting to a new market, the Resnicks ran the risk of a cash flow gap until they had actually penetrated that market. They worked hard at attracting the luxury trade they sought, and "hung on by the skin of our teeth" until they succeeded.

Innovation is a common response of entrepreneurs to business trouble. Has the familiar approach stopped working? Then try something new! But don't wait too long. Many entrepreneurs try something new only when the situation has reached a crisis. The crisis itself gets in the way of sound judgment and productive action. We have encountered entrepreneurs who seem to think that "something new" is whatever the competition is doing. Imitating the other fellow can lead to the folly of repeating someone else's blunders.

The Resnicks did not make either mistake. They carefully studied the kennel industry and looked for ideas. When they came across what looked like a good idea, they tried to find out how it worked and why it worked, and they asked themselves whether and why it might work in their particular operation. Their objective in looking around in the industry for ideas was to find and add services that could meet the needs and preferences of the kinds of customers they sought.

The Resnicks never got to the desperation stage that is experienced by so many first-time entrepreneurs. They thought the venture through together, they planned realistic marketing objectives, they worked very hard toward their goal, they kept close track of expenditures, and because they always stayed on top of the job they had set for themselves, they were able to maintain a sense of confidence in eventual success. This latter point illustrates the value of a positive mental attitude in coping with the stresses and strains of those early months and years in a new business.

Many of the innovations the Resnicks tried did not work out, but some became permanent features of their business. In the early months, they concentrated their advertising in the Yellow Pages. They also promised their customers that they would feed the pets whatever special diet the animal got at home (the customer had to supply the rations). They promised that if the animal required veterinary care, they would take it to its usual vet. They made sure the veterinarians in town knew of this policy, thus ensuring good, reliable sources of referrals. They established the practice of bathing and grooming the animals before they went home. They offered classes in behavior and show handling. They set up a shop that carried pet paraphernalia, knickknacks, and books. The business took off and has been free of serious problems since the third year.

MONEY, PEOPLE, AND LIGHTNING

Samuel Wallace, of Xodex Enterprises, Ltd., has been less fortunate. His setbacks and surprises were numerous and seriously threatening. He ennumerated them for us:

1. The demand in his area for market research services was less developed than he had anticipated, and as a result his business has grown less swiftly than he had anticipated, forcing staff reductions.
2. His partners did not work out, and he has had to get rid of them.
3. His reluctance to borrow money in the early stages weakened the business and left Wallace unable to find additional needed capital later on.
4. "We never recognized how important the political aspects of the environment we work within would be. . . . This has required a total reorganization of how we do business."
5. The recession of the early 1980s hampered growth and left the business ill-equipped to grow once the recession was over.
6. "The most difficult aspect of the business is the ability to attract persons with the skills as well as the financial resources to be able to maintain themselves while the business is in the growth period. . . . Thus the business has attracted no new partners."

Wallace's solution to these problems has been straightforwardly simple. He has reduced Xodex to a one-man operation, and he is struggling to make it work. His greatest asset may be his ability to persevere.

Judith Kaplan, of Action Packets, mentions the difficulty of attracting competent, energetic people from urban areas of the country to the relative isolation of Ocala, Florida. Another of our respondents, who prefers to remain anonymous in this particular context, has a similar problem. His company is located in a remote section of the country. He reports that attracting technical and administrative managers is difficult.

In today's atmosphere where references describe only the positive qualities of an individual and seldom any hint of shortcomings, recruiting, especially by an inexperienced entrepreneur, can be very hazardous. There can be many positive reasons why a seemingly well qualified person might want to join a new venture, and there can be one or more negative reasons; drinking is the most common. Our anonymous remote respondent tells us that individuals "with quite attractive experience and resumes . . . have on several occasions had such problems, and we have had to release them."

Our anonymous respondent adds a word of advice for entrepreneurs who are setting up in remote areas: the most successful employees seem likely to be people who are "returning home . . . they were raised in the area or a similar one . . . or they have had their fill of city life . . . or they just want to return to their roots."

Thomas Lisle, of Cruisers, Inc., reports that most of his setbacks and surprises have been fairly ordinary. He cites quality control problems, employee problems, inventory shrinkage, and poor accounting, any of which can hold real dangers for the first-time, inexperienced entrepreneur.

One of Lisle's surprises was not so routine. He had labored hard to end the company's losses. He had weathered the recession of the early 1980s. The business was just beginning to take off when a bolt of lightning struck a warehouse and factory building. This immense disaster, Lisle recalls, "taxed both our personal and financial resources." He credits "extraordinary efforts by our employees" to maintain operations while replacement facilities were built. The "pull-together" attitude (noted in Chapter 7) that Lisle had fostered among the employees early in the enterprise paid off in overcoming the emergency.

Larry Gleeson of Maine Hydro-Electric Corporation in Belfast, Maine, has suffered no real setbacks, but there have been a few surprises. The greatest has been community reaction to his development of hydroelectric power facilities. He had long thought of hydroelectric power as a benign energy source, but, he has found, lakeside property owners object to changes in water level and sportsmen object to whatever they perceive as spoiling fishing or duck-hunting. At his Belfast site, he found that a dispute over the uses of the water from the lake that feeds the stream on which one of his powerhouses sits had gone on for years, and when he entered the picture, it focused on him. Feelings ran so high that his facilities were actually vandalized.

Environmental groups also raised a surprising number of obstacles. Larry notes that the groups that feel their interests are adversely affected are the ones you hear from during licensing hearings, and that as soon as you resolve matters with them, others appear, offended by the solution.

RELIGION

Bill Wernsing, of Williams Laboratories in Ithaca, New York, insists that failure in one sense is impossible. His belief is that "given a valid attempt, any result is success. The point is to play the game as best as you can." Thus, though his business has gone up and down over the years, he sees no failures, no setbacks, not even surprises. The difference between one year and another for Wernsing is between good and not-so-good, not between good and bad.

Still, those not-so-good years are what others call setbacks. Wernsing tells us that about 1980, he had saturated the market for his oil seal analyzer. He had seen this situation coming, and he had started working on a computer printer device as his new sustaining product. About that time, daisy-wheel printers came on the market, and his efforts on the computer printer device proved to have been wasted. That setback brought on a couple of years with no income, and Wernsing went deeply into debt. "You get used to the ups and downs," he says, "But you can still get pretty tense."

The crisis ended with the development of Bytewriter, the gadget that converted an electric typewriter into a computer printer. Innovation, ingenuity, new product development, these are the keys to Wernsing's success. They can be the ingredients in the success of just about any entrepreneur who is willing to develop and apply whatever talents he or she possesses. Persistence and hard work are necessary adjuncts to talent.

Bill Wernsing and his wife insist that these qualities are not less important in success than religious faith. They both believe in a personal, concerned God, and prayer, Wernsing says, gives him confidence and calm, especially in times of anxiety.

Religion seldom comes up in discussions with entrepreneurs. Nevertheless, most people are religious, and many are devout.

Therefore, we believe that a thorough study of religion as a factor in business success is long overdue.

BIG SURPRISES AND BIG SETBACKS

Ron MacCrae, of RAM, Inc., Atlanta, Georgia, did not have time to pray the day of the coup in Nigeria. The crisis was over before he knew it had begun, and his small company was out a $5 million contract to do computer systems design for the Nigerian government. What did MacCrae do? "We about lost our shirt. . . . We worked a little harder and tried sweet-talking our banker. . . . We also took loans out on our houses." RAM was undercaptitalized from the beginning, and when the Nigerian crisis hit, MacCrae realized that the company should have obtained more investors "to better capitalize the company."

Ralph Brown was working hard and expanding rapidly toward a goal of $10 million in annual sales when, without warning, cheap imitations of his unique products hit the U.S. market from the Far East. He explains that one of the firm's mass market lines was thoroughly derailed by foreign "piracy" imports. Ralph's response was to fight the imports through government agencies and in the federal courts (the results are still pending), and "to broaden our design base with items less easy or fruitful to copy."

SMALL SETBACKS AND FEW SURPRISES

Katie Crane of Crane Marketing Communications, White River Junction, Vermont, had no serious setbacks or unpleasant surprises in her first two years. In fact, she started out believing that "there would be no problems if I was completely in control" And that is pretty much the way things have gone for Katie. So far (1985) the problems have been manageable ones. "I've had clients who didn't like the designer I hired to do a job; I've had to reprint a brochure at my expense because there was a mix-up; I've had a personal run-in with one designer. . . . Each of these things caused me considerable distress and tension, but all were satisfactorily resolved and the business survived." Katie explains that so much of what she is doing

"parallels what I have always done that I have very few surprises."
She is very much in control as a one-person business, and that is how
she intends to keep it."

Ellen Green of Allied Systems Design, Bangor, Maine, also
knows exactly what she is doing and what she wants to do. She
avoids problems and the wrong kinds of surprises by being her own
most severe critic. "One product came out horribly even though my
customer didn't think so." She reports that her biggest surprise as a
new entrepreneur was "who my contacts turned out to be and the
[positive] feedback on my professional reputation," earned before
she went into business for herself. She says with justifiable pride, "I
never knew how well known I was before being on my own."

SETBACKS THAT HAVEN'T HAPPENED

Several of our subjects have been successful almost from the
point of start-up. Two of them worry about the setbacks and surprises
that have not happened to them, and they have included contingency
planning in their preparations for the future. Pat Heffernan is a careful planner and a thorough manager. She tries to anticipate problems,
and probably that is one of the reasons she has had so few. "The fact
that I have had no setbacks makes me nervous, and so I am constantly planning how I'll handle any setback. . . . My greatest fear is
failure because of the pleasure in what I am doing."

Win Cross of Cross Publishers tells us that the setbacks for his
new (1984) company have been "relatively minor." But, he says, "in
a small organization even minor ones can be important. . . . Our
approach has been to take a long-term view of our business, knowing
that there will be surprises along the way and to address each of them
to the best of our ability when they arise. . . . The setbacks included
our having to let a secretary go, and some defective product which
caused us to force a supplier to replace the product at their cost . . .
in each case, we tried to concentrate on resolving the problem, and
not dwell on its effects."

CONSTRUCTIVE MISTAKES

In addressing the question of setbacks and surprises, several of
our subjects put them in the category of legitimate trial and error.

Greg Kravitt says that there were "many initial blows to the ego and many mistakes." But, he added, "Mistakes are constructive if you're not too hard on yourself and if you learn from them." That is exactly the point that Ellen Green expressed when she told us that many of her successes "came from mistakes. . . . I learn things that help my next project. It seems the next time around that the lesson proves invaluable."

This is the spirit that leads entrepreneurs time and again to eventual success. We noted earlier that many entrepreneurs fail their first time around, but not on their second or third. This is because, for many, the first attempt is a learning experience. Like John North, they gain a valuable education. However, the financial and personal cost of tuition can be very high. It thus seems wise for entrepreneurs to learn all they can from books, courses, advisers, and job experience *before* they make mistakes. Even so, there can be no substitute for experience.

CHAPTER 9

Growing Pains:
Coping With Success

Despite setbacks, despite surprises, most of the entrepreneurs with whom we talked have not failed. They have succeeded to some degree, and in the process they have had to cope with other problems.

What kinds of problems can success bring? It is easy to imagine a few. Some people thrive on uncertainty, and when things settle down, they suffer greater stress than before. Such people enjoy the challenge of adversity; they would rather struggle than win. Some people experience serious problems going from poverty to affluence.

Other people can handle winning, making it big in business. Once they have made it, they have to cope with the issues of new wealth. Successful entrepreneurs must face basic decisions such as whether to expand their businesses, to grow and diversify, or to stay small. Successful entrepreneurs must learn to manage increasing demands on their time and energy, to hire and manage executives, to coordinate larger production lines and sales forces.

They must learn to find and use new sources of funding, new markets, new strategies. In short, they must face the problems of change from small entrepreneur to big business person. Some entrepreneurs do not want to take on the problems of big business and so they remain small or they sell out to someone who does or to a large company that needs the product or the expertise. Some small entrepreneurs who have built a successful business, and then sold out, take the capital and begin a new enterprise.

Our subjects provide us with several examples of coping with the problems of success. First, let us review the stages of business growth as developed by Churchill and Lewis (1983). They studied 83 selected companies in order to understand the life cycle of small businesses. They found that most companies progress from an "existence" stage through survival, success, and take-off to resource maturity.

STAGE ONE. The existence stage is the start-up, whose main problem is finding and serving customers. The company's structure is simple with the owner doing almost everything. One example among our subjects is Ron Slatin, whose Medimicro Systems, Inc., has just one product, a computer software program for interpreting pulmonary function diagnostic data. The company has one marketing agent, and Slatin and his colleagues do all of the work that goes into refining and producing the program, keeping company records, and so forth.

Another of our subjects, Samuel Wallace of Xodex Enterprises, was also in the existence stage at this writing (1985). He is still struggling to get his business established.

STAGE TWO. In the survival stage, the company has developed a market. It is selling product or service successfully. Its main problem is maintaining sufficient cash flow to cover expenses and to finance enough growth to make the business pay a reasonable return on investment and entrepreneurial effort. Greg Kravitt, of North American Group, Ltd., got through the survival stage by consciously learning from his mistakes. It is essential, he counsels, "Never to lose sight of your objectives." Ron MacCrae would probably be beyond the survival stage by now if the Nigerian contract had not been torpedoed by a coup against the government. Win Cross, by his own estimate, will probably not be on solid ground before his fifth year in business as a publishing house. Larry Gleeson, of Maine Hydro-Electric Corporation, may be nearing the end of this stage, for he now [1985] has several powerhouses on line and is becoming more prosperous each year.

STAGE THREE. At stage three, the business is established, and the entrepreneur faces the crucial question of whether to seek outside funding for further growth, aiming perhaps at becoming a big business. The alternative is maintaining the business at the current level.

Churchill and Lewis divide stage three into two substages which they label Success-Disengagement and Success-Growth.

In Success-Disengagement, the business is stable and profitable and can remain so for the foreseeable future. If the business is put into the hands of professional managers who are content with a policy of no-growth stability, the entrepreneur can be free to pursue other interests, perhaps developing another business. Under the entrepreneur's personal management, the business can be a source of support and professional satisfaction indefinitely. Two of our subjects, the Resnicks and Bill Wernsing, have chosen this formula for their businesses.

More of our subjects have chosen Success-Growth. They are using funds generated by their businesses to expand in production, markets, and subsidiaries. The problems of this stage center on maintaining the vitality of the basic business, finding and retaining growth-oriented managers, and planning effective strategies. The risks involved are similar to those of the start-up. Ralph Brown broke with two partners in succession over the issue of working toward growth and expansion. The second partner specifically argued for retrenchment and comfortable, steady profit making over reinvestment and expansion. Ralph had to go it alone as the entrepreneur and look for growth-oriented managers to help him. J. W. Anderson never has stopped planning new ways of giving life to his wealth of ideas. As of this writing, he is looking for backing to set up "Robot World, Orlando", an entertainment-oriented, high-tech tourist attraction set near Walt Disney World in Florida. Pat Heffernan considers her Heffernan & Associates to be a success and annually reassesses expansion objectives for the future.

STAGE FOUR. In the take-off stage, the commitment to growth changes the entrepreneur's definition of success. Now success requires growth, preferably rapid growth, and so the key problem is financing and managing that growth. The company takes off, climbing quickly into the rarefied heights of wealth. The owner must delegate more and more responsibility to hired managers, impose tight controls on expenses and investments, and may decentralize the corporate structure. Success is measured by the price of the eventual buy-out.

STAGE FIVE. In the stage of resource maturity, a company must consolidate the financial and other gains made during the stage of rapid growth. It must, say Churchill and Lewis (1983), expand its management force to maximize efficiency and professionalize its management practices, planning, and budgeting. The company's original entrepreneurial character may slip away in this stage. By now, the owner has given up much of his or her personal involvement, and the business is yielding great wealth.

Churchill and Lewis warn of loss of creativity and ossification at the resource maturity stage if the company does lose its entrepreneurial character. The danger of ossification is that the company will soon become vulnerable to growth-oriented competitors whose forte is rapid response to opportunities in the marketplace.

Churchill and Lewis (1983) remark that the sequence of stages can be interrupted or reversed at any point. They are not immutable. For instance, a company that fails in an attempt to grow may drop back to the survival stage, or even to the existence stage. Businesses may halt at any stage, as we see in the distinction between Success-Disengagement and Success-Growth. Such halts are not irreversible decisions, as we will see in the case of the Resnicks.

GETTING OVER THE HUMP

Moving from the start-up (existence) stage to later stages means getting over the hump, reaching a condition in which success seems not merely conceivable, but likely. This process can be very quick, as it was in the case of Pat Heffernan, who realized a profit in the first month and also in the first year of operation. Win Cross reached the second, or survival, stage within the first year of operation with several early, successful books.

Getting over the hump can take years. Larry Gleeson has struggled for more than a decade against the vicissitudes of the energy market, regulators, and citizen groups. Greg Kravitt started The North American Group with one partner, who put up the capital, and a small crew of employees. He tells us that the pressure to survive was intense. With limited start-up resources, more responsibilities had to be assumed by everyone. The biggest problem in this period was conflicts growing out of conflicting objectives among partners and investors. Kravitt survived the first few years because of careful preparation and planning, choice of the right partner for his needs, keeping his nerve when the going got rough, compromising when he couldn't get his way, learning from errors, and never losing sight of his own objectives.

We asked our respondents, "What problems of success did you encounter, and how did you handle them?" Not all of our respondents consider themselves to have arrived at that happy stage, and so from some we got very short answers:

> Gleeson: "Hasn't been a problem so far!"
> Kravitt: "I should live so long!"
> MacRae: "I would like to have some of those problems . . ."
> Sakurai: "When I got my first outplacement contract, I felt like stopping. . . ."
>   Green: "No problem yet!"
>   Slatin: "Ha!"

Several of our subjects consider themselves to be on the way to success. But the problems en route can be vexing and unsettling. Win Cross, publisher, cites fund raising as one task that kept him in constant uncertainty for much of the year of planning and preparation. "On a personal level, raising capital, although successful, was an emotionally trying experience. . . . It means putting yourself—your capabilities, your integrity—on the line with each investor. . . . It caused a lot of sleepless nights and a lot of stress." How did Cross handle the stress? "I felt that a stepped up exercise program—one hour a day, 5 or 6 days a week—helped relieve some of the tension." Ellen Green walks to and from work to deal with the stress of her first two years.

Katie Crane reports that she is just beginning to encounter her first problem of success: "Where local people are turning to others for help before me because they assume I'm too busy with bigger fish!"

HOLDING PATTERNS

Mike Resnick's goal was to provide the financial security to support a shift from hack writing to serious writing. He figured that the Briarwood Pet Motel enterprise would be a natural for him and Carol because of their experience as dog breeders.

Mike tells us that he was perfectly willing to stay away from the typewriter so long as he and Carol were fighting for survival. But when the business doubled twice in the first three years, Mike refused to continue putting in the long hours that had built the business. Mike and Carol therefore promoted their two best employees to manage the business. Although they continued to live on the grounds and to deal with emergencies, they gradually disengaged. "Actually," says Mike, "Carol gradually disengaged; I signed a four-book contract with a major science fiction publisher and was gone in a flash."

Briarwood continued to generate money, and the Resnicks expanded the grooming room and then the cattery. They added a unique pet store, and along the way made the decision to plow more than half of the profits back into the business. Briarwood continues to expand. The Resnicks now plan to computerize all of the operations, including reservations, feeding and medication charts, store inventory, and so forth. Carol is thinking of building other branches in nearby cities.

Mike, on the other hand, is opposed to expansion. After all he is comfortably situated with several new book contracts and has all the money he wants from Briarwood without branches. Be that as it may, Mike expects Carol to have her way about the expansion and branches.

What all this amounts to is that the Resnicks have reached the stage of Success-Disengagement. At least Mike has. They have delegated management in return for an ample income from the business. Have they rejected expansion? Mike surely has, but Carol surely has not. So is it Success-Disengagement or Success-Growth? Mike thinks it will be the latter. Carol thinks so too. For the present their situation could be described as a holding pattern.

We can see a second example of a holding pattern in the case of Bill Wernsing. He set up Williams Laboratories as a vehicle for his own talents as an engineer and inventor. His company's sole real asset is Bill Wernsing, idea man. The products he develops are extensions of himself, and they bring in the income.

Wernsing's goal has been to support himself and his family by doing what suits him best, and he has succeeded. Despite years of sparse income, he says, he has averaged about the same income as he would have made had he remained with GE. He seems content.

Much of Wernsing's success has been fairly recent. It was his Bytewriter computer-typewriter interface that made him "comfortable.'' Now that that product has reached the end of its marketability, Wernsing is looking to the next product to maintain his success.

Asked about problems of success, he replies characteristically, ''Problems? What problems?'' Pressed, he grows serious and says, yes, there are problems, but he does not want to talk about problems. Would there be a problem in losing the ground he has gained? He concedes, ''When I didn't have it, I didn't worry about it. Now that I have it, I don't want to lose it. In a sense, I don't feel any more secure than I did before.''

Despite the uncertainty, Wernsing says he does not want to become a big corporation. In an interview, he brushed aside the subject of market expansion with the comment, ''Now you're trying to turn me into a big business!'' He says bigness is not what he wants. He insists that his sole aim is to keep within the limits of a comfortable status quo.

What Wernsing would do if he hit upon a product that took off into a major market is an open question. His tentative answer is that he might license such a product to a larger company. He says he would never sell the product—any of his products—to anyone. A rationale for such a sale would be cash for expansion, which he says he does not want. Also, he explains, his products are the fruits of his personal skills and therefore the foundation of his business. In fact, the closest he has come to the sale of a product was to sell the rights to the name ''Bytewriter'' to a Japanese maker of computers and printers who wanted to avoid a trademark conflict over their product name, ''Brite Writer.''

Several of our subjects are in the stage of Success-Growth. When Thomas Lisle took over Cruisers, Inc., the company was in the survival stage, and in trouble. Lisle's first task was to get the company out of trouble, that is, beyond the struggle for survival. He succeeded, and within three years the workforce tripled. After the first year and a few setbacks, the company became increasingly profitable. Once the company had emerged from the survival stage, Lisle concentrated on growth, and from that point on the problems centered largely but not entirely on expansion and facilities acquisition.

Labor problems came hand in hand with profitability. The company was no longer in that ''shallow pocket,'' and the employees knew it. New employee demands have become one of Lisle's toughest problems in the expansion stage. At this writing (1985), Lisle was still in the midst of grappling with all of these growth-associated problems. We hope to check back with him in a few years to learn the outcome of his efforts.

J. W. Anderson's ShowAmerica, Inc., has been growing steadily ever since its start 19 years ago and is on the verge of an attempt at take-off. Anderson has considered selling out, but he has rejected that course of action. "As I've gotten older [he was 56 in 1985], I find I've satisfied my economic demands—car, house, long vacations—and time is becoming very important. . . . Yet due to my discipline and personal drive, I would just starve to death if I didn't have the day-to-day involvement in the business that I have now." Anderson added that while he might sell for the right offer, he would feel compelled to get right back into something else to "occupy my energies, drives, ambitions, and goals."

Anderson's ShowAmerica has been on a strong growth pattern for several years. He reports 12 percent growth in 1982, 26 percent in 1983, and 30 percent in 1984. The heart of his business is his industrial film and radio-TV commercial awards-competition festivals, which have been solid successes. The remote-control robots he rents to trade shows, mall openings, and the like have been popular. With these successes firmly established, Anderson is on the lookout for new directions in which to expand. He says, "We have the brain-power, the vehicles, and we want to use them."

ShowAmerica's success owes much to Anderson's dedication to serving people, "to working effectively to provoke a positive response from clients and their customers." Anderson is a promoter and a very effective one. He is also prompt and efficient. Answers to queries go out the same day, even, he claims, when the queries come in five minutes before closing time. The company attitude is summed up in a plaque on Anderson's office wall (presented to him by his employees): "No task shall be avoided simply because it is impossible."

The crisp efficiency of ShowAmerica's operation is due in no small part to the role played by Anderson's wife in overseeing day-to-day business. Anderson's son personally arranges and supervises most of the robot exhibitions at client trade shows, etc. This dedicated family involvement has freed Anderson to expand the business and to develop plans for new directions.

One new development is an electronics sweepstakes machine for giving away door prizes. Another is the plan for an entertainment complex featuring the company's robots, for which Anderson is seeking several million dollars in venture capital.

This latter development is what could move ShowAmerica into the take-off stage. If the robot entertainment complex attracts the necessary capital, Anderson says he will turn over most of the responsibilities for the on-going operation of the business to his son and wife and concentrate his personal efforts in the new venture. He says he will decentralize, tighten up on finances, and do what is necessary for a take-off to be successful.

Larry Gleeson does not contemplate parting with his operation in the foreseeable future, but he says that he has already sold off bits and pieces, in the form of particular hydroelectric sites, often in return for a measure of assured income. He has also had inquiries that amount to invitations to go into the franchising business, but so far he has turned them all down, having no wish to package his expertise in that way. He may in the future, however, decide to pursue that path.

TAKING OFF

Judith Kaplan and Action Packets, Inc., seem to be in the take-off stage. The process began a few years ago, when the business had grown enough to need warehouse space. Kaplan met that need by moving to Florida where the required space was available at rates the business could afford.

In time, Action Packets needed more money to finance growth than the business itself could supply. This is a common problem of businesses in the growth stage of development. Kaplan's solution was to take the company public, raising nearly a million dollars in a stock offering.

Action Packet's move to Florida and growth has presented Kaplan with some unwelcome personnel problems. We noted earlier the difficulties she has encountered in attracting key employees to Ocala. That is a problem of location. A problem of growth for Kaplan is the inevitable "distancing" from employees. She finds that she can no longer be a friend to most of the people who work for her. Unlike the Resnicks, Kaplan had always managed to have close relations with Action Packet employees without feeling any handicap in her role as boss. In the rapidly expanding business, Kaplan reports frustration at being cut off from personal relationships with and interest in employees.

Judith Kaplan has been in great demand as a speaker in the wake of her fame as an unusually successful business person. She denies that the increased demands on her time present a serious problem, for the speaking opportunities support the idealism that motivated her business efforts in the first place. She aggressively seeks to present herself as a role model for other women. Kaplan's solution to the increasing time demands from the business and her speaking activities is beginning to be evident in her efforts to attract and train a small corps of key employees who could become the future management group of Action Packets.

SOME OTHER PROBLEMS OF SUCCESS

Judith Kaplan talks about another kind of success problem, one that could be called role conflict. She has come to believe that "other people, such as employees, feel you are above them, you don't understand them and their problems . . . you are 'different'. . . . But I try to empathize with people—all people." Of course, the boss is the boss with the power to call the shots, to run things, to hire and fire. The boss has the economic lives of her employees in her hands. It follows that she will be considered to be above them and "different." The hierarchy is built into the situation, and all the benevolent employer can do is to be fair and firm at the same time, and to maintain that social distance the Resnicks found so necessary.

Pat Heffernan is a success in her own eyes. Indeed, she is a success by any measure. So, when she came to our question on problems of success, her mind went to the problems of image she has encountered in her small Vermont community. Some of the problems of success, she reports, "have been other people's assumptions. . . . One assumption is that you are personally wealthy. . . . Another is that you have ample time and money for community organizations and worthy causes. . . . A third is the assumption by some that all business people are constantly cheating on their taxes and making legal arrangements that are unethical. . . ."

The other problem of success that Pat says she had not expected to face so soon in her business is the one of growth or no growth. She tells us that she handles it "by comparing the implications of expansion and growth with my personal short-term and long-term goals. . . . I do this generally during an annual assessment in which I review (with my husband) where I am, and where I want to go, and how the past year was, and any changes I want to make."

Most entrepreneurs would not mind having such problems. However, there are problems no one wants. Ralph Brown, our back-country toy maker, won success after years of dedicated work building a national and international market for his products, but at the cost of a divorce. He says that he "married the factory. . . . My wife of 10 years . . . became a factory widow. . . . We never succeeded in mutually solving the needs of both marriage and factory. . . . It is notable that our best marriage years were in poverty, as were also the early entrepreneurial years. . . . With success, oncoming of money, and building a new house, came unresolvable discontent." Now in his second marriage he is trying to strike a balance between the demands of a still growing business with those of his personal life.

It may be that entrepreneurs find fewer problems in success than in failure, but the problems of success are by no means simpler or less frustrating. Perhaps the lesson to take from this chapter is that problems are an inevitable part of the hard-driving life of an entrepreneur. They come in business and at home, with struggle and with success and they must constantly be dealt with. So be prepared.

CHAPTER 10

Doing it Differently

Hindsight is cheap. It is easy to look back over one's life and career and say, "If only I had. . . ." If there is any point in mulling the past, it is to analyze mistakes and missteps. The lessons we all learn from our successes are a valuable foundation for continued success, but the lessons of mistakes and failure are potentially even more valuable. Climbing a treacherous mountain without a slip may be a matter of luck, but if the climber interprets an initial success as purely a matter of skill, he or she may be in for trouble the next time up, when the odds of a slip or two are increased by over-confidence.

In our interviews with entrepreneurs, we urged each of them to share with us for the benefit of our readers the lessons, both good and bad, that they learned from their experiences of cutting loose. Most were candid with us and so we are able to describe in this concluding chapter some experiences that may help you to anticipate, prepare for, and—we hope—avoid certain problems that every entrepreneur encounters sooner or later in launching a new business. We offer, so to speak, a map of the mountain with some of the hazards marked.

Thomas Lisle, of Cruisers, Inc., is the climber who went up the mountain, well prepared, without any serious slips. He was our respondent who said, "While my partner and I have made numerous errors, strategically we have made the right moves." So, we ask, for the purpose of a chapter on "Doing It Differently," does Lisle have anything to teach us? He and his partner did make the right moves in market anticipation, asset management, accounting, manufacturing, and so on. You can tell they made the right moves because their success to date is the evidence. The errors of which they speak had to have been so insignificant hardly to have affected the outcome. Recall that Lisle's only reported setback was the lightning bolt, which he survived by making a whole series of "right moves." So we leave Lisle and partner to their success, and move on to other subjects who did experience setbacks that offer valuable lessons.

John North's disastrous experience has more useful lessons in it than several success stories combined. He says that his experience has left him less susceptible to flattery, and probably better able to evaluate an enterprise objectively. On doing things differently, he says he would put the original company into bankruptcy immediately as the principal strategy of reorganization. That maneuver, he says, might have enabled him to start over soon enough to save the company from going under.

He would not employ friends. He would minimize expenses, doing without a large office, a company car, and so on. He would keep the operation of the company on a small scale, applying sound planning and planned objectives to develop a track record before attempting to seek investors and expand nationwide. He would develop a good business plan as a chart to future growth, and then seek funding from a venture capital company.

If he had it to do over again, he would be more willing to surrender equity in return for assistance, and he would not accept a greedy partner (but how can you tell in advance?). His criteria for employees would be imagination, sincerity, expertise, and discipline. He now considers money and good advice to be crucial commodities in any enterprise.

Most readers are likely to say, "Of course, those are all good lessons. But they are also common sense, and I doubt that I need John North to tell me about them." Probably John North would have said the same thing before his sad experience, because he did, after all, believe himself to be a competent and sensible person . . . until he got part way up the mountain without enough equipment and preparation. The entrepreneurial business may look easy, but it is not so easy as it looks. Take it from John North and his "worst case" experience.

A little more from John North and then we will look at some less depressing second thoughts. North learned the hard way, but he learned many of the same lessons more fortunate entrepreneurs pick up on the job working for someone else or in business school. His "would haves" sound like run-of-the-mill prescriptions for sound business practices, which says a lot to us about the value of negative experiences—if someone is willing to learn from them and move on to new ventures. Will North? Time will tell. Greg Kravitt did.

Ralph Brown has few regrets about the way he built his toy manufacturing business. He stuck to the goals of his "idealistic and enlightened capitalism within the confines of reality." Ralph is that rare combination of idealism and realism that we also see in Judith Kaplan. Ralph reminds us in responding to our question, "What would you have done differently? that he was "energized to go into business by financial need, health problems related to physical labor, boredom at being a cog in a big machine, and failure at homesteading." He explains that he "brought these problems onto an acceptable and rewarding course through entrepreneurship."

Although neither of his partners worked out as permanent and satisfying relationships, Ralph feels comfortable in retrospect about the essential role both partners played while they were involved. "I had to attempt to share that whole spectrum from wealth to danger in exciting brotherhood with others. . . . This attitude came in part because I felt incapable alone of piloting the company to success, inexperienced as I was, partly because of my natural repugnance for 'big-shot' trappings and milieu. . . . In any case, I believe that the burdens of sole proprietorship in the early years might have broken and destroyed the company."

He has one regret about an early decision to pass up a large, old, abandoned mill in favor of an abandoned gas station for his initial operation in Maine. He considers the decision both as costly mistake (in hindsight) and at the same time as a trivial regret in the overall perspective of what he has accomplished. He says the choice of the old mill "would have saved a fortune in loan payback and interest and the personal financial liability which is the legacy of our new plant [built in 1984], as well as years of inefficient bursting at the seams at the old [gas station] plant." But, he explains, "at that early time of decision, I could not imagine the growth in store for our company. . . . What I saw [in the abandoned mill] was a decrepit 'white elephant' of five times the size we needed, whose upkeep would decimate our resources and divert our time and attention, so I shunned it.''

Before Ralph leaves the question of doing things differently, he comments again on the effect entrepreneurship can have on marriage. ''At times I ponder at the danger of entrepreneurship to marriage wherein the couple are not actively involved together—indeed a delicate, poignant and very personal question.''

Kravitt tells us that he made many mistakes in setting up and operating his North American Group, but, he goes on to say, ''I truly believe that mistakes are a necessary part of the growth process . . . From an overall perspective, I would not do anything differently . . . Pain and all, the experience was worth it.'' Kravitt adds that he had to learn ''to develop the ability to separate oneself mentally and emotionally from one's work when playing or resting.''

Samuel Wallace of Xodex Enterprises, Ltd., would agree that mistakes are educational, though he says he would have been better off if they had been avoided. Hence, he told us, ''There are a number of things we would have done differently if given the opportunity.'' He now says that he should not have taken friends as partners. He also says that he would require that every key employee have at least a bachelor's degree, ''and hopefully an MBA in marketing.'' He says he should have explored the geographic and economic aspects of the regional market more thoroughly than he actually did.

He would raise more start-up money, and he would establish relationships with two or three banks ''to provide us with backup alternatives should one or the other not prove supportive.'' He would also set the firm's rates initially higher, offer ''more tangible products than intangible consulting services,'' and find means of heading off political-type problems within the firm.

Wallace is looking at the problems that hampered his business— money, competence, marketing, internal controversy—and wishing he could have avoided them. Many of our subjects seem to have made fewer or less damaging mistakes and to talk less about regrets, though some of them are willing to look back and comment on whether some things could have been done differently and better.

Judith Kaplan wishes she had learned to manage people earlier, ''to allow people to grow earlier.'' She wants to ''drive people to perform to their highest potential'' so that she can trust them to do more and do less herself.

Mike Resnick's sole regret is that he and Carol did not take out their original loan for 35 years instead of the 20 they insisted upon. "I wish I was still deducting the interest that I deducted a few years ago!" he exclaims.

Bill Wernsing cites the mistakes he has made in product choice. He now knows more about the time that is involved in developing a product and marketing it. He would in hindsight avoid some of his most time-consuming projects. His greatest error, he says, was na-ivete. At one point, he sold a British distributor $25,000 worth of his Bytewriters, having been "lured into believing" the distributor was honest. It took him two years of court battles to recover payment. He comments, "You learn to spot crooks," and to balance trust and distrust.

Wernsing's essentially positive attitude about his experiences is a prerequisite for the would-be entrepreneur. It is belief in oneself, confidence, that makes the risks seem acceptable, and even some-times trivial.

When J. W. Anderson of ShowAmerica looks back, he laughs at the disparity between his present business and his original degree in ornamental horticulture. He says he might have sought a more gen-eral degree, or one related to business, but he notes philosophically that the degree would have been ideal if he had wound up running a greenhouse business. "You never know," he observes, "when your training, experience, and dedication are right. . . . Only in retrospect can you tell. . . . I feel fortunate that what I have done has been successful. . . . It's clicked, it's worked, it's made me quite well off and independent, and I honestly don't know what I would have done differently other than the education."

On further reflection, Anderson says that he could have started his business earlier. But then he shakes his head. He did try. As a new college graduate, he set up a business, but it lasted only two years, and that was the end of it. He did not have the capital to make it work, and he lacked experience. That experience was itself neces-sary to the much later success of his film festivals and show robots.

Ron Slatin of Medimicro Systems, Inc., of Tucson, Arizona might have tried to market his pulmonary function interpretation pro-gram ten years earlier. "However," he adds, "I am satisfied that waiting out the development has produced a good program, and at least I didn't have to go mad trying to keep all the customers updated everytime a new mistake was found in the program!"

Sandy Sakurai, Career Counselor in Baltimore, Maryland, ran into a misunderstanding about a state license as she was preparing to accept clients. The result was an awkward confrontation with state authorities who challenged her right to practice. She was able to explain that she had inquired about state licensing procedures at two state licensing offices and had been told that she did not need a license if she was operating at home. In retrospect, Sandy says she should have gone first to the state agency that had been responsible for closing down her former employer to ask for guidance. That move would have saved several weeks of delay occasioned by the licensing challenge. Sandy also mentioned the need to set more definite goals early on "to keep things moving."

Win Cross's big regret is that he did not plunge directly into lining up outside financing prior to starting up the business. "This would have resulted in a less stressful start-up period and would have enabled me to spend more time on the business instead of raising funds," he says.

Pat Heffernan would do two things differently. She would have taken a course on how to sell oneself, and she would have allowed some early "slow time" for advanced marketing and "personal joy sharing."

She would have wanted the course on how to sell herself to "force me repeatedly actually to stand up and sell myself and my services." She says that while she has had "a plethora of standard marketing courses" and is considered an accomplished speaker, still "in all those situations one is selling a cause or a theory, not yourself." She explains, "I have found personal selling awkward and I therefore put it off and I don't do as much of it as I should. . . . I think if I had had such an exposure or training before starting out, I would have felt much more comfortable."

Pat says that she wished she had allowed more time for advance marketing and personal joy sharing. She means simply that she would actually have sent out all those announcements about the opening of her business that she kept putting off until it was too late. She would have had a party for her family and friends to celebrate her big move. The announcements and the party are what she calls "joy sharing." And she feels she missed the chance by starting off full tilt and leaving friends and family in a cloud of dust. We have a suggestion, Pat. Celebrate your Heffernan & Associates fifth anniversary in 1987 along with the 200th birthday of the Constitution. We'd like to be there.

Asked about doing things differently, Larry Gleeson of Maine Hydro-Electric Development Corporation mentions the franchising opportunities he has passed up. They were, he says, chances to do things differently, but they never seemed right for him at the time. Perhaps someday, he adds.

He also mentions money. It would have been useful to have had more capital, but those who might have provided it wanted too much equity. He does not think he would pay that price, even with the benefit of hindsight. He enjoys too much owning the operation himself.

And he mentions trust, pointing to the would-be investor we mentioned in Chapter 7. He says he might have played his cards a little closer to his chest, at least with some people.

But overall, like so many of our subjects, he would not change much in his past. He has enjoyed his entrepreneurial voyage, even though it has been at times a struggle.

The entrepreneurs we interviewed have each learned much from their various experiences. Most of the lessons echo common themes from books of business advice. The most important of these lessons are the value of planning and of objectivity. Yet though most of our entrepreneurs recognize past errors, they are not inclined to go back and change them. The main lesson these entrepreneurs offer is that no entrepreneur should worry excessively about being right at every step of the way. No one can always be right. You cannot avoid being wrong, at least some of the time.

Aim your efforts toward your desired goals. Focus on what needs doing. When mistakes occur, correct them or move beyond them. If you cannot correct them, do not eat your heart out over them. Do not waste your personal and corporate resources in endless analysis and recrimination.

You can overcome mistakes best by learning from them and moving on. You can be defeated by them if you do not. Remember, mistakes are essential to growth. They turn into disaster only when you refuse to use them to increase your knowledge and wisdom. This is what our respondents mean when they say that despite some mistakes they wouldn't change a thing.

APPENDIX

<hr>

QUESTIONNAIRE FOR
Cutting Loose:
Making the Transition
From Employee
to Entrepreneur

<hr>

DATE: _______________________

1. We seek reflective, discursive, even anecdotal responses to the questions below. Please ignore questions or parts of questions that do not apply to your case. Give as much detail as you are comfortable revealing. If we wish more detail, we will follow up this questionnaire with one or more phone calls. Please write below when are the best times to reach you at which phone number(s):

____

May we have your permission to use your name and that of your company in the text of our book and in the book's advertising? If so, please sign here:

____

You will also receive an acknowledgement in the book's preface. If you do not wish your name mentioned, even in that way, please sign here:

____

2. Please describe your current entrepreneurial activity or business. How long has it lasted?

3. What factors—dissatisfaction, opportunity, job loss, search for joy or fulfillment, creative urge, etc.—made you want to become an entrepreneur?

4. How and where did you find the idea for your entrepreneurial activity? How did you evaluate its potential?

5. What were your qualifications—education, managerial experience, past entrepreneurial efforts, etc.—for trying your entrepreneurial activity? What qualifications did you lack?

6. Please outline the planning process you undertook before beginning your entrepreneurial activity. What did your planning cover? Where did you find the necessary information? What good did your planning do you? What developments did your planning fail to anticipate?

7. How did you obtain necessary funding or seed money? How did you decide how much money you would need? What expenses did you foresee? What expenses did you fail to foresee? How did you use your expense forecasts?

8. Entrepreneurs often manage to set up their businesses while still employed, perhaps using—with or without approval—their employer's facilities or resources. Even when they leave their jobs before setting up their businesses, they use contacts, ideas, and expertise gained while employed. How did you handle the ethical problems implicit in such "borrowings"? How did you handle the problem of competing with your employer?

9. When and why did you incorporate? If you did not, why not?

The next few questions relate to the human dimension of entrepreneurship. Your answers may help future would-be entrepreneurs decide whether they really wish to be entrepreneurs; they may also help future entrepreneurs cope more effectively.

10. What problems did you encounter in working with employees, partners, and investors? How did you handle these problems?

11. What problems did your entrepreneurial activity generate in your personal life—personal finances, family, friends, leisure, health, etc.? How did you handle them?

12. What setbacks and surprises (including failure) did you encounter? How did you handle them, on both personal and business levels?

13. What problems of success did you encounter, and how did you handle them?

14. Many entrepreneurs wind up dissolving or selling their companies. If you have done so, please explain the reasons and results.

15. What would you have done differently, and why?

Thank you.

Thomas A. Easton
Ralph W. Conant

References

Baty, G. B., Entrepreneurship for the Eighties (Reston, VA: Reston, 1981).

Boyd, D. P., and D. E. Gumpert, "Coping with entrepreneurial stress," Harvard Business Review, March–April 1983, pp. 44–64.

Broehl, Jr., W. G., John Deere's Company: A History of Deere & Company and Its Times (New York: Doubleday, 1984).

Brown, D., The Entrepreneur's Guide (New York: Macmillan, 1980).

Bulfinch, T., The Age of Fable (New York: Heritage Press, 1942).

Burlingham, B., "Let them make mudpies," Inc., July 1983, pp. 65–74.

Churchill, N. C., and V. L. Lewis, "The five stages of small business growth," Harvard Business Review, May–June 1983, pp. 30–50.

Coll, S., "When the magic goes," Inc., October 1984, pp. 86–97.

Collins, O., and D. G. Moore, The Organization Makers: A Behavioral Study of Independent Entrepreneurs (New York: Appleton-Century-Crofts, 1970).

Cooper, A. C., "The Entrepreneurship-small business interface," in C. A. Kent, D. L. Sexton, and K. H. Vesper, eds., Encyclopedia of Entrepreneurship (Englewood Cliffs, NJ: Prentice-Hall, 1982), pp. 193–205.

Drucker, P. F., "Our entrepreneurial economy," Harvard Business Review, January–February 1984, pp. 59–64.

Easton, T. A., and R. W. Conant, Using Consultants: A Consumer's Guide for Managers (Chicago: Probus, 1985).

Friedman, R., "63,000 entrepreneurs," Inc., May 1984, pp. 14–16.

Gilder, G., "Fear of capitalism," Inc., September 1984, pp. 87–94.

Gumpert, D. E., and D. P. Boyd, "The loneliness of the small-business owner," Harvard Business Review, November–December 1984, pp. 18–24.

Hershey, Jr., R. D., "Going hammer and tongs for small business," New York Times, Sept. 5, 1984.

Kennedy, A., Interview, Inc., April 1984, pp. 108–117.

Kirzner, I. M., Perception, Opportunity, and Profit: Studies in the Theory of Entrepreneurship (Chicago: University of Chicago Press, 1979).

Kirzner, I. M., "Entrepreneurship and the future of capitalism," in J. Backman, ed., Entrepreneurship and the Outlook for America (New York: The Free Press, 1983), pp. 149–172.

Kravitt, G. I., J. E. Grossman, K. P. Keller, K. Mitra, E. A. Raha, and A. E. Robbins, How to Raise Capital: Preparing and Presenting a Business Plan (Homewood, Il: Dow Jones-Irwin, 1984).

Ledoux, D., "A shaky start, but ideas, energy power Michaud's American Stabilis," Maine Today, December 1983, pp. 20–21.

Levinson, H., "Conflicts that plague family businesses," Harvard Business Review, March–April 1971, pp. 90–98.

Levinson, H., "A second career: The possible dream," Harvard Business Review, May–June 1983, pp. 122–129.

Lindsey, J., "Acquisition crazy," Venture, March 1985, pp. 63–65.

Mamis, R. A., "The Pied Piper of Sunnyvale," Inc., March 1983, pp. 57–66.

Mamis, R. A., "New money," Inc., April 1984a, pp. 93–100.

Mamis, R. A., "Sparring partners," Inc., March 1984b, pp. 43–50.

Mescon, T. S., G. E. Stevens, and G. S. Vozikis, "Women as entrepreneurs: An empirical evaluation," Wisconsin Small Business Forum, Winter 1983/84, pp. 7–17.

Pinchot III, G., Intrapreneuring: Why You Don't Have to Leave the Corporation to Become an Entrepreneur (New York: Harper & Row, 1985).

Posner, B. G., "In search of a better business plan," Inc., September 1983, pp. 136–138.

Richman, T., "Will the real SBA please stand up?" Inc., February 1984, pp. 85–90.

Russell, S., "Being your own boss in America," Venture, May 1984, pp. 40–52.

Shapiro, M., "The entrepreneurial individual in the large organization," in J. Backman, ed., Entrepreneurship and the Outlook for America (New York: The Free Press, 1983), pp. 55–80.

Silver, A. D., Up Front Financing: The Entrepreneur's Guide (New York: Wiley, 1983).

Silver, A. D., The Entrepreneurial Life: How to Go for It and Get It (New York: Wiley, 1983).

Simon, J. L., The Ultimate Resource (Princeton, NJ: Princeton University Press, 1981).

Sinetar, M., "Entrepreneurs, chaos, and creativity—Can creative people really survive large company structure?" Sloan Management Review, Winter 1985, pp. 57–62.

Smith, I., Diary of a Small Business (New York: Scribner's, 1982).

Solomon, S., "Out on a limb," Inc., August 1984, pp. 77–83.

Spanner, R. A., "Improvements on the noncompetition agreement," Harvard Business Review, March–April 1985, pp. 8–10.

Steingold, F. S., "Competing with your former employer," Inc., January 1983, pp. 91–92.

Stevenson, H. H., and D. E. Gumpert, "The heart of entrepreneurship," Harvard Business Review, March–April 1985, pp. 85–94.

Thurston, P. H., "Should smaller companies make formal plans?" Harvard Business Review, September–October 1983, pp. 162–188.

Vesper, K. H., Entrepreneurship and National Policy (Chicago: Heller Institute for Small Business, 1983).

Waters, C. R., "Going private," Inc., February 1983a, pp. 41–47.

Waters, C. R., "Banking on the entrepreneur: The leveraged buy-out boom," Inc., September 1983b, pp. 46–53.

Waters, C. R., "Fleshing out an empire," Inc., October 1984, pp. 53–61.

Welsh, J. A., and J. F. White, The Entrepreneur's Master Planning Guide (Englewood Cliffs, NJ: Prentice-Hall, 1983).

White, Jr., R. M., The Entrepreneur's Manual (Huntington Beach, CA: Chilton, 1976).

Index

Blessing *La Política*

BLESSING *LA POLÍTICA*

The Latino Religious Experience and Political Engagement in the United States

Carlos Vargas-Ramos
Anthony M. Stevens-Arroyo
Editors

PRAEGER

AN IMPRINT OF ABC-CLIO, LLC

Santa Barbara, California • Denver, Colorado • Oxford, England

Copyright 2012 by ABC-CLIO, LLC

All rights reserved. No part of this publication may be reproduced, stored in a retrieval system, or transmitted, in any form or by any means, electronic, mechanical, photocopying, recording, or otherwise, except for the inclusion of brief quotations in a review, without prior permission in writing from the publisher.

Library of Congress Cataloging-in-Publication Data

Blessing la política : the Latino religious experience and political engagement in the United States / Carlos Vargas-Ramos and Anthony M. Stevens-Arroyo, editors.

    p. cm.

Includes bibliographical references (p.   ) and index.

ISBN 978–0–313–39389–1 (hard copy : alk. paper) — ISBN 978–0–313–39390–7 (ebook) 1. Hispanic American Catholics—Religious life—Congresses. 2. Hispanic American Catholics—Political activity—Congresses. 3. Voting—United States—Congresses. 4. Catholic Church—Political activity—United States—Congresses. 5. Christianity and politics—United States—Congresses. I. Vargas-Ramos, Carlos. II. Stevens Arroyo, Antonio M.

BX1407.H55B54   2012

261.7089'68073—dc23   2012004646

ISBN: 978–0–313–39389–1
EISBN: 978–0–313–39390–7

16 15 14 13 12   1 2 3 4 5

This book is also available on the World Wide Web as an eBook.
Visit www.abc-clio.com for details.

Praeger
An Imprint of ABC-CLIO, LLC

ABC-CLIO, LLC
130 Cremona Drive, P.O. Box 1911
Santa Barbara, California 93116-1911

This book is printed on acid-free paper ∞

Manufactured in the United States of America

Portions of Chapter 3 are reused from Carlos Vargas-Ramos, 2003, "The Political Participation of Puerto Ricans in New York City." *CENTRO Journal*, 15(1): 41–71.

Contents

PART III: 2004 ELECTIONS

Preface

The annual meeting of the Society for the Scientific Study of Religion/ Religious Research Association held in Kansas City, Missouri, in 2004 was the spark that ignited the long process that has produced this volume. Dr. Anneris Goris of Brooklyn College had convened a panel in which to engage, with empirical evidence, Sidney Verba, Kay Lehman Scholzman, and Henry E. Brady's influential work *Voice and Equality: Civic Voluntarism in American Politics*. The panel's members were Latino and Latina scholars whose purpose was underscored in the panel's title: "Latino/a Catholic Political Involvement: *Voice and Equality* Revisited." From different perspectives, the panelists challenged some assumptions and conclusions made by the Ivy League research team led by Dr. Verba.

Although the panel took a critical view of the previous study, there was general recognition of the importance of *Voice and Equality* for those studying political participation in the United States. Verba and his colleagues proposed the *civic voluntarism* model to move beyond what had been the standard socioeconomic status model of political participation. While never denying the role of greater income and more education as major factors promoting political awareness and voting patterns, Verba et al. had focused upon how contact with and participation in various organizations can elevate political participation.

Their model proposes that voluntary associations such as communities of faith help members acquire civic skills and the motivation to engage in political activity. In a short, one of Verba and colleagues' contributions to political science was to outline how communities of faith might level the political playing field, even when the membership may reflect socioeconomic disparities that contribute to the stratification of society. Faith communities provide an advance of political action because they often nurture leadership and civic skills to which the less educated or those involved in less prestigious or complex occupations might otherwise not have access. Communities of faith, as a type of nonpolitical voluntary association, expose congregants to political stimuli. Sermons that explain how the faith should be applied to actual circumstances often foster informal political discussion or extend a network of friends and acquaintances for organized action in groups with solid norms of trust and reciprocity. Sometimes churches contribute to political involvement merely by providing a space where congregants may be recruited for political activity.

The panel members, most of whom eventually contributed their insights to this book, did not dispute the key points of the civic voluntarism model. Their critique was delivered upon Verba et al.'s findings about Latinos and especially about Latino Catholics. Verba et al. reported that while Latinos showed high levels of attendance to church, their involvement in ancillary church activities was low. In contrast, wrote Verba and his colleagues, African Americans were more likely to develop and practice civic skills acquired in these communities of faith to a greater degree than non-Hispanic whites and Latinos, reducing their disparity in the total number of skills they possessed relative to non-Hispanic whites. In searching for an explanation of this difference between Latinos and African Americans, who usually occupied the same social space, Verba and his colleagues concluded that "[p]art of the explanation for this pattern seems to lie in the fact that Latinos are much more likely than African-Americans or Anglo-Whites to be Catholic rather than Protestant" (1995: 245).

The panelists at the 2004 academic conference dissected this conclusion. As noted by David Leal, who participated that day, and by Carlos Vargas-Ramos, who is coeditor of this volume, the explanation about Catholicism's lowering effect on Latino political participation proposed by Verba et al. was not supported by findings in other important surveys of Latinos and Latinas on political participation. Anthony M. Stevens-Arroyo explained that the PARAL Study had intentionally posed to the heads of faith communities the same questions used by Verba's team; yet, it had not been able to corroborate the supposed Catholic disadvantage. Moreover, onsite participant observer studies of Latino faith communities were equally challenging to Verba et al.'s characterization of Latino Catholicism. From her observations of the mobilization of Mexican Catholics in Los Angeles, Cristina Mora offered a very different description of the political vibrancy within the church; they organized to protest unjust immigration laws. On the East Coast, Samiri Hernández reported that Caribbean believers in Connecticut suffered from few of the drawbacks that had figured in Verba and colleagues' study of Catholic participation.

The purpose of this book is then to continue the scholarly discussion that began with that 2004 panel, now sharpened by additional research and mutual insights and offered for examination in written form. Enriched by a contribution from Frank Ridzi and Matthew Loveland's study of data on Hispanic Catholic voting in the 2004 presidential election, this book constitutes a multi-disciplinary examination of the political mobilization of Latinos and Latinas. Furthermore, by examining patterns among Mexicans and Chicanos in California and linking these to studies of Puerto Ricans and Dominicans on the East Coast, this volume gives greater attention to intra-Latino issues than was possible for Verba et al.'s initial study.

This book goes beyond a monodimensional reporting of voting statistics to enter into the cultural and structural factors of political mobilization. There is also an extensive treatment of the premise that underlies much comparative research on Catholics and Protestants, namely that Catholicism is less "modern" than Protestantism. This premise, along with its origins and its fallacies, is examined in detail in the introduction to this volume, which was written by Anthony M. Stevens-Arroyo, a coeditor of this book and distinguished pioneer in the field of Latino religion.

To some, this volume may appear audacious: Latino and Latina scholars challenge the findings of an eminent professor from a leading U.S. research university. However, there is no claim here that Latinos and Latinas are more trustworthy when studying Latinos and Latinas just on account of a shared ethnicity. In fact, the panelists confessed to an initial intention to support rather than challenge the civic voluntarism model. Notable in this attempt to validate Verba et al.'s findings is a seminal article by Michael Jones-Correa and David Leal that figured largely in the panel, but for technical reasons was not included in this volume.

Jones-Correa and Leal set out to specifically test the hypotheses regarding religious affiliation, attendance to religious services, and political activity outlined by Verba and his colleagues using two distinct data sets: the Latino National Political Survey and the American National Election Studies (Jones-Correa and Leal 2000). These data sets were national in scope, as was Verba et al.'s Citizen Participation Study. Moreover, the Latino National Political Survey is a large probability sample of the Latino population in the United States, which captured more than 90 percent of the country's Latino population. With these datasets, these scholars were able to test the proposition about Catholicism and political participation not only among Latinos but also among non-Hispanic whites. Jones-Correa and Leal found that denominational difference did have some explanatory power for Hispanic political participation, but not in the manner anticipated by Verba and colleagues.

Specifically, Jones-Correa and Leal found that being Catholic did not have a statistically significant impact on overall political participation, voting for president, or being registered to vote. However, when being Catholic did have a statistically significant impact (as in voting for candidates for Congress or school boards), the effect was positive rather than negative. Among non-Hispanic whites, denominational affiliation did not have any significant impact, either. On the other hand, Jones-Correa and Leal found that the role of churches as civic associations explained political participation to a greater extent than denominational affiliation. Greater attendance to religious services had a positive effect on several measures of political participation for Latinos and non-Hispanic whites, even while holding denominational affiliation constant. This effect was more pronounced among Latinos than among non-Hispanic whites. This effect of attendance on Latino participation is derived, Jones-Correa and Leal hypothesize, from the centrality of communities of faith as voluntary associations. That is, as non-Hispanic whites have a more extensive membership in a variety of civic association than do Latinos, churches tend to serve a disproportionate associational role for Latinos.

Vargas-Ramos provides an even more direct challenge to the findings of Verba and his colleagues. Using a probability sample of New York City residents, he finds that being Catholic does not have a negative impact on several measures of political participation. In fact, being Catholic has no impact on participation among New York City residents and Latinos specifically. When this religious affiliation does have an effect, it is one that promotes rather than impedes Latino involvement in political activity. Thus, Verba's results are not supported even when controlling for the effect of attending religious services. In fact, frequency of attending religious services has no statistically significant effect on any measure of political participation among all New Yorkers, including Latinos.

Ridzi, Loveland, and Ruhland enter this debate by tracing—through quantitative analysis—the bases for policy positions of U.S. Catholics and establishing how Latino Catholics are a distinct group insofar as policy preferences are concerned. They analyze in chapter six data collected by Zogby in political polling, and show how Catholic and Protestant differences are represented in choices about government-based policies of social insurance in contrast to a neoliberal-inspired individual-based capital investment preference state. Ridzi et al. found a consonance between the material conditions of Latinos and Latinas and Catholic Church teachings on social justice. Among Latino Protestants and Evangelicals, the social justice concerns were generally overshadowed by political choices made by priority given to family values. Latino Catholics' stronger support for social justice issues, manifested through support of social safety net programs, distinguishes them not only from non-Latino Catholics, but also from Latino Protestants. Such distinctions make Latino Catholics (and Latino Protestants) distinct constituencies, which partisan organizations are likely explore and exploit.

For those interested in assessing the importance of sample size and methodology, this volume suggests that within Latino Studies, there are new studies and new scholars whose production needs to be included before making claims about political participation. Certainly, the scholars in this volume report findings that conflict with the interpretation initially offered by Verba and his colleagues, but the challenges to the earlier study ran within the parameters of academic exploration. It is our hope that the reader will apply the same scholarly acumen to our work as we did to that of Dr. Verba and his colleagues.

Finally, we hope that the reader will recognize the ground-up process that helped us assemble the chapters in this volume. Each chapter builds upon the others to provide statistical, historical, theoretic, and cultural evidence that Latinos and Latinas ought not be lumped together for political analysis. The religious factor is relevant; if it is not always shown in electoral results, it most certainly is in the way that Catholic and Protestant churches contact and mobilize their members. Just as travelers can choose different routes to arrive at the same destination, Latino Catholics and Protestants move through diverse paths on the way to political activism. This book has been written to give voice to those religious differences and invite readers to further explore this new perspective of an increasingly important set of political participants.

Carlos Vargas-Ramos
New York City

Anthony M. Stevens-Arroyo
East Stroudsburg, PA

Acknowledgments

Flowers come from seeds, and books like this come from collective expectation. We want to thank those without whose efforts this book would not be
a reality. First and foremost, we want to acknowledge our people of faith
who have committed themselves to combining their religion with politics in
the new and important ways outlined in this book. *Blessing* La Política is a cou-
rageous step, since the cliché holds that one should never discuss "religion and
politics." But tens of millions of Latinos and Latinas are mobilizing our rapidly
growing communities to put faith into action on the dangerous playing fields
of U.S. politics. Such is a worthy new development, especially when considering the many obstacles to full rights of our electoral participation, both in the
history of past injustices and in the present climate of anti-Hispanic legislation. Moreover, many of our newly arriving immigrants from Latin America
have had negative experiences with politics in their countries of origin. It
would demand remarkable fortitude for them even to think that politics—*la
política*—can be blessed. To each and all of these nameless heroes, we owe a
debt of gratitude and have tried our best to explain their cause.

In assembling this book, we want to thank the Program for the Analysis of
Religion Among Latinos and Latinas (PARAL) of the Center for Religion in
Society and Culture (RISC) at Brooklyn College. We came together when
PARAL sponsored a set of panel discussions at the annual meeting of the
Society for the Scientific Study of Religion (SSSR), which was scheduled to
take place the week before the 2004 presidential election. Specifically, we rec-
ognize Dr. Anneris Goris, associate director of research for RISC, who

moderated the panel that allowed us to begin engaging *Voice and Equality: Civic Voluntarism in American Politics*. One panel participant was Dr. David Leal of the University of Texas, who, with Michael Correa-Jones, had already published a seminal critique of the findings of Dr. Verba and his associates about the religious factor in Latino voter participation. That article initially served to define the parameters of our explorations. Dr. Leal's intellectual contribution set important parameters for the discussion that has resulted in this book, and for that we are thankful.

We want also to acknowledge Dr. Mark Gray of the Center for Applied Research in the Apostolate (CARA) at Georgetown University, who encouraged this project at a point when unfortunate timing in academics had dimmed the viability of publishing a book before the presidential election. We were reanimated by Mark's insistence that there was great value in publishing a distinct Latino and Catholic scholarly perspective about United States politics. In spite of his demanding workload, he found the time to accept our invitation and write the epilogue to this volume. It offers an updated 2011 commentary on the book's topic from his perspective as a political scientist and research specialist at a key Catholic institution.

Support also came from Dr. Edwin Meléndez, director of the Centro de Estudios Puertorriqueños at Hunter College in New York. He saw early on the value of this expansion for the research conducted at the Centro and allowed his associate, Dr. Vargas Ramos, to include within his workload much of the editorial preparation of this volume. Dr. Meléndez also opened the Centro to an important symposium on religion among Puerto Ricans held in May 2011 at which some of the findings in this book were discussed in a scholarly setting.

Our greatest thanks in this process go to Emily Birch, senior editor at Praeger Publishers. She favorably reviewed our manuscript, guided by her insightful understanding of the dynamics of political involvement and the role of religion among Latinos and Latinas in this process. She helped secure a contract with our publisher and was of great encouragement at every step of the way for a project that had been stalled by the vagaries typical of many collaborative academic projects. Emily moved on before this volume was published, but her key role will forever be appreciated. Marian Perales of ABC-CLIO and Beth Ptalis of Praeger assumed responsibilities for the editing and publishing of the final manuscript. It is always helpful at the end of the writing process to have competent and caring editors who know how to administer the final polish. To them and many others at Praeger whose names we do not know, *muchas gracias*. Nor can we fail to express our gratitude to PARAL and its chief foundation sponsor, the Lilly Endowment, for the financial support that allowed the contributors to meet for the first time at the SSSR meeting in Kansas City.

Carlos Vargas-Ramos and Anthony M. Stevens-Arroyo

Introduction

Anthony M. Stevens-Arroyo

The election of Barack Obama as the President in 2008 has proven to be a landmark moment in the history of the United States of America. Independently of any eventual policy achievements or failures during his term, the election alone proved historic. The significance of an African American as president reaped immediate and continuing attention from scholars of political science, newspapers and the media, talking heads on radio and television shows, and international heads of state. The pope compared the election to the fall of the Berlin Wall that symbolized the end of Communism. During the first months after the election, the recognition trickled down to common citizens everywhere, from barbershops and bodegas in city neighborhoods to country-club locker rooms and bridge parties in the fashionable suburbs.

The purpose of this book is modest by comparison. After embracing the symbolic value of electing as president a man of mixed race, this volume will examine the pattern of political participation of a very specific group of Americans—the 50 million people of Latin American origin or heritage. What engages Latinos and Latinas whose religious identification is Catholic to become involved with U.S. politics? The question merits attention because, as we hope to show, in addition to similarities, there are certain characteristics of political participation among Latinos and Latinas not reflected among other groups. The particulars shaping Latino Catholic political preferences have been developing unique contours over time and likely will continue in importance long after the 2008 election has been eclipsed by future developments.

As described in detail elsewhere in this volume, Latinos and Latinas voted decisively (67%) for Barack Obama, with Latino Catholics more pronounced in this tendency than Latinos of all other denominations. Moreover, the healthy margin of preference for the Democratic Party ticket among Latino Catholics was sufficient to move Catholics as a group from a majority of Euro-American Catholics (52%) for the Republican John McCain to an overall Catholic preference (54%) for Obama and the Democrats.

How Latinos and Latinas voted is of more than hothouse interest. With considerable justification, pundits point to the Latino vote in several key states that swung from the Republican column in 2004 to the Democratic column in 2008. The cases for Latino decisiveness are clearest in Colorado, Florida, Nevada and New Mexico, states that accounted for 46 total electoral votes. Those states had been in the GOP column in 2004 but switched to the Democrats in 2008. Their swing votes were a major part of Obama's impressive 365-to-173 vote edge over McCain in the Electoral College. Some might add Virginia (13 votes) and North Carolina (15 votes) to the list of Latino-influenced switches, which would add 28 more electoral votes to the Latino factor, but there is no need to include more than the first four obvious cases to make the point that the Latino vote had significant impact on the national scene.

The importance of the Latino vote in 2008 is augmented by the prospect of rapidly increasing numbers of Latinos and Latinas at the polls in coming years. Latinos and Latinas form the largest of U.S. minority groups, and alone among voting blocs of similar size, will grow significantly in each election cycle. This increasingly muscular political presence is the result of simple demographics: U.S.-born Latinos and Latinas represent an extremely young segment within the nation's population. Their impact will likely increase as large numbers of Latinos and Latinas come of voting age each year.

We will tiptoe around the temptation to overstate the importance of the Latino vote. Everyone agrees, for instance, that as the incumbent party at a time of great uncertainty, any Republican would have had an uphill battle to gain the presidency in 2008. Other specific issues, such as Obama's proficiency in identifying supporters, his ability to raise campaign funds, and the appeal of his speeches and relations with the media, were of undeniable relevance. But while each election has its own set of particularities, there are also gradually building and long-staying trends that survive a specific electoral cycle.

This volume proposes to make the case not only that the Latino Catholic vote was important nationally in 2008, but that it was the result of gradually emerging patterns of political participation. Even if Latinos and Latinas voters were not afforded major public attention until this last decade, the underpinning of today's relevance can be found in exploration of the past. Similarly, religious identity has always been a part of the electoral reality. The 2008 presidential election, however, occasioned a shift in how religious affiliation was viewed by each party. Obama and the Democratic Party engaged in a new kind of competition with McCain and the Republicans for voters motivated by religious concerns. Whereas religious issues had previously been centered on abortion and the use of embryonic stem cells—matters favorable to Republican candidates—religion in 2008 was presented as an interlocutor for environmental concern and basic issues of economic social justice, issues of wider electoral appeal.

Our concern here is the social dynamic among Latinos and Latinas that created an audience for this appeal. The area inhabited by religion is deep in the hearts of individuals and nourishes the sinew and muscle of grassroot social interaction for both private and public institutions. Among Latinos and Latinas, Catholic heritage is the lifeblood of many cultural traditions. In contrast to the United States, where Protestantism has shaped cultural presumptions, Latino social celebrations like *fiestas patronales*, family institutions like godparent responsibilities (*compadrazgo*), and individual rites of passage like the *quinceañera*, spring from a Catholic past. Thus, even for voters whose religion is mostly cultural, Catholic symbols and Catholic moral premises exercise a huge role. Moreover, Catholic parishes provide focal points for community organization and services, often paired with specifically religious agencies. Precisely because Latinos and Latinas lack many of the overtly political and secular organizations enjoyed by more economically privileged groups, both Catholic and Protestant churches figure hugely as players in forming Latino political attitudes.

The emergence of a "Latino Catholic vote" in the first three elections of the twenty-first century was not an *ex nihilo* event. The current Latino experience of politics and religion has some parallels with the past history of other groups, even if there are also salient differences. Within recent memory, general political opinion has gone from a premise in the 1950s that religious identification was losing its relevance to a consideration in the 1980s that Evangelicals would provide reliable winning margins to the Republican Party in most elections. In a similar way, beginning in about 1972, the first national polls to include voting Hispanics—they were called that—usually depicted an underperforming electoral force mostly limited to local politics in a few states such as Texas or New Mexico. But this neglect changed significantly in this century, in a new role for (now renamed) Latinos and Latinas as officially more numerous than African Americans in the United States.

This essay suggests that the best path to understand both the present and the past is derived from considering the complex history of religion, ethnicity, and race in politics during the twentieth century for all groups before arriving at the present historical moment in the first decade of the twenty-first century. An outline is offered here: first, of religious worldview and politics; next, of some American perspectives on religious factors in elections; and then, of an examination of the political role of ethnicity, which is linked to racial identity as well. Finally, the reader will be introduced to the most recently opened avenues in social science that have afforded a new set of tools to examine the Latino Catholic vote.

Religious Worldview and Politics

Even if attention to a distinction between Latino Catholics and Protestants is new, the relationship of religious worldview and political power is part of the birthright of modern social science. Max Weber (1864–1920) explored the contrast between Protestants and Catholics and established a premise that can still be found in many studies of political participation.[1] This Weberian premise holds that attitudes toward individuals and authority within organized religion carry over into civic behavior. Although politics is about human power over individuals and society, the theory states that religious conceptions of divine power shape human understanding of power in the public arena. The sociologist pointed out, for instance, that belief in God as king-over-all inclines support for an absolute monarch's power in actual social conditions. With considerable insight, Weber traced the essential theology of established faiths, looking for clues of how its adherents were inclined to certain perceptions about social power. He predicted that the political behavior of believers would vary in ways correlated to their doctrinal differences. At the distance of at least a century, even those who disagree with conclusions drawn by Weber recognize that he established for social science a linkage between religious conceptions and political presumption that always merits examination.

Relevant to the current topic of the Latino Catholic vote is how Weber assumed Protestantism to better fit modernity than Catholicism or Judaism. According to Weber, within democratic societies, Protestantism has significant civic advantages because it gives religious sanction to the exercise of individual freedom and rational thought for Protestant believers. He viewed other, more traditional religions like Catholicism as propagators of concepts that did not easily accommodate modernity. For instance, Weber contrasted Protestantism's doctrine of freedom of conscience with Catholicism's conception of a church hierarchy mediating individual contact with God. The former was open to the values of the modern world, while the latter was not. Control of belief by church authority, he suggested, was paralleled by control of political freedom in society. The Catholic attitude derived from a faded feudal system, Weber asserted. Reformation values, on the other hand, were more in consonance with modern freedoms.

Along with this premise favoring Protestantism over Catholicism was Weber's more subtle supposition that rationalism and scientific thinking were replacing faith and religious belief. Weber may have viewed Protestantism to have been more modern than Catholicism because it relied less on symbols, sacraments, and religious authority; however, he thought even Protestantism would eventually give way to secularism. The human freedom of the individual was for him the basic unit in defining social power. This aspect of Weber's thought would eventually evolve into a theory of secularization. In such thinking, organized religion continually retreats from social engagement in civic and public issues until faith is reduced to little more than personal and private conviction.[2] Doubtlessly, Weber's anticipation of an inevitable secularization was fed in the first decades of the twentieth century by Freudian psychology that in parallel with political secularization likewise substituted reason for faith in understanding human behavior.

In the United States, sociology in the 1920s was born with the birthright of Weber's premise about Protestantism and Catholicism. Weber's theories about religion did not receive a *carte blanche*, however. The inevitability he assigned to secularization met resistance in the early sociology of the United States. Unlike many European experiences wherein Protestant denominations fought among themselves, in the United States, it was said, the denominations had found an exceptional formula of coexistence. Denominational tolerance had separated church and state, allowing both to prosper in the United States. On this account, many considered that the United States had achieved social tolerance for religious differences in ways that were superior to those of Europe. The boast was that the U.S. religious experience had achieved a modern separation of church and state, without the need of eliminating one or the other as in Europe.

From this mind-set sprang the concept of American Exceptionalism, fully mature and as the defining trait of the American Protestant experience. Europe's history of sharp and historical conflict among religious denominations had been avoided in the United States, it was thought, thus proving that the exceptional case of religious tolerance in the United States had reduced the need for antireligious secularization in the body politic. Congregationalists and Episcopalians, Methodists and Baptists were united by a common *Protestant* bible and a reliance on individual freedom of interpretation of Scripture in ways unmatched in Europe.

Despite this praise of its exceptional case of tolerance in academia and *belles lettres*, every day events painted a different picture. America had entered the century with the historical burden of significant prejudice against non-Protestant groups. The nineteenth century had exhibited scant remorse for ugly discrimination and sporadic violence against Catholics and Jews. This anti-Catholic prejudice proved stubborn and was undeniably influential in the 1928 defeat of Catholic Al Smith, a candidate for the presidency. For those embarrassed by such prejudice, the Weberian principle with its attendant presumption of gradual secularization provided a way to relativize these ugly chapters. If Catholics and Jews belonged to religions with antimodern and anti-American traits, the thinking ran, then one might say that discrimination against Catholics and Jews had been provoked *by the victims*. Since the U.S. society was modern in ways that these other faiths were not, there was no reason for Protestant Americans to retreat from their views of religion's proper role. It was the task of the non-Protestant believers to adjust to the national norms, not vice versa.

Even without succumbing to Weber's anticipation of religion's marginalization in a modern secular state, there was support for the notion that the minority should modify its behavior. Since the majority in the country professed Protestantism, political thinkers in the first third of the twentieth century generally argued that Catholic and Jewish immigrants would have to water down some distinctive religious practices in order to adjust to the established values and institutions of the Protestant majority. Walking in the footsteps of Protestantism was the only path toward becoming truly American.

Gauzy clichés were spun out of the premise of social assimilation. Terms such as "melting pot," "nation of immigrants," and "Americanization" were used to describe how Jews and Catholics were to adjust to life in the United States. They were to follow the path to social homogeneity taken by Protestant denominations toward an amalgamated generic "-ism." This premise induced social science to measure the behavior of immigrant groups against a composite White, Anglo-Saxon, Protestant core. The closer any immigrant group came to WASP behavior, it was reasoned, the more it could be said to have been assimilated into United States society. It was "for their own good," one might say, that they would lose their religious distinctiveness. The hard edges of this assimilationist view were somewhat cushioned by a distinction between conforming behavior in the public square, on the one hand, and the private right to religious freedom, on the other. In other words, Catholics and Jews could celebrate their differences once behind the closed doors of church or synagogue. But when exercising public duties, they were supposed to be indistinguishable from their Protestant neighbors.

By *Protestant*, most commentators clearly meant the historical denominations (mainline Protestantism) that conformed to the definition of *modern* Weber had suggested. The brand of Protestant Christianity that had achieved this intra-religious equilibrium conformed to the paradigm of an increasingly rationalistic modernism, à la Weber. These mental gymnastics preserved the conceit that the religious and cultural matrix of the country was irrevocably identified with liberal Protestant Christianity, and therefore the standard to be used in measuring the American experience.

Sociology and Protestantism

The content of this favored version of Protestantism was to undergo modification as all of America trudged through the Great Depression, experienced a restructuring of the political establishment by the New Deal, and fought a World War on two fronts. These earthshaking events were concentrated into the decade and a half from 1930 until 1945. Whether jostled in the same breadlines, joined by union pickets, or shivering in the same foxhole during the war, men and women from diverse religious and ethnic groups had been pressed together by a common history. Their forced interaction as social actors compressed the process of assimilation, significantly reducing the social distance in religion and ethnicity for white Americans. The gaps that had separated denominations and nationalities in earlier periods had now been reduced. In a sense, the result for Jews and Catholics was not assimilation into Protestant mold, but a more flexible "accommodation" that left diversity in place—but without rough edges. While the impact was less telling on groups defined racially such as African and Asian Americans, as well as Latinos, there was no denying the leveling of the social terrain that had long separated Protestants—predominantly of Northern European stock—from Catholics and Jews of more recent Mediterranean and Eastern European immigration.

Sociology in the United States rose to the challenge of changing times. From his perch in the Ivy League halls of Harvard, Talcott Parsons (1902–1979) developed an approach focused by social functions. His 1937 book, *The Structure of Social Action*, laid out key social science categories that proved useful in analysis of the changes of those times. Over the next two decades, Parson's influence over American sociology grew mightily. Many scholars adopted Parson's slant on the principle that human beings had multiple reasons for behaving as they might, each at a different level of relevance.

Added to the techniques for observation of social process, Parsonian sociology included a judgmental element. Societies would function most smoothly when group behavior was definable by rational premises for social action, it was suggested. Groups with the most clarity about means and ends were those best able to function in society. Parsons imagined that this trend defined Western Civilization and he considered it the standard with which to measure all societies everywhere.

While religion was one of the entries on the list to measure social behavior, it was neither the only, nor even the decisive one. When it came to examining political behavior, other characteristics were more useful than classification based exclusively on membership in a religious denomination. Income, education, and the like were added as factors that shaped social interactions under the religious umbrella. It became important to look at whether a Baptist was a city dweller in a Northern city or a rural sharecropper in Mississippi. Neither the generic label of Protestant nor a denominational commitment was to be considered in isolation from other social factors.

Although these insightful measures enhanced an emerging Sociology of Religion, Parsons's admiration for Euro-American society privileged liberal Protestants, thus implicitly creating hegemony among religious groups. Liberal Protestant socioeconomic and educational achievements generally coincided with the highest ranks in the Parsonian scheme. In a sense, Parsons had refined but not eliminated the existing predilection for approximation to a WASP core as a measure of modernity.

To the Weberian premise, Parsons had added large dollops of concepts taken from Émile Durkheim (1858–1917), one of Weber's European contemporaries. Citing Durkheim, Parsons painted religion as a stabilizing force that allowed individual actions to benefit the equilibrium of the larger society. The Durkheimian notion that religion helped harmonize social forces replaced the prominence Weber had given to secularization. Because liberal Protestantism in the United States was considered to be the functional equivalent of European secularization, liberal Protestants were considered to be both modern and religious. Their faith functioned to unite believers and secularists in maintaining social harmony. Whereas European politics were measured by degrees of secularization (e.g., the most secular being considered the most progressive), in the United States it was liberalism, both in an out of the churches, that gauged social progress.

This intellectual nimbleness blurred the boundary lines separating secularism and religion. By emphasizing function and observable consequences, Parsons had measured Protestantism as much for its works as for its dogma. In other words, religion was judged by its empirical acts toward improving society. In this perspective, social activism was the principal function of religion, while belief was a private matter not terribly important to social science. In the post–World War II *Pax Americana* and the attendant prosperity after 1945, Parsons's view of progressive society enjoyed considerable popularity in scholarly circles and trickled down into the popular mind-set that saw the United States as the heir to Northern Europe's world hegemony.

Liberal Protestant hegemony, however, was not welcomed by Evangelical Protestants. Evangelical Christianity opposed secularization and interfaith cooperation. For Evangelicals, such modern trends constituted a surrender of vital religious principles. These Evangelicals had been forced into retreat from politics by the symbolism of the Scopes Trial (1926) that amounted to public rejection of Bible truth as a substitute for science. Prohibition, which began in 1920, was also identified with this brand of Protestantism, so that repeal by the New Deal in 1933 further eroded Evangelical political influence. Likewise marginalized in national politics for the first half of the twentieth century were denominations like the Church of Latter-Day Saints and Pentecostals. The Protestant establishment had long believed these groups to profess a lesser form of religion, at times questioning the authenticity of their Christianity. Religious fervor for all these groups generally required a sharpening rather than a blurring of religious differences. In some instances, they viewed themselves as the truest of Protestants, precisely because they held to the traditional norms of hegemonic Protestantism rather than seek accommodation with the post–World War II changes. The generation-long isolation of Evangelicals from national politics may have sheltered them from continued ridicule from secular forces but it had also left the role of religious hegemony to liberal Protestantism. Thus, it should be stressed, the hegemony of liberal Protestantism as the essence of U.S. Christianity did not apply to all Protestants.

Liberal Protestantism's standing as the measure for U.S. religion was not without its internal critics, however. White Protestant scholars like the theologian Reinhold Niebuhr and the sociologist Robert Bellah challenged the notion that Christianity could *ever* become identified with U.S. culture. Economic and social inequalities received new attention from these critics, invading the feel-good zone for Protestant hegemony. Religious belief and political interests, it was said, had become conflictive forces; they could never be totally reconciled in the United States. Protestant individualism of conscience had to be matched with generalized altruism. Thus, a more just public society became a principle goal for religious activity. This trend became inescapable with the rise of the civil rights movement in the 1950s (and would intensify in the anti–Vietnam War efforts leading into the 1970s). Religious crusade for change was necessary, it was argued, precisely because the United States was not heeding religion's message for social transformation. Thus, hegemony had brought Protestantism a burden. Religion ought not seek to be rewarded with privilege in the politics of the republic, but understand its obligation to stand outside the halls of power and pester like a gadfly.

Most pretensions for Protestant hegemony within U.S. politics came unhinged in 1960, when the United States elected John F. Kennedy as the first Catholic president. True, there were dissenting voices during the campaign that attempted unsuccessfully to revive the prejudice leveled in 1928 against the Catholic, Al Smith. For some liberal Protestants and secularists, Catholicism still remained too traditional and authoritarian to represent the nation. Evangelicals also joined this sentiment, often with stronger condemnations that insisted that Catholicism was the "whore of Babylon" of the Bible.[3] However, with an eerie anticipation of 2008's welcome of Barack Obama as the first African American president, Catholic John F. Kennedy's election was viewed by most Americans as a triumph for the U.S. political system, rather than as its undoing. Kennedy obliged this fame. Far from causing general unease, his popularity made the administration into a political version of the legendary Camelot.

If Catholicism were no longer characterized as an antimodern faith in U.S. politics, the change was matched in theological circles soon after the 1960 election. In 1962, Pope John XIII opened an ecumenical council that would recast Catholic institutions. Catholicism's goals were redefined in more modern terminology, with clearer accommodation to science, technology, and global communications. The Second Vatican Council stressed the need for Catholics to be more engaged with the modern world and with politics. In effect, the official church had turned the page on outspoken Catholic conservatives like Father Charles Coughlin (1891–1979), whose radio messages had railed against the New Deal policies of Franklin Roosevelt. Papal encyclicals like *Mater et Magistra* of Blessed Pope John XXIII endorsed many of the social justice principles of the Council's documents. The new vision for Catholicism undermined the claims to represent church teaching by intellectual conservatives like William F. Buckley, Jr., whose influential *National Review* famously challenged Pope John XXIII with the quip, "Mater, sí; Magistra, no," as well as defending the anti-Communism of Senator Joseph McCarthy and segregation as a legal necessity to preserve social order.

By 1970, the changes in Catholicism and U.S. Judaism had undercut the bias that these faiths could not be "modern." In fact, in rising to the moral challenges of the civil rights movement and opposition to the Vietnam War, progressive Catholics and Jews had proven to be solid allies with progressive Protestants. Bellah's *The Broken Covenant: American Civil Religion in Time of Trial* was published in 1975 and helped define for social science the end of pretensions about Protestant political hegemony. Using the expression of Princeton University's Robert Wuthnow,[4] who is a master of the sociological *bon mot*, American religion had undergone a "restructuring." *Civil religion* now included more than just Protestantism, and the progressive role of the churches was to critique U.S. policies whenever they failed.

Within a decade, however, Bellah's view that progressive religion would lead the way met an irresistible force. During the 1980s, Evangelical organizations like the Moral Majority were victorious in the combat with liberalism in politics and religion. Entering the electoral arena during the Reagan years, these conservative expressions of Christianity bestowed religious legitimization on right-wing politics. Remembering the Parsonian emphasis upon progressive social action, Bellah lamented the lack of political muscle among religious progressives in his 1985 book, *Habits of the Heart: Individualism and Commitment in American Life*. The exit of liberal Protestant hegemony and engagement with Catholics, Jews, and unbelievers, he noted, had opened the door to less progressive religious groups to replace them as principal actors on the political stage.

Ironically, the 2008 election is now being seen as a tipping point for hegemonic religious ranking in the United States, reversing the enthronement of the conservatives in 1980. It is noteworthy that from retirement after the November 4, 2009, election of Obama, Bellah provided a commentary on the significance of the election, vindicating his earlier perspectives. The cycle in which individualism replaced social commitment for religious people in the United States has come full circle, suggests Bellah, and the election of Obama has once again given religious social solidarity a more prominent role than individualism. Relevant to our subject of Latino Catholic political behavior, Bellah (2009) credited Catholicism with having spearheaded the social justice foundation of modern European society and believed Obama's campaign voiced the principles of Catholic social justice rather than the themes of Protestant individualism. The two trends—Protestant individualism and Catholic social commitment—are now restored to progressive balance within U.S. civil religion, he said. However, before addressing how the 2008 election reintroduced topics first limned by Bellah, this essay will outline social science consideration of ethnicity's role in past politics.

Religion and Ethnicity

Ethnicity had been generally absent from pre-1960s discussions about Protestant America. Episcopalians, Presbyterians, Methodists, Congregationalists and other charter members of establishment Protestantism were seldom seen as anything but "American." While most Lutherans in the United States may have been German or Scandinavian in heritage, any unique beliefs or practices were more likely to be classified as "Lutheran" than as "ethnic." Similarly, Baptists were divided into American, Southern, and Black denominations, and their differences in political outlook or racial membership formed part of the list of attributes to be analyzed with Parsonian tools. Judaism and Catholicism, on the other hand, were often considered religions of non-American immigrants well into the 1940s.

For sociologists who utilized Parson's set of categories, ethnicity was often reduced to a set of functions, much as with religious identification. This approach of the 1950s, however, did not always escape the ethnocentric bias of Parsonian categories. Rather frequently, ethnicity was measured as the stubborn persistence of cultural traits that differed from the WASP core. *Ethnic* and *American* were mutually exclusive terms: one could not be both at the same time.

Defense of a flexible accommodation in America's religions, rather than total assimilation, fell to scholars of non-Protestant groups. The dilemma they faced was difficult: If approximation to the WASP core was left as the unchallenged measure for Americanization, then could Catholics and Jews ever be completely "American"? Unless Americanization could be redefined *without including Protestantism as an essential requirement*, fidelity to the traditional religion would forever impede Catholic or Jewish absorption into the fabric of United States society.

Until Kennedy's 1960 election, this question about the character of Catholicism in the United States was particularly vexing. Long before it became a matter of sociology, it had been a contentious matter of Catholic pastoral vision. The nineteenth century had been dominated by two major but contradictory attitudes toward Americanization within the United States Catholic Church. One wing had tried to approximate Protestantism in style if not in substance, while an opposing wing had adopted a triumphalistic and polemic defensiveness about Catholic differences from Protestantism. The debate had orbited around a necessary judgment as to whether accommodation to Protestant social conventions in the United States—which seemed inescapable—also constituted a weakening of the Catholic faith.[5] (The very similar debates within U.S. Judaism were no less important, but fall outside the focus on Latinos and Latinas that belongs to this essay.)

In order to focus upon the political science impact of such research on Catholicism, it may be useful to examine the work of William Halsey in his award-winning evaluation of Catholic identity in the United States from

1920 until 1940.[6] He focuses upon Catholic intellectual thought in the same decades in which sociology emerged as an accepted discipline within academia. His book suggests the Catholic solution: separate ethnicity from religious belief. Catholic sociologists preferred to study Irish, Italian, Polish, and German immigrants who were Catholics confronting assimilation. This emphasis on ethnicity and its cultural diversity, sidestepped the Weberian premise about Protestantism's better fit for modernity. Instead of agreeing that Protestant civic prominence was due to doctrinal differences with Catholicism, these scholars of the Catholic experience went in another direction. They argued that American Protestant aptitude for modernity came from social conditions, rather than from religious beliefs. The demographic concentration of Catholics in urban areas, the variations in social preparedness before emigration, the evolution of political traditions in the homeland, and the like, were the factors that determined political behavior—not Catholic dogma. The lack of modernity among American Catholics, it was said, lay not with the faith, but rather with ethnic Catholics not yet being American enough.

Halsey's book ends without putting intellectual cudgels to the 1950s. However, he lays the foundations for understanding why the mid-century Protestant doubts about civil religion like those of Niebhur and Bellah induced some Catholics eventually to conceive of themselves as more American than the American liberal Protestants. Popularized by such public figures as Monsignor Fulton Sheen, whose weekly television lectures would rival the comedy hour of Milton Berle, the theology of Thomas Aquinas was presented as the source of just social and economic policies that sailed the middle passage between Communism and laissez-faire Capitalism. Rather than be threatened by Catholic tradition, it was suggested, American virtue was saved by it.

Thus, by the 1950s, Catholic intellectuals had reconciled the two sides of the nineteenth-century dilemma about whether to imitate Protestants or instead to preen superiority for Catholic traditions. Catholics had no need to imitate Protestants in order to be Americanized, it was reasoned, because Catholicism was itself a more sure guarantor of American values than an uncertain Protestantism. Between a too secular liberal Protestantism and a too narrow Evangelicalism, Catholicism traveled the centrist golden mean.

Ethnicity and Race

The racist theories of 1920s had invoked science to argue for racial superiority. While Hitler's Aryan preachments are the most familiar of this unfortunate trend, there were other effects. Despite the ways in which Irish and Italian Catholics had been considered "nonwhite" in the nineteenth century, sociology was pushed toward creating clearer distinctions between race and ethnicity. Once this became the trend, Protestantism chose to focus more on race than on ethnicity. Protestantism was, in fact, segregated at least in part by churches that had been organized in ways that segregated black and white believers. Understandably, race along a black-and-white divide was a more important concern for Protestantism than ethnicity.

Racism was considered permanent because racial differences were also permanent. Ethnicity, on the other hand, was generally left out in the cold in this Protestant self-examination. Being an ethnic American was considered a temporary condition because time might lift the differences that caused discrimination, especially if the ethnics cooperated by trying to become *more American*. Discrimination against Italians or Slovaks could be remedied by educating those persons in how they could best assimilate by modifying their cultural behavior and by persuading the majority to afford time for the assimilation. The idea was to lose the hyphen in *Irish-/Italian-/Slovak- American* and become just plain *American*. No such easy option was open to people of color.

Exchanging Ethnicity for Civil Religion

U.S. politics has always been pragmatic. As such, elections in the United States embraced ethnic voters. Concerned with results rather than theories, many politicians cultivated ethnicity and its symbols, rather than avoid them. As far back as the end of the nineteenth century, America's politicians had been engaged by the impact of ethnic identity in the voting booth. Newspapers showed candidates wearing outlandish hats, munching on ethnic culinary delights, and marching in ethnic parades. By showing themselves to accept and enjoy ethnic contributions, members of the political establishment confirmed the practical truth that intellectuals ignored into the 1950s: ethnic differences were *already* assimilated into U.S. society. Thus, for instance, the St. Patrick's Day parade became a symbol of sanitized Irish ethnicity. Politicians marched in the parade, not to endorse Irish Catholicism but to reach out to voters of second and third U.S.-born generations. Since it was but one day in the year, the saint's parade did not so much symbolize separation from the American society, but rather inclusion within it.

In the postwar optimism of the 1950s, Will Herberg published *Protestant, Catholic, Jew*, a book that popularized an upbeat version of assimilation in terms of *both* ethnicity and religion.[7] Raised within conservative Judaism, Herberg had a personalized perspective on the interplay of ethnicity and religion. His book advanced the idea that in the aftermath of World War II, ethnicity had lost much of its earlier influence on social behavior. What was left, he stated, were versions of Judaism and Catholicism that had homogenized the original ethnic differences into a set of religious practices accommodated to United States's society.

The second and third generations born in this country had ceded to religion the preservation of ethnic traditions, said Herberg. Italian and Irish Catholics (like Russian and Polish Jews), had become less Italian or Irish (less Russian or Polish) because of their birth into the American nation. Often enough, these U.S.-born generations married across ethnic boundaries with combinations like Irish Italian, or Russian Polish. However, they also married within their religious faiths. The common denominator in such intra-denominational marriage was the faith, and religion preserved only those ethnic traditions that were found in both nationalities. An Italian Irish Catholic in a second or third generation would identify with the Catholic religion more than with the ethnic heritage. After all, the first was clearly defined, which ethnicity was muddled because it was shared.

Religion had become the container into which ethnicity had been poured, filtering out the most alien elements, but distilling essential differences. The Protestant majority should tolerate these brands of Catholicism and Judaism, it was proposed. After all, the process underway among Jews and Catholics reflected the earlier process within Protestantization that had homogenized previously well-marked ethnicities like Welsh Methodists, Scottish Presbyterians, Dutch Calvinists and the like. Just as Protestantism had softened earlier ethnic boundaries into a generalized American identity, now Catholicism and Judaism were doing the same for their ethnicities.

Herberg promoted the sociological concept of an *American civil religion* but instead of placing only Protestantism at the core, he defined it as a blend of Americanized versions of Catholicism, Protestantism, and Judaism. No single religion need be hegemonic, since all these denominations shared a common function within American society. The accommodation of distinctive ethnic identities became acceptable under the umbrella of religious tolerance. In fact, the mutual tolerance had created a three-headed civil religion to dethrone the earlier exclusivity of Protestantism alone. This religious diversity was more manageable than ethnic conflicts. It was also an alternative to the stifling forms of assimilation. Ethnic awareness might endure, but it would do so in watered-down versions acceptable to all.

While more popular than sociological, Herberg's work nonetheless led political science into temptation. There was now a *Catholic* vote and a *Jewish* vote to be measured against Protestants who were represented, if unevenly, in both the Democratic and Republican Parties. Political science was directed by a presumption that a second generation of Catholic and Jewish immigrants could best be identified by religious affiliation rather than by ethnic roots. The immigrants had approximated the Protestant majority by finally having subsumed ethnicity into homogenizing religions that made them American enough to fit into Herberg's comfortable triad.

Social science tested Herberg's insights by asking if ethnicity was losing importance among generations born to immigrants in the United States. The efforts of Milton Gordon addressed this issue,[8] as did the popularized version of Gordon's approach in *Beyond the Melting Pot* by Nathan Glazer and Patrick Moynihan about ethnicity and religion in New York City. The suddenly popular view of ethnicity-becoming-civil religion was reflected in books about ethnic groups on the road to Americanization. Writ large in books like *Beyond the Melting Pot* is the issue of political participation among the various religious groups, rather than on separate nationalities in the City of New York.

The optimism about gradual homogenization of U.S. society held out by Herberg's was to quickly sour. His vision of an expanded civil religion with fading ethnic subdivision was undercut by a newly resurgent militancy about cultural, racial, and social divisions in U.S. society. By the second edition of *Beyond the Melting Pot* published in 1970, the authors suggested that "religion as a major line of division in the city is for the moment in eclipse."[9] Race and culture were more secular, less reconcilable, and more divisive than religious differences had been. New York's Irish Catholics, it was said, had subordinated their ethnic awareness in order to accommodate their culture under a religious mantle. This strategy had once been successful, gaining political power for them. That trade-off, however, had robbed them of something valuable in the changing society now charged with heightened racial awareness. Thus, the path Irish Catholics had taken to political influence would not be the same for New York's Puerto Ricans.

Race, it was said, had prevented assimilation to the WASP core. But with President Lyndon Johnson's declaration of a War on Poverty in 1964, racial identity became an advantage in securing federal funding for local organizations delivering social services. The self-help provisions of the new legislation aimed at what was called the *inner city* effectively provided racial minorities with resources that exceeded their share in the old ethnic politics.

The emphasis on race as a condition for governmental largesse presented a dilemma to Latinos and Latinas who were identified with faith-based organizations. The conditions for accepting federal funds at that time prohibited any use for specifically religious goals. Should religious Latinos and Latinas surrender their ties to the churches in order to utilize these resources? The answer by some Catholic leaders within the Latino communities was to echo the confidence of liberal Protestantism that one could work for God's cause within a secular city.[10] Thus, there was greater advantage to Latinos and Latinas projecting themselves as an ethnic/racial minority rather than as a Catholic religious group.

Such an approach was contested in the 1970s. Some Catholics feared that attention to racial divisions within the church would spoil the profile of a Catholicism that had successfully Americanized the immigrant. While he was probably not the best of Catholic sociologists with this focus, Father Andrew Greeley certainly was the most prolific. Making adept use of survey data where religious identification was available, Greeley produced books, monographs, and a weekly column in diocesan newspapers that reported on Catholicism among the descendants of ethnic immigrants from Europe. In his writings, Catholic voting patterns were analyzed in comparison with those of Protestants.

In agreement with this perspective, but without sociological precision, were the books on ethnicity from Michael Novak, who first gained fame as an advocate of change in accord with the teachings of the Second Vatican Council. Politics figure more prominently in his commentaries on U.S. Catholics than with Father Greeley. Moreover, Novak was not shy about projecting his observations into partisan considerations. While defending Catholics as the *unmeltable ethnics*, Novak lamented the attention given to racial groups who, with varying degrees of disloyalty, protested against the Vietnam War and attacked American social values and its economic system. Novak took particular exception to the tendency of some angry voices that lumped generations of white immigrant Catholics with the Protestant establishment. Novak complained that it was the Protestant majority that had written the legal rules for discrimination, not the Catholic immigrants. Why should black radicals blame slavery upon Polish Catholics whose grandparents had come to America long after the Civil War? As had been argued earlier in the 1950s, Novak offered reasons why Catholic white ethnics were more loyal to the true values of the country than racial radicals and their left-leaning liberal Protestant allies. In the 1970s, both Greeley and Novak had the effect of popularizing a Euro-American Catholicism that was not going to submerge itself within a liberal Protestant paradigm. Sadly, the rapidly growing Latino and African American members were nearly invisible in these profiles of American Catholicism, which left out more than one-third of all Catholics at that time.

Since the Reagan years, Novak has marched so far from the center as to take up his current residence as guru at a right-wing conservative think tank, the American Enterprise Institute. Greeley's frequent reports on survey data sometimes drifted toward a similar political interpretation. While never allowing himself to be put into the kind of box that Novak now inhabits, Greeley often mixed into his sociology sundry attacks and biting ridicule against enemies real and imagined. As a result, he sometimes undid with one hand what he had accomplished with the other. Strangely for a gifted sociologist, most of his output today can be found on lists of paperback fiction.

To his credit, these works of Greeley and others like them provided a common ground where studies of Catholicism and Protestantism could compare and contrast the same issues, employing similar scholarly methodologies. With such resources, social science acquired a literature that examined religion in America comprehensively but without burying important denominational differences. Had religion in the United States been made up of only Euro-American Catholics, Protestants and Jews, their contributions might have proven more enduring. However, these thinkers were penalized by the lack of a theory that accounted for growing influence of Latino groups on Catholicism.

Finding the U.S. Latinos and Latinas in Catholicism

The first significant analyses of Catholic Latinos and Latinas are found in the work of two pioneering sociologists; Patrick McNamara, of the University of New Mexico and the Fordham University Jesuit Joseph P. Fitzpatrick. When both authors began their careers, the-immigrant-becoming-American was the premise of sociology. However, McNamara and Fitzpatrick described how, among Latinos and Latinas, the trajectory had not been the same as for Euro-American Catholics. The distinctions they identified in their early work are still relevant when profiling Latino religious differences.[11]

McNamara deserves credit for measuring the social distance created between Mexican American Catholics and the Church. He had contributed a chapter on religion to Leo Grebler's major study of Mexican Americans.[12] Limited in scope by the preset definitions of the research, McNamara's article nonetheless contrasted the functions of Catholicism among Mexican Americans to its role among Euro-Americans. McNamara pointed out that in California, Texas, and New Mexico, the Catholic immigrants were the Euro-Americans, who had arrived in after the wars against Mexico. The Mexican Americans had been the first Catholics in these regions and could not be considered to be the "newcomers." Later, McNamara focused on the traditions of Catholicism before the invasion and annexation of Mexican homelands by the United States in the nineteenth century.[13] The religious experiences of the Mexican Americans, he pointed out, often referred to places, buildings, and events within the United States and differed from the "old country" nostalgia of European groups. He demonstrated that the most effective ministers to Mexican American Catholics were found among the clergy that adapted their pastoral approach to preexisting traditional and institutional expectations.

Father Joseph P. Fitzpatrick smuggled a similar perspective about Puerto Ricans into his analysis of the migration to the United States after the Second World War. Fitzpatrick refused to call Puerto Ricans *immigrants*, pointing out that they were U.S. citizens by reason of Congressional fiat in1917.[14] The Jesuit stressed that Puerto Rican assimilation did not face legal status issues that had usually prevented immediate participation by immigrants as voters in the United States. Their cultural persistence, therefore, could not be explained away as a temporary inability to overcome political boundaries as immigrant noncitizens. Since their cultural identity was not going to disappear, attitudes about religion and ethnicity needed to be rethought. Fitzpatrick extolled the advantages of understanding the transnational aspects of Catholicism and was most influential in establishing a training program for New York's priests. The clerics and members of religious congregations for women prepared for ministry in the United States by studying the Catholic religion as practiced on the island of Puerto Rico. Cultural differences were to become a resource for, rather than as an impediment from, promoting the faith.

Both Fitzpatrick and McNamara wrestled with the *Protestantization* of Puerto Ricans and Mexican Americans. Rather than *modernization* of Latinos and Latinas, they saw conversion away from Catholicism as an abandonment of culture. The two scholars argued for cultural maintenance within Catholicism of a vision that today would be called *multiculturalism*. This was advocacy for the application in the church of a new 1970s element in the construction of social identity.

A United States in which Latinos and Latinas did not have to assimilate acquired a potent intellectual component when universities began creating departments for Chicano and Puerto Rican studies. For the generation that came of age during the protests against Jim Crow and the Vietnam War,

Latinos and Latinas were soldiers in the struggle to change history and realize the vision of "freedom and justice *for all*." Racism, imperialism, economic exploitation through capitalism and cultural genocide were the rallying calls for Latino studies in key institutions of higher learning. Thus, to the already palpable Latino militancy in communities across the nation, books on the people's history, literature and politics gained a foothold in academia.

Sadly, in these new fields of inquiry, Catholicism suffered from inattention. The Catholic faith was often cast as part of the problem, not of any solution to injustice. It is not as if the works of McNamara, Fitzpatrick, and a cohort of pastorally inclined sociologists of religion were worthless: rather they lacked visibility in the new generation of scholars of the Latino experience. One possible explanation is that the two pioneers of a sociology of Latino religion had not utilized race or class theory. These ideologically slanted methodologies had become mainstays of the emerging new field of Latino studies. Although the messages of McNamara and Fitzpatrick were consonant with the thrust of the new Latino scholarship, they were not coded with the same disciplinary language. Because they used the language of the establishment, some thought that McNamara and Fitzpatrick were the establishment. Moreover, the fact that most published studies on Catholicism had been produced by non-Latinos with Irish surnames did not help promote the works of McNamara and Fitzpatrick in the reading lists generated by Latino studies.

Consider, for instance, the narrow religious concerns in the otherwise pioneering survey—the Latino National Political Survey.[15] Produced by a national consortium of universities with key scholars in Latino studies, this survey explored Latino particularities with admirable insight and professional excellence. It deserves an important prominence in the history of research among Latinos and Latinas. However, this creativity stalled on issues related to Latino religion. The items included in the survey were limited to standard identification of religious membership borrowed from other political science surveys of participation patterns. While adequate for basic information of religious affiliation, the survey missed an opportunity to explore important Latino experiences of syncretism, dual religious loyalties and popular religiosity.[16]

Unfortunately, attention to religion continues to lag within Latino studies. While naming names and books might demonstrate the scope of these omissions, it is more politic to invite the reader to scour the index of any favorite text on Latinos and Latinas and decide if religion has been addressed adequately. What we have a right to expect are social science data that derive their categories of analysis and survey questions from the lived experience of religious Latinos and Latinas. On the premise that since the 1970s, our religious believers have been formed by distinctly Latino influences, we need data that accurately reflect these differences from others within the general U.S. religious community.

Ironically, the lack of traction in Latino studies for the serious social science work of both McNamara and Fitzpatrick also impeded general acceptance of their work among their non-Latino peers. Greeley published *The American Catholic*[17] intending that this book would summarize the standing of Catholicism upon the 200th anniversary of the nation. Astoundingly, his book *excluded* Latinos and Latinas! Greeley opined that racial factors skewed the influence of ethnicity when measuring assimilation into U.S. society. On that basis, he eliminated "blacks and the Spanish-speaking" from his definition of "the American Catholic." Elsewhere we have questioned Greeley's logic that made speaking Spanish into a *racial* category.[18] The justification for his strange stance appears to have been ignorance of the work of Fitzpatrick among Puerto Ricans and McNamara among Mexican Americans. Greeley comments: "In the Northeast, for example, there is a deliberate attempt to create a Spanish-speaking ethnic group (an attempt that is not supported, incidentally, in the Southwest)."[19] Perhaps because his survey data on Euro-American Catholics provided little insight into the special issues that confronted Latinos and Latinas, he was inclined to avoid including unfamiliar data. But one would think it is up to the social scientist to change his or her categories when they do not fit the reality, and not vice versa. Intelligent readers in the public could not justify elimination of (then) 30 percent of American Catholics from consideration as to membership in the church, and Greeley's work was poorly received.

The Latino Religious Resurgence

Ironically, *The American Catholic* ended a historical phase in the study of U.S. Catholicism, rather than set the tone for future research. Moreover, Greeley's outdated views of ethnicity and Americanization were challenged by a nation-wide mobilization of Latinos and Latinas within Catholicism. The movement has been baptized with the name, "the Latino Religious Resurgence."[20] The Religious Resurgence might be described as the Catholic Church version of the Latino cultural, social, and political movements in the United States during the same period. For example, after the implementation of affirmative action policies within the larger society, the Resurgence's leaders argued that the Catholic Church should have Latino bishops in proportion to the percentage of the laity who were Latino. While cultural leaders sought money from secular sources for community programs to protect and cultivate Latino art, church activists advocated diocesan financial support for pastoral training centers (like the Mexican American Cultural Center in San Antonio), where the language and culture of Latinos and Latinas would be cultivated and communicated by native Latino and Latina faculty. Relevant to the issues of religion and politics, these efforts of the Resurgence resulted in a network of centers, movements, personnel, and resources directed by Latinos and Latinas for Latinos and Latinas. For example, the Hispanic Liturgical Commission devised a ritual for use in church celebrations of the *quinceañera*, a coming-of-age ceremony popular among teenage girls. This effort took the commission well beyond a secondary role as merely translating into Spanish what had already been approved by the English-speaking hierarchy. In this case, the ritual originated with and was developed by Latino leaders.

It would be counterproductive to describe the results of the Resurgence as "a church within the church." However, it is fair to conclude that by 1990 enough institutions, programs, and agencies had been created for and by Latinos and Latinas to ensure that the socialization of Latino Catholics would be different from that of non-Latinos within the church. More or less the same might be said of various Protestant denominations as well, since their generally liberal traditions gave them significant opportunities to shape policies within their churches. Political scientists might compare these pockets of real autonomous Latino power within churches to the functions of political parties or special interest caucuses within such parties.

Social science nourished the rise of these Latino caucuses, organizations, and ecclesiastical leaders. Everyone wanted demographic and other sociological data for planning purposes and to justify calls for greater proportion of denominational resources. This interest was not limited to Latinos and Latinas. After the attention to the Catholic future that was part of the Call to Action Program of 1976,[21] virtually all of Catholic groupings and many Protestant ones as well have gradually grown more interested in Latinos and Latinas. For example, the books on Catholic laity authored by William D'Antonio, Dean Hoge, Ruth Wallace, and other colleagues have afforded Latinos and Latinas growing importance.[22]

The Program for the Analysis of Religion Among Latinos and Latinas

It was only after 1988 with the creation of the Program for the Analysis of Religion Among Latinos (PARAL),[23] that scientific study of religion among

Latinos and Latinas was coordinated at a national level. While previously there had been scholars within social science interested in this topic, there had been scant coordination of research efforts that traversed the nation and treated all the different Latin American nationalities. Beginning in 1991, private foundations, most notably the Lilly Endowment, funded scholarly analysis of Latino religious experiences in the United States. PARAL adapted an existing body of sociological work on Latino religion to the premises of colonization and oppression that had given birth to Latino studies as a field. In offering an example of this approach, we hope to be excused a certain partiality toward the book, *Oxcart Catholicism on Fifth Avenue* by Ana María Díaz-Stevens.[24] It was among the first full-length books to spell out what was until then found principally in dissertations and monographs on Latino religion. *Oxcart Catholicism* earned significant awards and has retained its importance in the field. Díaz-Stevens, who was among the last of Fitzpatrick's doctoral students at Fordham University and among the first in PARAL, linked the Puerto Rican Catholic experience in New York to those of the Euro-American immigrants. Unlike Fr. Fitzpatrick's work, Díaz-Stevens wrote unencumbered by a need to link the U.S. Catholic Church with Americanization. Instead of repeating Fitzpatrick's theme of what the church had done (and still needed to do) for the Puerto Ricans, Díaz-Stevens described instead what the Puerto Ricans had done (and would continue to do) for the church. With her deft treatment, U.S. Catholicism emerges as an institution whose future membership depends upon adaptation to new challenges. Herstance—like that of a growing number of scholars—challenges American Catholicism to become less American and more Catholic.[25]

Liberation from linkage to Americanization framed the contributions of PARAL to the field of sociology, but it also found echo in the revisiting of ethnic religious experience for other Catholic groups. For instance, the work of Robert Orsi on Italians in New York ripened into a new look at the enrichment of U.S. Catholicism by a focus on devotions like that to St. Jude, Patron of Hopeless Causes (1996).[26] With similar effects, there is increased attention to something called "material religion," meaning the use of pictures, statues and other artifacts of belief and devotion.[27] There seems not to be very much difference in material religion from what Latino and Latin American scholars call "popular religiosity."

Rather than apologize for the ethnic component within religion, the newer approach has been to see it as a factor that multiplies or divides the impact of doctrinal positions. Moreover, it is relatively easy to understand how such practices link religion in the United States to the sources of nationality and ethnic identity. Religious attentions to weeping *Madonnas* among Italian Americans, pious pilgrimages to ethnic shrines among Poles in the United States, and the notion of Celtic spirituality for the Irish Americans are increasingly common. In a sense, the 1950s' view of assimilation has been turned on its head. Instead of examining how such non-Protestant, non-American traits are discarded by Latinos and Latinas, it is now supposed that customs linked historically with ethnicity are on the rise, even among non-Latinos and non-Latinas. Moreover, by focusing upon religion as it is *lived* rather than as it is fostered by *institutions*, issues like gender relations, racial identities, and doctrinal hybridity are studied along with religious factors. In sum, the old paradigms flowing from the Weberian premise about Protestantism and Catholicism are no longer hegemonic in the field.

Religion and Latino Politics

It is timely for this volume to focus upon the linkages between Latino religious identities and politics at a time when new theoretical perspectives are emerging. As always happens with paradigms, they reach a point when they no longer efficiently explain a reality. Stephen Warner summarized the nearly a century's work in the sociology of religion by encapsulating much of the questioning that was nibbling at the reigning paradigm and called for a new one.[28] He has reunited religion and ethnicity, but in ways that generally avoid the pitfalls of past efforts. Wade Clark Roof reaffirmed the same need and outlined how study of the Latino reality was indispensable to forming a picture of all of religion in the United States.[29] Warner's later research accomplishments,[30] like those of Helen Rose Ebaugh,[31] consider ethnicity (and race) to be operative not only in Catholicism or faith communities created by immigrants, but also as new forces within Protestantism and Islam. Professor Nancy Ammerman of Boston University has underscored the need of liberal Protestantism to adjust to new social trends, as has Mark Chaves's exploration of what congregations actually accomplish in terms of U.S. culture.[32] The 2005 book by Wuthnow on religious diversity adds him to the list of scholars reexamining multiculturalism within U.S. religion.[33] With their visibility within the highest echelons of the field,[34] as well as their warm support for PARAL, they have contributed to a recasting of ethnicity and religion in the American context for all scholars, no longer neatly divided into opposing camps of Catholics or Protestants. Moreover, over the past decade and a half, the ethnic focus has grown at the expense of the purely racial. The term *black* was been virtually replaced by *African American* in every day parlance. In fact,

Obama ran not so much as a black man, but as a racially ambiguous mixed-race candidate who was ethnically African and American.

This new direction in mainstream sociology and empirical study of religion is a promising one. PARAL took us on a path through Latino studies in the 1990s to apply concepts used to analyze our people's experience for an understanding of religion. We now meet non-Latino scholars coming around the bend on the same road to a better appreciation of all religion in the United States. They are increasingly concerned with issues of race, culture, diversity, language, and musical types, just as we have been. Along with them, we seek a new paradigm, no longer for just our particularized focus, but for the entire field. This is the spirit of collaboration and openness that has generated this volume on religion and politics. Happily, this book joins a growing number of scholarly publications that fill a void.

Where to Go from Here

We can summarize the trends that have shaped this book. Firstly, ethnicity and denominational affiliation are considered to affect each other. Gone is the conviction that ethnicity is doomed to disappear from religion because assimilation or Americanization are believed inevitable. Secondly, race has entered the building without divorce from ethnicity. It is common to find Hispanics/Latinos as a category distinct from African Americans, Asian Americans, or all others. Thirdly, it is increasingly difficult to consider ethnicity as only an immigrant experience. At least one secular interpretation of being American—multiculturalism—fosters the adoption of ethnicity as part of a ritualized social order. Thus, on St. Patrick's Day we are all Irish, and during Kwanza we are all African American, and to mark the Chinese New Year we go to a Cantonese restaurant. Indulging such permeable boundaries of ethnic identity, it is sometimes said, is a special characteristic of the United States. Fourthly, religion has made a comeback. Not only are faith-based institutions occupying an increasingly prominent place in the civic arena, religious expression has become more visible in multicultural America. Although doctrinal controls are asserted with fire and brimstone on occasion, religion in the United States today includes eclectic choices from individuals who assemble new personalized forms of faith in defining the sacred for themselves. While secularization of *religious institutions* continues apace, individuals profess an increasingly diverse mix of *personal faith expression*. The term most often applied here is to "cafeteria Catholics," who pick and choose the religious practices most appetizing to them. Rather a term for those with weak religious commitments, it often describes religious creativity and the power to innovate that comes from lived religion. Fifthly, among Latinos and Latinas it appears the tug of the country of origin has extended itself beyond the first and second generations of Latin American immigrants. The families of successful middle-class Latinos and Latinas, who would have been expected to be the most assimilable, often seek to reclaim their roots by identifying themselves socially with Latin American culture. This is more than transnationalism, which is pictured largely as a phenomenon among immigrants who do not cut the ties to the old country. Finally, we face a society in which race, religion, and ethnicity are seldom attacked. It appears instead that politics is the only tribalism where vitriol is allowed.

This volume examines how each of these trends has developed the political participation for Latinos and Latinas. Simultaneously, the robust institutions and traditions of Catholicism have functioned in ways that differ from the trends among Latinos of all other denominations. To understand politics today, it is not enough to count Latino votes every four years. Hopefully, this introductory chapter has prepared the way to see how contemporary religion—particularly Catholicism—exercises significant influence in shaping the Latino future.

Notes

1. The literature on Weber's positions is vast, and is available to those interested in exploring this complex theme apart from its application to the issue of Latinos and Latinas.
2. *See* Casanova 1994.
3. Rev. 17: 4–18.
4. Wuthnow 1988.
5. This issue is explored succinctly in David O'Brien's article (1990).
6. Halsey 1980.
7. Herberg 1955.
8. Gordon 1963.
9. Glazer and Moynihan 1970: ix.
10. *See* Cox 1965, 1985.
11. *See* McNamara 1995.
12. Grebler 1970.
13. McNamara 1973.
14. Fitzpatrick 1971.
15. De la Garza et al. 1992.
16. Ironically, it was the reluctance of the organizers in the Inter-University Program for Latino Research (IUPLR) to include scholars of religion that opened the door

for funding of PARAL by the Lilly Endowment and the Pew Charitable Trusts. To its credit, however, the IUPLR did make a seed grant to the organizers of PARAL to draft the proposal to the foundations.

17. Greeley 1976.
18. Díaz-Stevens and Stevens-Arroyo 1998: 42–43.
19. Greeley 1977: 15.
20. Díaz-Stevens and Stevens-Arroyo 1998.
21. The Call to Action Conference was supported by the U.S. bishops as part of the bicentennial observance for the country in 1976. It followed a consultation process very similar to what had been used by the *Encuentros*. For more details of this comparison, see Stevens-Arroyo (1980) 270, 306–311, 314–15. Currently, there is the lay organization that can be traced to this conference and uses the name of "Call to Action," but which does not have official recognition from the bishops.
22. D'Antonio, Hoge, Wallace, and others 1989, 1996, 2001.
23. *See* Díaz-Stevens and Stevens-Arroyo 1998.
24. Díaz-Stevens 1993.
25. Stevens-Arroyo 1995.
26. Orsi 1985.
27. Taves 1986; McDannell 1995.
28. Warner 1993.
29. Roof 1998.
30. Warner 1997, 1998.
31. Ebaugh 2000.
32. Chaves 2004.
33. Wuthnow 2005.
34. Professors Ebaugh, Roof, Warner, and Wuthnow have served as presidents of the Society for the Scientific Study of Religion. Professor Chaves has won awards with both the best book (1999) and the best article (1988) in the field. All have participated in PARAL events. Moreover, each has played a role within the Religion Section of the American Sociological Association.

Part I

Theoretical and Historical Issues

Chapter 2

The Political Persuasions of Latino Faith Communities

Anthony M. Stevens-Arroyo

The Program for the Analysis of Religion Among Latinos (PARAL) Study was one of several coordinated efforts to study religion at the start of a new Christian millennium. As noted in the introduction to his volume, PARAL was formed to foster social science analysis of religion from the unique perspectives of the Latino experiences. Beginning with its first meeting in 1997, the scholars of PARAL aspired to a national study of religion among the various nationality and regional Latino groups. It became apparent, however, that such an ambitious effort would simultaneously have to rebut certain biases and general unfamiliarity with Latino religiosity in much of the academic community. When the PARAL national study was launched during 2001, with funding from the Lilly Endowment and the Ford Foundation,[1] it had the dual purposes of surveying Latino faith communities and also a testing of existing presumptions.

In shaping the survey questions on political participation, therefore, the PARAL Study combined both new and standardized perspectives. In particular, it tested the findings of the Citizen Participation Study, a major undertaking to explain political and civic participation in the United States.[2] The PARAL Study included two national survey questionnaires: one of the leaders of Latino faith communities and the other of practicing believers within their parishes and congregations. To supplement the reliability of the sample, the researchers added a phone survey of the religious identification by Latino individuals, and seven community studies with thick description of interactions at a local level. Moreover, the PARAL Study was designed and conducted by a team of Latino and Latina scholars.

By securing lists from denominations of all the faith communities considered to serve Latinos and Latinas, we made the leadership in these churches and congregations the unit of analysis. In the first questionnaire, we surveyed the heads of each of the worshiping Latino faith communities that participated in the study. We declined to call these heads of the faith community "pastors" because terminology differed from church to church. Rather than enter into theological refinements about the meaning of such terms, the questionnaire was directed to "the person with the chief responsibility to organize and lead the Latino faith community." With the second questionnaire, we surveyed lay or volunteer leaders from among the responding churches and congregations. This dual approach gave us relevant socioeconomic data with the insights of the pastor or minister and opinions from lay and volunteer leaders in the same faith communities.

The list of the participating institutions whose responses from Latino membership are included in the report follows below, with the response rate in parentheses:

American Baptist Church (37%)
Christian Reformed Church (55%)
Disciples of Christ (41%)
Evangelical Lutheran Church in America (38%)
Roman Catholic (48%)
Seventh Day Adventist (29%)
United Church of Christ (46%)
United Methodist Church (46%)
Presbyterian Church, USA (51%)

The Roman Catholic churches were surveyed with a representative sample, as were the Seventh-Day Adventists. All the other denominations were surveyed by sending questionnaires to 100 percent of their congregations, basically because the total numbers were too small for sampling.[3] Subsequent to the data processing, additional responses were received, to raise the overall response rate to 47 percent. A significant limitation of the study is the absence from the Protestant sample of denominations considered Fundamentalist/Evangelical or Pentecostal.[4] Nonetheless, the results from the nine denominations represent approximately 85 percent of Latinos in affiliated churches.

The PARAL Study closely followed both the American Religious Identification Survey (ARIS) and the cooperative congregational study directed from the Hartford Seminary entitled on "Faith Communities Today" (FACT).

The latter was conducted during 2000 by an impressive list of U.S. religious denominations that pooled expertise and devised common questionnaire items in order to produce a series of denominational studies with comparative religious data that could be used to interpret the 2000 U.S. census.

The PARAL Study benefitted from both ARIS and FACT. Specifically, we included survey items from FACT out of the Hartford Seminary, but with the questions expanded or narrowed in order to explore issues special for Latinos and Latinas. For instance, while the Hartford Seminary's effort asked general questions about social services in faith based congregations, the PARAL Study specified programs for immigrants, English language lessons, citizenship, etc., all of which are particular to ethnically identified communities.

The survey components of the PARAL Study were initially reported as the National Survey of Leadership in Latino Parishes and Congregations (NSLLPC).[5] The NSLLPC had larger samples than the earlier Citizen Participation Study (CPS) by Sidney Verba and his associates. While the CPS's findings depended on less than 400 Latinos and Latinas, we had 883 valid responses from the heads of Latino faith communities. Within that number were 496 Catholic parishes and 387 Protestant congregations. We labeled the Latino Protestants as "all other denominations" (AOD) in order to be able to aggregate those who called themselves "Evangelicals," "Pentecostals," "Protestants," and "Christians." The second survey, which was conducted among lay and volunteer leaders, had 824 valid responses, of which 80 percent were from Roman Catholics. It replicated the two questions of CPS verbatim.

Testing for Political Involvement

Like Verba et al.,[6] the NSLLPC tested only those engaged in ministry—not those whose Catholicism might be considered merely "nominal." With the intent of testing Verba et al.'s findings, the NSLLPC asked the same key questions about political involvement as in the CPS. The heads of the faith communities were asked to what degree leadership opportunities in the church helped teach lay people "skills for addressing civic and social issues" (see Table 2.1). This question subsumed the two items used by Verba's team. The respondents were able to indicate the intensity of the experience by choosing among "very much help," "some help," "not much," and "not at all."

The heads of the Roman Catholic parishes were less likely to see "very much help" (24%) when compared with AOD ministers (36%). But in responding "some help," the numbers were alike: Roman Catholics at

TABLE 2.1 Leadership opportunities and skills for civic and social issues of faith community heads, by denomination (in percentages)

	Roman Catholic	All Other Denominations
Very much	24	36
Some	46	42
Not Much	22	16
Not at all	4	3
No Answer	4	3

Source: PARAL study, Table *11.5.5*

46 percent and AOD at 42 percent. Overall, a healthy majority for both RC (70%) and AOD (78%) reported there were positive opinions about church involvement as training in civic skills. These numbers suggest a less salient difference between Protestants and Catholics than was reported by Verba et al. Moreover, the rates of positive response in the PARAL Study are nearly twice as high as the Citizen Participation Study's findings in its two items for Latino Protestant members and about three times as high for Latino Catholics.

Of course, one needs to recognize that heads of faith communities may exaggerate the usefulness of their ministries. Thus, the PARAL Study repeated the same questions about participation to the lay and volunteer leaders as Verba et al. had posed to individual respondents in the CPS. These concerned democratic decision making and skills employed in conducting meetings. Notice that the response from these lay and volunteer leaders did not include a measure of intensity but sought only a factual, yes-or-no answer. For technical reasons,[7] the results of the PARAL Study group together both RC and AOD. In fact, the respondents were overwhelmingly Roman Catholic. Table 2.2 shows that the democratic process of making decisions by majority vote was experienced by 83 percent of all respondents; only 16 percent said that they had not had such an experience. In the item about public speaking, conducting a meeting, or planning activities, the responses were even more positive. Those who reported "yes" were 91 percent of respondents and those with "no" were 8 percent (see Table 2.2). It bears repeating that these high rates of positive experience were from a mostly Roman Catholic lay leader base.

Thus, the data of NSLLPC do not confirm the CPS's findings on two counts. First, the heads of the faith communities in both RC and AOD denominations report a higher percentage of civic participation for their members than suggested by the Citizen Participation Study. Second, the mostly

TABLE 2.2   Democratic involvement and use of skill within church (in percentages)

	Yes	No
Participation in Democratic Process	83	16
Use of Leadership Skills	91	8

Source: PARAL study, tables III.9.2, III.9.3

Catholic lay and volunteer leaders give such high incidence of leadership experience so as to be virtually indistinguishable from the rates among AOD leaders reported by Verba et al.

Only one of the results of the NSLLPC finds a salient discrepancy that ranks Catholics lower than Protestants. This concerns the inquiry about the degree of leadership preparation taking place in the faith community. Heads of AOD faith communities reported a rate of "very much" preparation for leadership that was 12 percent higher than among RC faith communities. RC communities, on the other hand, reported a slightly higher rate for "some" preparation than AOD (46% to 42%). Overall for both "very much" and "some," the net difference between the two denominations for leadership preparation is 8 percent higher among AOD denominations (RC: 70%, AOD: 78%). This one result, however, measures only intensity *as perceived by the head of the faith community*—which is salient, as I hope to suggest— but does not support Verba et al.'s conclusions about actual practice among lay and volunteer leaders.

To explore the notion of actual civic and political activism as members of a faith community, it is necessary to turn to the PARAL Study's data about services and civic engagement at the local level. The questionnaires divided such services into two categories: those that required professionally trained personnel and those that did not. In addressing the material needs of the people, the heads of the faith communities were asked to choose from a list of possible venues for such services: *services delivered locally in the parish or congregation; referred to a religious agency for service delivery; or referred to a secular agency for service delivery.* Table 2.3 offers an overview of the nonprofessional services for three of the most significant categories. Roman Catholic parishes were more likely (70%) to distribute clothes and food locally than all other denominations (57%). When adding references to other religious agencies to these highly visible ministries to the local services in the faith communities, the survey found that 85 percent of Roman Catholic faith communities and 70 percent of those of all other denominations practice charity in this direct form.

TABLE 2.3 Non-professional services, by denomination (in percentages)

		Offered	Referred to Religious Agency	Referred to Secular Agency
Distribution of clothing/food				
	RC	70	15	4
	OAD	57	13	7
Sports Groups				
	RC	37	7	20
	OAD	40	7	13
Scouts Groups				
	RC	37	7	20
	OAD	40	7	13
Excursions				
	RC	50	5	11
	OAD	60	3	10
Disaster Victims				
	RC	54	16	9
	OAD	57	14	9
Join Civic Marches				
	RC	34	7	10
	OAD	40	3	9
Support Candidates				
	RC	12	3	17
	OAD	21	1	16

Source: PARAL study, Table 1.8.1

The two areas of difference concern politics. Latino faith communities of all other denominations were somewhat more likely (40%) than Roman Catholic ones (34%) to join in civic marches. These same AOD Latino faith communities were significantly more likely to support candidates in elections (21%) than Roman Catholics (12%). Although in both cases the support came from less than a quarter of all Latino faith communities in each denomination, this finding indicates a greater inclination from AOD faith communities to engage overtly in political activities. I believe this difference can be linked to the finding of greater intensity among AOD heads regarding the civic leadership opportunities to their members. Whereas most Catholics have reservations about direct church endorsements of specific candidates, it appears there is less reluctance among AOD. Notice that the two categories of difference in terms of such nonprofessional services concern both civic and political awareness, suggesting that the AOD leadership sees partisan politics as part of general concern for public policy.

Table 2.4 reports on services that generally require professional training. This is the area that is a step above such volunteer efforts as collecting food or clothes. Of the services that usually require trained personnel, more than a quarter of all Latino faith communities are most likely to provide within their own facilities at the local level ministries that address the following: lead-

TABLE 2.4 Professional services, by denomination (in percentages)

		Offered	Refered to Religious Agency	Referred to Secular Agency
Senior Citizens				
	RC	40	12	20
	OAD	27	13	24
Shelter Homeless				
	RC	14	26	36
	OAD	11	21	34
Immigration				
	RC	29	33	22
	OAD	30	16	26
Housing				
	RC	13	24	41
	OAD	9	14	42
AIDS Programs				
	RC	10	20	36
	OAD	11	15	35
Family Violence				
	RC	24	20	35
	OAD	35	13	17
Job Training				
	RC	8	14	50
	OAD	13	13	36

(Continued)

TABLE 2.4 (CONTINUED)

		Offered	Refered to Religious Agency	Referred to Secular Agency
Health Clinic				
	RC	16	18	47
	OAD	21	10	38
Rehabilitation				
	RC	10	15	47
	OAD	11	19	35
Day-Care/Pre-School				
	RC	35	9	28
	OAD	21	13	25
English Classes				
	RC	38	13	29
	OAD	32	9	26
Literacy Classes				
	RC	20	14	36
	OAD	22	9	28
Leadership Training				
	RC	45	19	12
	OAD	65	7	7
Youth Conferences				
	RC	55	21	5
	OAD	59	11	4

Source: PARAL study, Table 1.8.2

ership training, youth conferences, senior citizens, English classes, immigration, family violence, and day care/preschool. However, while Roman Catholics (45%) are considerably less likely to offer leadership training in the local parishes than all other denominations (65%), they are also more likely (19%) to refer leadership training to a religious agency, (i.e., a diocesan or national movement) than all other denominations (7%) and to send young people to a center or program outside the parish (21%) than all other denominations (11%). While both AOD and RC Latino faith communities avail themselves of national and regional youth movements, the training for Catholics is almost twice as likely to take place in these larger settings than for AOD youth.

Thus, we find two important trends here. The first is categorized as "intensity" in which Latinos of AOD congregations report higher levels of awareness for civic and political items. The second is the tendency among RC parishes to refer members to faith-based professional agencies for social services beyond those offered by the parish.

Not surprisingly, the PARAL Study found that outreach ministries correspond to particular needs of the Latino faith community. This is similar to what FACT reported for congregations located in cities and the historically black Protestant churches. Such racially designated congregations were found to be more likely to sponsor social justice programs than the national average.[8] In the Latino cases studied by PARAL, more than a third of all Latino faith communities provide English classes at the local level. Moreover, virtually 30 percent of all Latino faith communities nationwide provided immigration services, which is higher than the national average for the congregations surveyed in 2000.[9] Thus, supporting a finding of a more general survey, the PARAL Study provides additional specificity about the special character of the material needs addressed by Latino faith communities as well as for the acquisition of leadership skills.

Under George W. Bush (2000–2008), the U.S. federal government made an effort to channel public funds through faith-based communities as social service providers. In 2001, when the PARAL Study was conducted, that effort was just beginning, and less than 2 percent of Latino faith communities reported receiving government funds for ministries related to educational and social services. Somewhat surprisingly, the paucity of government funds to local communities does not translate into an absence of outside funding. Nearly half the Latino faith communities (44%) said they received some subsidy, grants, or funding. However two-thirds (66%) of this funding was from a denomination or other religious sources. The remaining parishes and congregations with outside sources of funding attributed 16 percent to private foundations, 11 percent from other charitable sources, and only 6 percent from government.

In all, one-third of faith communities receive a denominational subsidy, making this the most important type of additional funding. Only a quarter of Roman Catholic Latino faith communities (25%) received denominational subsidies, contrasted with nearly half (44%) of Latino faith communities in all other denominations. Of the two-thirds that did not receive a denominational subsidy, about 17 percent received grants or funding from other sources in order to serve Latino needs.

Most subsidies are not large. In 1999, the median amount of denominational subsidy to Latino faith communities was $17,500; for grants from sources other than the denomination, the median was $9,500. The bulk of grants and funding went to supplement religious education. The data showed that 27 percent of Latino faith communities surveyed had a school. However, this was chiefly a Roman Catholic experience, since 86 percent of Latino faith communities with a school in 2001 were in a Catholic parish. With the establishment of more charter schools under faith-community sponsorship, these percentages have likely changed, since the funding mechanism for charter schools begun under the Bush administration makes it easier for the AOD congregations to affiliate with such institutions. Still, a religious school remains a mostly Roman Catholic experience for Latinos and Latinas.

Rather than subsidy, however, the substantial difference between Roman Catholic and all other denominations in sponsoring private elementary schools may be explained by the size of the faith community. Nearly half (49%) of Latino faith communities sponsoring schools were large or mega-communities with 1,000+ Latino members. Only 9 percent of small Latino faith communities with fewer than 100 members sponsor schools; this small number includes churches with 1,000+ total members, but with only 100 Latinos and Latinas.

There appears to be linkage between openness to government funding for social ministries and support for school vouchers. The PARAL Study reported that 74 percent of those in favor of government funds for social services also support vouchers for private religious schools. Support for vouchers was about evenly split among those faith communities which did not already have a school: 49 percent say they would start a religious school if there were government funds such as vouchers for private education; 44 percent would refuse such funds. Presumably, these attitudes carry over to congregational sponsorship of a charter school. The heads of Latino faith communities, both RC and AOD, who are open to vouchers also consider it important or very important to use government funds for social ministries (49%).

The openness to government funding of schools is highest among the lay and volunteer leaders. Three quarters of those responding welcomed the use of government funds to accomplish the work of the churches. Half of these respondents (50%) say it is "very important" to receive governmental funds to do ministries, and another 24 percent say it is simply "important" to do so.

In speculating on the causes for their finding of disparity between Roman Catholics and Protestants in individual civic participation skills, Verba et al. also suggested that size might be an important factor, but in a different way. He suggested that fewer members provided more leadership opportunities for members, while larger communities would tend not to ask the same persons to assume more than one leadership role. The PARAL Study also found size was important to social ministry, but with opposite results as those of the CPS. Looking at the faith community as the unit of analysis, the PARAL Study found that greater size *enhanced rather than diminished* civic engagement when addressing material needs. In general, Catholic parishes not only have more members than Protestant congregations, they also enjoy a larger physical plant and much higher income from weekly donations. The PARAL Study found that larger size of the membership and the physical plant of the church buildings were more likely to affect the delivery of services to the material needs of the people than dogmatic considerations.

For instance, the PARAL Study reported that day care/preschool services were offered in only 18 percent of small faith communities but in 41 percent of megafaith communities. Similarly, English classes were offered in 26 percent of small but in 44 percent of megafaith communities, and immigration services were found in 20 percent of small but in 38 percent of megafaith communities.

Confirming the trend cited above, Roman Catholic faith communities were also more likely than AOD to refer clients to religious-based agencies outside of the local community. With the assistance of an organization such as Catholic Charities, Catholic Latino parishes were able to refer clients to a professional agency outside the parish facilities but still related to church work. This was an advantage over AOD churches, which often faced the choice of either providing a service locally or referring believers to secular and public agencies (see Table 2.4 above). The most striking instance of this tendency is in terms of immigration services. These are more than twice as likely to be offered through a reference to a Roman Catholic religious agency (33%) than through references to religious agencies for all other denominations (16%). The pattern is reversed, however, for rehabilitation from drugs and alcohol and job training, wherein a reference to secular agencies is considerably higher for Roman Catholics than for AOD. Despite the RC tendency to refer to secular agencies, however, there is no proportional difference between the denominational groups for references to religious agencies for substance abuse and job training. In other words, while both RC and AOD pay attention to these issues at about the same rate, the RC parishes are more likely to use referrals to a secular agency than the AOD, which greatly prefer religiously inspired forms of rehabilitation. It may be that all other denominations have a theological perspective different from that of Roman Catholics on the local church's role in the cure of addictions. This finding also holds for forms of job training and may be related to the desire to couple material success with church membership that is discussed below.

Nonetheless, the typical Catholic parish and Protestant congregation generally shared the same list of priorities for the people's social and civic needs. While there are some differences in perception or incidence of certain social services between the RC and AOD groups, the PARAL Study does not corroborate Verba et al.'s contention that Latino Protestants receive better training in leadership skills, at either an individual or congregational level. It is true that we found a greater inclination to be overtly political among Latinos and Latinas of AOD, a trait we have called "intensity." However, this does not have an effect on either the services actually rendered or the extremely high rates of leadership experiences among lay and volunteer leaders. In addition, the data did not support Verba et al.'s contention that the generally smaller size of Protestant congregations provided more leadership opportunities than the larger Catholic parishes. In fact, the greater size of the parishes often *increased* the opportunities for participation in services requiring professional training.

Women as Leaders of Faith Communities

Verba and his associates noted the Catholic Church's exclusion of women from ordination and clerical status, suggesting this may explain their findings of a lower level of leadership training among Latino Catholics. Once again, this hypothesis was not supported by the PARAL Study's findings. It will be remembered that the NSLLPC surveys avoided titles such as "pastor" or "minister" in seeking the "head," i.e., the person principally responsible for the organization and worship of the Latino faith community. This made it possible for the study to engage the observations of Dr. Ruth Wallace's *They Call Her Pastor.*

In her pioneering book, Dr. Wallace noted that with fewer priests able to meet the ministerial needs of Latino faith communities, in some places women trained in ministry function as heads of the Hispanic segment of the parish membership. Such ministry appointments do not violate canonical rules requiring ordination in order to exercise the office of pastor. Wallace's study focused on parishes where there was no resident priest, usually because the male cleric was official pastor for more than one faith community. In the parishes she studied, women in ministry lived permanently in the parish while they supplied for leadership functions of organization and worship ordinarily provided by resident clerics. In effect, such women are heads of Catholic faith communities, complementing the work of priests and supplying ministry to the faithful under the guidance of the bishop. As the title of her book suggests, in most of these circumstances the parishioners call these Catholic women "pastor," even if the title is not official.

Overall, the PARAL Study reported a woman as head in nearly one in five of Latino faith communities (18.5%) nationwide. The Roman Catholic percentage of women in such a post (19%) is proportionately the same as the general average. It would also be a misconception to characterize all such Catholic women heads as "nuns," as if they could not be considered true laity. While the Catholic half of the male heads of Latino faith communities were celibate priests, only 21 percent of women heads of Latino faith communities were celibates because of vows in a religious community of sisters or nuns. Other salient characteristics of all these Latinas are listed below:

- There is no proportional difference from males in age distribution.
- Women heads are slightly more likely to be married (49%) than men (44%), but considerably more likely to be single (18%) than men (4%).
- Women heads of Latino faith communities are slightly more likely to be of Latin American heritage (53%) than men (47%).
- There was no proportional difference for men or women heads of faith communities in reference to the country of birth.
- Women (15%) are more likely than male heads of Latino faith communities (5%) to have some college training or to have a college degree (26%) compared to male heads (18%).
- Male heads of Latino faith communities are significantly more likely (50%) to have a master's degree than women (31%).
- Nearly half of all women heads of Latino faith communities (47%) have an advanced degree.

The PARAL Study reported that women were less likely (17%) than men (23%) to be heads of the faith community when the faith community had been founded within the past five years. This would seem to indicate that women often assume leadership of already functioning parishes and congregations, while men are more often the first such organizer. Moreover, contradicting Verba et al.'s suggestion that Catholics were less open to female church leadership, both Roman Catholic (75%) and respondents of all other denominations (77%) agreed most strongly that women should be equally represented with men in faith community leadership.

The PARAL Study did distinguish between allowing women to be "leaders" and considering them "heads of the faith community." Roman Catholics were considerably less likely to agree that women should be pastors of the faith community (32%) than heads of all other denominations (78%) (Table 2.5). Reflecting current Roman Catholic practice of ordaining

TABLE 2.5 Faith community heads' opinion on acceptance of women as heads of faith communities, by denomination and gender (in percentages)

	Roman Catholic	All Other Denominations	Female	Male
Agree Strongly	32	78	60	51
Agree Somewhat	17	12	12	15
Disagree Somewhat	13	4	9	9
Disagree Strongly	24	4	12	16
No Answer	14	2	7	9

Source: PARAL study, Table II.4.2

only males, Roman Catholics were six times more likely (24%) to strongly disagree with women as heads of faith communities as those of all other denominations (4%).

It should be noted, however, that a third of RC respondents "strongly agree" with women's ordination, exceeding the quarter who "strongly disagree." The 18.5 percent of female heads also showed some differences from the male heads but few salient differences among themselves. Women (60%) were more likely than men (51%) to "strongly agree" that women should be accepted as heads of faith communities and somewhat less likely (12%) than men (16%) to "strongly disagree." In sum, while Verba et al. correctly link Catholic exclusion of women from *ordination* to general ideas about clergy roles, this theological prohibition makes for no difference between Catholics and Protestants in *actual service* or support for gender equality in nonordained ministries.

Since the two suggestions of Verba et al. about the size of a congregation and women's ordination are not substantiated as explanations for differences between Latino Roman Catholics and those of all other denominations, a search for causes of difference must turn elsewhere. We have already seen a tendency among AOD leaders to be more overtly civic and political in church identification of how best to serve material needs. Does this represent some ideological difference that reflects party politics?

Faith Commitments and Political Activism

The PARAL Study understood that political involvement presents a challenge to faith communities. On the one hand, the trust placed in the churches by their Latino and Latina believers give them influence in the civic forum. On the other, politics usually involves siding with a particular candidate who may support only some of the beliefs of the faith community about social policies. Avoiding the term "moderate" in order to sharpen the categories, we asked if respondents considered themselves liberals or conservatives before entering into questions about partisanship (i.e., Democrats or Republicans). Most heads of Latino faith communities (54%) avoided being "very liberal" or being "very conservative": the largest categories were either simply "liberal" (33%) or simply "conservative" (29%). One-fifth of the heads of Latino faith communities said they had no political preference (21%) or did not answer the question (10%). Only 2 percent classified themselves as "very conservative"; less than half as many as those who said they were "very liberal" (5%).

The findings for heads in terms of ideological tendencies can be compared to the findings for lay and volunteer leaders (see Figure 2.1). Lay and volunteer leaders are generally more *conservative* and *very conservative* (43%) than the heads of the Latino faith communities (31%). Whereas one out of three heads were liberal, only one out of four lay and volunteer leaders classified themselves in this way. Lay and volunteer leaders were more likely to have *no political preference* (30%) than the heads of Latino faith communities (21%).

These findings about political preferences did not show any proportional difference between RC and AOD. However, it bears repeating that the PARAL sample greatly underrepresents Southern Baptists, Pentecostals, or nondenominational Latino congregations, which likely are the faith communities most likely to be conservative or very conservative.

FIGURE 2.1 Ideological preferences: Leaders and heads of Latino faiths communities (in percentage)

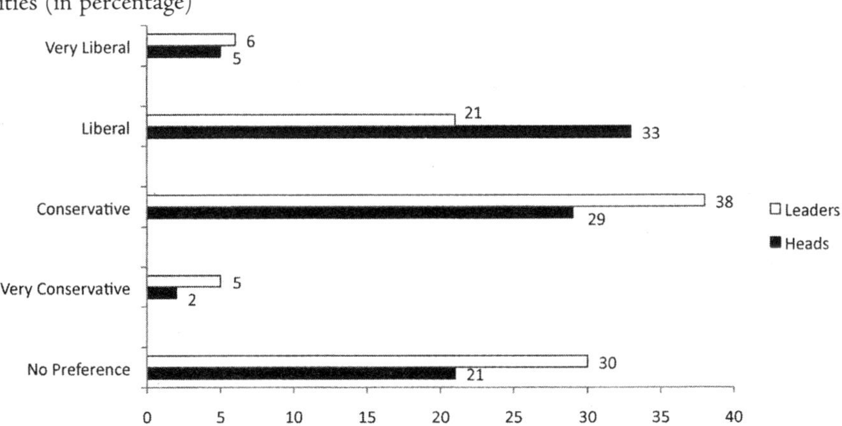

Source: PARAL study, graph III.8.4

The PARAL Study also asked the heads of the Latino faith communities: Which political party helps the most? We provided the opportunity to make both parties the same:[10]

+ 12 percent said that neither helped.
+ 13 percent said both helped the same.

Nonetheless, 40 percent of the heads of Latino faith communities had no opinion about politics or did not answer. For those who identified a political party as the helper of Latinos, there was a huge advantage for the Democratic Party, six times larger than the GOP:

+ 30 percent said that the Democratic Party helps the most.
+ 5 percent said that the Republican Party helps the most.

Table 2.6 shows opinions about political parties by denominations. There is no difference between Roman Catholics (30%) and all other denominations (30%) in viewing the Democratic Party as the one that helps Latinos the most. Heads of Latino faith communities from all other denominations are more likely (7%) than Roman Catholics (4%) to consider the Republican Party to help Latinos and Latinas the most, although both percentages are considerably lower than those viewing the Democratic Party favorably. Heads of Latino faith communities from all other denominations are also slightly more likely (34%) to not be sure or have no idea about political parties than among Roman Catholics (30%). This contrasts with the earlier reported findings that AOD were more inclined to be overtly connected to the civic and the political. An intervening factor may be the length of time as resident in the United

TABLE 2.6 Faith community heads' opinion on help provided by political parties to Latinos and Latinas, by denomination (in percentages)

	Roman Catholic	All Other Denominations
Democrat	30	30
Republican	4	7
Both The Same	12	14
Neither	13	11
Not Sure/No Idea	30	34
Other	1	–
No Answer	10	5

Source: PARAL study, Table II.5.1

FIGURE 2.2 Lay and volunteer opinion on political parties that help Latino/as (in percentage)

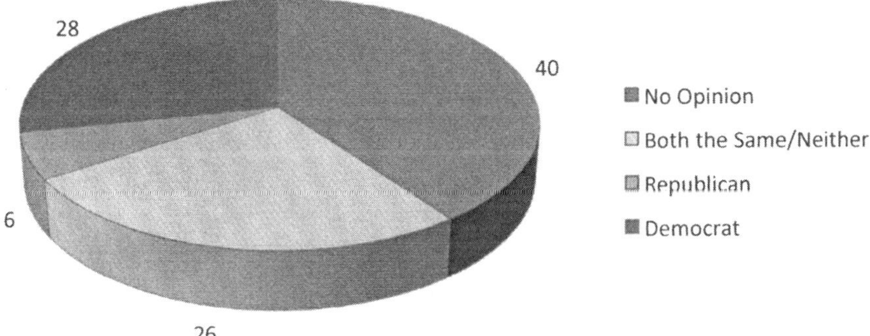

Source: PARAL study, graph III.8.3

States, which was mostly measured in the PARAL Study by language prefer-ence as analyzed below.

Even though the lay and volunteer leaders tend to be more conservative than the heads, they also saw the Democratic Party as helping Latinos and Latinas more than the Republican Party by a wide margin (see Figure 2.2). Although just like the heads of the faith communities, the largest group of lay and volunteer leaders had no opinion about politics, they were more likely to identify themselves by membership in the Democratic and Republican Par-ties (40%) than they were to respond to their ideology as either liberals or conservatives (30%). Since these respondents were mostly Roman Catholic Latinos and Latinas, this finding suggests that the Latino Catholic laity is more involved with partisan political choices than the heads of the parishes.

There is an important caveat before interpreting either lack of preference for a party, or the opinions *both are the same* or *neither helps*. Many studies based on interpretations of political participation in the United States pre-sume that voting for candidates of the Democratic or Republican Parties indi-cates political maturity. Nonparticipation in elections, on the other hand, is attributed to lack of awareness of politics. The PARAL Study challenged this premise by allowing responses of "helps the same" and "neither helps," thus distinguishing between people who were skeptical about the U.S. political sys-tem and those who have "no political preference." In some circles, skepticism about the two-party system becomes a more sophisticated political attitude than voting for either of the two major parties. About a quarter of Latinos and Latinas of faith fall into this category, and it may reflect the sophistication of active participation in Latin American politics, where electoral abstention is often invoked as political protest.

TABLE 2.7 Partisan identification by language preference (in percentages)

	Only English	Mostly English	Equal	Mostly Spanish	Only Spanish
Democrat	23	37	31	24	16
Republican	8	5	6	4	–
Both The Same	15	12	14	11	11
Neither	19	17	11	9	16
Not Sure/No Idea	25	20	31	48	58
Other	2	–	–	1	–
No Answer	8	10	8	4	–

Source: PARAL study, Table II.5.2

The most relevant factor to opinions about U.S. political parties, whether Democratic or Republican, was language preference (see Table 2.7). The Democratic Party fared best among those who spoke mostly English (37%) or spoke both languages equally (31%). The highest rating for the Republican Party (8%) came from those Latinos who spoke only English. A near majority of those who spoke mostly Spanish (48%) and a majority of those who spoke only Spanish (58%) were not sure or had no idea of which political party helps Latinos and Latinas. Since English language proficiency generally increases with the years spent living in the United States, the data may be interpreted to show that before English is mastered, many Latinos and Latinas have little identification with U.S. political parties, and that Republicans fare best among those who no longer use Spanish at all.

Somewhat surprisingly, the self-definition as "conservative" did not predict identification of the Republican Party (12%) over the Democratic Party (17%) as the one that most helped Latinos and Latinas (see Table 2.8). Only those who were "very conservative" chose the Republican Party (29%) over the Democratic Party (14%). A majority of those who said they had no political preference were not sure or did not have an idea of which political party helped the most. They were joined by a third of those who were "conservative" (36%) and "very conservative" (33%) who were not sure or did not have an idea of which political party helped the most.

Perhaps the most relevant conclusion to be drawn is that most Latino faith communities (66%) are headed either by persons who do not have political preferences (40%) or who believe that there is no difference in the way the parties assist Latinos (26%). These categories may represent very different political outlooks, however, since the opinion that the parties are no different

TABLE 2.8 Partisan identification by ideological leaning (in percentages)

	Very Liberal	Liberal	No Preference	Conservative	Very Conservative
Democrat	70	55	10	17	14
Republican	5	1	2	12	29
Both The Same	–	10	11	21	5
Neither	7	10	14	13	14
Not Sure/No Idea	14	20	55	36	33
Other	–	–	1	–	–
No Answer	5	2	4	2	5

Source: PARAL study, Table II.5.4

from each other may come from significant experience and a resulting skepticism about the U.S. system, while lack of political preferences may be the consequence of unfamiliarity. Note as well that considering the Democratic Party to help Latinos more (30%) than the Republican Party (5%) does not define personal political preferences as liberal or conservative.

It ought to be remembered that transnationalism exercises increasing influence on the Latino population in the United States. Latin American countries like the Dominican Republic and Mexico today frequently recognize joint citizenship with the United States. At present, the majority of foreign-born Latin Americans in the United States are eligible for dual citizenship, which means the right to vote in the elections of two countries and to travel freely between them, carrying two passports. While the data provided in the PARAL Study provide no clear handle on transnationalism, the skepticism toward U.S. party politics and it possible linkage with voting participation in the country of origin may be worthy of future investigation.

Shaping Political Attitudes for Believers

What are the ordinary sources of political attitudes for believers? Of course, secular society provides the major influences, but the association of faith and politics is often imparted by sermons. The PARAL Study asked the heads of the faith community about the frequency of certain topics featuring in their sermons (see Table 2.9). In interpreting these results, it is important to note that the pretesting for the PARAL Study taught us not to indicate *which opinion was voiced in the sermon*, since that question tended to make respondents suspicious that the survey was intentionally biased. Potential respondents

TABLE 2.9 Frequency of Sermon Topic by denomination (in percentages)

		Always	Often	Sometimes	Never	No Answer
Social-Political Issues						
	RC	6	24	57	9	5
	OAD	9	28	50	10	3
Critique of US Policy						
	RC	1	7	55	28	8
	OAD	2	14	49	30	5
Abortion						
	RC	13	24	52	5	5
	OAD	7	21	55	14	4
Immigration						
	RC	6	14	59	17	5
	OAD	10	21	52	14	3
Bilingual Education						
	RC	8	12	49	25	7
	OAD	13	25	48	11	3
Affirmative Action						
	RC	10	16	49	19	6
	OAD	18	23	42	15	4
Support of Local Groups						
	RC	13	24	48	10	6
	OAD	21	26	43	6	3
Electoral Procedures						
	RC	6	13	48	27	6
	OAD	11	16	47	24	4
Homosexuality						
	RC	3	7	68	16	6
	OAD	6	15	61	14	4
Reforms Against Poverty						
	RC	18	24	47	7	5
	OAD	24	27	38	7	3

TABLE 2.9 (CONTINUED)

		Always	Often	Sometimes	Never	No Answer
Domestic Violence						
	RC	23	30	39	3	5
	OAD	29	33	32	3	4
Gender Equality						
	RC	24	31	37	3	5
	OAD	34	29	32	2	4
Family Unity						
	RC	43	34	18	1	4
	OAD	58	24	14	1	4

Source: PARAL study, Table I. 10.1

rejected formulations that favored one or other conclusion, particularly those with partisan political implications. In conducting the survey, therefore, only the fact of addressing the topic rather than the content of the sermon is recorded. In other words, the data indicate only that there are sermons on abortion but not that the preacher was either pro-choice or antiabortion. (Cross-tabulation with the other categories of liberal and conservative elsewhere in the questionnaire provides a way to interpret the ideological direction of the sermon.) Finally, note that not all of the sermon social topics were political.

The highest scores for appearing in sermons of a majority of Latino faith communities were family unity (79%), equality between men and women (58%), and the denouncing of family violence (57%). The social issues that most frequently figured in sermons but not in majority of faith communities were reforms against poverty (46%), support for neighborhood groups (41%), and abortion (34%). The issues that are most likely to never be mentioned in sermons were a critique of U.S. policy and electoral procedures.

The differences between RC and AOD heads of faith communities figured prominently in abortion, a topic which is almost twice as likely to *always* figure in a sermon for Roman Catholics (13%) when compared with all other denominations (7%). In contrast, Latino faith communities of all other denominations are nearly three times more likely (14%) to avoid preaching on abortion as Roman Catholics (5%). Combining categories of "always" and "often," Table 2.9 shows that Latino faith communities of all other denominations (AOD) are more likely than Roman Catholic ones (RC) to include in sermons the political topics of immigration, bilingual education, affirmative action, support for local groups, electoral procedures, and reforms against poverty. There is also a more intense feeling about gender equality among the AOD than among the RC. A more significant finding is that preaching in critique of U.S. policies either "always" or "often" is twice as likely for Latino faith communities of AOD (16%) are twice as likely than Roman Catholic ones (8%). The AOD also more frequently include homosexuality in sermons (21%) than RC (10%), although it ought to be remembered that here, as in the critique of U.S. policies, this indicates only the frequency, but not the content of preaching. Thus, for instance, critique of government policies considered too liberal may be as likely as those who criticize the government for being too conservative.

In sum, while there is a trade-off for abortion (more common among RC) and homosexuality (more common among AOD), the Latinos of AOD have a pronounced tendency to speak from the pulpit more frequently about core social issues. They are also twice as likely to criticize U.S. policies in sermons. These findings strengthen the premise that intensity about civic and political issues among Latino Protestants carries over to the choice of sermon topics.

The lay and volunteer leaders were also asked about which sermon topics they wanted to hear and how frequently.[11] The most popular sermon topics were:

+ In favor of family unity (87%)
+ Against domestic violence (64%)
+ In support of equality between men and women (58%)
+ In support of reforms to end poverty (54%)

The leading topics respondents said should *never* be in sermons were:

+ Criticism of U.S. policies in Latin America (39%)
+ Instruction about the electoral process (26%)
+ Homosexuality (24%)

The PARAL Study data may also explain how the Latino AOD congregations reinforce each other regarding their more intense commitment to civic and political issues. Latino faith communities of all other denominations are far more likely to report ecumenical participation in social causes than are Roman Catholic parishes. The findings of the PARAL Study suggest that RC parishes are more likely to cooperate with each other than they are with Protestant or interfaith groups. The PARAL findings for the AOD ecumenical participation, on the other hand, are virtually identical with the national average reported in FACT, where a majority of participating faith communities were of all other denominations, i.e., Protestant denominations (Figure 2.3).

It is likely that this solidarity and cooperation with other denominations intensifies a sense of civic engagement for these Latino AOD congregations with each other. Such a pattern may reflect the historic status of Protestantism as the hegemonic religion in the United States. But while the data suggest that Catholic Latino faith communities are less likely to cooperate with AOD congregations, it needs to be added that RC Latino parishes interact with other Catholic parishes on matters of social justice with as much frequency as the AOD with AOD. Thus, it is more the nature of the partners than actual patterns of cooperation that distinguish the AOD from the RC Latino faith communities. Moreover, the reported cooperation of RC Latino faith communities includes programs with non-Latino parishes as well, such as in "twining" diocesan programs where an affluent parish is linked in social justice programs with a poorer, more diverse parish.

Finally, some attention needs to be paid to common theological influences. If sermons shape attitudes for members of the faith community, the sermon givers are themselves shaped by their theological training. The PARAL Study inquired about the seminary and pastoral training of the respondents. One can argue whether the version of theology of liberation referred to by the respondents is the same as the earlier radical version using Marxist theory as a tool of analysis that emerged in Latin America nearly 30 years ago.[12] As seen

FIGURE 2.3 Churches with social ministry partnership with other denominations (in percentage)

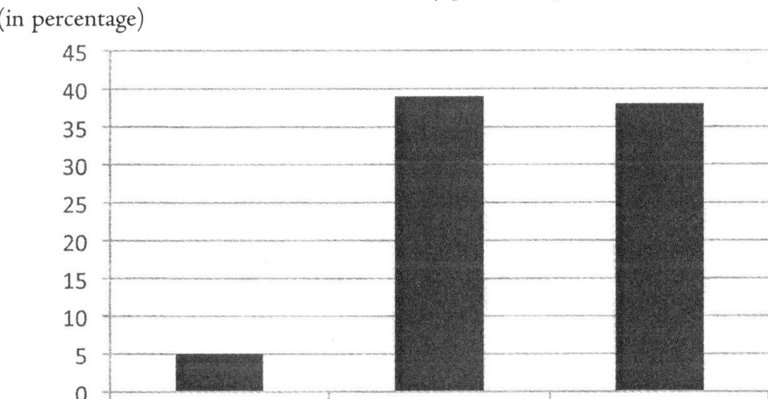

Source: PARAL study, graph I.7.2

above, sermon topics that criticized U.S. policies were generally avoided by preachers and disliked by listeners.

Despite the inevitable caricatures, however, the theology of liberation is not based exclusively on anti-imperialist notions. Its general premise intends to remove the doctrinal boundaries that previously separated "sacred history" from "human history." Such a separation of "what is Caesar's and what is God's" was a strategy to silence the Latin American church from criticism of social injustice. With the theology of liberation, however, governments are judged as morally legitimate to the degree that they utilize resources to reconcile class differences and reduce the suffering due to unjust economic structures. Church leaders who follow the theology of liberation are expected to make a "preferential option for the poor" and prioritize programs that benefit the poor over those that serve the rich as matters of governmental policies. Moreover, this theology is usually accompanied by a *pastoral de conjunto*, which is a process of dialogical planning among all persons involved in ministry.

If nothing more than the bare bones of these theologies are incorporated into the practice of Latino parishes and congregations, it seems safe to say that the traditional boundaries of politics and faith have been recast.[13] Within such a theological outlook, the use of static and partisan terms such as "Republican/Democrat" or "conservative/liberal" may be insufficient to capture the politicizing impact of nonpartisan theological ideology.[14]

Certainly, future research would do well to explore this theological nexus with the same vigor used to register the actual confluence of dogma and democracy for Latino Catholics.[15] For the time being, we have some data that suggest its current impact on Latino faith communities. As shown in Table 2.10, 59 percent of both RC and AOD heads knew about the theology

TABLE 2.10   Level of contact with theology, by denomination (in percentages)

	Theology of Liberation		*Pastoral de Conjunto*	
	Roman Catholic	All Other Denominations	Roman Catholic	All Other Denominations
Know About It	59	59	41	25
Took Training/ Studied It	21	22	11	6
Never Heard of It	12	14	37	59
No Answer	9	5	12	10

Source: PARAL study, Table II.3.10

of liberation. Not only was knowledge level both high and equal among both groups, but an additional one-fifth of respondents in both groups (RC, 21%; AOD, 22%) had taken training in or studied theology of liberation. In sum, even when we admit that "knowledge of" is not the same as "agreement with," four out of five of heads of Latino faith communities in both RC and AOD denominations recognize what is meant by the "theology of liberation." While less visible overall, *pastoral de conjunto* is familiar to about a third of the Latino AOD heads of faith communities and 40 percent of the Catholic ones.

In light of the visibility of the theology of liberation, it is not surprising that the Mexican American Cultural Center (MACC), in San Antonio, Texas, was recognized by so many of the heads of Latino faith communities. Founded in 1972 on the grounds of the archdiocesan seminary by the legendary Father Virgilio Elizondo, MACC pioneered in the postconciliar promotion of the theology of liberation as a guide for pastoral training in the United States. It was known to a majority of Roman Catholics (60%) and a significant number of those of all denominations (29%). Moreover, one in eight of Roman Catholic heads of faith communities (16%) were trained by, or studied at, MACC. When one considers that about half of Roman Catholic parishes do not have a majority of members of Mexican heritage, it likely that as many as one in three of parishes serving Mexican-heritage Catholics are led by someone trained at MACC.

Perhaps, rather than focus upon challenging the hypothesis of Verba and his associates about a better civic preparation for Hispanic Protestants over their Catholic peers, the PARAL Study can be mined for the differences in the theological mind-set of these two groups. First, the PARAL Study suggests that in actual practice, the preparation of Latino Catholics for civic participation is not very much different from that for Latino Protestants. The AOD members, however, *feel more strongly* about their politics. This tendency has been reported in many other surveys wherein intensity is almost always stronger among AOD than among Catholics.[16] Since the activities and functions are virtually the same for both groups, what appears here may be more connected to subjective perception than objective reality. Perhaps the measure of intensity—to consider something as "very important" rather than just "important"—is characteristic of the theology of Latinos of AOD.

The PARAL Study also shows a greater tendency for Hispanics of AOD to include partisan politics and civic electoral participation as directly connected to ministry. Doubtlessly, theology shapes this attitude, but imitation may also be a factor. In the community study conducted in Boston by Nancy López of the University of New Mexico for the PARAL Study, López reported a conscious effort from Latino Protestant and Evangelical leaders to imitate African American pastors. Let us posit here that for historical and social reasons, black pastors frequently represent their communities in politics and government. Rather than be constrained by an established tradition of political reticence, their political involvement is often expected, often leading them to simultaneously hold elected office. Moreover, there are fewer restrictions placed by their denominations upon such participation when compared to the absolute prohibition of canon law on Catholic clergy running for office.

Related to this more direct political attitude of Latino AOD is the tendency of Latino Catholics to consider action for social justice as nonpolitical. For example, Latino Catholics engaged in sponsoring a soup kitchen, referring the needy to a Catholic Charities agency for immigration, and sponsoring neighborhood housing construction may not consider such activities to be "political," but rather commitment to a social justice apostolate. The same Catholics may consider themselves to be acting politically only when writing petitions to end abortion. Latinos and Latinas of AOD, on the other hand, may see both social service delivery and letter writing to be "political" and thus report higher rates of civic participation.

While not detailed in the PARAL Study, pretesting of the NSLLPC questionnaire by Dr. Anneris Goris, the study's associate director, indicated that the different mind-sets could affect the perception of what was acceptable to religious commitment. Consider a question found in many Protestant-oriented surveys: *Have you experienced an increase in wealth since joining this congregation?* In assessing the pretesting, Dr. Goris reported that such a question was considered insulting by most Catholics. On the other hand, Latino Protestants objected to inquiries about civic practices like the *fiestas patronales* that depend upon statues, rosaries, or processions. Although such examples are derived from the connections of dogma to civic practice among Latinos and Latinas in faith communities, there are wider theoretic explorations of such linkages to dogma and practice.[17]

Finally, the PARAL Study shows that although relatively few in number, the differences between Latino Catholics and members of all other denominations are notable. The results from the 2001 survey become all the more provocative when cast against findings from surveys conducted in connection with the 2004 presidential election. Titled "The American Religious Landscape and Political Attitudes: A Baseline for 2004," this report by John C. Green for the Pew Forum on Religion & Public Life examined the response of Hispanic Catholics and Hispanic Protestants to several key political issues. The PARAL Study had

TABLE 2.11 Religious landscape and self-identified partisanship (in percentages)

Partisanship	Overall	Republican	Independent	Democrat
Denomination		38	20	42
Protestant				
Evangelical	26.3	56	17	27
Traditionalist	12.6	70	10	20
Centrist	10.8	47	22	31
Modernist	2.9	30	26	44
Mainline	16	44	18	38
Traditionalist	4.3	59	10	31
Centrist	7	46	21	33
Modernist	4.7	26	20	54
Latino Protestants	2.8	37	20	43
Black Protestants	9.6	11	18	71
Catholic	17.5	41	15	44
Traditionalist	4.4	57	13	30
Centrist	8.1	34	19	47
Modernist	5	38	11	51
Latino Catholic	4.5	15	24	61
Other Christian	2.7	42	36	22
Other Faiths	2.7	12	33	55
Jewish	19	21	11	68
Unaffiliated	16	27	30	43
Believers	5.3	28	37	35
Secular	7.5	29	27	44
Atheist, Agnostic	3.2	19	27	54

N=4000

Partisan leaners included with Republicans and Democrats; minor party affiliation included with independents.
Source: Fourth National Survey of Religion and Politics, Bliss Institute University of Akron, Table 1 (2004)

already separated Latinos and Latinas into separate religious groups, but this religious distinction in 2004 was an important innovation for a well-established political survey.

Table 2.11 is taken from this survey and discloses the important variations made by the survey's authors within the larger denominational groupings. Although most of the labels for the subcategories are self-explanatory, the reader is referred to the complete study for more complete definitions of each.

This survey identifies Latino Catholics as 4.5 percent of the voting public and Latino Protestants as 2.8 percent. While these proportions might be examined more closely from a methodological viewpoint, they suggest that in 2004, Latino Protestants formed a larger percentage of political partisans than their actual numbers in the population. Even though more Latino Protestants considered themselves Democrats (43%), they were more than twice as likely to identify with the Republican Party (37%) than Latino Catholics (15%). At 61 percent, however, Latino Catholics were more likely to vote for the Democratic Party candidate for president, John Kerry, than any other Catholic group. In fact, only Jews (68%) and Black Protestants (71%) were more loyal to the Democratic Party in the 2004 election.

Latino Catholics and Latino Protestants showed striking differences of opinion in two categories explored by Green: support for the Bush policies on government spending, and for tax cuts. Respondents were asked if the government should spend less, the same, or more on social programs. While Latino Protestant opinions about government spending approximated the responses of the entire sample in virtually all categories, Latino Catholics were notably different (see Table 2.12). They were the least likely of all U.S. religious groupings to want less government spending and the one to most desire an increase. Although the Latino Protestant category was new to the 2004 survey, the Latino Catholic category had been used previously. Green reported that the net change for Latino Catholics from 1996–2004 was also significant. There was a negative difference (−18%) of those wanting less government spending in 1996 when matched with opinion in 2004. Correspondingly, the number of Latino Catholics asking for higher government expenditures had grown by 23 percent in the same period. Thus, it can be suggested that since 2001, when the PARAL Study was conducted, and the 2004 election, the differences grew significantly between Latino Catholics and AOD, i.e., Latino Protestants, in support of governmental spending on behalf of social justice programs, even if both remain generally in favor of such programs.

TABLE 2.12 Support for government spending (in percentages)

	Overall	Latino Protestants	Latino Catholics
Less	26	24	16
Same	40	36	36
More	34	40	48

N= 4000

Source: Fourth National Survey of Religion and Politics, Bliss Institute University of Akron, Table 9 (2004)

TABLE 2.13 Foreign policy opinion, by religious group

Issue	All Voters	Latino Protestants	Black Protestants	Modernist Catholics	Latino Catholics
US Should Go It Alone	28	37	27	17	17
Pre-Emptive War Justified	62	70	55	50	43
Iraq War Justified	58	72	34	39	37
Approve Bush Foreign Policy	45	52	17	25	28
Bush Doctrine Score*	50	61	38	39	46

*Other issues calculated to arrive at Bush Doctrine Score: Favor Israel in Middle East and US Has Special Role in World
Source: Fourth National Survey of Religion and Politics, Bliss Institute University of Akron, Table 1 (2004)

Another important ideological tendency reported by Green concerned foreign policy and the U.S. role in world affairs. Table 2.13 shows that opinions about foreign policy in 2004 had wide divergences between Latino Protestants and Catholics in virtually every one of the survey's categories. Significantly, Latino Catholics were more faithful to papal teaching opposing preemptive war and the War in Iraq than any other Catholic groups. Seven out of ten of Latino Protestants, on the other hand, supported the morality of preemptive war and the War in Iraq. Differing significantly from Black Protestants (17%), more than half Latino Protestants (52%) supported the Bush foreign policy, while only about a quarter of Latino Catholics (28%) did so. Along with what were classified as modernist or liberal Catholics, Latino Catholics were not inclined (17%) to support an effort for the United States to "go it alone" without international support. More than double that number (37%) of Latino Protestants felt that the United States did not need international support.

Conclusion

Such findings in the 2004 survey confirm a increase of the differences in political perceptions initially recorded by the PARAL Study in 2001. While both RC Latinos and Latinas and those of all AOD engage in the actual delivery of services to address material needs, and are equally concerned for ministry, the ideological—or theological—basis for each group's political thinking seems to have diverged. By 2004, Latinos and Latinas of all other denominations reported different visions of political involvement for themselves and much higher levels of approval for the Bush foreign policy than Latino Catholics. In fact, Latino Catholics seem to have moved in an opposite direction, becoming more tied to the Democratic Party and closer to the progressive social vision of the popes. Moreover, Latino Catholics tend to agree on issues with so-called liberal Catholics more than with traditional or centrist Catholics. Such agreements are all the more remarkable since Latino and liberal Catholics tend to come from different social and economic classes, with Latino being among the poorest of the U.S. population and liberal Catholics the better-off in a suburban middle class.

In conclusion, we might return to the departure point of Verba et al.'s supposed better civic preparation of Latino Protestants over Latino Catholics. Even if this was more of a subjective disposition than an objective reality in 1995, it appears that the seed of difference has grown into an intriguing conundrum for today. The inclination of Latino Protestant leaders to join Evangelicals in political participation has received attention and faith-based initiative funding from Washington. The result is that a religious segment of the Latino population nationwide supported less government spending (except in aid to faith-based programs), preemptive war, and a messianic role for the United States in world affairs, independent of international support. The Catholic segment, on the other hand, was the most supportive for active government support to address social inequalities and the most loyal to a transnational and papal opposition to interventionist war.

Perhaps the differences initially reported by Verba et al. can be linked to what became in the Bush administration directly funded support for social services controlled by the faith-based congregations. But in such a case, the issue becomes whether support for the Bush policies constitutes "civic leadership" or just enlistment in a political strategy dictated from a party's establishment. If the latter is the case, then the substitution of Republican influence in Washington would likely explain why Latinos of AOD have drifted away from support for specifically Republican issues since 2008.

As reported by other scholars contributing to his volume, each of the faith communities have different patterns of political mobilization in accord with internalized cultural and theological norms. The PARAL Study and subsequent research on similar terrain offer a road map for how people of faith travel from religious convictions to political action. It appears these religious routes to the voting booths may be more important for understanding Latino attitudes than overtly political maneuvers imposed from outside. Religious people are, after all, religious.

Notes

1. Stevens-Arroyo et al. 2002–2003.
2. Verba et al. 1995.
3. For instance, with the Presbyterian Church, USA, we had 66 congregations, of which 3 turned out to have moved. To the valid questionnaires, 32 responded. From the United Methodist Church, we had 119 responses from the 263 Latino congregations we contacted. Because most Latinos and Latinas are Roman Catholic, we contacted a sample of 1,036 from just about 3,000 parishes serving Latinos and Latinas nationwide. From the Roman Catholics, we had 496 responses.
4. Although the Hispanic Homeland Ministry agency of the Southern Baptist Convention cooperated, as did a comparable office with the Pentecostal Church of God, the response rates from each (8 percent) was considered too low to be as reliable as the other denominations.
5. Stevens-Arroyo et al. 2002–2003.
6. Verba et al. 1995: 559.
7. These are mostly related to the bombing of the World Trade Center and subsequent anthrax scare regarding the mail. The response to this questionnaire, sent out the second week of September 2001, had a poorer response rate than the 47 percent obtained for the survey of heads of the faith community.
8. *FACT*, Figure 4.17: 48.
9. *FACT*, Figure 4.12: 46.
10. This question, original to the 2001 PARAL Study, was later used in a survey conducted for the *Wall Street Journal* in May 2010 by HART/McINTURFF (Study #10316). It read as follows: "When it comes to (READ ITEM), which party do you think would do a better job—the Democratic Party, the Republican Party, both about the same, or neither?"
11. The PARAL Study, Table III.6.3.
12. Berryman 1984; Maduro 1982.
13. Cadena 1989. For a debate over civil religion and its accessibility to Latino Catholics, see Bennett (1993) and Hammond (1989).
14. *See* Deck 1995.
15. Just such a discussion has begun; *see* Peña 1997. This is fitted into theological issues explored by Bevans (1992) and Schreiter (1985).
16. Robert Bellah et al. (1985) explore much of the Protestant ethic as it has evolved at the end of the twentieth century in the United States.
17. Luhmann 1984; Bourdieu 1980/1990.

Part II

Community Perspectives

Chapter **3**

Latinos, Religion, and Political Participation in New York City

Carlos Vargas-Ramos

As a group, Latinos in the United States have lower rates of political involvement than the population as a whole as well as subpopulations such as non-Hispanic whites and blacks.[1] Latinos are less likely to turn out to vote[2] as well as to contact elected officials, participate in informal community activity, contribute money to a political campaign or candidate, engage in general campaign work on the behalf of a political candidate or party, or sign petitions. Explanations to account for this lower level of political participation among Latinos have included the language barrier; the youthfulness of Hispanics; lower levels of educational attainment; lower income levels and free time to devote to political activities; lower levels of associational membership and involvement; lower levels of exposure to skill-acquiring and skill-exercising activities useful in politics; greater membership in the Catholic Church; lower levels of exposure to mobilizational appeals to political activities; lower rates of citizenship and naturalization; shorter length of residency in the country; and institutional barriers to participation (e.g., literacy requirements, poll taxes, and intimidation).[3]

Long-standing empirical models of political participation have provided consistent explanations for differential levels of political activity in the United States as well as in other countries. The standard socioeconomic status (SES) model[4] has shown empirically how higher levels of participation are strongly and positively correlated with higher levels of education, income, and occupation.[5] Refinements to the SES model highlight the roles that associational involvement and education play in fostering higher levels of participation.[6] Political activity, it is argued, is affected by the skills and the resources people have at their disposal, how psychologically in tune they may be to political affairs and the political system in which they live, and whether and how people are asked to participate and become involved in politics. Education and income afford individuals the resources of time, money, and *civic skills* (i.e., communication and organizational abilities) that are conducive to participation. Higher educational attainment has a positive impact on a person's earnings, and more formal education imbues an individual with language and communication skills. Moreover, higher earnings show a positive relationship with membership in social organizations, where individuals acquire, develop, and/or put into practice communication and organizational skills that become useful and are transferable to political activity.

From this socioeconomic status perspective, as Latinos exhibit lower income levels, lower educational attainment, higher rates of participation in the service economy and placement in unskilled or semiskilled occupations, higher unemployment rates, and higher rates of poverty than the country's majority population (i.e., non-Hispanic whites) and some other minority groups (e.g., Asian Americans),[7] they would be accordingly expected to engage in political activity at lower levels. Moreover, Latinos would be less likely to have the time, the money, or to have developed the communication and organizational skills that result in actual and effective political activity; and, as a group that is less likely to join social or civic organization as other ethnic or racial groups (i.e., African Americans), Latinos would also miss the opportunity to occupy an environment where they might be able to develop or enhance "civic skills" that overcome or compensate for their lower income or educational attainment.

Other models of political involvement have attributed the dwindling involvement in politics generally noted in the United States to the steady erosion of a sense of community generated and reinforced by associational activity.[8] The diminishing *social capital* (i.e., social networks, trustworthiness, and norms of reciprocity) across communities has had negative consequences on the nature of civic relations and civic responsibilities, which in turn have turned people away from one another and the political sphere. As people become socially disengaged, their involvement in politics declines as well. Further refinements to these "associationist" approaches accentuate the political features that membership in associations provides. However, more than the social capital that belonging to an association may afford, or the ability to develop, put into practice, or sharpen politically relevant organizational and associational skills, it is the *political capital* that gives a boost to an individual's involvement in politics particularly in "poor urban ethnic communities."[9]

Religion and Participation

Particularly provocative has been the explanation that Latinos may exhibit lower levels as a result of their proportionally broader confession in the Catholic Church. The civic voluntarism (CVM) model, expounded by Sidney Verba, Kay Lehman Schlozman, and Henry Brady,[10] stresses the role of belonging to a religious denomination and mobilization for political action. The type of association (i.e., denomination) matters as well. Thus, whereas African Americans were able to develop politically relevant skills in the purportedly more participatory and socially active congregation-based Protestant churches, Latinos, who are overwhelmingly Catholic, were less likely to develop organizational and communication skills in the Church, due to its more hierarchical and institutionalized structures. Thus, Catholics generally, and Catholic Latinos specifically, are expected to participate at lower rates than non-Catholics.

The argument proposed by Verba and his colleagues is not one that highlights the cultural aspects of religion and their effect on participation. Their focus is rather on the extent to which belonging to communities of faith, as particular types of social institutions, may potentially exert an effect on how politically relevant resources, particularly civic skills, are acquired or developed and as locations that serve to facilitate political mobilization and engagement. As a result, they examine how belonging to a particular faith, attending religious services, participating in nonservice-related activities in the religious congregation and contributing to the economic sustenance of these organizations relate to the level of communication and organization skills, time, and money people have. The importance of these religious institutions for political activity rests on how they come to supply an individual with resources, which, while not necessarily oriented to political activity, are fungible and therefore pertinent for political activity, particularly for those individuals who are at a deficit of politically relevant resources (e.g., income and education) given how resources are distributed in a society such as that of the United States. In a resource rich, but inequitable society, particular social groups (e.g., women, Latinos, blacks) are at a disadvantage in relation to non-Hispanic whites males.

As robust as these arguments and the empirical findings by Verba et al. are,[11] more recent research on religion and Latino voting has challenged these results.[12] Jones-Correa and Leal have in fact found that being Catholic does not make Latinos (and even Anglos) less likely to vote, but on the contrary more likely to vote in congressional and school board elections. The content of this chapter and others in this volume contribute to a body of literature that examines more closely and more subtly the impact that religion may have on civic involvement.

Elsewhere,[13] I have tested the factors that have been highlighted by the socioeconomic status model,[14] its refinement—the civic voluntarism model[15]—as well as postulates of akin "associationist" models, such as those that rely on social capital explanations[16] and its refinement—the political capital model.[17] Therefore, in the rest of this chapter, I will focus more closely on the impact that church affiliation, and particularly membership in the Catholic Church, has on political participation among New York City residents. I rely on data collected in a survey conducted in New York City in 1997 by the Barnard/Columbia Center for Urban Research and Policy: the NYC Participation Survey.[18]

Why limit the focus of the analysis to a locality, even a large one as New York is, when there are datasets that are national in scope that can account for the behavior of people throughout the country? The Citizen Participation Study, which provided the data to test the civic voluntarism model developed by Verba et al.,[19] is undoubtedly a major accomplishment in political science quantitative research. It provided a wealth of cross-sectional data from an enormous group of respondents, which allowed for a very sophisticated multivariate analysis of factors and processes that affect the political involvement of individuals. However, the acts individuals engage in to influence the public decision-making process involved in governance is seldom, if ever, a national endeavor in federal systems such as the United States. The large number of overlapping jurisdictions in which residents of the United States find themselves in creates numerous political arenas in which those individuals may become involved. But there is no national jurisdiction as such. Even the election of the president is institutionally circumscribed to the level of the state by the Electoral College. At best, the largest political jurisdictions in which U.S. residents tend to participate are the states, from which both the president and U.S. senators are elected. Even when lobbying Congress or agencies of the federal government, which may involve the concerted effort of people from different states, the ultimate pressure plays out at election time when it is the registered voters of a Congressional district or a state who decide the fate of the elected federal officials. Thus, what takes place in lower jurisdictions, from school or zoning districts, to local county or state legislatures, may be determined by factors that differ from those that appear salient at the *national* level.

Moreover, context matters. Since V.O. Key's path-breaking study of politics in the U.S. South, quantitative studies of political behavior at the national level have controlled for geographical region as an important explanatory factor.[20] More recent research has highlighted the independent role that local context or environment has on political participation.[21] By limiting the focus of analysis to a locality, one is able to control for a variety of contextual factors that may impact participation at a national level and may not be captured even by a sophisticated model. Furthermore, given the robustness of the civic voluntarism model and its findings nationwide, or any other explanatory model with general applicability, one would expect these results to be found elsewhere, even in smaller jurisdictions such as a city. Thus, the findings that Catholic tend to have lower levels of political participation than Protestants and that Latinos are particularly susceptible to this denominational effect on their participation should be manifest not just in a nationwide representative survey but one localized in New York City as well.

Latino Political Participation in New York City: A Descriptive Analysis

The New York City Participation Survey was conducted in the late summer of 1997, and it consisted of a sample of 1,480 people, 18 years of age or older, who resided in any of the five boroughs of the city.[22] The sample was 26 percent non-Hispanic white, 24 percent non-Hispanic black, 11 percent Puerto Rican, 19 percent of other Latinos, and 20 percent of other backgrounds (e.g., Asians, other race). Table 3.1 shows the percentage of respondents by racial/ethnic category that engaged in different forms of political activity.

According to the survey, voting is the most common form of participation for all groups in New York City, a finding consistent with other research. It is in registering to vote that the lower rates of citizenship and naturalization among Latinos, other than Puerto Ricans, distinguish them from other groups in New York. Whereas non-Puerto Rican Latino respondents informed that they were citizens at a rate of 69 percent, for non-Hispanic blacks the proportion was 83 percent and for non-Hispanic whites, 92 percent.[23] As a result, the rate of voter registration for other Latinos stood at 57 percent compared to 81 percent for Puerto Ricans and 73 percent for all respondents. Consequently, the proportion of other Latinos that voted for president in the 1996 elections was 48 percent, compared to 61 percent for Puerto Ricans, 64 percent for non-Hispanic blacks, and 79 percent for non-Hispanic whites.[24]

After voting, contacting elected officials was the second most common political activity in which respondents engaged. About a quarter of

TABLE 3.1 Political activity in New York City by ethnicity (in percentages)

Activity	All Respondents	Non-Hispanic Whites	Non-Hispanic Blacks	Puerto Ricans	Other Latinos
Registered to Vote***	73	81	75	81	57
Voted (for President in 1996)***	65	79	64	61	48
Campaign Work	8	6	10	7	11
Campaign Contributions	17	20	16	13	16
Political Fundraising	11	10	14	11	11
Attended Political Rallies*	14	10	18	12	16
Attended Political Meeting*	15	11	19	17	15
Contact Elected Official**	24	30	25	18	19
Protest	13	10	17	13	13

*p ≤ 0.1; **p ≤ .05; ***p ≤ .01
Source: Barnard/Columbia Center for Urban Research and Policy, 1997

respondents contacted a government official about a problem or need during the previous year. This rate was two-thirds lower than the rate of voting for all respondents. Among Latinos, the rate of contact was even lower, with less than a fifth of Latinos turning to their elected officials to address their concerns. Non-Hispanic blacks make contacts at a higher rate (six percentage points) than Latinos, and non-Hispanic whites contact at rates higher than any other group in New York City (11% higher than Latinos; 5% higher than non-Hispanic blacks)—a statistically significant finding. This implies that non-Hispanics (black and white) convey more information about their wants and needs to elected officials than Latinos, and that whites also have an advantage over blacks on this count.

For all respondents, the third most common political activity was contributing money to a political campaign or candidate, at 17 percent.[25] However, for Latinos, the third most common political activity were other forms of electoral politics: in the case of Puerto Ricans, this was attending a political meeting, such as a city council or board of education hearings; for other Latinos, this was attending political rallies. Non-Hispanic blacks were the New Yorkers most likely to attend such a political meeting (19%), followed by Puerto Ricans (17%) and then other Latinos (15%)—a statistically significant finding. Those attending political rallies were more likely to be non-Hispanic blacks (18%), followed by other Latinos (16%) and then Puerto Ricans (12%)—also statistically significant differences. Non-Hispanic whites were the least likely to attend these two types of electoral activities as well as volunteer in political campaigns, although the differences in proportions for the latter activity are not statistically significant.[26] Other activities for which the differences were not statistically significant were participating in a protest or political demonstrations, making campaign contributions, and attending fundraisers for a political campaign or candidate.

Political participation is also gauged by measuring the total number of activities an individual undertakes. To this end, I constructed three indices of participation: one that measured overall political participation, and two that measured separately the most common forms of participation—voting and contacting.[27] For overall participation, of a maximum 11 political activities an individual could engage in, the average participation was in 2.4 activities (with a standard deviation of 2.3 activities). For non-Hispanic whites, the average participation was 2.7 activities (sd = 2.1); for non-Hispanic blacks, 2.5 (sd = 2.4); for Puerto Ricans, 2.3 (sd = 2.2); and for Latinos, other than Puerto Ricans, 2.1 (sd = 2.7). This means that Puerto Ricans, other Latinos, and non-Hispanic blacks participate in fewer political activities than non-Hispanic whites, at rates of 15 percent, 22 percent, and 7 percent lower, respectively. This lower participation in political activity by Latinos and non-Hispanic blacks is also evident in the indices of voting participation and contacting government officials. Puerto Ricans and non-Hispanic blacks turn out to vote at a rate that is 14 percent lower; for other Latinos the rate is more than 36 percent lower than non-Hispanic whites. Non-Hispanic blacks make contacts at a rate that is 29 percent lower than non-Hispanic whites; for other Latinos the rate is 32 percent lower and for Puerto Ricans, 40 percent lower.[28]

What can be concluded from these data is that non-Hispanic whites have an edge over other groups in New York City insofar as political participation is concerned. This advantage is notable in the most extended forms of political engagement: voting and contacting. This advantage in communicating political preferences (i.e., contacting) and in exerting political pressure (i.e., voting) has the potential to translate into higher degrees of influence for non-Hispanic whites in the selection of government officials and policy outcomes than there is for others,[29] particularly Latinos. And while the political dynamics need not result in zero-sum games between racial and/or ethnic groups, differing degrees of incorporation into the networks of government tend to result in disproportionate allocations of government resources to different groups in the polity.[30]

Overall, Puerto Ricans lagged behind other groups in New York City, including other Latinos in contacting elected officials, consistent with previous findings.[31] They outperformed non-Hispanic whites in attending political rallies and meetings, a contrast to findings elsewhere,[32] but trailed non-Hispanic blacks in both activities. Finally, Puerto Ricans were out-voted by both non-Hispanic blacks and whites. Thus, the *voice* that Puerto Ricans may have relative to other groups in the city is not silent, but it is dampened. The activities in which Puerto Ricans, and other Latinos, engage in to communicate preferences to government officials may convey sufficient information to them, but may bring little pressure to bear on those officials, although Puerto Ricans exert more pressure politically than other Latinos because of their higher turnout rate.

Latino Political Participation in New York City: A Bivariate Analysis

The remainder of the analysis will concentrate on the role that religious identification plays in influencing political behavior in this process of giving voice (or dampening those voices) to different ethnoracial groups in New York City's political system. The analysis will proceed in three stages. I will first test bivariately for the relevance of factors on political participation variables on the larger survey sample, and then test bivariately the same factors on the political participation variable for each of two subsamples: one made up of all Latinos and another including Puerto Ricans exclusively.

Table 3.2 shows the strength of the relationship, as measured by correlation coefficients, between sociodemographic, socioeconomic, institutional, and psychological variables described above and three measures of political participation—overall political participation, voting, and contacting elected officials—for the entire sample. With a few exceptions, the coefficients indicate a positive association between the variables.

One of those exceptions is for those respondents who identify as Catholic. The correlation with overall participation is negative, albeit weak.[33] That is, being Catholic is weakly (but statistically significantly) associated with lower overall participation. The variables with the most robust correlation with overall participation are those that highlight an associational affiliation (e.g., membership in organizations, in unions, etc.), particularly those that are political in nature (e.g., membership in politically active organizations). Socioeconomic variables (e.g., income, education) and psychological engagement variables (e.g., interest in politics, political discussion) also have strong (and positive) correlations with overall participation. These correlation patterns are

TABLE 3.2 Pearson's correlation coefficients for politically relevant variables (Citywide sample)

	Overall Participation	Voting	Contacting
Age	.239**	.394**	.098**
Education	.083**	.151**	.108**
Income	.243**	.142**	.211**
Employment Status	.136**	.026	.016
Gender (Female)	.003	.034	.025
Non-Hispanic White	.085**	.196**	.128**
Non-Hispanic Black	.025	.007	−.038
Latino	−.092**	−.226**	−.051
Puerto Rican	−.033	.007	−.061*
Length of Time in City	.231**	.458**	.102**
Length of Time at Address	.193**	.343**	.116**
Homeowner	.163**	.192**	.161**
Citizenship	.341**	.604**	179**
Catholic	−.081**	−.012	−.064*
Membership in . . .			
Labor Union	.228**	.18**	157**
Organization (general)	.52**	.213**	.389**
Non-Political Organization	.248**	.106	.2*
Politically Active Organization	.493**	.169**	.327**
Mobilized	.237**	.223**	.168**
Interest in Politics	.37**	.336**	.25**
Political Efficacy	.127**	.139**	.093**
Political Discussion	.33**	.139**	.222**
Family Members Usually Vote	.262**	.359**	.127**
Friends Usually Vote	.191**	.272**	.111**
Co-Workers Usually Vote	.187**	.254**	.104**

*p ≤ 0.1; **p ≤ .05; ***p ≤ .01
Source: Barnard/Columbia Center for Urban Research and Policy, 1997

replicated when the political activity of interest is contacting elected officials. Identifying as Catholic also has a negative and weak (but statistically significant) correlation with contacting officials.[34] On the other hand, measures of associational affiliation and, to a lesser extent, those gauging socioeconomic

status and psychological engagement are those with the strongest (and positive) association with contacting elected officials.

For the voting measure, however, the pattern shifts somewhat. Being
Catholic has no statistically significant association with voting; whereas in
New York City, a city with a large nonnative population, citizenship has the
strongest effect on voting. Ethnicity and race also have significant correlation
with voting, so that being non-Hispanic white is positively correlated with
exercising the franchise, while being Latino actually reflects a turning away
from the voting booth.

I now turn to replicate the bivariate analyses on two smaller samples. It
would be expected to note the same effects in the smaller Latino subsamples
as in the overall citywide sample. Table 3.3 shows the Pearson's correlation
results for both Latinos (including Puerto Ricans) and for Puerto Ricans
exclusively. The pattern that emerged in the citywide sample is by and large
repeated in both subsamples. The "associationist" variables have strong correlations with overall participation and contacting, but those that are strictly
political in focus have more robust associations.

The role of religion in political life, with Verba and colleagues indicating
the depressing effect that being Catholic has on political involvement among
Latinos,[35] is borne out in this bivariate analysis of the larger Latino subsample.
Being Catholic is associated negatively with overall participation and contacting among Latinos. The association is moderately weak for overall participation[36] and contacting,[37] but statistically significant. As with the larger
sample, being a Catholic Latino is not associated with voting, whether negatively or positively. Among Puerto Ricans, as an exception to the findings in
the citywide sample and the all-inclusive Latino subsample, the association
between identifying as Catholic and participation (overall participation and
contacting) is positive, although the association is not statistically significant.
However, there is a moderate positive correlation between voting and identifying as Catholic among this particular subgroup of Latinos.[38] These unexpected
findings for Puerto Ricans may be the result of the largely nominal character of
Catholicism among Puerto Ricans. The lesser the influence of institutionalized
Catholicism on Puerto Ricans may result in a smaller, if any, depressing influence on political participation. These results are thusly an interesting contrast
to those highlighted in the literature for all Latinos.

But is it, in fact, the case that the Puerto Ricans are only nominally Catholic
or less institutionalized in the Catholic Church in relation with others in New
York City? Table 3.4 shows the responses to a religious preference question.
Most respondents to the survey identified as Catholics (42%), followed by
those who stated they had no religious preference (14%) and those who

TABLE 3.3 Pearson's correlation coefficients for politically relevant variables (Latino and Puerto Rican samples)

	Latinos (including Puerto Ricans)			Puerto Ricans		
	Overall Participation	Voting	Contacting	Overall Participation	Voting	Contacting
Age	.226**	.356**	.063	.223**	.399**	.049
Education	−.042	.096	.015	.221*	.32	.269**
Income	.397**	.188**	.305**	.262**	.173*	.259**
Employment Status	.103*	−.01	.087	.141	.189*	.065
Gender (Female)	.033	.017	.039	.003	−.07	0.026
Length of Time in City	.027	.372**	−.012	.241**	.396**	.151
Length of Time at Address	.128**	.265**	0.075	.255**	.293**	.158*
Homeowner	.109*	.094	.128**	.231**	.134	.162*
Citizenship	.323**	.609**	195**	.01	.229**	.01
Catholic	−.142**	.025	−.114*	.1	.207**	.13
Membership in . . .						
Labor Union	.355**	.246**	.265**	.285**	.282**	.208**
Organization (general)	.631**	.222**	.487**	.421**	.19**	.432**
Non-Political Organizatiom	.221**	.023	.142*	.073	.002	.116
Politically Active Organization	.646**	.225**	.453**	.394**	.208*	.305**
Mobilized	.346**	.22**	.239**	.223	.194*	.186*

(*Continued*)

TABLE 3.3   (CONTINUED)

	Latinos (including Puerto Ricans)			Puerto Ricans		
	Overall Participation	Voting	Contacting	Overall Participation	Voting	Contacting
Interest in Politics	.349**	.283**	.242**	23**	.184*	.138
Political Efficacy	.018	.089	.026	.129	.148	.118
Political Discussion	.429**	191**	.309**	.279**	.08	.216**
Family Members Usually Vote	.248**	.31**	144**	.155	.258**	.172*
Friends Usually Vote	.168**	.208**	.146**	.131	.168	.176*
Co-Workers Usually Vote	.22**	.236**	.161**	.217*	.229**	.134

*p ≤ 0.1; **p ≤ .05; ***p ≤ .01
Source: Barnard/Columbia Center for Urban Research and Policy, 1997

TABLE 3.4   Religious preference in New York City by ethnicity (in percentages)

Denomination	All Respondents	Non-Hispanic Whites	Non-Hispanic Blacks	Puerto Ricans	Other Latinos
Protestant	13.9	10.4	25.4	7.2	8.4
Catholic	42.4	42.5	16.8	63.5	62.2
Jewish	8.1	23.2	0.3	1.8	0.8
Muslim	1.7	0.5	3	2.4	1.2
Other	18.9	7.6	38.9	10.8	14.3
No Religion	14.3	15	15	13.8	12.7

Pearson's Chi-Square score= 402.57; p≤ .01
Source: Barnard/Columbia Center for Urban Research and Policy, 1997

TABLE 3.4   (cont.) Religious preference in New York City by Latino origin (in percentages)

Denomination	Dominican	Central American	South American	Mexican	Cuban	Other
Protestant	4	4.1	6.4	0	0	18.3
Catholic	73.3	51	57.4	69.2	81.8	31.3
Jewish	0	2	0	0	0	9.6
Muslim	0	0	0	0	0	1.7
Other	9.3	28.6	21.3	15.4	9.1	21.6
No Religion	13.3	12.2	14.9	15.4	9.1	16.8

Pearson's Chi-Square score= 146.66; p ≤ .01
Source: Barnard/Columbia Center for Urban Research and Policy, 1997

identified as Protestants (14%). Jews represented 8 percent of the sample, and Muslims 2 percent. Those who offered other religious preference (e.g., Jehovah's Witness, Christian Scientist, Hindu, Christian, Buddhist, etc.) represented in the aggregate 19 percent of the sample. Table 3.4 also shows that the vast majority of Puerto Ricans and other Latinos was Catholic, and in proportions greater than others in the New York City.

A measure of integration and institutionalization within a community of faith is the frequency with which people attend religious services. Table 3.5a shows how frequently different groups in New York City attended religious services. Most respondents attended religious services every week (27%) followed by those who attended services a few times a year (27%). Eighteen percent attended once or twice a month, while 13 percent attended several times a week. Nine percent never attended services, while 6 percent attended almost every week.

Puerto Ricans and other Latinos, along with non-Hispanic blacks, are overrepresented among those who attended weekly or more than once a week. These respondents are evenly represented among those only attended a few times a year. Puerto Ricans are also evenly represented among those who never attended services as well as among those who attended once or twice a month. But denominational differences within these groups may result in disparities in their attendance to religious services with the potential that these disparities underscore different rates of integration and institutionalization in

TABLE 3.5A Attendance to religious services in New York City by ethnicity (in percentages)

	All Respondents	Non-Hispanic Whites	Non-Hispanic Blacks	Puerto Ricans	Other Latinos
Several Times a Week	12.5	7.6	13.4	14.6	17.1
Every Week	27	22.3	31	28.5	27.6
Almost Every Week	6.3	5.7	6	4.9	8.3
Once or Twice A Month	18	14.6	21.1	18.8	18.4
A Few Times A Year	26.7	36.6	22.5	22.2	20.7
Never	9	12.7	5.6	9.7	7.4

Source: Barnard/Columbia Center for Urban Research and Policy, 1997 Pearson's Chi-Square score= 49.308***
*p ≤ 0.1; **p ≤ .05; ***p ≤ .01

TABLE 3.5A (cont.) Attendance to religious services in New York City by Latino origin (in percentages)

	Dominican	Central American	South American	Mexican	Cuban	Other
Several Times a Week	12.3	11.6	5	9.1	10	12.6
Every Week	35.4	30.2	37.5	27.3	20	24.2
Almost Every Week	12.3	4.7	5	0	10	6.3
Once or Twice A Month	20	18.6	22.5	36.4	20	17.5
A Few Times A Year	15.4	27.9	25	9.1	30	28.1
Never	3.1	7	5	18.2	10	10.8

Source: Barnard/Columbia Center for Urban Research and Policy, 1997

TABLE 3.5B Attendance to religious services in New York City by ethnicity and denomination (in percentages)

Ethnicity Denomination	All Respondents[a]		Puerto Ricans[b]		Non-Puerto Rican Latinos[c]	
	RC	AOD	RC	AOD	RC	AOD
Several Times a Week	7	18	5	43	8	39
Every Week	33	21	30	24	33	16
Almost Every Week	7	6	7	0	9	7
Once or Twice A Month	21	16	21	14	24	7
A Few Times A Year	24	29	26	11	22	16
Never	8	10	10	5	4	15

[a]Pearson's Chi-Square = 47.64***
[b]Pearson's Chi-Square = 35.59***
[c]Pearson's Chi-Square = 45.07*
Source: Barnard/Columbia Center for Urban Research and Policy, 1997
*p ≤ 0.1; **p ≤ .05; ***p ≤ .01

the communities of faith. By and large, the pattern of attendance to religious services among Catholics of different ethnic origins does not seem to vary much (see Table 3.5b). Therefore, the hypothesis that Puerto Ricans, who tend to be largely Catholic, have different participation patterns from other Catholics because they may be only nominally Catholic is questioned. Given these bivariate results, why then do we observe differing rates of political participation among Catholics, especially among Catholic Latinos?

Moreover, there are notably large differences in the pattern of attending religious services between Catholics and members of other religious denominations within the different ethnic groups. Indeed, the frequency of attending religious services does have a positive impact on several measures of political participation, but not for all political activities or ethnic groups. Correlation coefficients show that the more frequent the attendance to religious services is for respondents of the citywide survey, the greater their overall political involvement and their likelihood to contact elected officials, even if slightly.[39] However, attendance to services shows no significant association with voting. This pattern is also evident among Latinos as a group,[40] but not among Puerto Ricans.[41]

Latino Political Participation in New York City: A Multivariate Analysis

These bivariate analyses have highlighted the impact that individual participatory factors may have on the three measures of participation presented.

However, to ascertain the *independent* effect that each variable may have on participation a multivariate analysis is needed. Bivariate associations may mask the impact that other underlying factors may have on variables. For instance, the length of time a person has lived in the community may operate positively on voting as a result of the age of the respondent, and vice versa. The older one is, the more likely it is for that person to turn out to vote. But the older a person is, the more likely it is that such a person has lived in his or her community longer than a younger person. Thus, age as well as other hypothesized participatory variables need to be included in a model in order to control for their effects on each other and on the dependent variable. Given these intervening factors, a multivariate analysis will allow us to control for intervening effects and isolate independent impacts on the dependent variable.

Ordinary–least–square regression models were run separately for the citywide sample and the subsamples of all Latinos and Puerto Ricans. As I have conducted a comprehensive analysis of the impact of independent variables on political participation elsewhere,[42] the focus below will be exclusively on the impact of being Catholic. Table 3.6 shows the unstandardized coefficients of the regression's results for the citywide sample.[43] Once a host of theoretically and empirically relevant independent variables have been taken into account in a model that explains 40 percent of the variance in overall participation, it is observed that being Catholic has no statistically significant impact on participation. This is the case for the larger measure of participation (overall participation) as well as for voting and contacting. These findings hold for overall participation and contacting officials while controlling for attendance to religious services.[44] Yet Catholics turn out to vote more often even when holding attendance to services constant.[45]

For the Latino subsample, results are similar in the overall participation model as well as in the contacting model: being Catholic has no statistical impact on participation (see Table 3.7). However, on the voting measure, and unlike the results in the citywide sample, being Catholic does have an impact, and it is a positive. While this positive effect of being Catholic on voting is at a lower level of statistical significance, it counters what was expected by the civic voluntarism model. Moreover, the effect of being Catholic holds while holding constant attendance to religious services.[46]

Among Puerto Ricans, the impact that being Catholic has on political participation, measured along three models for three populations in the same locale, is very consistent. Contrary to what Verba, Schlozman, and Brady have postulated, being Catholic does not have a negative effect on participation (see Table 3.7), even when controlling for attendance to religious services.[47] In fact, being Catholic in New York City does not have any effect on participation

TABLE 3.6 Political participation (OLS regression: Citywide sample) (Unstandardized regression coefficients; standard error in parenthesis)

	Overall Participation	Voting	Contacting
Constant	−3.441** (1.055)	−1.965** (.422)	−.534 (.415)
Age	.013 (.012)	.019** (.005)	.0023 (.005)
Education	.034 (.043)	.045** (.017)	.0033 (.017)
Income	.022 (.069)	−.00312 (.028)	.014 (.027)
Gender (Female)	−.0596 (.286)	.09 (.114)	.11 (.112)
Catholic	−.158 (.302)	.152 (.121)	−.138 (.119)
Latino (Other than Puerto Rican)	.248 (.446)	−.310 (.178)	.0083 (.175)
Puerto Rican	.549 (.522)	.244 (.209)	.039 (.205)
Non-Hispanic Black	.342 (.356)	.152 (.142)	−.033 (.14)
Length of Time at Address	.056 (.089)	.073* (.035)	.008 (.035)
Homeownership	.16 (.3)	.027 (.12)	.149 (.118)
Citizenship	1.578* (.468)	1.75** (.187)	.284 (.184)
Membership in Labor Union	.272 (.297)	.064 (.119)	.123 (.117)
Membership in Non-Political Org.	519** (.129)	.048 (.051)	.151** (.051)
Membership in Politically Active Org.	.492** (.1)	.068 (.04)	.104** (.039)
Mobilized	.16 (.32)	−.128 (.128)	.251* (.126)
Interest in Politics	471** (.173)	.104 (.069)	.122 (.068)
Political Efficacy	.153** (.048)	.022 (.019)	.026 (.019)
Political Discussion	.028 (.051)	−.0108 (.02)	−.0083 (.02)
Family Members Usually Vote	.465 (.354)	.220 (.142)	−.101 (.139)
Friends Usually Vote	−.331 (.411)	−.0491 (.164)	−.0052 (.161)
Co-Workers Members Usually Vote	−.318 (.571)	.041 (.228)	−.012 (.224)
R^2	0.454	0.577	0.256
Adjusted R^2	0.399	0.534	0.181
F ratio	8.24**	13.521**	3.415**
Degrees of Freedom	229	229	229

*p≤ 0.1; **p≤ .05; ***p≤ .01

TABLE 3.7 Political participation (OLS regression: Latino and Puerto Rican samples) (Unstandardized regression coefficients; standard error in parenthesis)

	Latinos (including Puerto Ricans)			Puerto Ricans		
	Overall Participation	Voting	Contacting	Overall Participation	Voting	Contacting
Constant	−5.974** (1.951)	−2.405*** (.697)	−1.779*** (.601)	−11.525* (5.52)	−1.307 (1.524)	−3.18** (1.374)
Age	.034 (.024)	.026*** (.008)	.0016 (.007)	−a (.053)	.027* (.015)	.0068 (.013)
Education	.089 (.074)	.034 (.026)	.047** (.023)	.297* (.167)	−a (.046)	.138*** (.042)
Income	.037 (.145)	−.0354 (.052)	.079* (.045)	.047 (.289)	.041 (.08)	.028 (.072)
Gender (Female)	.408 (.553)	.065 (.197)	.288* (.17)	1.456 (1.121)	−.428 (.344)	.228 (.301)
Catholic	−.34 (.545)	.337* (.195)	−a (.168)	1.179 (1.194)	.091 (.33)	.091 (.297)
Length of Time at Address	.085 (.168)	a (.06)	−a (.052)	.284 (.324)	−a (.089)	.32 (.913)
Homeownership	−.212 (.617)	−.192 (.22)	.067 (.19)	3.373* (1.874)	−.338 (.517)	−.145 (.466)
Citizenship	2.036** (.808)	2.18*** (.288)	.521** (.249)	n.a.	n.a.	n.a.
Membership in Labor Union	.325 (.539)	.176 (.192)	.29* (.166)	.69 (1.025)	.067 (.283)	.162 (.255)
Membership in Non-Political Org.	.25 (.22)	.065 (.079)	.173** (.068)	−a (.445)	−a (.123)	.23* (.111)
Membership in Politically Active Org.	.563*** (.206)	.085 (.074)	.1 (.064)	.449 (.484)	.112 (.134)	−a (.12)
Mobilized	.181 (.685)	.05 (.245)	−a (.211)	.897 (1.322)	.468 (.365)	−.111 (.329)
Interest in Politics	.378 (.301)	309*** (.107)	.112 (.093)	.008 (.673)	.308 (.186)	−.15 (.168)

TABLE 3.7   (CONTINUED)

	Latinos (including Puerto Ricans)			Puerto Ricans		
	Overall Participation	Voting	Contacting	Overall Participation	Voting	Contacting
Political Efficacy	.148* (.082)	.021 (.029)	.0065 (.025)	.078 (.223)	.102 (.062)	.0052 (.055)
Political Discussion	.018 (.107)	−.112** (.038)	−a (.033)	.096 (.213)	−.135** (.059)	.035 (.053)
Family Members Usually Vote	a (.568)	.199 (.203)	−.101 (.175)	.621 (1.346)	.104 (.372)	.027 (.335)
Friends Usually Vote	.272 (.83)	.0063 (.296)	.525** (.256)	.609 (1.562)	−.114 (.431)	.575 (.389)
Co-Workers Usually Vote	1.105 (1.147)	.756* (.41)	−a (.353)	−.419 (2.31)	1.221* (.638)	−.268 (.575)
R^2	.42	.655	.381	.478	.696	.593
Adjusted R^2	.275	.569	.226	.031	.435	.244
F ratio	2.9***	7.596***	2.459***	1.070	2.671**	1.699
Degrees of Freedom	90	90	90	39	39	39

*p ≤ 0.1; **p ≤ .05; ***p ≤ .01, a<.001

whatsoever, whether it is among a representative sample of city residents or smaller subsamples. When it does, as in the case for voting among Latinos, it is in a positive manner.

I nevertheless caution that the civic voluntarism model that Verba and his colleagues propose relies crucially on the impact of organizational membership on the development of skills that are useful politically. The present analysis has not tested this component. The New York City Participation Survey did not collect data on politically relevant skills, their acquisition, and exercise. To make inferences without actual evidence about the degree to which politically relevant skills may be acquired through active participation in communities of faith may lead to spurious conclusions. The hypotheses on the acquisition of skills and their exercise in civic associations need to be engaged head on. Unfortunately, with the tools I have had available, this remains a pending matter. Therefore, I must remain agnostic about the civic skills-building opportunities that communities of faith provide individuals and their differential impact on different believers and practitioners in New York City.

Yet, these findings challenge the overall conclusions of Verba et al. The findings may not trace the mechanism through which religious affiliation may operate in New York City. Nevertheless, they are consistent with those found in other analyses on the impact of religion on Latino political participation at the national level.[48] Yet while Jones-Correa and Leal find that attendance to religious services has an independent impact on several measures of political participation, this is not the case in New York City, whether it is for New Yorkers as a whole or Latinos more specifically. Jones-Correa and Leal reject that the difference in participation between Latinos and non-Hispanic whites is based simply on the acquisition of politically relevant civic skills, but rather argue that faith communities serve as another type of voluntary association in their promotion of political involvement particularly in voting.

The robust impact of voluntary associations, both political and nonpolitical, on political involvement is certainly evident in the findings presented in this chapter. But in reaching their conclusion, Jones-Correa and Leal relied on statistical controls that included two measures of religious involvement besides denominational affiliation and frequency of attendance to services. They also included in their analysis two additional measures of religiosity: the centrality of religion in their lives and whether they had a personal religious experience (e.g., born-again). Jones-Correa and Leal report that these two additional measures did not have an independent impact on political participation, leading them to reject the *intensity* of religiosity as a possible explanation in the difference in participation between Catholics and non-Catholics Latinos.[49]

Including these additional variables on religiosity in the analyses contributed additional controls, which likely highlighted the relevance of attendance to religious services. These additional measures were not available in the New York City Participation Study and therefore were not included in the present analysis. Yet, as Stevens-Arroyo argues in the preceding chapter, it may not be the intensity of the religious fervor Catholics and non-Catholics may feel what impacts their politics, but rather the intensity with which Catholics and non-Catholics hold their *political* convictions what may lead them to different rates of political participation.

Moreover, the additional measures of religiosity in Jones-Correa and Leal's study may not have had a significant impact on political participation because those measures were individually based rather than being measures of a communal experience. It may not be how deeply one's individual faith may be, but how such faith may be put into practice not simply in *ekklesia* (i.e., assemblies or congregations) but rather in *communities* of faith where solidarity and cooperation is fostered and practiced. The intensity of religiosity and its impact on political engagement and involvement is put into practice is outlined in Mora's chapter. Nevertheless, the question remains open for more extensive quantitative based analysis and testing.

Conclusion

The results presented in this work have shown how the characteristics of individuals affect their political participation in New York City. It has been shown how the characteristics of individual Puerto Ricans, and Latinos more generally, differ from those of other New Yorkers to an extent that makes their involvement in politics less frequent. However, one of those characteristics—Catholicism—does not have an independent impact on participation, and when it does, as on voting among Latinos, the effect is positive. This effect holds even as attendance to religious services is held constant. This measure serves as proxy for the extent to which individuals may be more or less integrated into and committed to their communities of faiths as sites where the norms of trust and reciprocity that form the core of social capital may be fostered.[50] These communities of faiths are also repositories of socially and politically relevant information and sites of exchange of such information as well as being sites of potential recruitment into civic and political activity. Thus, while increased attendance to religious services is associated with an increase in political activity, as established by the bivariate analyses, it does not show an independent impact on participation once other factors, including identifying as Catholic, are factored into the analyses.

One accounts for the disparities in the bivariate and the multivariate analyses by inferring that the largely negative, if small impact, that being Catholics has on political participation, evident in the bivariate analysis, is given by other factors that are associated with being Catholic in New York City but not by following that particular confession. The multivariate analyses point to the importance of associational variables, particularly those that foster not simply social capital, but political capital as well. Being part of voluntary associations does provide individuals with the wherewithal to be civically engaged. In this sense, the theoretical argument laid out by Verba and his colleagues remains a robust one, if not empirically applicable in its entirety to New York City. The compelling argument about politically relevant resources that may be acquired through associational membership, particularly in communities of faith, in smaller geographical settings awaits further research and empirical testing.

Appendix

Dependent Variables

The dependent variables (scales) were constructed by adding the scores to the following questions (dummy variables):

Contacting Scale:
Q: "Over the past year, have you contacted a local elected official about some need or problem?" (1 = yes; 0 = no)
Q: "In the past year, have you written a letter to a public official?" (1 = yes; 0 = no)

Voting Scale:
Q: "Are you currently registered to vote where you live?" (1 = yes; 0 = no)
Q: "In 1996, you will remember that Bill Clinton ran for president on the Democratic ticket against Bob Dole for the Republicans and Ross Perot for the Reform Party. Did you vote in that election? (1 = yes; 0 = no)
Q: "In 1993, you will remember that Rudolph Giuliani ran for mayor of New York City against David Dinkins. Did you vote in that election?" (1 = yes; 0 = no)

Overall Political Participation Scale: (This scale includes the variables in the two preceding scales, with the exception of the voter registration dummy variable.)
Q: "In the past year, have you worked as a volunteer for a party or candidate?" (1 = yes; 0 = no)
Q: "In the past year, have you contributed money to a political party or candidate?" (1 = yes; 0 = no)

Q: "In the past year have you attended a political rally for a candidate?" (1 = yes; 0 = no)

Q: "In the past year, have you attended a political meeting?" (1 = yes; 0 = no)

Q: "In the past year, have you attended a fundraiser for a political cause?" (1 = yes; 0 = no)

Q: "In the past year, have you made calls for a candidate or party?" (1 = yes; 0 = no)

Q: "In the past year, have you participated in a protest or political demonstration?" (1 = yes; 0 = no)

Independent Variables

Age—Q: "What is your age?" (in years)

Education—Q: "What is the highest level of education or schooling you finished?" (no schooling; grade1 through 12; junior/business college; technical/trade school; first, second, third year of college; college graduate; some graduate school; graduate school degree)

Income—Q: "In which of the following ranges does your family income fall? (1 = $12,000 or less; 2 = $12,001 to $20,000; 3 = $20,0001 to $30,000; 4 = $30,001 to $40,000; 5 = 40,001 to $50,000; 6 = $50,001 to $60,000; 7 = $60,001 to $80,000; 8 = $80,001 to $100,000; 9 = $100,001 to $150,000; 10 = over $150,000)

Employment Status—Q: "Are you currently working, or are you temporarily laid off, unemployed, retired, permanently disabled, a homemaker, a student, or what?" (1 = working; 2 = part-time; 3 = laid off; 4 = unemployed; 5 = retired; 6 = disabled; 7 = homemaker; 8 = student)

This variable was dichotomized into those working (1 = working and part-time) and those not working (0 = all else).

Gender—Interviewer coded the respondent's gender (1 = female; 0 = male).

Race/Ethnicity—Recoded into mutually exclusive categories from the following two questions:

Race—Q: "For statistical purposes, we'd like to ask you, are you white, black, or some other race? (1 = white; 2 = black; 3 = Hispanic/Latino; 4 = mixed; 5 = other)

Hispanic/Latino—Q: "Are you of Hispanic origin or descent, or not?" (1 = yes; 0 = no)

Puerto Rican—Q: "Did you say you are or are not Puerto Rican?" (1 = yes; 0 = no)

Length of Time at Address—Q: "How long have you lived at your present address?" (1 = less than six months; 2 = six months to one year; 3 = one to two years; 4 = three to four years; 5 = five to ten years; 6 = eleven to twenty years; 7 = twenty-one to thirty years; 8 = more than 30 years.)

Length of Time in the City—Q: "How long have you lived in New York City?" (1 = less than six months; 2 = six months to one year; 3 = one to two years; 4 = three to four years; 5 = five to ten years; 6 = eleven to twenty years; 7 = twenty-one to thirty years; 8 = more than 30 years)

Homeownership—Dichotomized in a single variable from responses to the following two questions:

> Q: "Do you or your family own your own home or pay rent?" (1= rent; 2 = own; 3 = neither)
> Q: "Do you rent from a private landlord, another family member, or from the public housing authority, or do you own your apartment? (1 = private landlord; 2 = another family member; 3 = public housing authority; 4 = own apartment)

Catholic—Q: "What is your religious preference? Is it Protestant, Catholic, Jewish, Muslim, some other religion, or no religion?" (Responses were dichotomized into 1 = Catholic and 0 = all else.)

Citizenship—Q: "Are you a United States citizen? (1 = yes; 0 = no)

Membership in Labor Union—Q: "Are you currently a member of a Labor Union?" (1 = yes; 0 = no)

Organizational Membership—Respondents were asked about membership in organizations or associations such as neighborhood; professional; religious or church based; sports clubs; service or fraternal; PTA; veteran's; hobby; civic; literary; and ethnic. The organizational membership scale was constructed by adding the number of "yes" responses to each one of these questions.

In addition, affirmative responses to the organizational membership questions were followed up with this inquiry: "Does this organization (group/club) engage in political activity?" The nonpolitical organization membership and politically active organization membership scales were constructed by adding separately the total number of negative and positive responses, respectively.

Mobilization—Q: "During the last presidential election did anyone telephone you about registering to vote or getting out to vote? (1 = yes; 0 = no)

Interest in Politics—Q: "Some people don't pay much attention to politics. How about you—would you say that you are very much interested in politics, somewhat interested, not much interested, or not at all interested? (1 = not at all interested; 2 = not much interested; 3 = somewhat interested; 4 = very much interested)

Political Efficacy—A scale was constructed adding the responses to the following three questions:

> Q: "Do you agree or disagree? People like me don't have any say about what the city government does."
>
> Q: "Do you agree or disagree? Sometimes city politics and government seem so complicated that a person like me can't really understand what's going on."
>
> Q: "Do you agree or disagree? 'I don't think local officials care much what people like me think.'"
>
> (1 = agree; 2 = somewhat agree; 3 = somewhat disagree; 4 = disagree)

Political Discussion—A scale was constructed adding the responses of the following three questions:

> Q: "How often do you discuss politics with family members: nearly every day; once or twice a week; less than once a week; or almost never?"
>
> Q: "How often do you discuss politics with friends: nearly every day; once or twice a week; less than once a week; or almost never?"
>
> Q: "How often do you discuss politics with coworkers: nearly every day; once or twice a week; less than once a week; or almost never?"
>
> (1 = never; 2 = almost never; 3 = less than once a week; 4 = once or twice a week; 5 = nearly every day.)

Family Members Vote—Q: "Do most members of your family usually vote?" (1 = yes; 0 = no)

Friends Vote—Q: "Do most members of your friends usually vote?" (1 = yes; 0 = no)

Coworkers Vote—Q: "Do most members of your coworkers usually vote?" (1 = yes; 0 = no)

Notes

1. When discussing political participation, I circumscribe the concept to activities by which residents of a society attempt to influence their form of government, how the people who run the government are selected, and/or the policies the government makes (Conway 1991; Verba and Nie 1972). The definition is limited to legally sanctioned activities, but much broader than activities that simply involve the election or selection of governing officials. In other words, the focus on political participation surveyed in this work will go beyond electoral politics, which is the form of political involvement that is analyzed most frequently. It will include nonelectoral forms of political participation, such as collective action to solve community problems, participation in protest activity, petition signing,

and contacting elected officials. It will not touch upon other activities that attempt to shape the policies, the form, and/or the selection of government— such as vandalism, sabotage, kidnapping, assassinations, riots, insurrections, or other forms of direct action—as the focus of this work is on secular or quotidian participation.

2. *The Washington Post* et al. 2000. The results for the turnout rate among registered voters, 18 years of age and older, was 68.4 percent for non-Hispanic whites, 65.7 percent for non-Hispanic blacks, 65.8 percent for non-Hispanic Asian-Pacific Islanders, and 59.4 percent for Hispanics (Day and Gaither 2000).

3. Calvo and Rosenstone 1989; Conway 1991; Rosenstone and Hansen 1993; Verba et al. 1993, Verba et al. 1995; Garcia 1997; Diaz 1996.

4. Lipset 1960; Verba and Nie 1972.

5. Conway 1991.

6. Verba et al. 1995; Nie et al. 1996.

7. Therrien and Ramirez 2001.

8. Putnam 2000.

9. Fuchs et al. 2000.

10. Verba et al. 1995.

11. Verba et al. 1995.

12. Jones-Correa and Leal 2001.

13. Vargas-Ramos 2003.

14. Verba and Nie 1972.

15. Verba et al. 1995.

16. Putnam 2000.

17. Fuchs et al. 2000, 2001.

18. The survey was conducted by telephone, in English, with respondents chosen randomly from households selected using a RDD procedure, between August 11 and September 8, 1997. The survey was a joint effort of the Barnard/Columbia Center for Urban Research and Policy and the Hispanic Education and Legal Fund Opinion Research Project.

19. Verba et al. 1995.

20. Key 1949; Hanson 1991; Brown 1988.

21. Gimpel 1999; Oliver 2000.

22. The original random sample for the survey was 1,123 New York City residents, 18 years of age and older, with access to a residential telephone. This sample was supplemented by an oversample of Latinos and blacks that yielded a total of 350 black and 453 Latino respondents.

23. The Current Population Report for the 1996 elections reports that in New York State, 35 percent of Hispanics, 19 percent of blacks and 10 percent of whites did not vote because they were not citizens (U.S. Census Bureau 1998). The slightly higher rate of citizenship among Latinos in the sample may be attributed to the fact that the survey was conducted in English, therefore selecting a particular segment of the Hispanic population of New York City.

24. A note of caution is in order. The Current Population report for the 1996 elections shows that the percent of Latinos, 18 years of age or older, that voted in those elections in New York State was 29 percent, compared to 42 percent for blacks and 55 percent for whites (U.S. Census Bureau 1998). Studies on voting validation have shown that "Latino turnout was much lower than estimates based on self-reporting" (Shaw et al. 2000). Another explanation for the higher percentages of Latinos that responded to have voted may be the fact that the New York City survey was conducted in English, again selecting out a sample of the Latino population more likely to vote.

25. The survey only probed for whether a respondent had contributed to a campaign or candidate, but it did not inquire as to the amount of the contribution.

26. Lack of statistical significance in these proportions means that the differences that exist between groups, while observable, cannot be attributed confidently to the independent effect of a respondent's race or ethnicity. Other factors may operate in accounting for the discrepancy, including chance.

27. The three measures of political participation are additive scales of dichotomous variables. The scale for overall political participation is made up of voting in the 1993 mayoral elections, voting in the 1996 Presidential elections, working as a volunteer for a party or candidate, contributing money to a political party or candidate, attending a political rally for a candidate, attending a political meeting, attending a fundraiser for a political cause, making calls for a candidate or party, writing a letter to a public official, contacting a local elected official, and participating in a protest or political demonstration—all in the past year. This 11-point scale had an internal reliability (Chronbach's alpha) score of 0.7858, and all factors loaded onto the dimension at 0.5 or better. (Protesting had the lowest loading, at 0.481.) It accounted for 32 percent of the variance. The voting scale was made up of registering to vote, voting in the 1993 mayoral elections and voting in the 1996 presidential elections. Its internal reliability score was 0.8401 and it accounted for 16 percent of the variance. The contacting scale added writing a letter to a public official and contacting a local elected official about some need or problem. Its internal reliability score was 0.6731 and it accounted for 9 percent of the variance.

28. The average for the voting scale was 1.9 activities (with a standard deviation of 1.2 activities). Among non-Hispanic whites, the number of voting activities was 2.2 (sd = 1.1); for non-Hispanic blacks, 1.9 (sd = 1.2); for Puerto Ricans, 1.9 (sd = 1.1); and for other Latinos, 1.4 (sd = 1.3). The average for the contacting scale was .5 activities (sd = .74); For non-Hispanic whites the number of contacting activities was .62 (sd = .8); for non-Hispanic blacks, .44 (sd = .72); for Puerto Ricans, .37 (sd = .64); and for other Latinos, .42 (sd = .74).

29. Verba and Nie 1972.

30. Browning et al. 1984.

31. De la Garza et al. 1992.

32. De la Garza et al. 1992.

33. Pearson's r = −0.08.
34. Pearson's r = −0.06.
35. Verba et al. 1995.
36. Pearson's r = −.14.
37. Pearson's r = −.11.
38. Pearson's r = .23.
39. Pearson's r = .118 and .071, respectively.
40. Pearson's r for overall participation = .165; for contacting elected officials = .138.
41. Attendance to religious services is only statistically associated with contacting elected officials (Pearson's r = .162).
42. Vargas-Ramos 2003.
43. Non-Hispanic white is the omitted category on which the comparisons with other ethnic groups are made in the regression equation.
44. Regression results are not shown.
45. Unstandardized regression coefficient for Catholic is B = .276 (s.e. = .124, p = .027).
46. Regression results are not shown. Unstandardized regression coefficient for Catholic is B = .442 (s.e .= .258, p = .092).
47. Regression results are not shown.
48. Jones-Correa and Leal 2001.
49. Jones-Correa and Leal 2001.
50. Putnam 2000.

Transnational Religious and Sociopolitical Dynamics of a Racialized Puerto Rican Community in Connecticut

Samiri Hernández Hiraldo

The town of Loíza, nestled among palm trees on the northeastern coast of the island of Puerto Rico, may seem very different from frosty New Haven, Connecticut, the working class and congested city surrounding the Ivy League's Yale University. Yet the transnational dynamics of today's Latinos and Latinas have linked Puerto Ricans in both places through religious traditions that carry within them both cultural and racial identities that have political consequences.[1] The significant link between Loíza and the Puerto Rican community of New Haven is the popular festival of *Santiago Apóstol* (Saint James the Apostle). A complex tradition with roots in medieval Spain, the festival has been carried by Loizans who have migrated to the United States. This chapter is a brief exploration of how the festival of Santiago articulates the Loizans' social, economic, political, and religious experience back home and their experience in their new surroundings.

As a reader of Chapter 5 (by G. Cristina Mora) will understand, this festival of Puerto Rican migrants shares some similarities to the experience of Mexican Catholics living in Los Angeles who are devoted to Our Lady of Guadalupe. However, uniquely for Puerto Ricans, an African racial identity figures prominently in the Santiago festival because of Loíza's mostly black population.[2] Although most Puerto Ricans claim a legacy from the *jíbaros*, or mountain-dwelling peasants of uncertain mixed racial heritage, in the common vernacular, Loíza, among towns with large black populations in the island, is considered to best represent the African influences upon Puerto Rican culture.[3] This festival, in particular, is widely considered to reflect the traditional idea of Puerto Rico as a cultural mix of the Indian, Spanish, and African elements and to simultaneously epitomize Afro-Puerto Rican culture.

The Origins of the Loizan Festival of Santiago Apóstol

Max Harris has examined the role of the festival of Santiago in medieval Spain and how the celebration was perpetuated in Mexico.[4] He describes a picture of fourteenth-century Iberia in which the masqueraders dressing as Spanish knights ritually fought and conquered those wearing Moorish disguises. Among the functions of these rituals, however, was one that served to integrate the winners with the losers into the same community. For him, the medieval Spanish feast fostered a unifying rather than a divisive social function. The festival among Christians and Muslims, he says, "celebrated a vision of *convivencia* rather than a memory of bloodshed."[5] With its importation to the Americas, the same unifying function endured but acquired a racial dimension as well. The transformation of Iberian Moors into Mexican Aztecs gave a new local meaning to the festival once it crossed the Atlantic.[6] The celebration in Mexico, like its medieval Spanish antecedent, recognizes past historical differences at the same time that it reconciles contemporary social unity. In fact, by adapting the religious functions that integrated Moors and Christians in Spain, *convivencia* in the New World took the form of ethnic and racial integration. Significantly, the equality between the ethnicities and races represents the undoing of the conquest of natives by Spanish whites. When celebrating Santiago Apóstol, the conquered Mexican descendants become equal with their European *conquistadores*, even if symbolically. Even today, says Harris, Mexicans celebrate the festival of Santiago in order to "draw on the repertoire of Aztec ritual to imagine a world of local authority free from external control."[7]

The symbolic functions of social unity, racial integration, and reversing the power structures are found with stark clarity in the Loizan experience and cultural expression in general. The African heritage of the town is celebrated as an identity just as worthy as a Spanish one. The celebration of the African heritage is a local example of the official view advanced by the pro-Commonwealth government in the 1950s, which made official the representation of Puerto Rican culture as the harmonious coexistence of the Indian, Spanish, and African elements of society With the migration of the festival to the United States, one can argue that the aforementioned functions have acquired the political dimensions of the civil rights movements of the past half century. As I hope to show, moreover, these functions are not a mimicry, nor automatic. Both Loizans on the island and those who migrated to New Haven have contributed to the construction of this special African identity within the generic Puerto Rican one. Consistent with Harrison's perspective that rituals do not necessarily reflect reality, but temporarily alter it, many Loizans insist that the festival should transcend the level of symbolic and mobilize people for a profoundly important political struggle.[8]

Settled originally by the Taíno natives of the island before the arrival of the Spaniards, Loíza derives its name from a woman *cacica* or chieftain, who figured prominently in the island's earliest colonization accounts. The contemporary town is located 15 miles east from the city of San Juan, Puerto Rico's capital. It is separated from the rest of the island by a vast expanse of mostly empty land to its south. Bordered on the north by the Atlantic Ocean, Loíza is west of the municipality of Río Grande and north of Canóvanas. The west is bordered by the large and suburbanized municipality of Carolina.

The Puerto Rican Catholic celebration in honor of Santiago Apóstol is explained in greater detail elsewhere.[9] In short, it can be seen that the Puerto Rican festival of Santiago Apóstol in Loíza is cut from the same cloth as the Spanish and Mexican traditions. The pattern of the imported Spanish celebration of Christians and Moors allowed for a Puerto Rican accommodation to the African peoples similar to the Mexican accommodation to the Aztecs. The festival in Loíza became a vehicle to recognize racial differences while still celebrating social and religious unity.

While the masks used by Puerto Rican revelers to represent Santiago are very similar to what was used in medieval Spain and in contemporary Mexico to represent the Apostle as a medieval Spanish knight, in Puerto Rico there is representation of neither Moors nor Aztecs.[10] Instead, the opposing figure is a *vejigante*, a word derived from *vejiga* or animal bladder that was used like a bagpipe to produce a bellowing sound.[11] The *vejigantes* wear masks that suggest a grotesque, animallike face and colorful pajama-like costumes with billowing sides, somewhat like the wings of a bat. Loizans identify with the masquerade of the Catholic saint, Santiago, as witnessed by the festival groupings: Santiago of men, Santiago of women, and Santiago of children. The statues are kept by local *mantenedores* (i.e., families who take care of the statues). However, *vejigantes* have become the most typical characters of the Puerto Rican variant of this festival. Zaragoza calls them both "ritual clowns" and "devils,"[12] and common culture often identifies them with the *cuco* (i.e., boogeyman or prankster). I argue that their mediating position in relation to and aside from Santiago makes the symbolic identity of the *vejigantes* ambiguous. The meaning of *vejigantes* as both good and bad and Christian and non-Christian (e.g., pagan or secular) is an example of their social and political malleability. In this way, they stand as effective vehicles to represent the complexity of the Loizan reality.

The festival claims its Puerto Rican origins with the miraculous rescue of an image of Santiago Apóstol in 1832.[13] According to this documented account, although it had been transferred to a more dignified resting place in the church, the statue of Santiago was mysteriously returned at night to the beach settlement at Las Carreras (literally, where the horse races were held). In recognition of the saint's desire to have his statue venerated in the outskirts of town, where many poor blacks lived and where horse races were held, the townspeople celebrate his feast day on July 25 each year with activities held in this section of the beach in the Medianía Alta *barrio* of Loíza.[14]

There are several salient issues of historical nature that highlight the political import of this feast. First, the festival of Santiago is not in honor of the town's patron saint. The parish church was named after St. Patrick as long ago as 1645, in response to the protection that spared the cassava crop—then a staple in Puerto Rico—from a plague of worms (although the popular version says ants).[15] Second, although the town of Loíza was incorporated as early as 1719, its most significant growth took place during the nineteenth century with the development of a sugar industry based on slave labor in Puerto Rico at a time when the slave trade was in the process of being outlawed in the British Caribbean. Fugitive slaves from other Caribbean islands, like Haiti, also populated the town.

Moreover, the most important sugar plantation owners in the region in the nineteenth century were of Irish descent, and they promoted the devotion to St. Patrick as the parish patron saint. Saint Patrick and his seventeenth-century miracle with the cassava enabled Irish immigrants and Spanish *hacendados* to fashion the religious festival into an image of their own social prestige. That left a void for the African people to find a patron and a celebration to reflect their racial identity. Third, the eclipse of the sugar industry after the abolition of slavery in 1873 led to the impoverishment of most of Loíza's African inhabitants. Fourth, the transfer of power from Spain to the United States after 1898 introduced Protestantism, both mainline and Pentecostal, to the town as competitors with a traditional Catholicism that had suddenly been stripped of its social preeminence. Moreover, the introduction of Protestantism was accompanied by political opportunities for elites that professed belief in spiritism, belonged to Masonry, and often were overtly anticlerical. Finally, the wealthier segments of the region's population had moved to Canóvanas, one of Loíza's barrios, which was separated politically from Loíza in 1971, making each town less diverse racially. Canóvanas was whiter and richer; Loíza was blacker and poorer.

These developments form the background for the racialization of Loizan identity, especially in comparison with Canóvanas. Elsewhere, I have provided an extensive description of the cultural results: Loíza is poor, noticeably black in racial heritage, and characterized religiously by the coexistence of spiritism, African religions (this includes *Santería* from Cuba and *Vodou* from Haiti), Catholicism, and Protestantism (including Pentecostalism), and by their syncretistic mix.[16]

The Racialization of the Loizan Festival of Santiago Apóstol

Whatever the exact historical origins may be, the twentieth century pushed this festival toward racialization. As suggested above, when Puerto Rican ceased to be a Spanish colony and became an American one after 1898, the historic religious hegemony of Catholicism was ruptured. With a weakening of institutional controls, forms of popular religiosity reemerged or gained new strength as a response to the rapidly shifting sands of cultural, political, and social identities.

In 1910, the local administration and a group of landowners decided to transfer the administrative center and the parish seat to Canóvanas, which as mentioned earlier, was home to a relatively large group of prosperous families of Spanish and Irish descent. After the administrative transfer, the area of Canóvanas improved economically until the desperate years after the Great Depression of 1929. The transfer and the Great Depression, moreover, continued to debilitate the socioeconomic condition of original town, reaching a nadir when it came to be known as "Loíza Aldea" (literally, Loíza hamlet). Loizans disliked the word *aldea* because it identified them with a primitive life outside the flow of social progress. In the postwar 1940s, when the island country began to move toward an industrialized economy by developing a more stable political relationship with the United States, there were movements by the disadvantaged Loizans to transfer the administrative center back to its original location. Loizans expected this transfer would help improve the town's general situation. As a Loizan elder put it to me, "With everybody else moving toward progress, we did not want to be left behind."

Simultaneous with the economic developments of the 1940s and 1950s, the Catholic Church began to assist in the efforts to restore the structure of the parish in downtown Loíza. Chief among the efforts was a restoration in the center of Loíza of the former church building, named after the Holy Spirit and Saint Patrick, but which had suffered various natural disasters in the nineteenth century, rendering it unusable. The restoration of the church building was considered necessary to revive official Catholicism, which was considered "dead" since the parish seat was transferred to Canóvanas. Part of this effort stressed devotion to Saint Patrick as the official patron saint of Loíza. Interestingly, the priest in residence during the first phase of my research had requested that a famous local artist, Samuel Lind, paint a portrait of the saint with dark skin, and this was placed on the church's altar. Committees were formed with Loizan and non-Loizan residents to help this cause in the late 1960s. Even the Irish Catholic community and members of Saint Patrick's Cathedral in New York City offered spiritual support and financial assistance.

In Loíza, there are differing positions regarding these and other issues. To give an example, Las Cuevas is a neighborhood in the urban zone and seat of the town's administration, and is quite different from the outlying barrio of Medianía Alta where the image of Santiago first appeared. A good number of Las Cuevas's residents described the people of barrio Medianía Alta as backward and superstitious. The former view the latter as clinging to a traditional mentality, and, therefore, as being responsible for the slow development of the town. In my interviews, Las Cuevas's residents described the Medianía Alta people as being "very black" or "blacker." They made fun of the speech style of the Medianía Alta people, referring to this barrio as "almost another world."

Also during the 1940s and 1950s, Medianía Alta residents sought the foundation of a new local parish in honor of Santiago that would help legitimize the festival and their Catholic practice in general, creating an impact on their self-esteem and sense of community. The idea of a new parish of Santiago Apóstol in Medianía Alta also became part of a significant effort by the Catholic Church to cope with the rapid penetration of Pentecostalism at the time, especially in the area of Medianía Alta. The foundation of the Parish of Santiago would address, on the one hand, Medianía Alta residents' suspicions of the Catholic Church's favoritism toward Canóvanas and, on the other, provide the people of Mediania Alta with the same ecclesiastical attention that was being given to the Catholic community in downtown Loíza.

Some Medianía Alta residents believed that the foundation of the Parish of Santiago was intended by the church to eclipse the popular religiosity of the African heritage traditions within the devotion of Santiago. People were on both sides of this issue: that is, some wanted the African-ness subsumed within a more established devotion to Santiago, while others preferred the popular version of the celebration to be kept independent of the church, without completely disregarding its religious significance.

In the 1950s, Loíza gained much academic attention from scholars of Puerto Rican island culture, precisely because the racialization of the festival preserved facets of local identity rapidly disappearing in a rapidly industrializing society. This recognition helped solidify a specifically Loizan identity as one that is simultaneously religious, cultural, and racial during a time when migration to the United States was assuming mass proportions. Despite or because of this, in the past decades, Loíza has tried to develop a strong tourism industry centered on the special African qualities manifest in the celebration of the festival of Santiago. These efforts have been at the forefront of a notable controversy involving concerns as diverse as racial and environmental issues.

Loíza and Canóvanas each became a separate municipality in 1971, following the recommendations by the Commonwealth government's *Junta de Planificación* (i.e., planning board) office. Under the pro-Commonwealth *Partido Popular Democrático* (PPD), the planning board assigned fewer funds and less land to Loíza than to Canóvanas, despite the larger population and greater needs of Loíza. These developments gave Loíza a lower financial status than any other town in Puerto Rico save the small island of Culebra, resulting in high unemployment and poverty rates. Loizans accepted these conditions because of the state government's promise of aid, Canóvanas's promise of a gradual separation, and the future possibility of developing a strong tourism industry that would help Loíza's economy.

In an official document prepared by the planning board, the terms of the separation seemed to be justified by a description of Canóvanas as more economically developed and geographically closer to the metropolitan area. The people of Canóvanas were characterized as self-sufficient, distant from traditions, independent, practical, less subordinated to the social group, and puritanical. Opinions associated Canóvanas's socioeconomic progress with the rapid growth of Protestantism in the area since the beginning of the century. In contrast, Loizans were described as subordinate to the social group (which is cohesive, integrated, homogeneous, and isolated) and inclined to a bohemian lifestyle, use of alcohol, carnal pleasures, and free love.[17]

Loíza's slow economic development is often attributed to a generalized backward and superstitious mentality and a belief in witchcraft that is associated with African traditions. This is also similar to the correlation normally established between Haitian Vodou and the country's serious economic and social problems.[18] This is, of course, an unfortunate stereotype that persists despite the strong influence of Pentecostalism among the townspeople. It is true that many Loizans agree that Loiza can be considered more African than its former partner, Canóvanas, and most of the rest of Puerto Rico. It is also true that forms of spiritualism and African-based religious practices became more pronounced with the difficulties of institutional Catholicism in the first quarter of the twentieth century. Yet, as I hope to show, these special conditions are more a part of the identity complex of Loizans than strict doctrinal definitions.

The separation between Loíza and Canóvanas had the support of the upstart pro-statehood party, the *Partido Nuevo Progresista* (PNP). In fact, the PNP characterized itself as siding with Loiza and contrasted itself with the PPD, the party that stipulated the terms of the separation. (This explains the majority support that the PNP has enjoyed over the years.) Thus, the division between the two classes and races was dealt a partisan political face as well. The division also acquired a religious dimension because when Canóvanas finally separated from Loíza in 1971, the parish of Santiago was finally created in the barrio. This happened more than a decade after the official reopening of the parish downtown, but at last the Catholic community of Loíza regained its parish seat lost with the municipal seat of government's transfer in 1910. A few residents said the new parish of Santiago would coopt emerging protest movements against aspects of institutional Catholicism.

In summary, it can be seen that from its inception long ago, the festival of Santiago Apóstol has had sharply defined cultural, racial, economic, and political functions. Moreover, even before considering its impact on migrants from Loíza, the celebration had been much more than merely a relic of quaint folklore; rather, it was a vehicle that used the "religious repertoire" referred to by Harris with cultural, racial, economic, and political purposes.[19]

I cannot close this overview of the festival without including a reference to a similar process among the leaders of the Catholic Church of Miami who sought to distinguish between the worship of Our Lady of Charity and Ochún, a Yoruba goddess in Santería, originally from Cuba.[20] In order to blunt the syncretism of Santiago with Changó, a chief *orisha* in Santería, there was also a big campaign on the part of the Catholic leaders in Loíza to establish the festival of Saint Patrick as a "religious" (or spiritual) celebration as opposed to the festival of Santiago as a "traditional" (or cultural) celebration. To further the identification of St. James with Catholicism and not with Santería, the image of Santiago was placed inside the main parish downtown Loíza during Mass.

Moreover, the rivalry between Canóvanas and Loíza was extended by the use of competing symbolic identities. In some of Loiza's festival parades it is common to see children dressed up like Indians. According to Loizans, these parades are necessary because the people of Canóvanas have appropriated the Indian identity as if they were the only ones with an Indian ancestry. At the main entrance of the town of Canóvanas there are two big statues: an Indian woman and an Indian man. The people of Canóvanas commonly refer to themselves as the Indians of Canóvanas. This is understood as complying with the romantic view of Indians as superior to blacks in Puerto Rico, as it has happened in other Latin American and Caribbean countries.[21] However, this view of the Indian has encouraged some Loizans to affirm their African legacy all the more adamantly.

Why and How Did Loizans End Up in Connecticut?

The 1952 creation of the Commonwealth, which granted Puerto Rico self-governance under the auspices of the U.S. government, happened in the context of a broad initiative to enhance the country's difficult social and economic situations during a push toward industrialism, although the movement toward industrialization did not happen in a linear fashion in Loiza. As Giusti has shown and elder Loizans confirmed, since earlier times, Loizan men and women have engaged in various alternate economic activities (e.g., fishing, farming, animal husbandry, small market, and domestic jobs) in order to survive.[22] Puerto Rico became a showcase for successful U.S.-driven progress. As of today, Puerto Rico is almost completely dependent on U.S. imports and a majority of the country's exports are sent to the mainland United States.

The new relationship of Puerto Rico with the United States encouraged the massive migration of Puerto Ricans to the mainland. Puerto Ricans had been given U.S. citizenship in 1917, but only after World War II did large groups of Puerto Ricans migrate to the United States to work on the farms, in manufacturing, and in other low-income jobs. This migration was orchestrated by the United States in partnership with the Puerto Rican government. Between 1990 and 2000, the Puerto Rican population in the United States grew from 3.2 to 3.4 million, compared to the population of 3.8 in Puerto Rico. Indeed, the Puerto Rican population in the United States surpassed the four million mark in 2010. Puerto Ricans continue to migrate to the United States. A relatively new trend, as identified by Duany and Matos-Rodríguez, is the large number of Puerto Ricans that have made Florida their new home.[23] Puerto Ricans in general also continue to be involved in a circular, although not always consistent, migration pattern.[24]

In 2010, Connecticut had the sixth largest Puerto Rican population in the United States. The total number of Puerto Rican inhabitants was 252,972 (or 7% of the state's population) making it the state with the largest percentage of Puerto Ricans compared to total population. In New Haven County, the Puerto Rican population was 77,578 (9% of the county's population), and in the city of New Haven it was 20,505 (15.8% of the city's population). There is evidence of Puerto Rican migration to Connecticut as early as the early nineteenth century. However, as with other states, most Puerto Rican migrants came after WWII; in the case of Connecticut, they migrated in order to do farm work. These individuals were from the interior parts of the island and had the light skin of the poor white and mixed race segments of the island's population. Identified with the mountain-dwelling *jíbaro*, or peasant, these early migrants demonstrated a preference for the jíbaro traditions in music and cultural expression. The gradual loss of job contracts in Connecticut farms in the late 1960s and early 1970s forced many of these agricultural workers and their families to move to cities such as New Haven to look for other job opportunities, such as manufacturing or industrial work.[25]

By the 1970s, moreover, the patterns of Puerto Rican migration to the United States had significantly changed. Global economic structures not only induced Puerto Ricans to migrate to the United States, but during this same period the number of Puerto Rican returnees began to surpass those leaving for the United States.[26] In the midst of these structural changes in Puerto Rican migration, a significant number of Loizans established themselves in Connecticut. During my field study, there were about 1,500 Loizans in New Haven, many of whom lived in Kensington and on Church Street South, two residential projects in downtown New Haven.

In Loíza, I found that a significant number of its residents had migrated to other towns in Puerto Rico and to other states in the United States, for example, Massachusetts. I also found that a good number of these migrants were professionals. These Loizans migrated for the following reasons: (1) under- or unemployment, (2) crime, (3) family issues, and (4) a change of lifestyle in general. As a reader of this collection will likely understand, the situation of Puerto Rican migrants and their celebration of the festival of Santiago bears comparison with the experience of other Latinos and Latinas in the United States, such as Mexican Catholics living in Los Angeles.

The first Loizan known to have migrated to the area of the city of New Haven (within New Haven County) in Connecticut was Ezequiel López from Medianía Alta. López was a soldier in the Korean War, and after the war he returned to his hometown of Loíza. A few years later, he and his brothers moved to Maryland to work as farm workers. However, the difficult employment situation in Maryland forced them to search for better jobs and living conditions. Thus, they settled in New Haven in 1960 to work on farms there; they felt they found the best situation under the circumstances. Sometime later, López asked his wife, Luz Selenia Osorio, to move to New Haven with him, and there they started a family. Other family members followed them not too long after. Some members of the family still remember that at that time, there were only a few other black Puerto Rican families in the neighborhood and that some "white" and "mixed color" Puerto Ricans discriminated against them. Considering this, it is not hard to understand their involvement in FLECHAS.

What Is FLECHAS?

During the middle 1970s, as the Loizan population continued to grow in New Haven, the festival of Loíza became important in its own right. Like López, a good number of these Loizans came from Medianía Alta, where the festival of Santiago first originated. In 1977, the state of Connecticut registered FLECHAS as a community organization, deriving the name as an acronym for *Fiestas de Loíza en Connecticut en Honor al Apóstol Santiago* or "Festival of Loíza in Connecticut in honor of St. James the Apostle." In 1999, FLECHAS became a not-for-profit 501(c)(3) cultural and educational organization. As posted on the FLECHAS's website (www.flechasct.org), the organization promotes awareness of the Spanish, Indian, and African legacies. (At the bottom of the seal it reads, "A Puerto Rican expression of three cultures.") However, the organization is emphatic that its main goal is to document, preserve, and promote the significance of African elements in Puerto Rico's culture through history and the arts and by using classes, workshops, exhibitions, and performances in schools and for the general public.

FLECHAS emphasizes the Loizan version of Afro-Puerto Rican identity; the Afro-Puerto Rican identity is quite strong and visible in other parts of Puerto Rico. This emphasis is apparent in the great significance given to *vejigante* parades and crafts, *bomba*[27] performances, and other Afro-Puerto Rican folk arts. The organization also puts emphasis on the other two perspectives of Afro-Puerto Rican culture. One is the sociohistorical perspective represented by slavery. Instead of opting for denial, which is what happens among some Loizans in Loíza, every March 22, FLECHAS commemorates the celebration of the abolition of slavery in Puerto Rico and raises awareness about the reality of slavery. There is the cultural modern perspective represented by the internationally known Afro-Caribbean music genre of *salsa*, which is also considered a symbol of Puerto Rico and Latino culture in general and which is performed in the festival.

The festival is considered by the media and by state officials as the number one festival in New Haven. It is generally better organized and attended by people from different cultural and ethnic backgrounds than the Puerto Rican parade (celebrated since 1964). In the last years, the average attendance has been 60,000 people. The festival has received numerous recognitions and awards and relies on large sponsors such as Telemundo (a Hispanic channel of NBC), MTV Español, and the Comcast Cable Company.

The Socioeconomic and Political Significance of FLECHAS

Many Loizans I spoke with agreed that FLECHAS came about because of their need to re-create and experience Puerto Rico while in the United States. As they were traveling back and forth, they also realized the significance of demonstrating Puerto Rican identity outside of Puerto Rico. It was important for them to show their Puerto Rican identity and to establish a critical perspective on the idea of national identity back home, which required residency on the island.

In New Haven, Loizans were presented with another dilemma. Many other Puerto Ricans living in Connecticut came from the interior part of Puerto Rico, where there is a high concentration of light-skinned residents and a strong preference for the jíbaro traditions. Loizans needed to be in unity with their Puerto Rican compatriots, but they also needed to distinguish themselves from these compatriots and from African Americans. African Americans became more visible in New Haven at the end of the 1970s, while competing with Puerto Ricans for social and political recognition and resources.

This distinction is considered an important issue today, according to older generations, because over the years more young Puerto Ricans have been identifying with the African American contemporary lifestyle and leaving their culture's original traditions behind. Nevertheless, many individuals in New Haven believe that the similarly difficult social and economic experiences of Puerto Ricans and African Americans and a common cultural background have contributed to growing African American support for the festival of Santiago and have helped create a unified search for a stronger affirmation of ethnic/racial identity and a better socioeconomic situation for all minorities in New Haven. More significantly, Loizans and many non-Loizan Puerto Ricans in Connecticut, who can relate to the African/black side of Puerto Rico, have felt the responsibility to affirm both the African/black side of Puerto Rican culture, which has been marginalized, and the Loizan identity, for which Loizans have been discriminated against inside and outside Loíza. This is even truer for the residents of Medianía Alta who have been discriminated against by other Loizans.[28]

In New Haven, there is an established critical connection between the festival, cultural/ethnic recognition, and political power. The leaders of FLECHAS see political power as an essential step toward the economic stability of the *whole* Puerto Rican community, especially when considering their position in the United States as "marginal" or as a "minority" (despite their U.S. citizenship by birth). This middle step between cultural recognition and financial stability is easily disregarded, since it requires the leaders to consider the voice of the people. I found that this is an area in which many Loizans in Loíza and Connecticut claim Loíza's municipal government has fallen short; such assessment is currently an issue of contention in Loíza's politics.

Such an association between cultural recognition, political power, and economic stability is also believed to encourage the unity between generations, which, as Glasser confirms,[29] has become an important issue in Connecticut because of a growing socioeconomic and geographical gap between various Puerto Rican sectors. The leadership of FLECHAS has fought hand in hand with local residents and Hispanic elected officials for important causes in New Haven, such as Puerto Rican history, culture and bilingual education (begun in 1977). It should not be surprising that increasing the rate of property ownership for Hispanics has been an important concern of the FLECHAS leadership. To accomplish these goals, FLECHAS has tried successfully to recruit members of the academic community in the state of Connecticut (e.g., Yale University and the University of Connecticut), including Puerto Ricans and other Hispanics.

After many attempts to obtain the recognition and support of the Puerto Rican government, on June 17, 2002, the governor of Puerto Rico proclaimed July 11 as the official day of the festival of Loíza in Connecticut. The leadership of FLECHAS has worked to establish solid economic and social relationships between New Haven and Loíza, but, according to former Loíza's PNP mayor, Ferdín Carrasquillo, Loíza's urgent needs and priorities have always interfered with these efforts. A few years ago, Loíza's mayor carried the saint during the festival's procession in New Haven. Ironically, FLECHAS has recommended a limited role for Loíza's mayor, asking him to come "wearing only his cultural hat" to avoid *partidismo* (i.e., partisanship) or promoting any personal political agenda. Loizan artists such as the musical bomba group *Balet folklórico de los hermanos Ayala* have participated in the festival, and Loizan artists like Samuel Lind and Evelyn Vázquez have participated as members of the board of FLECHAS.

The festival in Connecticut is usually celebrated on a weekend in the middle of July to avoid interfering with the July 25 celebration in Loíza. Loizans and non-Loizans travel from Puerto Rico and other states to participate and vice versa. The festival in Connecticut, like its Loizan counterpart, includes a variety of activities, but unlike the festival in Loíza, which lasts 10 days, the festival in Connecticut lasts only 3. This happens in spite of tempting offers to FLECHAS by sponsors to extend the festival to attract the youth clientele.

FLECHAS is careful to safeguard the theme of the festival and also the Puerto Rican image and cause in general. This is especially so in light of the statistics concerning the prevalent negative stereotypes associated with the generally poor economic status of Puerto Ricans in the United States. The organization has also taken note of the unfortunate events associated with Puerto Rican parades around the nation, some of which have been covered by the media. The festival in Loíza in the last several years has been associated with the controversy surrounding the local government's plans for the town's development by using Loíza's natural resources and its unique culture. The festival is considered to best serve these purposes, only to benefit a few Loizans and outsiders. (In the last decade, Loiza has attracted a significant number of new residents through the construction of tourist residential and multipurpose buildings.) There has also been an increase in criminal activity in Loiza related to the festival.

In this chapter, I can provide only a truncated account of the challenges surrounding FLECHAS. What is clear is that in New Haven, as in Loíza, some Puerto Ricans, including Loizans, claim that the festival or too much attention to culture in general diverts attention from real issues, such as unemployment or underemployment, poor housing and social services, and that the money could be used for solving many of these immediate problems. Loizans have reacted to this criticism by pointing out the fact that the festival, among other things, promotes culture in a way that makes possible to *ganarse unos chavitos* (make some money) by marketing culture and other things. Some criticize the festival's African emphasis, and there have been attempts to create organizations that emphasize Loiza's Indian and Spanish heritage, although these have had little success.

In New Haven, there are Pentecostals, who have openly defended the Puerto Rican African heritage; some of them are educated religious leaders. However, also as in Loíza, a large group of Pentecostals, including a good number from Puerto Rico and Loíza, associate the African elements of the festival—particularly the *vejigantes* and the very percussive and danceable rhythms of *bomba*—with evil forces and subsequently, with Loizans' socioeconomic problems. These Pentecostals have publicly attacked FLECHAS and politicians who have supported the organization's priorities and agendas. These accusations have used a religious premise. Regarding the latter, the leaders of FLECHAS and its political supporters have been publicly referred to as pagan. This information has been used during the campaign season in public communications to discredit both politicians who have supported FLECHAS and the projects that are supposed to benefit the Puerto Rican and Latino communities in general.

The news spread rapidly when, during one of the festival's processions, a Pentecostal leader publicly attacked members and supporters of FLECHAS over loudspeakers. FLECHAS's founding member and leader Menen Osorio has been accused repeatedly of being a witch and a *santera* because of the way she dresses (she told me she often wears all black, white, or red), her hobby of making black dolls, and her having created an alleged Santería altar in the office of FLECHAS (according to her and other members of FLECHAS, this is instead a permanent exhibition of Afro-Puerto Rican arts and crafts). These attacks continued despite her public Catholic affiliation and denials. However, the controversy is broader and quite complicated as the voice of nonchurchgoers, the nonreligious sector, and different religious and political sides clamor to be heard.[30]

Politicians have taken note of the steadily growing Hispanic Pentecostal sector in New Haven and now give serious consideration to the Pentecostal point of view. Some of these Pentecostals, including a good number of Puerto Ricans, are politically active and also have promoted certain (Hispanic) political leaders and agendas during their meetings. A few years ago, FLECHAS was involved in a legal battle for permanent possession of the building where its office had been located. Residents who supported FLECHAS claimed that New Haven's government was not facilitating this acquisition in order to satisfy Pentecostal voters, especially the members of a Pentecostal church who wanted the building for their permanent use and who have accused members of FLECHAS of paganism. Other Pentecostals, though, prefer to stay neutral regarding the festival, and FLECHAS in general. These individuals respect and support the things the organization has done for the community (e.g., educating the community on Puerto Rican culture, and social and political issues, and fighting for better social services and housing rights). A few residents try to stay optimistic and consider these conflicts as an opportunity for interreligious dialogue. Some efforts in this direction seem to be moving forward, both for the community and key individuals.

The Religious Implications of FLECHAS and the Transnationalization of Puerto Rican Folklorized Culture

In New Haven, the festival is generally considered more cultural than religious. As is the case in Loíza, this view, which disassociates tradition from religion, justifies some Catholic and even Protestant participation. Especially from the Protestant and even the Pentecostal perspective, as a tradition, the festival does not represent a threat or competition at the spiritual level. At the same time, the official religious aspect is encouraged by some as part of the festival, especially by those members or supporters of FLECHAS who are members of Saint Rose of Lima Parish. In Loíza, the existence of a parish in honor of Santiago does not eliminate the need for this religious encouragement. This is because of the common view that the parish is more of a "real (spiritual) thing" than the festival, especially when considering that in the last several years the festival has increasingly adopted a secular character.

This promotion of the official religious aspect of the festival in New Haven, through the celebration of a Mass in St. Rose of Lima Parish, is also intended to give more credibility and seriousness to the festival and to encourage the participation of a group of people who otherwise would not have an interest in the festival, Puerto Rican identity, or the African/Loizan experience. The Catholic Church obviously benefits from these events by keeping people close by. However, unlike in Loíza, the low attendance at the Mass and lack of interest in this component in New Haven may be an indication, among others, that most are comfortable dissociating official religion from tradition or culture.

The tension between cultural and religious celebrations may be considered an aspect of both nationalization and transnationalization. When local folk religion is considered as a manifestation of traditional values, then festivals like Loiza's become instances of cultural preservation and identity disappearing in other aspects of a rapidly industrializing society. As discussed elsewhere,[31] at the end of the 1960s Puerto Rican folklore in general gained significant media attention. Loíza's and Medianía Alta's folklore in particular included *vejigante* crafts and local *frituras* (i.e., local fried fast food) and was identified as a source of townspeople's pride and an important means of survival.[32] Still, as Dávila has demonstrated, the African or black component (as well as the subject of slavery) has been marginalized or disregarded for the most part.[33]

The media attention to Loíza and Medianía Alta was consistent with a developing folklorization of culture. According to Dávila, the folklorization of Puerto Rican culture at the time was not unique to Puerto Rico, but part of a concurrent worldwide trend that has been linked to a reconfiguration of hegemonic centers and to global economic changes.[34] Dávila defines folklorization as a turn to those aspects that were deemed authentically Puerto Rican, while alluding to Puerto Rican ethnic building blocks. The media and government organizations greatly contributed to this process of folklorization, and Loíza became a venue and an example of it.

The successful selling of folklore during the 1970s by foreign (i.e., U.S.) and local corporations, although not unique to Puerto Rico, had to do in great part with the island's colonial context. As Duany observes, defending Puerto Rican national culture has been the official rhetoric of the three main parties—

pro-Commonwealth PPD, pro-statehood PNP, and pro-independence PIP—regardless of their political stance vis-à-vis the United States.[35] The selling of culture was spurred on by the economic recession of the time.[36] Informal economic activities, including those related to the country's folklore, became a means of survival for many families.[37] Therefore, during this time, it was common to see Loizan families and individuals selling "local culture" on the streets and outsiders wanting to visit Loíza to taste "authentic" or "very traditional" (Puerto Rican) culture. It is not surprising, therefore, to see similar usages of culture and religion among the Loizans in Connecticut, while expressing a tension between the two. In fact, the travel back and forth from both locations tends to reinforce the need for maintaining the festival as a unique symbol of African-based Puerto Rican identity and as a means to counter marginalization and economic deprivation.

Conclusion—"Looking Back in Order to Move Forward"

Loizans in New Haven can be credited for retaking a process of self-identification that they left behind or started in Loíza. This political process clearly refers to the strategic "self-identification" model developed by Scherer in his characterization of the Chinese Cuban dynamics of identity.[38] The model is also intended to critique Said's popular book—*Orientalism*.[39] Orientalism is understood as a product of the West derived from an essentialist view of both the East and the West (or the Orient and the Occident) while ignoring the *different* and *multigeographical* (my emphasis) voices of the "Orientals" themselves. In a similar way, Loizans' self-identification is not isolated from external representation, but it is neither homogeneous nor straightforward. Their capacity for "self-orientalization" should be emphasized considering that most of the literature about black Puerto Ricans like the Loizans ignores how they represent themselves. Over a long period of time, as traced in my work, they continue to fashion an identity that fits both a transnational context and the diverse exigencies of everyday life.

Moreover, the case of FLECHAS refers to various interrelated self-identification strategies. First is the use of a popular symbol, a religious tradition that was already culturally, socially, and politically meaningful to Loizans, under some kind of relationship with official religion. One can see that this strategy makes an issue of the distinctions between secular and religious, official and popular, ideal and actual, symbolic and practical. Even though I cannot elaborate further on this here, the case of FLECHAS demonstrates how both popular and official religion answers the challenge to their integrity and authenticity.

Here I would like to react to Harris's use of James C. Scott's distinction between public transcript and hidden transcript.[40] The first refers to the way power relations manifest openly and where the perspective of the oppressor is what matters. The second refers to the ways the oppressed confronts the oppressor offstage, where the power holders cannot see it. Harris considers this distinction useful to better interpret the meaning of the festival of Santiago celebrated in Puerto Rico. While recognizing his invaluable (but unchallenged) contribution, Harris has targeted Puerto Rican anthropologist Ricardo Alegría for his simplistic portrayal of the festival as the syncretic mixture of Spanish and African traditions.[41] According to Harris, Alegría's portrayal is more along the lines of the idea of the festival held by those in positions of authority (religious and government officials and scholars). Therefore, it corresponds to public transcript. Harris sees Loizans' actual participation and performance in the festival as a true manifestation of hidden transcript. However, as I have attempted to demonstrate here, the Loizan experience articulates more of a dynamic than a "neat" distinction between the two types of transcripts, between the powerful and the powerless, the ideal and the actual, the symbolic and the practical. In fact, Loizans in Loíza and New Haven subscribe to both transcripts and make good and "on stage" use of a kind of negotiation between the two. (Loizans do not necessarily need me to read and interpret the hidden transcript for them. My job is to put it all together on paper.)

The events around FLECHAS are not far from the usual understanding of ethnicity as the enhancement of collective political and economic interests. Raising African/Loizan cultural/ethnic pride by celebrating a festival that is capable of symbolizing social unity, racial integration, and a reversal of power structures is a major step in making these functions actually happen during, before, and after the celebration. This is the second strategy. Loizans have surely experienced discrimination. Even though race has not been as a strong issue in Puerto Rico as in the United States, in Connecticut the significance of race is strategically minimized or used less consistently than cultural/ethnic identity. As a Loizan explained it more fundamentally: "Still today, many Americans do not believe that we are Puerto Ricans [because of our skin color and facial features]." Ironically, discrimination against Puerto Ricans can be seen in the fact that in the United States, Puerto Rican literature and the Afro-Puerto Rican theme has not been as good a "cultural capital" as Cuban American literature and the Afro-Cuban theme.[42]

The issue of national identity in relation to FLECHAS brings to mind Duany's popular distinction between cultural nationalism and political nationalism.[43] This opens discussion of the third strategy: the use of Puerto Rican experience or identity as referent, while critiquing it and simultaneously redefining it. According to Duany, cultural nationalism is opposed to political nationalism, which promotes a concrete nation-state. Cultural nationalism has been pushed forward by the pro-Commonwealth PPD since the 1950s as a collective label for the majority of Puerto Ricans in the island and the mainland. Puerto Rico's distinctive collective identity is capable of political critiquing even without the support of a Puerto Rican nation-state. I argue that the experience of Loizans refers to cultural nationalism not so much because of the assertion of Puerto Rico's distinctive collective identity, but because of a critique against this collective identity. In this case, I agree with Duany's contention of cultural nationalism by arguing that Loizans' cultural nationalism is not a lesser or minor form of political nationalism. Instead, it is as political as it can be without a sovereign state being their ultimate goal or an issue at all.

I also agree with Duany when he sees the "strong" potential of cultural nationalism to subvert ideologically the colonial regime in Puerto Rico. I underscore the word "ideologically" because as Duany himself states in his conclusion, a big impediment for political nationalism is the "different" everyday life experience of migrants.[44] They include both Puerto Ricans who once migrated from the island and those who have never been on the island, a distinction that merits emphasis. Moreover, the power of religion to represent transnationalism in geographical terms also may be used to transcend political boundaries.

In summary, the nature of the festival and the goals of FLECHAS—religious expression, cultural celebration, and public entertainment, with political and economic consequences—refer to a building process that adds new elements. Simultaneously all of these reflect upon the experience back in Puerto Rico. In other words, Loizans and other Puerto Ricans support the goals of FLECHAS because they fit not only their life in Connecticut but also resonate with Loizans' past experiences on the island. This is especially significant because of the elements linked to ethnic/cultural background, race/color and town identity, religious practice, economic well-being, and the political meaning of current events in Loíza.

In special ways, the social and political activities of FLECHAS have generated conflicts with racial or ethnic overtones. The conflicts are echoed in friction between Catholics who support the festival's organizers and Pentecostals in New Haven who reject it. As already hinted, these conflicts have pushed FLECHAS supporters to become even more politically active. More recently, the threat of turning the political activism around FLECHAS into strict party politics has created a greater division and decreased support for the festival by the larger community, which includes Loizans. There have been talks about creating another Loizan (or Puerto Rican) festival. However, steps have been taken to deal with the above issues, for example, bringing about a complete change in the leadership of FLECHAS and creating an interparty and interreligious dialogue. We will have to wait for the future to determine how the relationship between FLECHAS and religious groups (whether Catholic or Protestant) will develop and which route FLECHAS will take politically.

This chapter has presented the interconnectedness of the transnational Loizan experience, which is never well understood by an exclusive focus either only on the island or life in Connecticut. However, at a time when the newness of transnational links are overemphasized, as Hamilton and Stolz Chinchilla remind us, the important thing is not to probe transnationalism by showing (or even forcing) connections, but to stress the active role of international immigrants in shaping their own experiences within transnational contexts, while transforming both the receiving and sending societies in the process.[45] Clearly, the time limitation of my research did not allow me to examine the full extent of this "shaping" and "transforming." Future research should consider that transnationalism is manifested differently among communities, and at different levels (i.e., birthplace, ancestry, blood relations, sentiments, attitudes, communication, and physical interactions). Thus, Loizans in Connecticut experience Puerto Rico and Loíza basically at the first six levels, while encouraging more physical interactions with Puerto Ricans and Loizans in the island. It will be useful in future research to compare how Loíza is being transformed by the events of FLECHAS and its efforts for interaction with similar processes among other transnational groups.

All of the above goes back to the frequent omission or superficial analysis of the Diaspora in the Puerto Rican experience/identity. Other times, precisely in reaction to this omission, connections between Puerto Ricans in the mainland and the island are assumed or forced. The findings here are also significant when considering that Puerto Rican politics on the island and of the Diaspora are mainly understood as an issue of nationalism and in terms of the country's relationship with the United States or *los americanos* (who are usually portrayed by Puerto Ricans, including scholars, as an homogeneous group).

This chapter may have posed more questions than given answers. Some of these questions may be answered in other chapters of this book. One of these questions is: If Catholics are as political as Protestants, what are the real differences? Studies of Latino religions describe general patterns, but they also should note differences between Latino Catholic and Protestant sociopolitical participation and within each group. These differences may be subsumed among racial, ethnic, and religious symbols, but they are nonetheless essential to understanding Latino politics. Examining these circumstances can shed more light onto Latinos' redefinitions of what is political, what is religious, and the relationship between the two.

Notes

1. Fieldwork in Loíza spanned more than 12 months between 1996 and 2003. It involved historical, literary, Internet, and audiovisual research, open-ended conversations, formal and informal interviews (some of which were conducted in more recent years), a survey, questionnaires to individuals and religious groups, and participant observation. I conducted literary research and interviews with people in New Haven. I would like to thank Loizans in Loíza and in New Haven and members of FLECHAS for their participation in this research project. I draw special attention to informants Menen Osorio and Kevin Díaz. The information in this chapter is more extensively discussed elsewhere (Hernández Hiraldo 2006: 32–69, 120–40).
2. Loizans use a wide variety of racial terminology. In my survey, there were at least 30 color classifications. Elsewhere (Hernández Hiraldo 2006: 37–40), I have analyzed the meaning of this pattern in relation to Puerto Rico.
3. Dávila 1997: 93.
4. Harris 2000.
5. Harris 2000: 36.
6. Harris 2000: 18–21, 31–36 et passim.
7. Harris 2000: 250.
8. Harrison 1985.
9. Hernández Hiraldo 2006: 99–114; Zaragoza 1995: 58–65, et passim.
10. In fact, a controversy related to this issue surfaced in the town of Comerío in 1971. It resulted in the expulsion of the Dominican friars from their administration of the parish (Díaz-Stevens 1993).
11. Zaragoza 1995: 72.
12. Zaragoza 1995: 101, 56.
13. Zaragoza 1995: 62; Alegría 1954: 22–25.
14. Editor's note: Presently, July 25 has other political connotations for Puerto Rico, related to Puerto Rico's status with the United States. On July 25, 1898, U.S. troops landed in the southern coast of Puerto Rico, beginning the Puerto Rican campaign of the Spanish–Cuban–American War, which resulted in Puerto Rico becoming a territory of the United States. On July 25, 1952, Puerto Rico inaugurated its Commonwealth status under which it attained self-government over local matters as an unincorporated territory of the United States. July 25 is therefore a state holiday in Puerto Rico.
15. *See* Romberg, 2003: 16, 36–37.

16. Hernández Hiraldo 2006.
17. Estado Libre Asociado de Puerto Rico, Junta de Planificación 1968: 21–22.
18. Hurborn 2001: 121.
19. Harris 2000.
20. Tweed 1999: 142.
21. Duany 2002: 261–80.
22. Giusti 1994.
23. Duany and Matos-Rodríguez 2006.
24. Duany 2002: 208–35.
25. *See* Glasser 1997.
26. Duany 2002: 211.
27. *Bomba*, a drumming with dance, is associated with different Afro-Puerto Rican towns in the island. There are at least two kinds of Loizan bomba: the *seis* and the *corvé*. Loíza's bomba is commonly known as a faster rhythm and with stronger and deeper drum sound than other kinds of bomba.
28. Loizans are convinced they have suffered a double discrimination at the personal level, directly and in subtle ways: one for being black and the other for being a black Loizan. I heard many stories relating to this issue, although every now and then I also encountered an attitude of denial (even after admitting having experienced discrimination personally). This is similar to the denial one encounters when talking about slavery, and it seems to come from a belief that admitting racism is a way of supporting it or complying with it. However, the issue is further addressed elsewhere (Hernández Hiraldo 2006).
29. Glasser 1997: 175–177.
30. For more information about this controversy, *see* "Lawsuit claims 'voodoo' slander" by Angela Carter in *New Haven Register*, November 15, 2003 and in www.yale.edu/tnj/35-3/bcontent.htm/.
31. Hernández Hiraldo 2006: 46.
32. *El Mundo*, July 13, 1968: 1, 3, and 5.
33. Dávila 1997: 43, 71–73, 177–182.
34. Dávila 1997: 64–65.
35. Duany 2002: 17.
36. Dávila 1997: 169–189.
37. Scarano 1993: 815–816.
38. Scherer 2001.
39. Said 1978.
40. Harris 2000: 23–25.
41. Harris 2001.
42. Flores 2000: 177–179.
43. Duany 2002: 17, 123–124.
44. Duany 2002: 282, 284.
45. Hamilton and Stolz Chinchilla 2001: 10–11.

"It's a Calling to Get Involved . . . " The Catholic Charismatic Movement and Civic Engagement among Mexican Immigrants

G. Cristina Mora

Every Wednesday evening, about 30 Mexican immigrant gardeners, factory workers, housewives, and janitors convene in a small Knights of Columbus civic hall in Paxton Heights,[1] a Mexican immigrant community in Los Angeles, California. Upon entering the meeting space, this group of immigrants transforms into a vital Catholic Charismatic faith community called *Sangre de Cristo en el Barrio* (Blood of Christ in the Neighborhood). For three hours, Sangre de Cristo members sing, dance, pray, and give testimonials about the "power of the Holy Spirit" in their lives. After the final closing prayer, as members gather their belongings, announcements are given about the upcoming events at Santa Lucia, the group's affiliated Catholic parish. The events range from monthly parish fundraisers, to parenting and marriage counseling classes, to neighborhood vigils against gang violence. With each announcement, a sign-up sheet is distributed and Sangre de Cristo members are recruited to help organize and lead the different events.

Indeed, parish and community service, and civic engagement more generally, are important aspects of Sangre de Cristo. In an interview, one long-time member described the importance of service by noting that "being a Catholic and a Charismatic requires that we serve . . . it's a calling to get involved and to help the community." When asked what service meant, he elaborated that "it means . . . providing the Eucharist to the sick, becoming a

Catechist, organizing the food and clothing drives [for the homeless] . . . and just taking steps to make sure that you help [to improve] the community."

This chapter explores the issue of religion and civic engagement among Latino immigrants by examining the case of Catholic Charismatics. While high-profile works have theorized that Mexican immigrants' relatively low-levels of civic engagement, especially their low rates of voluntarism and political participation, is connected to their Catholic faith,[2] cross-sectional research,[3] and Catholicism's contemporary immigrant advocacy role suggest otherwise.[4] Nonetheless, several questions remain about *how* immigrants reconcile religious beliefs with civic engagement, or service to their communities, and about how U.S. Catholicism facilitates this behavior.

Drawing on interviews and ethnographic data, this chapter examines these issues among Mexican Immigrant Catholic *Charismatics* [hereafter, Charismatics]. I argue that Charismaticism provides immigrants with a new vocabulary with which to connect community service to spiritual growth, while the organizational structure of Charismatic prayer groups provides members with the skills, information, and resources that are necessary for civic engagement. In this manner, Sangre de Cristo members not only develop an understanding that serving others is integral to their relationship with the sacred, but also become invested in maintaining an organizational environment that facilitates volunteerism, social activism and other forms of civic activity. In the following pages, I first discuss the literature on Catholicism and immigrant civic engagement. Second, I describe the Catholic Charismatic movement and note how it has increased exponentially within the Latino immigrant community. Third, I detail the frames that Charismatics develop, and show how they provide an impetus for community service. Last, I delineate how the organizational structure of Catholic Charismaticism facilitates civic engagement by providing resources and opportunities to become civically involved. I conclude by discussing the implications of this study for understanding Latino civic engagement more generally.

Religion, Civic Engagement, and Latino Immigration

Historically, immigrant religious organizations have contributed to the civic development of their communities by mobilizing constituents for political action, and by providing an infrastructure that promotes service activities.[5] These churches have thus led efforts toward reforming union and local government politics, so as to funnel resources to the immigrant community, and have developed their own direct, social service programs. Of course, immigrant churches have varied in their civic involvement—for example, while some congregations directly aligned themselves with political campaigns and causes, others have preferred to provide their members with the information to independently participate in civil society.[6] While it has been documented that immigrant mainline Protestant and Pentecostal churches have historically encouraged civic involvement among Latinos,[7] the Catholic Church has been the subject of much debate.

For the most part, scholars agree that, historically, the U.S. Catholic Church was a conduit for civic engagement among European immigrants. Perhaps the best example of this is the nineteenth-century U.S. Irish Catholic Church, whose mission it was to improve the condition of Irish immigrant communities. Irish Catholic clergy not only encouraged parishioners to protest and demand more resources, they also helped Irish Catholics to run for office and transform political institutions from the inside.[8] Works on the Polish immigrant Catholic Church identify the same phenomena and note the important role that the Polish clergy played in reproducing machine politics in Chicago.[9] In addition, scholars have documented how the Italian immigrant Catholic Church trained its laity to provide social services to the Italian immigrant community.[10]

The Church's history of direct advocacy work on behalf of Latino immigrants, however, has been mixed. The practice of segregating Latino parishioners in basement churches,[11] creating *separate but equal* classrooms within Catholic schools, and prohibiting Spanish on school and parish grounds ostracized Latinos from the Church during the first half of the twentieth century.[12] These practices were met with loud disproval from Latino immigrant leaders, who coordinated sit-ins in Catholic churches and demanded that the clergy become more responsive to Latino immigrant communities.[13] Indeed, it was Latinos' popular religion, centered on ethno-religious symbols and festivals, which helped them to remain Catholic despite facing hostility from American churches.[14]

The 1960s was a watershed in Latino–Catholic Church relations: Latino activists, like César Chávez, crafted mobilizing frames that linked social activism to moral and religious arguments.[15] More importantly, while not having the formal support of the Catholic Church, activists learned to use ethno-religious symbols, like the *Virgen de Guadalupe*, to galvanize Latinos.[16] Gradually, as these movements gained wide recognition, clergy began publically supporting Latino causes and called for change within the Catholic Church.[17] By the mid-1980s, the Church hierarchy had established a Secretariat for Hispanic Affairs and had begun to institute programs that targeted Latino immigrants. Moreover, individual parishes in Latino neighborhoods began to develop their laity and promoted the idea of civic engagement, including voluntarism and community advocacy, among parishioners.[18]

For the most part, the study of religion and Latino civic engagement has been purview of Catholic theologians.[19] This work has argued that Catholic spirituality plays a role in positively shaping immigrants' civic attitudes and political inclinations as they are manifested both domestically and transnationally. Despite this, some frame Catholicism as a cultural problem for Latino civic involvement. Specifically, the comparatively low rates of Latino immigrant voluntarism and political participation are often viewed as a direct extension of their *otherworldly* faith and popular religiosity.[20] Thus, Huntington distinguishes between Latino Catholicism and "American Catholicism" and argues that the latter is decidedly different from its Latino version because it is less reliant on papal authority and, thus, promotes a type of self-reliance that encourages individuals to participate in civil society. Additionally, Huntington contends that Latinos' dependence on a Catholic-like salvation theology reproduces notions of fatalism that are fundamentally incompatible with the American creed. Quoting political pundits, he suggests that Latinos lack a sense of civic duty because they "accept poverty as a virtue for entrance into heaven" and lack ambition.[21] For Huntington, it is the unique combination of Latino culture, which leads people to accept their lot, and Catholicism, which is paternalistic and authoritative, that hinders their civic participation.

Others draw a more structural link between Catholicism and the low levels of Latino civic activity. Verba et al. argue that the structure of U.S. Catholicism promotes a dependence on clergy and therefore inhibits opportunities that otherwise motivate community individuals to volunteer and become politically involved.[22] Specifically, they posit that because Latino Catholic churches, more so than mainstream churches, adhere to a strict, hierarchical structure, there are little opportunities for immigrants to learn skills and to take on leadership roles. As such, they contend that Latino Catholics, more so than mainstream Catholics, are less likely to receive, and know how to act on, invitations to become civically involved.

However, both Huntington's and Verba et al.'s studies are short on empirical evidence. Various scholars have noted that Huntington provides little primary data to support his controversial claims about Latino culture.[23] Moreover, Verba et al.'s assessment of Latinos fails to control for pertinent factors that influence civic participation, such as church attendance and length of stay in the United States.[24] Thus, Jones-Correa and Leal's 2001 study on Latino civic involvement found that both church attendance and Catholicism were *positively* associated with civic engagement among Latinos. Nonetheless, there are still several unanswered questions about *how* religion can inspire community involvement. The following sections address this issue by focusing on Mexican Catholic Charismatic immigrants.

Catholic Charismaticism

Sangre de Cristo is one of over 30 different Catholic Charismatic prayer groups affiliated with Santa Lucia, and it forms part of a religious movement that is growing rapidly within Latino immigrant neighborhoods. The Pew Hispanic Research Center estimates that more than half of U.S. Latino Catholics, over 15 million persons, self-identify as Charismatic.[25] By this statistic, there are more Latino Charismatics than Muslims living in the United States, and the number of Latino Catholic Charismatics rivals the number of U.S. Jews. In contrast, Charismaticism has only grown moderately among non-Latino Catholics, as only about 12 percent of non-Hispanic Catholics are Charismatic.[26]

Charismatic worship differs starkly from traditional Catholicism. As a revival movement, it emphasizes the development of a personal relationship with God made possible through a *born-again* or *renewal* experience.[27] The new relationship with the sacred is publicly expressed through charisms, or gifts of the Holy Spirit, which include the ability to speak in tongues, experience visions, and even prophecy.[28] Sustained through interdependent prayer groups, Charismaticism also promotes a level of member-to-member intimacy not available in traditional Catholic services.[29] Thus, within the familiar space of the prayer group, members often refer to one another as *brothers* and *sisters* and share testimonials about their private lives.[30] In addition, Charismatic immigrants adhere to strict moral codes that, in turn, inspire a disciplined adherence to prayer and religious service.[31] Indeed, unlike traditional Catholics, Charismatics often attend religious functions several times a week and engage in various prayer rituals.

Despite these differences in worship, Charismatics strive to maintain a connection between the movement and traditional Roman Catholicism by stressing their adherence to the Catholic mass and their loyalty to a Catholic parish. Perhaps most important for Latino immigrants, Charismatics also stress the importance of the Marian devotion.[32] While non-Catholic Christians consider images and statues of the Blessed Mother as, at best, a Catholic addition to faith in Christ and as, at worst, a form of idolatry, Charismatics consider them important symbols of Christian devotion and Catholic loyalty. Latino Charismatics, then, often uphold Marian devotion in order to highlight their connections to Catholicism and to distance themselves from Pentecostal Protestants, whose worship style parallels Catholic Charismaticism.[33]

Among Latino immigrants, the Charismatic movement has also inspired the establishment of various formal umbrella organizations, such as *El Sembrador* and *Carisma en Misiones*, that endorse service within immigrant communities by providing classes that teach Charismatics, among other things, how to lead youth and family outreach programs through their parishes. Latino Charismatics in Los Angeles have even created their own satellite television station, whose 24-hour program lineup includes lectures and focus groups that discuss current events.[34]

At the parish level, Latino Charismatics are often active lay members and help in various activities from fundraising to building maintenance. Indeed, despite often juggling full-time jobs and family obligations, Charismatics are among the most active members in Latino Catholic parishes.[35]

Data and Methods

Using data gathered from in-depth interviews, this work provides a glimpse of Charismatic life among Mexican immigrants and explores how it might relate to civic engagement. In the summer of 2005 and winter of 2006, I interviewed 22 women and 12 men. The interviewees ranged in age from 28 to 72 years, with the modal age at 45 years. All of the interviewees were *working class* or *poor*, and most had resided in Los Angeles for at least a decade. The interviews lasted between 30 minutes and two-and-a-half hours, and they took place wherever members felt most comfortable: in their homes, at parks, at coffee shops, at workplaces, and at the Knights of Columbus Hall. All interviews were conducted in Spanish, as only three of the interviewees spoke English fluently.

I also attended weekly Sangre de Cristo meetings, the weekly Charismatic mass at Santa Lucia, various Saturday seminars led by Sangre de Cristo members, and the national retreats sponsored by Catholic Charismatic umbrella organizations. This ethnographic data allowed me to contextualize much of the interview data that I collected. In the following pages, I detail how Charismatics describe their spirituality and show how it is linked to civic engagement, in particular to parish service, community volunteering, and social activism.

Catholic Charismaticism and Sangre de Cristo Members

Sangre de Cristo's Wednesday night meetings are organized by a six-person, core leadership team and usually begin a little after seven in the evening. The first half hour of the meeting is allocated specifically for *alabanzas* [praises], a combination of singing and intermittent, spontaneous prayer. The next hour is allocated for public testimonials. If there are no testimonials, a group leader or a member who has been recognized by the group as possessing the gift of preaching will select a Bible passage and discuss its meaning. The last hour of the meeting is dedicated to deep prayer. The hall lights are turned off, and members pray softly while that week's speaker takes the microphone and encourages group members to "open their hearts to the Lord." In this hour, newer members are asked to kneel in the front of the hall as senior members place their hands atop them and pray. At the same time, some members speak in tongues, and others become so deep in prayer that they often *fall in the spirit.*

Despite being baptized Catholics, the tenets of Charismaticism encourage immigrants to form a new individualized relationship with the divine that is based on a "conversion-like" experience. For many, the experience of initially falling in the Lord denotes their moment of rebirth and the beginning of their Charismatic spirituality. Often people describe this experience as cloaked in mystery and miracle. Carlos, a 38-year-old construction worker, describes his experience:

> They were praying for me, and I felt a droplet of water; and I turned around and nothing. But that droplet continued. I remember that I thought I was going crazy but I kept trying to concentrate. They kept praying and I felt a chill inside me, deep inside me, like if the droplet was penetrating me inside. But when they finished praying it was amazing—I suddenly realized that I had just been reborn. I felt a change in my life, but a change so huge that I can't even explain it.

These experiences mark Charismatics' entrance into the movement. For Carlos, it was a mysterious drop of water that only he could feel that let him know a miracle was taking place; for others it is the apparition of the Lord's face or the sudden feeling of peace and "falling in the spirit" that authenticated their renewal/rebirth. Charismatics believe that experiences serve as proof that they are called on to develop a new relationship with the sacred.

"Falling in the spirit" marks the beginning of a *spiritual journey,* or a quest to continuously grow in faith.[36] Like other Charismatics, Sangre de Cristo members believe that one must continuously witness these seemingly miraculous experiences in order to mature spirituality and thus stave off evil forces. Indeed, Charismatics claim to develop a heightened awareness of the devil and the destructive forces that distract their spiritual journey.[37] Even Carlos, who stated he felt that his life had changed since entering the movement, noted that he had to "keep struggling" to maintain his change. He confessed:

> I see [that] the devil wants to stick in his tail and wants to separate me from my walk with the Lord. He wants to trip me and tell me, "Hey come over here— you were here once before. . . ." He wants to lure me to hell once again.

Charismatics also learn that following certain disciplinary codes helps them stay on their path of spiritual growth. Sangre de Cristo members thus learn that certain dress styles are *wordly* and not becoming of a person who is spiritually reborn; tank tops, shorts, and oversize pants are frowned upon. Secular activities like dancing and listening to non-Christian music, wearing too much make-up, drinking, and gambling are also restricted. Moreover, Charismatics learn that they must develop a spiritual discipline by praying and, more importantly, conversing with God on a constant basis.

As a result of these experiences, Charismatics claim to develop a new understanding of the sacred. For example, when asked to describe how her understanding of God changed since she became a part of Sangre de Cristo, Elvia, a 40-year-old housewife, stated:

> I had grown up believing the Lord was a punishing Lord. In my private moments, I would pray to La Virgen de Guadalupe—I felt that she was the one who was always with me. And whenever something bad happened, I would attribute it to God punishing me for something I had done in the past—and I would pray to the Virgin to help me in these times.
> *What kind of "bad things" would happen?*
> Like, for example, when my daughter would act up and when she ran away from home, I felt it was God that was punishing me because I had been so rebellious towards my own mother. So I felt he was finally punishing me for having been so bad in the past.
> *And now, what kind of relationship do you have with God?*
> Well, now that I am in the movement I know that God is love, that God is all around me and that God cares. . . . I think of him as someone that is my friend, my father, my savior, and my partner. I feel that with him that anything is bearable and nothing is impossible. And now instead, when I am having problems with my husband or my children, I talk to the Lord because only he knows what his plan is.

According to Elvia, becoming Charismatic allowed her to rearrange her relationship and perception of God. Her former notion of God as vindictive and punishing has since given way to a new notion of God as supportive and loving.

Thus, for Charismatics, being a part of their movement means learning to develop a new kind of spiritual discipline and a new relationship with the sacred. In the following sections, I outline how Charismatics translate their spirituality into a calling to serve.

The Spirit as Energy

To protect themselves from evil, Charismatics believe that they must learn to "fill themselves with the Spirit" and constantly pray in order to find peace in daily situations. The emphasis on continuous prayer and peace is an integral part of a frame, what I call the "Spirit as energy" frame, which Charismatics employ often. In fact, during their meetings, Sangre de Cristo members frequently commented that "the spirit" gave them the energy that they needed to endure their often onerous workday and make time for service. For example, during one particular session, as the lights dimmed and members began to pray, Julio, a long-time member, took the microphone and prayed:

> Holy Spirit, fountain of life and healing, we put all of our tired hands before you. Our hands that are callused and tired from gardening, from housework, from moving stones and laboring all day and we give them to you. Take our tired hands and breathe new life and new energy into all of us here today because we are gathered here to serve you . . .

In the interviews, members also spoke of the "Holy Spirit as energy" frame. Carlos explained that he often works long shifts lifting bricks and heavy bags of cement. When I asked how he liked the job, he stated:

> People think it's dangerous and that it's only job for new arrivals [new immigrants], but you'll see that sometimes on my lunch break me and two other guys get together and pray. And when the Holy Spirit becomes present, you actually begin to see that those bags are not so much of a problem anymore; they actually begin to feel lighter . . .

By offering their tiredness to God, Charismatics believe that they will become renewed, better, and more energized persons filled with peace and security.

Charismatics believe that the energy that the Holy Spirit provides not only helps them endure work, but also allows them to carry out religious and community service. For example, when describing a typical week day, Ruth, a 56-year-old janitor, stated:

> When I get home from work I kneel down and I say, "Thank you, God, for having given me this job and for letting me get home safely. I give you my weariness because you know how tired I am." . . . See, when I come home from work my back hurts and my fingers are always swollen, but when I kneel down and offer my weariness to God . . . I feel that I rest. [God takes] my tiredness and I become ready for the group [Sangre de Cristo] and anything else I have planned.

Indeed, Ruth not only attends prayer groups twice a week, she also helps provide clean-up duty one weekend a month at Santa Lucia and is an active member of the Santa Lucia prison ministry.

Ultimately this new understanding of faith helps Charismatics see themselves as capable of having the time and energy for service. Indeed, Julia, a

42-year-old factory worker who has been the movement for over 15 years
spoke of the importance of service to the parish community.

> Lots of people come in [to the Charismatic Movement], I guess, because they
> like the emotions and the warm feelings of community and because it's some-
> thing different for them. But we find that many of them quickly leave when
> they realize that being a Charismatic also requires that we serve in the church
> and in the community.

The question remains however, why is *service* a part of Sangre de Cristo?

Reinterpreting the Clergy and Organized Religion

The practice of developing an individualized relationship with the sacred can
often make for tense situations when Sangre de Cristo Charismatics interact
with non-Charismatic Catholic priests. When I asked members, especially
those who had been in the Charismatic movement for decades, what the relationship between Santa Lucia clergy and Charismatics was like, they all noted
a history of tension. In fact, less than five years ago, a visiting priest threatened
to break up Sangre de Cristo because he felt that the group's worship was too
eccentric. Sangre de Cristo leaders asked members to pray so that the clergy
would not dissolve the group. In the end, the visiting clergy's aggressions
toward Sangre de Cristo subsided, and the group remained.

Although it is difficult to find direct evidence to corroborate this in the Santa
Lucia case, evidence from studies of non-Hispanic Catholic charismatic prayer
groups suggests that clergy will often try to incorporate Charismatic groups
within the church laity, and thus provide them with service responsibilities, in
order to assure some level of control over the group.[38] It is possible, then, that
the focus on service within Sangre de Cristo, and other Santa Lucia charismatic
groups, stems from the parish clergy's desire to keep prayer groups connected to
the parish. At the same time, however, Sangre de Cristo members might simply
represent an easy target for clergy who find them easy to contact and thus
extend more invitations for these organized groups to take part in parish and
community service activities. More research is needed to discern this issue.

What is certain, however, is that the historical tension between Sangre de
Cristo and the clergy provides Charismatics with new understanding of organized Catholicism. For example, Gabriel, a 52-year-old gardener who has been
in the movement for about 17 years, stated:

> Some Catholics have these ideas that the priest is really sacred. We hold them
> up like saints, or even like gods. And when they say something we don't agree

with, we think that we are the ones that are wrong; that we must repent for disagreeing. And now, since I have been in the [Charismatic] renewal, I have come
to realize that priests are human just like everyone else and they are only trying,
trying their best to interpret the word and lead their parishes. They are not per-
fect and they are not gods.

It is this new perception that allows Charismatics to ignore priests who are
hostile to the movement. One member confessed that she switched parishes
because clergy in her former church disapproved of Charismaticsm. When
asked why she thought some priests were hostile toward the movement, she
commented:

> Well, there are some priests that, I don't really know why, but they just don't
> agree with the Charismatic groups. I don't know if it's that they think that we
> are unworthy of having the spirit manifest itself within us. You know the spirit
> resides in all of us, not just the priests, and, well, the Charismatic knows special
> ways—through prayer and service—we know of ways to live the spirit by exam-
> ple. Look, we don't just go to mass, we get together and pray with each other,
> we walk around the neighborhood to spread the word, we visit the sick
> and we spend our weekends serving others. Now if a priest can't appreciate all
> that we do, well, we just need to pray for them and help them to bring out their
> inner spirit, because priests can also make mistakes . . .

Indeed, many Charismatics feel that priests who are not supportive of the
movement have not fully developed their relationship with the Spirit and have
thus been deprived of the intimate encounters with the divine. Yet at the same
time, they hold them in reverence and understand that priests are important
for Catholicism.

Frames about the Holy Spirit, new interpretations of organized Catholicism, and invitations to serve, however, are likely not enough to maintain Sangre de Cristo's focus on service. I argue that it is also the Charismatic
movement's organization structure that helps facilitate civic involvement
among immigrants.

The Charismatic Prayer Group Structure

For the most part, Catholic Charismatics exercise their faith through small
prayer groups that are connected to larger Catholic parishes. Santa Lucia parish clergy mandate that prayer groups remain relatively small (fewer than 30)
because they contend that this helps encourage testimonial sharing and facilitates intimacy among members. For Sangre de Cristo, it is both the small
prayer group structure and the affiliation with Santa Lucia that facilitates civic
engagement among members.

Learning New Skills in Charismaticism

Indeed, one of the most important things that the small prayer group structure affords Sangre de Cristo members is an opportunity to learn new skills. These skills are usually honed within the confines of the prayer group and then transferred to volunteer opportunities provided by Santa Lucia or other Catholic parishes. For example, Alberto confessed that before he joined the movement, his life was "routinized" and dull. He recounts that:

> I used to work a lot so when I would come home I just wanted to drink beer and relax. I was also addicted to *telenovelas* [Latin American soap operas]. I used to come home every day after work and just sit in front of the television for a few hours and see the seven o'clock, eight o'clock and nine o'clock soap operas. That was my life: just work and television. I had no real conversations with my wife or the rest of my family.

As a Sangre de Cristo preacher now, Alberto notes that he no longer has time to keep up with soap operas. He adds that "every day there is something new to learn in the Bible." For his preaching, Alberto notices that he spends much of his free time reading not only scripture but also newspapers and books in order to help inspire his frequent Charismatic lectures at Sangre de Cristo. He states:

> For each lecture, I have to prepare for at least two weeks. This means reading the Bible, and examining and concentrating on current events, and thinking about what God's word means right now. I get out my notebook and organize all of my thoughts so that I'm always prepared for Wednesdays. And then I give it to God, I pray that God helps me to impart his word in a way that he thinks it is needed. Sometimes it takes a while. I have to think for 10 days before I can start writing the speech; and at other times it all comes right away. That's just how the Holy Spirit works; it's when God wants it and thinks the speech is ready—not when I want it.

It is questionable whether Alberto would have gained these public speaking skills if he were not involved in Sangre de Cristo. On the one hand, the belief that he is reborn and has an intimate relationship with the sacred likely affords him the confidence he needs to develop public speaking skills. On the other hand, the relative smallness of the Sangre de Cristo group affords him a comfortable and familiar learning environment, as well as a small, yet receptive audience that likely supports his public speaking activities. If nothing else, Sangre de Cristo provides Alberto with a microphone, an audience, and a regular opportunity to speak in public.

Another member, Elvia, observes how the belief that God speaks through her to spread his word inspires her to transfer the social skills she develops in Sangre de Cristo to other settings. Indeed, Elvia takes part in the neighborhood evangelization ministry, which requires that she visit homes in the Santa Lucia neighborhood and speak to her neighbors about 'the power of the Holy Spirit." She says of this experience:

> I'm from a small ranch in Mexico. I learned not to speak unless I was spoken to and that women belong in the house. You would never see women walking in the streets by themselves and just talking to other people. So at first I was very shy and would always go out with a senior [neighborhood ministry] member. But when you begin to ask people about what is troubling them and you hear how there is so much sadness and pain that comes from being an immigrant, you can't help but to do your best and really ask God to help you give them your best prayer. So I close my eyes and just let God do the praying through me.

Elvia, then, believes that her involvement in the neighborhood ministry is possible because God works through her. What is interesting about Elvia's experience, however, is what happens during visitation. When I asked her to describe her last few visitations, she mentioned that she not only prayed with neighbors but also referred them to the various social services and resources offered by Santa Lucia. For example, she noted that during one particular visit, a community member confessed that she was having difficulty maintaining the mortgage payments on her home because her work hours had been reduced. Elvia not only prayed with the woman and invited her to Sangre de Cristo, but she also provided her with the contact information for the home-loan refinancing counselor affiliated with Santa Lucia.

Sangre de Cristo members also participate in events that are not affiliated with Santa Lucia. Carlos, for example, lives about seven miles away from Santa Lucia, yet only one mile away from Saint Peter, a Latino Catholic Church that does not have a Charismatic ministry. On Wednesdays, Carlos attends Sangre de Cristo, but on Thursdays he helps organize a men's group at Saint Peter. He explains that "we call it the school of the cross, because it's not really a prayer group, rather a series of bible meditations and a space to talk about being a father, a husband, a son." Once a month, Carlos guides the group: he picks out a Bible passage for members to discuss and prepares questions about how the passage might speak to group members' daily life.

Indeed, for Alberto, Elvia, and Carlos, Sangre de Cristo provides not only a space for them to hone new social and public speaking skills, but also the opportunity to transfer these skills to other settings. While most of their service work is affiliated with a parish, Sangre de Cristo members nonetheless learn to develop a confidence in their ability to help and engage others.

Resources for Civic Engagement

In addition, the prayer group structure of Sangre de Cristo provides Charismatics with the information and resources necessary to engage in religious and community service. As mentioned, Sangre de Cristo members, and Charismatics associated with Santa Lucia more generally, are strongly encouraged to volunteer within the Church *and* to assist the efforts of local nonprofits affiliated with Santa Lucia. Members of Santa Lucia's community service ministry thus make bimonthly announcements at Sangre de Cristo and other prayer groups and provide information on how Charismatics can volunteer at food banks and shelters associated with the Church.

The small-group structure of Sangre de Cristo helps members act on this information, because the intimacy that emerges among members facilitates the sharing of resources. For example, I observed that announcements were often followed by ride-sharing discussions. These conversations were particularly prominent with respect to announcements about events that would be held in relatively distant areas. Thus, after an announcement about a fundraiser that would be held in a town about 15 miles away, the proceeds of which would go to help an Santa Lucia-affiliated battered women's shelter, Carlos stood up and proclaimed that he could fit several people in his van. Gladys, a Sangre de Cristo member who does not own a car, motioned toward Carlos and, smiling, noted loudly that she would help to lead the *alabanzas* [hymns] during the ride. While a different organizational structure might also have led to ride-sharing, it is the small-group set-up of Sangre de Cristo that fosters intimacy and allows members to comfortably offer and accept resources from one another.

In addition, the small-group format of Sangre de Cristo provided opportunities for Charismatics to filter in new information, especially that which is not directly connected to Santa Lucia. Indeed, it was not uncommon for Sangre de Cristo members, especially those like Carlos who were also involved in other parishes, to make announcements about events being organized by other churches. At times, members also shared information about activities organized by nonreligious organizations. For example, after one Sangre de Cristo session, a member made an announcement about the upcoming U.S. citizenship courses that would be offered at Santa Lucia on weekday evenings. Quickly after that member returned to his seat, another Sangre de Cristo member rose and provided information about a similar U.S. citizenship course offered at a local community center. In effect, we could imagine that a larger group structure might not have the flexibility to provide opportunities for members to make spontaneous announcements or to share information.

Last, the small-group structure of Sangre de Cristo provides Charismatics with spontaneous opportunities to help fellow persons in their broader (non-religious) community. Because Charismatics often discuss personal dilemmas in their testimonials and because the small-group structure facilitates intimacy among group members, Charismatics are sometimes moved to help the family and friends of members in an unplanned or unforeseen manner. Thus, during one prayer group session, Carmen, a relatively new member, revealed that her mother had recently been diagnosed with cancer and would be undergoing major surgery. During her testimony, Carmen confessed that, because she was a single mother and worked full-time, she felt guilty about not having the time or the means to care for her mother post-surgery. Even though Carmen's mother was not a member of Sangre de Cristo, some Charismatics made plans to help and, unbeknownst to Carmen, agreed to prepare meals and visit the elderly woman. While these spontaneous moments of assistance were few (in a three-month period I counted two instances of help), they are significant, considering that scholars have documented that Latino immigrants have significantly low levels of volunteerism.[39]

Indeed, although there is no formal mechanism for forcing members to volunteer or participate in some kind of service activity, Charismatics craft a spiritual link between religion and service. In addition, the small group structure of Sangre de Cristo helps provide the resources, opportunities and information necessary to serve.

Opportunities for Political Action

While the structure of Sangre de Cristo facilitates volunteering, it is the prayer group's link to the Santa Lucia parish that plugs Charismatics into political activities. During the summer in which I observed Sangre de Cristo, Santa Lucia clergy held several meetings with immigrant rights activists and had agreed to support some of the marches and demonstrations that would be coordinated in downtown Los Angeles on behalf of immigration reform. In fact, the immigrant rights organizations handed out flyers outside of Santa Lucia and made regular announcements about upcoming rallies during Sunday mass. The clergy even allowed the activists to use parish facilities to plan their events. Specifically, activists organized bus trips from the Santa Lucia parking lot to the immigrant rights rallies in downtown Los Angeles in hopes of increasing support for their cause.

In the weeks leading up to one of the major marches, the coordinators of Sangre de Cristo made announcements and asked that members "get on the bus" and help support the cause. An activist even showed up at Santa Lucia's weekly Charismatic mass to answer questions about the event: some Charismatics were particularly worried that undocumented Charismatic protestors might be deported. On the day of the event, eight Sangre de Cristo members, as well as several Charismatics from other prayer groups, showed up to demonstrate.

In effect, it is unlikely that Sangre de Cristo members would have shown up in such high numbers if their parish clergy had not sanctioned the event. While the clergy could not provide them with exact assurance that participating in the marches would not lead to any negative outcomes, such as the deportation or arrest, clergy could assure them that the marches were worthy causes. Additionally, Sangre de Cristo members were likely emboldened to participate because they knew that other prayer groups and other Santa Lucia members would also be supporting the event.

Accordingly, Sangre de Cristo members developed links between spirituality and political activism. Thus, when I asked members, including those who did not demonstrate, about their feelings toward the immigrant rallies, they consistently stated that it was the Church's duty to protest on behalf of immigrants. Jesus, a 41-year-old gardener who had recently become a U.S. citizen, told me:

> The church is called to aid the needy. Even Moses, when he realized that he was an Israelite, he stood up for his people. He went to the pharaoh and demanded that he free his people. . . . I think that the church should be called to defend and to free the most needy.

Maria, a 44-year-old factory worker and 14-year veteran of the movement stated:

> You know Jesus was also an immigrant. Yes, he was Jesus of Nazareth and he and his family moved around when he was young, and he faced discrimination for being a Jew. So in that sense, I think that it's the church's duty to intercede on behalf of immigrants and the *pueblo* [community] . . .

Charismatics not only felt that it was right for the Church to stand up for social justice, but they perceived it as a sort of spiritual obligation. Being a good Christian, according to their beliefs, was tied to social activism.

Interestingly, Charismatics also drew a line between religion, politics, and community issues. Thus Catherine, a 64-year-old retiree who has been in the movement for the longest time offers her opinion:

> I don't think that the church should be involved in telling the government who should be elected or anything, but I do think that it's part of the new life being brought to the church . . . I think that the church should continue to help, to be a voice for the helpless, and the people in the community. Look around us! We need to do something about the city streetlights, and the graffiti and the gang violence . . . And the priests should be helping us, not just preaching that we need to go, but actually going to city hall with us . . . But this is not called politics, this is called defending one's *pueblo*.

Catherine noted that while she resented what she often interpreted as priests' apathy toward community involvement, she also recognized that many of the younger Charismatic priests helped organize street vigils against gang violence and often attended the immigrant rallies. According to Catherine, and other Charismatics, the Church should advocate for social justice, and not doing so would be, as Catherine elaborated, "committing a sin of omission because . . . the injustices continue."

Conclusion

In the last two decades, the Charismatic movement has grown exponentially within the Latino Catholic community. At the same time, the Catholic Church has taken a more vocal and active stance on immigration rights and immigrant services. These two shifts have arguably created unprecedented opportunities for Latinos to connect religion and civic engagement and thus become active members within their parish and immigrant communities. On the one hand, Charismaticism provides Latinos with a vocabulary about spiritual growth as well as a small-group structure, both of which facilitate Charismatics' ability to take part in service activities. On the other hand, the Catholic Church now sanctions social justice causes as moral endeavors and thus provides Latino immigrants with the motivation to help effect social change.

Of course, there is still much to be learned about how religion and civic engagement are linked. While cross-sectional research suggests a positive relationship between Catholicism and civic engagement among Latinos, more work is needed to identify which Catholic immigrants are motivated to serve. Indeed, it is still unclear from this study whether Sangre de Cristo Catholic Charismatics are a self-selected group of volunteer-minded and civically engaged persons, or whether it is that increased religiosity led to their interest in community service. Future longitudinal and comparative studies on the topic more generally might help address these issues. Additionally, future research might explore just which type of service activities are more likely to be pursued by Latino Catholics. This study suggests that immigrants mostly engage in service to the parish, volunteer service to the community (which is often connected to the parish), and, only recently, political action. Further studies might uncover patterns in these behaviors and examine how, for example, community service might lead to electoral participation.

Nonetheless, for the immigrants in this study, Catholic Charismaticism seemed to instill a confidence and provide the resources and the opportunities necessary for them to get involved. Their commitment to serving was impressive. Juggling one (sometimes two) jobs, family obligations, and the pressures inherent in being a first-generation Mexican immigrant in America, they still found time to give of themselves to their prayer group, their parish, and their community. When I asked how Charismatics found the time to do so much, one member responded best when she quipped " . . . it's not us, it's the Spirit that calls us and makes the time."

Notes

1. The actual names of neighborhoods, prayer groups, churches, and interviewees have been changed. Paxton Heights is a working-class Latino immigrant "neighborhood" located in northeast Los Angeles, California. 2000 Census figures for the Paxton Heights neighborhood show that it is 89 percent Latino and has a median income of about $40,000 (U.S. Census, 2000).
2. Huntington 2004; Verba et al. 1995.
3. Jones-Correa and Leal 2001.
4. Hondagneu-Sotelo 2008; Espinoza et al. 2005.
5. Hirshman 2004; Ecklund and Park 2005; Kurien 2004.
6. Verba et al. 1995.
7. Sandoval 1990.
8. Olson 1987; Ignatiev 1996.
9. Liptak 1989.
10. Nelli 1970.
11. Diaz-Stevens 1993a.
12. Lopez 2009; Lint-Sagarena 2009.
13. Sandoval 1990; Lint-Sagarena 2009.
14. Acuña 1972.
15. *See* Espinoza et al. 2005.
16. Ganz 2009; Lloyd-Moffett 2005.

17. Leon 2005.
18. Espinoza et al. 2005.
19. *See* Stevens-Arroyo and Díaz-Stevens 1994; Hondagneu-Sotelo 2008.
20. Huntington 2004.
21. Huntington 2004: 253.
22. Verba et al. 1995.
23. Centeno 2005; Massey 2004.
24. Correa and Leal 2001.
25. Pew 2007.
26. Pew 2007.
27. Lawson 1996.
28. Csordas 1994; Lawson 1996.
29. Hervieu-Lever 1997.
30. Mcguire 1982; Nietz 1987.
31. Martin 2001; Chesnut 2001.
32. Laurentin 1977.
33. Laurentin 1977.
34. The station, *El Sembrador Nueva Evangelización,* airs entirely in Spanish and is run by the Catholic Charismatic Organization, *El Sembrador.*
35. Pew 2007.
36. Wuthnow 1998.
37. Lawson 1996; Nietz 1987.
38. Nietz 1987.
39. Verba et al. 1995.

Part **III**

2004 Elections

Standing Up for Social Justice: Catholic Voting Patterns and the Latino Effect in the 2004 Presidential Election

Frank Ridzi, Matthew T. Loveland, and Jillian Ruhland

Despite a history of racial and religious discrimination within a nation with a Protestant majority, Catholics have risen to political prominence in the United States.[1] Their current importance within the political process is attributable not only to their sheer size at a quarter of the United States population and generally strong turnout in voting, but also to their concentration in densely populated states with high numbers of electoral votes.[2] Catholics have traditionally sided with the Democratic party due in part to its pro-immigrant platform dating back to the nineteenth century and its more recent history of concern for the working classes through programs of social betterment funded by government.[3] Catholic support for the party, moreover, was at its highest in the 1960 election of John F. Kennedy, the first Catholic to become the president of the United States. Into the last quarter of the twentieth century, therefore, it was commonly assumed that Catholics constituted a staunch and reliable segment of the Democratic party.

A more careful scrutiny, however, reveals a shifting tide. Beginning with the presidential election of 1952 (Eisenhower vs. Stevenson), and continuing up to the 2004 presidential election (Bush vs. Gore), Catholic support for the Democratic party can be described as "lukewarm."[4] Further, in recent years, Republicans have transparently attempted to curry favor with a growing number of Catholics, enticing them away from Democrat loyalty. In fact, as of spring 2004, the Pew Forum on Religion found that 41 percent of U.S.

Catholics self-identified as Republican as compared with 44 percent who self-identified as Democrat.[5] This is a clear change from the early 1970s when the Democrat party claimed over 50 percent of Catholics, while Republican support from them rumbled about in the teens.

These trends of Catholic voters to move incrementally toward the Republican party help frame our research question: *How did Catholics vote in 2004?* The issue is highly relevant, not only to Catholics, but to U.S. politics in general because Catholics are such a large percentage of voters who are very likely to turn out (i.e., *likely voters*), and the growing sense that the Catholic vote is in play between Democrats and Republicans. Clearly, this work does not presume that Catholics ought to be considered a simple block of voters. It is necessary to explore demographic, social, cultural, and theological divides within the Catholic community that help explain voting patterns. Latinos and Latinas are of growing importance within United States Catholicism—demographically, culturally and now, politically. As already suggested in this book, the political mobilization of Latino Catholics needs to be examined as a vital element of the Catholic reality. Indeed, as insightfully analyzed by Michael Jones-Correa and David Leal, certain presumptions about a lack of political preparedness among Latino and Latina Catholics may be erroneous.[6]

Fault Lines

In the first chapter of this book, Anthony Stevens-Arroyo shows how social scientists studying American religion write of how the twentieth century has registered dramatic change in its attitudes toward the interplay of ethnicity and religion for U.S. Catholics. In contrast to the nineteenth century and first quarter of the twentieth century, when they were viewed as anchored into poverty and immigrant status, the majority of Euro-American Catholics have come to attain high levels of economic and social progress. By most accounts, modern Catholics are most similar to liberal and mainline Protestants in terms of educational attainment and occupational prestige,[7] although always with caveats. The dramatic rise in the number and visibility of Latinos and Latinas within the church since the 1960s[8] has made palpable the cleavages between a largely middle-class segment of European descent and a working-class, often immigrant, Latin American membership. The varieties of experience in the Catholic constituency have stirred both the Republican and Democratic parties to fashion special messages in attempting to bring Catholics to their sides. In this chapter, we focus our attention on two factors: (1) the politically conflicted nature of Catholic social and economic values, and (2) the growing segment of Latino Catholics.

A Split Constituency

On issues like abortion or gay rights, official Church teachings have a natural affinity with the Republican party platform. Wuthnow suggests, however, that individual beliefs are more predictive of social attitudes and behaviors than denominational affiliations.[9] What matters, he says, are not official denominational positions, but instead the preference of the individual believer. To illustrate the point in the Catholic context, suppose an election gave voters an option between a Republican candidate who stressed a reversal of *Roe v. Wade* and a Democrat candidate who campaigned on outlawing the death penalty. The Catholic Church's consistent life ethic creates a distinct problem for the Catholic wishing to follow church teaching.[10] Each Catholic voter must decide on his or her own which issue takes precedent because official teachings can be interpreted to benefit contrasting political positions.[11] That is to say, a likely election scenario would bring a Republican candidate to stress the moral position of opposing abortion in line with Church teaching, while a Democratic candidate would emphasize his allegiance to the Magisterium's teaching against the death penalty. Similarly, the Republican might cite opposition to government licensing of marriage for persons of the same sex, while a Democrat would stress the need to address poverty by supporting initiatives that resonate with the Church's preferential option for the poor. As Weber and others conclude,[12] the result is a Catholic swing vote that is simultaneously *socially conservative* (e.g., antiabortion, antisex and antiviolence in the media but in favor of traditional family structure), and *socially concerned activist* (e.g., pro-safety net for the poor, progressive taxation to make the rich pay more, favorable legislation for labor unions, and increased government regulation of corporations). While this description is theoretic, it is based upon scrutiny of platforms for actual Republican and Democrat candidates, respectively. The result during the past decade especially is to create a zero-sum game in competition for the Catholic vote that simultaneously risks alienating the socially conservative side of Catholic voters when appealing to the socially concerned activist side.

Ethnicity and the Catholic Vote

It stands to reason that the needs and interests of Catholic voters themselves have changed due to a transformation in Catholic ethnic demography. The large-scale immigration of Irish and Italian Catholics during the nineteenth and twentieth centuries has long since subsided. As these groups have attained increasing economic and social capital, they have ceased to be targets of labor market discrimination and social exclusion.[13] This change in itself suggests the likelihood that classic Democrat concerns such as poverty and inequality have decreased in salience among these Catholics. As a result, Catholics of European descent (i.e., Euro-Americans) have likely come in recent years to more closely resemble Nixon's silent majority of suburban white voters than pro–Great Society and social spending activists.[14]

Irish and Italian Catholics make up the most affluent segment of U.S. Catholics, but more recent immigrant populations are in different economic and social positions. Twentieth-century Mexican immigration and Puerto Rican migration to the United States constitutes the primary demographic switch in U.S. Catholicism in recent years.[15] As explained by others,[16] the Latinos and Latinas in these two major groups cannot properly be labeled as "immigrants." While both groups may occupy a low social and economic position familiar to previous immigrant populations, for historical reasons neither is composed of a majority of noncitizens or newcomers to U.S. society. Unique among ethnic groups, both Mexicans and Puerto Ricans were inhabitants of homelands annexed to the United States after wars of invasion. Regardless of one's interpretation of the historical events, the reality today serves to distinguish the majority of Latinos and Latinas from previous Euro-American immigrant Catholics.

In addition, regardless of immigrant status, Latino Catholics and European Catholics are viewed in significantly different ways within society because of racial perceptions. Certainly, the economic and social exclusions encountered by Euro-American Catholics during their initial clash with the U.S. Protestant hegemony carry several similarities to the contemporary experience of Latinos and Latinas. Indeed, racist attitudes have dominated U.S. culture since colonial times.[17] Nonetheless, racial perceptions persist for most Latinos and Latinas but not for Euro-Americans today. This is ironic in that in some instances, some Latinos as a group have lived in U.S. territories far longer than Euro-Americans. Such a disparity in experience of daily life within the United States suggests that the political views of Latino Catholics may be more in favor of government intervention and a traditional social safety net policy. For the nearly 30 percent of Latinos and Latinas who are foreign-born immigrants, this may be even more likely. A recent Pew Poll reported:

> Issues like abortion are more closely contested than social welfare issues in part because of the shifting allegiances of minorities. Latinos and Blacks tend to take the "conservative" view on life and family matters, but they are on the "liberal" side on questions of social welfare.[18]

However, grouping all Latinos together is misleading. This same Pew poll found that while only 15 percent of Latino Catholics identified as Republican, 37 percent of Latino Protestants did, suggesting that Republican efforts to gain the support of Protestant ethnic minorities through faith-based funding and other initiatives have made notable progress. Furthermore, there are distinct variations in the area of social safety net preferences, with Latino Catholics being more in favor than Latino Protestants of fighting poverty by taxing the middle class (50 to 43%) and the wealthy (64 to 57%). These complex tendencies create a backdrop for the research presented in this chapter and locate our work within a broader debate surrounding the combined role of religion and ethnicity in political participation.

As frequently stated in previous chapters, Sidney Verba and his associates have set forth the proposition that Latino Catholics are less active in non-electoral political activities because the institutional practice of Catholicism does not facilitate the development of civic skills to the extent that participation in the institutions of Protestantism does.[19] Beginning with the article of Jones-Correa and Leal and highlighted in the analyses of Carlos Vargas-Ramos and Anthony M. Stevens-Arroyo in this book, the discrepancy in civic skills between Latino Catholics and Protestants does not find support in most other relevant survey data. This is not to say that no differences were found between Hispanic Catholic and Protestant membership in churches. These differences, however, do not appear to affect the role of parishes and congregations as training grounds for political mobilization. Rather, as we will suggest, the differences lie in the issues. Most Latino Catholic believers have a different list of the important issues than their Protestant counterparts.

Widening the focus to include not only the differences between Latino Catholics and Protestants but also those between Latino and Euro-American Catholics, we explore political response to issues within U.S. Catholicism. Perhaps the political information in Latino-dominated Catholic congregations may be more, or less, focused on some issues, such as social justice. This possibility evokes a second proposition discussed by Jones-Correa and Leal but not tested in their article, which questions Verba et al.'s proposition that lack of political involvement is characteristic of Catholics regardless of ethnicity. It is to this proposition that the present chapter responds, comparing Catholic support for social safety nets on the basis of ethnicity as well as other demographic and ideological characteristics. The issue of whether government has a responsibility to afford social safety nets for the less fortunate is, in fact, an important aspect of the current political climate.

A Changing Social Safety Net and Catholic Stance on Public Policy

In her presidential address to the American Sociological Association, Jill Quadagno claimed that the U.S. social safety net is in the midst of a transition.[20]

The social insurance welfare state that had been reluctantly adopted with the New Deal and then solidified with the Great Society initiative, she said, is undergoing fundamental changes. In its place, a series of privatizing and investment proposals beckon a shift toward a capital investment welfare state, or what President George W. Bush referred to as an "ownership society."[21] The capital investment approach includes health savings accounts, personal investment Social Security accounts, and religion-based social welfare programs. In contrast, the social insurance effort emphasizes preservation of Social Security and Medicare programs as currently instituted. The contrast in the two approaches carries a series of other rhetorical and real oppositions: personal risks associated with market failure vs. a collective response to Social Security funding; personalized medical savings accounts re-centering the responsibility of well-being on the individual within a neo-liberal framework vs. social commitment. This trend is grounded in a popular resurgence of ideological support for the classical liberal, laissez-faire philosophy to replace the social insurance model inaugurated with the New Deal.[22] The Capital Investment approach is at odds with Catholic social justice teaching since Leo XIII's *Rerum Novarum*, which encouraged social safety net growth through anticapitalist stances that emphasize collective social security, community integrity, and communal responsibility over material accumulation. These principles rejected laissez-faire trust in market forces and self-reliance.[23]

Nonetheless, as suggested above, because the Republican agenda is paired with a set of social issues such as abortion and same sex marriage, its capital investment approach on economic issues has not prevented them from appealing to a Catholic voting public. For the time being, many of these measures remain the topic of debate, and as has historically been the case, public opinion will weigh heavily on the outcome.[24]

We chose to examine voting patterns among U.S. Catholics when deciding between these two sets of values. We use data from a national sample to assess the role U.S. Catholics are likely to play in this debate, and to provide insight into the beliefs and preferences of this diverse social group. Only recently have scholars begun to acknowledge the ways in which religious sensibilities underlie crucial components of contemporary U.S. social welfare policy debate.[25] In the wake of the 2004 election, it is clear that both major political parties are vigorously courting the Catholic[26] and also the Latino Catholic vote.[27] We seek to explore attitudes of U.S. Catholics of Latino and European descent to construct a fuller picture of differences not only between Latino Catholics and Protestants, but also Latino and Euro-American Catholics on matters of the social insurance approach to political issues.

This chapter will test the impact the following factors have on overall support for a government funded social safety net: we take into account hypotheses that suggest support for the social safety net is linked on the one hand to demographic characteristics, such as race, gender, age, and income, and on the other to ideological perspectives. Included in "support" are the principal items: preference for social safety net configuration vs. for privatization with individual accounts. We include other issues and relate these to voting priorities and choice of candidate in the 2004 election.

Previous research suggests that these attitudes will be greatly influenced by ethnicity and Catholic theological precedent. Consistent with the arguments of major welfare policy analysts, Mary Jo Bane and Lawrence Mead, we acknowledge that faith and religion provide underlying sensibilities that influence individual stances on public policy—particularly in matters that involve empirical uncertainty and ambiguity.[28] Many would characterize Catholics as conservative regarding issues of social liberties, such as the ordination of female clergy, acceptance of homosexuals, and willingness to diverge from orthodox or traditional leadership structure. When it comes to matters of social welfare, however, this is not necessarily the case.[29] In fact, there is strong historical precedent to suggest that the Catholic tendency is closer to ideals of social insurance than to capital investment. The reasons for this adherence to a Social Insurance agenda can be summarized as a "theology of charity."[30] In theological terms, this is the "preferential option for the poor," and it predisposes Catholics to support state-centered safety net policy.

The U.S. Social Safety Net in Global and Ideological Context

As noted earlier, the present direction of U.S. policy debate suggests considerable interest in favor of accelerating transition toward the liberal, Social Insurance model.[31] This discourse places the United States on a continuum of global social safety net ideal types. At one extreme, we find social democratic regimes (such as exist in Denmark, Sweden, and Holland) that are the strikingly community-centered. They deemphasize individuals' self-sufficiency and emphasize universal protection of individuals from market exploitation and commoditization. In the middle, one can describe conservative corporatist regimes (such as are present within Austria, France, and Germany), which, while valuing community solidarity and universal protections for workers, in contrast, also have social welfare benefit structures that are less apt to equalize inequalities between workers and are more apt to base eligibility for benefits on individual work history and tax contribution. The opposite extreme is occupied by neo-liberal safety net regimes,[32] such as are present within Australia, Canada, and the United States with George W. Bush as President. These are the most individual-centered in that they are designed with the ultimate end of making labor markets run smoothly. Within this context, the individual has the primary responsibility to be self-sufficient and to look after his or her own well-being.[33]

In order to gauge the role of U.S. Catholic public opinion in this debate between Capital Investment and Social Insurance, it is helpful to simplify these contrasting social safety net models to their root underlying values. Ellwood's analysis of values in the U.S. social safety net provides a useful conceptual framework.[34] In his analysis, autonomy of the individual, the virtue of work, primacy of the family, and desire for a sense of community underlie much of the philosophical and political rhetoric about poverty in the United States. These values, when applied to policy, often come into conflict.

As a result, Ellwood suggests, conundrums arise because two values cannot be simultaneously satisfied. One prominent example, the Security–Work Conundrum, arises from efforts to provide economic security to individuals in need (a community-centered value) which, by ensuring this well-being, have the latent effect of reducing pressure on needy individuals to work (work in itself is a virtue) and be autonomous. By providing increasing assistance to those in greater need, the rewards of working and the impetus to be self-sufficient are further reduced. Thus, the Security–Work Conundrum produces a conflict between the desire to help and the desire to encourage work and self-support. In other words, rugged individualism and interdependence, though counterparts, are both very much ingrained within the dominant ethos of American society.[35]

We build upon this conceptual conundrum to create a survey scale measuring U.S. Catholics' proclivity toward sympathizing with either of these two conflicting values. Specifically, the survey instrument is designed to compare the degree to which various Catholic constituencies support individualistic as opposed to communal responses to social safety net issues.[36] It delves into the heart of the issue that Lens encapsulates in the following words, "Social problems that involve a lack of something—such as health care, money, food, housing or child care—are inevitably framed by one basic question: Is it the individual's or the government's responsibility to provide it? Stated in this way, the answer is less empirical than ideological."[37] Our analysis makes explicit the shape and magnitude of social welfare ideology among diverse groups of U.S. Roman Catholics.

Method

The Sample

The Contemporary Catholic Trends project administers a national telephone survey of adult (18 and over) U.S. Catholics twice annually. Samples are randomly drawn from a Zogby International database of residential phone numbers of respondents who have previously self-identified as Catholic. The surveys employ sampling strategies in which selection probabilities are proportional to population size within area codes and exchanges. Weighting by region, age, race/ethnicity, and gender is used to adjust for nonresponse.[38] Spanish-language interviewers are provided for respondents who indicate that this is a preference. Cross-validation analyses indicate that CCT response patterns are highly consistent with other recent, major national surveys of American Catholics, including the 2002 General Social Survey Catholic subsample.[39]

Dependent Variables

Our primary dependent variable is a summary measure of overall support for each of the following representative social safety net programs: Temporary Assistance for Needy Families (TANF), food stamps, Social Security, and unemployment insurance. We adapt the work of Hasenfeld and Rafferty to account for public attitudes toward the social safety net with a series of measures.[40] The primary scale was constructed as follows: for each of these four programs, respondents were asked whether government spending should increase, remain the same, or decrease. If respondents selected increase, they were asked if they would be willing to pay for it through an increase in taxes. Respondents who selected decrease were asked if the savings from this reduced spending should be used to reduce taxes, decrease the budget deficit, or spend on other programs. Responses were configured into a support scale based on the following configuration developed by Hasenfeld and Rafferty: (1) decrease spending and decrease taxes; (2) decrease spending and reduce deficit; (3) spending should remain the same; (4) increase spending without an increase in taxes; (5) increase spending with an increase in taxes.[41] The scale was constructed by summing support of these four programs; scores ranged from 4 to 20.[42]

Preference for a social safety net configuration was measured using a question designed to reflect the three safety net configurations (i.e., liberal, corporatist, and social democratic) that literature has identified as dominating

Western states.[43] Respondents were asked which of the following they felt is the best way to distribute aid to individuals and families in need of financial assistance: through the free market (i.e., liberal), through employers that are regulated by government requirements (i.e., corporatist), or through government programs that are universal and open to all citizens (i.e., social democratic).

We also analyze a measure of voting priorities among four issues that the U.S. Catholic bishops have said should influence Catholic voting decisions: overcoming poverty, economic justice, abortion, and same-sex marriage. Respondents were first asked to indicate which of these issues is most important to them when making voting decisions. They were then asked to indicate which of the remaining choices was the "next most important." This question was repeated three times to produce a ranking of first, second, third, and fourth priorities for each respondent. The four options were rotated. A variable with three attributes was constructed as follows: those who selected overcoming poverty and economic justice (in either order) as their top two priorities were grouped as a social justice priority. Those who selected abortion and same-sex marriage (in either order) as their top two priorities were grouped as family values priority. Those with other configurations were assigned to a middle group.

Support for personal savings accounts was measured with the following question that asked respondents to strongly agree, somewhat agree, somewhat disagree, or strongly disagree: governmentally controlled programs such as Social Security and Medicare should be replaced with individually managed personal savings accounts.

Finally, choice of presidential candidate was measured by first asking respondents whether they voted in the recent presidential election. (It should be noted that over 93% of the sample reported voting.) Those who responded in the affirmative were asked which presidential candidate they voted for: George W. Bush, John Kerry, Ralph Nader, or other.

Independent Variables

For the analyses in this chapter we employ two types of independent variables: demographic characteristics and ideological perspectives. Demographic variables include the respondent's family income, education, age, gender, and race and whether he or she is receiving federal benefits. We include a dichotomous variable that indicates whether a respondent receives benefits. It is constructed by combining two questions and ranges from 0 (i.e., no benefits received) to 1 (i.e., some benefits received). The first asks if respondents have received benefits in the last year from unemployment insurance, workers' compensation, Social Security, Supplemental Security Income (also known as SSI), Medicare, or veterans benefits. The second asks if respondents have received benefits in the last year from Medicaid, food stamps, Temporary Assistance to Needy Families, or public assistance. Thirty six percent of respondents reported receiving at least one benefit.

The economic ideological perspectives variables include three scales developed by Hasenfeld and Rafferty.[44] The first measures the respondent's judgment of the responsibility of government to intervene in the economic order in order to bring about greater social equality. It consists of three items: the government has a responsibility to assist communities that have lost industrial plants, the government has a responsibility to reduce income inequality, and the government does not have a responsibility to enact affirmative action programs. For each of these questions, respondents could strongly agree, somewhat agree, somewhat disagree, or strongly disagree (the question on affirmative action was reverse coded before adding it to the scale). The scale ranges from 3 (low government involvement) to 12 (high government involvement).[45]

The second scale measures the respondent's perceptions of the bounds of socially legitimate state-guaranteed entitlements to citizens. It consists of three items: the government should guarantee jobs to insure a basic standard of living, the government should guarantee medical care, and the government should guarantee income security in old age. The scale ranges from 3 (no government guarantee) to 12 (government guarantee).[46]

A third independent variable, adapted from Feagin by Hasenfeld and Rafferty,[47] measures a respondent's attitude toward work and the causes of poverty to gauge the perceived causes of poverty as either structural or individual. The items included in the scale are: poverty is due to circumstances beyond one's control, and the poor want to get ahead as much as everyone else. The scale ranges from 2 (poverty is under individual control) to 8 (poverty is structural).[48]

A final independent variable measures perceived government accountability and efficiency in administering safety net programs. The scale includes two questions with the same stem: overall, how much waste and inefficiency do you think there is in the following group of programs? Unemployment insurance, workers' compensation, social security, Supplemental Security Income (also known as SSI), Medicare, and veterans benefits; Medicaid, food stamps, Temporary Assistance to Needy Families, and public assistance. For each of these questions, respondents could indicate either none, some, a considerable amount, or a lot. Scores on the scale range from 2 (a lot of waste) to 8 (no waste).[49]

Findings

Our study tests the hypotheses that demographic characteristics and economic ideological perspectives impact on political choices. Five dependent variables are included: 1) support for the social safety net; 2) preference for social safety net configuration; 3) preference for social safety net reform (i.e., privatization through individual accounts); 4) voting priorities; and 5) choice of candidate in the 2004 election.

Table 6.1 presents the preliminary bivariate relationships between race and each of the dependent variables. Prior to controlling for other personal characteristics, the following are significantly related to overall welfare support: race, being in favor of distributing aid through government programs, voting on the basis of social justice, and whether a respondent voted for Bush. These initial results provide evidence that Catholics are not a single voting block and, further, that ethnic differences matter. In the history of Catholicism, what have appeared as ethnic differences can often be explained by differences in social and economic status. Does this hold today, specifically in the case of Latinos?

Controlling for personal characteristics, we found that being a Latino Catholic was still a significant predictor for all five dependent variables (see Table 6.2). On the scale of overall welfare support, our model predicts that the average (scoring average on everything in the model) employed white female who has graduated from college will score a 13.1. If she was a Latina Catholic, however, our model predicts that she would score a 14.05. Thus, net of other factors, a Latino Catholic on average scored .95 points higher than non-Latino Catholics on the measure of overall welfare support. Our model of

TABLE 6.1 Catholic perspectives on safety net by ethnicity (in percentages)

	Overall	Latino	White	Other
Overall Safety Net Support***				
High	25	34	22	35
Medium	53	54	53	45
Low	23	13	25	20
Favor Distribution of Aid	65	75	61	77
Through Government Programs***				
Favor Individual Accounts	38	36	37	45
Vote on the Basis of Social Justice***	48	61	44	47
Vote For Bush***	45	19	51	61

* $p \leq 0.1$;
** $p \leq .05$;
*** $p \leq .01$

TABLE 6.2 Regression equations' results for the effects of personal characteristics on safety net related questions (unstandardized linear and logistic regression coefficients; standard error in parenthesis)

Dependent Variables	Equation 1 (OLS) Overall Safety Net Support	Equation 2 (Logit) Favor distribution of aid through government pro-grams	Equation 3 (Logit) Favor individual accounts	Equation 4 (Logit) Vote on the basis of social justice	Equation 5 (Logit) Vote for Bush
Independent Variables					
Constant	13.1*** (.81)	.48 (.41)	−.01 (.41)	−.69 (.39)	−.4 (.4)
Personal Characteristics[#]					
Latino	.95** (.39)	.66*** (.21)	−.54*** (.2)	.84*** (.19)	−1.61*** (.22)
Other	.42 (.54)	.7** (.3)	.38 (.27)	.19 (.25)	.2 (.26)
Male	.5 (.29)	−.32** (.14)	.71*** (.15)	.01 (.14)	.1 (.14)
Not Employed	−.11 (.37)	−.36** (.18)	.4** (.19)	−.09 (.17)	−.02 (.18)
Employed Part-Time	−1.02** (.47)	− .82*** (.23)	.11 (.24)	−.11 (.22)	−.36 (.22)
Receive Contributory Benefits	.51 (.39)	−.07 (.19)	−.38 (−.2)	−.06 (.18)	−.19 (.19)
Receive Mean-Tested Benefits	−.5 (.57)	−.16 (.29)	.22 (.28)	.15 (.27)	.61** (.28)
Income	−.09 (.11)	−.05 (.05)	.01 (.05)	.01 (.05)	.06 (.05)
Age	−.03*** (.01)	.01 (.01)	− .02*** (.01)	.01 (.01)	.00 (.01)
HS Grad or Less	1.25*** (.4)	.26 (.2)	.11 (.2)	−.28 (.19)	.48*** (.2)
Some College	.52 (.33)	.41*** (.17)	.14 (.17)	.08 (.16)	.18 (.16)
R^2	.056				

(Continued)

TABLE 6.2 (CONTINUED)

Dependent Variables	Equation 1 (OLS) Overall Safety Net Support	Equation 2 (Logit) Favor distribution of aid through government pro-grams	Equation 3 (Logit) Favor individual accounts	Equation 4 (Logit) Vote on the basis of social justice	Equation 5 (Logit) Vote for Bush
Adjusted R^2	.045				
F ratio	5.217**				
x^2		45.38***	58.28***	26.84***	88.17***
Degrees of Freedom		11	11	11	11
N	987	986	941	986	986

[#]Reference groups: White, Female, Employed Full-Time, College +

* $p \leq 0.1$;

** $p \leq .05$;

*** $p \leq .01$

favoring distribution of aid through government programs predicts that the average employed white female who has graduated from college (scoring average on everything in the model) has a 62 percent probability of favoring distribution of aid through government programs. If, however, she were a Latina Catholic, she would have a 76 percent chance of favoring distribution of aid through government programs. Furthermore, the same average employed white Catholic female has a 33 percent probability of voting on the basis of social justice issues, as compared to a 54 percent chance if she were a Latina Catholic.

For the average employed white Catholic female surveyed there is a 50 percent chance that she will favor individual accounts, as compared with a 37 percent chance if she were a Latina Catholic. With regard to presidential voting, the average employed white female would be 40 percent likely to vote for Bush, as compared to 12 percent if she were a Latina Catholic. Latino Catholics were, conversely, less likely to favor individual accounts and less likely to vote for President Bush than non-Latino Catholics. Overall, being a Latino Catholic makes one more supportive of safety net programs; this translates into being more likely to favor distribution of aid through government programs and to vote on the basis of social justice issues.

When measures of economic ideology were included in each of the above models, however, being a Latino Catholic was no longer a significant predictor of the dependent variables (with the exception of voting for Bush). This suggested that it is not ethnicity itself that impacts the dependent variables but beliefs or ideological positions that correspond with the Latino Catholic experience that predict the dependent variables. To explain how this occurs we employed a path model analysis. Figure 6.1 demonstrates that while being a Latino Catholic is not directly related to safety net support when economic ideology is controlled for, there are indirect effects. Latino Catholics are more supportive than non-Latino Catholics of social rights and government intervention, each of which are directly related to increased support for the social safety net. Thus, being a Latino Catholic means that the respondent was more likely to support guaranteed social rights, such as guaranteed jobs to insure a basic standard of living, guaranteed medical care, and guaranteed income security in old age. Being a Latino Catholic also means that the respondent was more likely to support government intervention, believing that the government has a responsibility to assist communities that have lost industrial plants to reduce income inequality and to enact affirmative action programs. This is consistent with expectations that Latino Catholics, whether individually poor or not, are citizens for whom issues of poverty and economic justice are salient.

FIGURE 6.1   Path Analysis Model

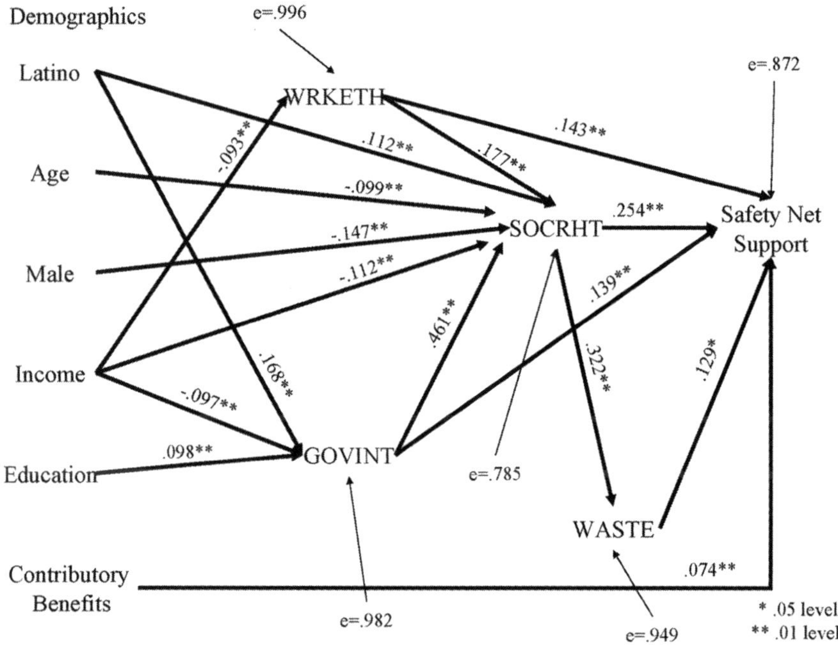

Conclusion

The reader can understand our conclusions about Latino Catholics best when placing the issues in context. First, notice that as a group, all Catholics are politically important within the U.S. political experience because of their numbers and high voter turnout rates.[50] Secondly, since decisions about social spending depend on public support, Catholic attitudes are key to the directions for current politics. Historically, Catholics have been supportive of redistributive policies thanks in large part to their heritage as a marginalized community. But Catholic perspectives today diverge on matters of social safety net policy. On the one hand, many Euro-American Catholics have or are rapidly moving into middle-class society.[51] However, although this group of Catholics is no longer part of the immigration flows and no longer experience significant social exclusion, Latinos and Latinas represent both a large segment of the Catholic population and a different social composite. Thus, knowing how U.S. Catholics diverge on these issues is of great importance to political assessment. Finally, our data paint a picture of more than one Catholic experience. Contrary to opinions such as Verba et al's, Latino Catholic identity is consequential for civic preferences and voting participation. Moreover, as indicated in the other chapters of this book, Catholicism is a significant predictor of Latino political participation.

The importance of churches lies in their role as conduits of political information and recruitment. The difference between Latino Protestants and Catholics is not that the former is being offered political skills and the latter is deprived of them. The differences appear, rather, in the choices made about issues. The data presented in this chapter provide evidence not only for the notion that the Catholic Church influences its Latino members on issues different from those emphasized among Protestant Latinos and Latinas, but also that Latino Catholics emphasize different aspects of Church social justice teaching than do non-Latino Catholics. For Latino Catholic parishes, social justice perspectives support a social insurance model for politics to a degree noticeably higher than among Euro-American Catholics.

It may be suggested that this emphasis on social justice issues today among Latinos and Latinas reflects a similar posture held in an earlier time by Irish and Italian Catholics. In the history of U.S. Catholicism, ethnic populations have embraced those elements of Catholic teaching that emphasize the social safety net and resonate with the traditional Democratic party platform. This loyalty to social justice and the Democratic party, it might be supposed, will continue as long as Latinos suffer from social inequalities produced by their perception as immigrants.[52]

Our results provide evidence that Latino support for social safety net activism is strong and statistically significant. The path analysis we provide allows us to further specify that the reason behind this statistical relationship is that Latino Catholics are more likely to support social rights and government intervention than other Catholics. It is not the purpose of this chapter to either prove or disprove the hypothesis that upward social mobility will change this alignment toward the Democratic party. Whether Latinos and Latinas are assimilating so as to lose their cultural identity is addressed more than adequately in most of the other chapters in this book. What can be stated here is that because Latino Catholics are an important and growing segment of the U.S. electorate with needs and priorities different from Euro-American Catholics, they cannot be ignored as a group deserving continuing study. In modern American society, to be Latino is to be familiar with poverty and discrimination. So while it is no surprise then that we see Latino Catholics standing up for social justice, it is important to note that Latino Protestants do not evidence the same set of commitments when they participate in electoral politics.

Notes

1. Feagin and Feagin 1999.
2. Menendez 2000; Weber 2000.
3. Menendez 2000.
4. Manza and Brooks 1996.
5. The Pew Forum on Religion & Public Life 2004.
6. Michael Jones-Correa and David Leal 2001.
7. Wuthnow 1988; D'Antonio et al. 2001.
8. *See* Díaz-Stevens and Stevens-Arroyo 1998.
9. Wuthnow 1988.
10. Perl and McClintock 2001.
11. Jelen 2003.
12. Weber 2000; McBrien 1983; Misra and Hicks 1994.
13. D'Antonio et al. 2000.
14. Jansson 2001.
15. Menendez, 2000; Paul 2003; Schaefer 2004; D'Antonio et al. 2000.
16. *See* Díaz-Stevens and Stevens-Arroyo 1998.
17. Feagin and Feagin 1999.
18. The Pew Forum on Religion & Public Life 2004:7.
19. Verba et al. 1993.
20. Quadagno 1999.
21. Stevenson 2004. [Editors' note: For the remainder of this article, the opposing terms shall be *capital investment* and *social insurance* without inclusion of the rest of the term, viz., *welfare state*.]
22. Quadagno 1999; Starobin 1998.
23. Misra and Hicks 1994; Stephens 1979; McBrien 1983.
24. DeVroye 2003; Jansson 2001.
25. Dionne et al. 2003.
26. Nichols 2001.
27. Paige 2002.
28. Dionne et al. 2003:11.
29. McBrien 1983; also *see* Burns 1992: 719.
30. Regnerus, Smith and Sikkink 1998: 484.
31. Quadagno 1999; Starobin 1998.
32. [Editors' Note: The term *liberal* has different meanings on each side of the Atlantic. Here, it is used in its classic European sense of laissez-faire capitalism, which approximates the contemporary approach of the Republican Party.]
33. Voorhis 2002; Amenta et al. 2001.
34. Ellwood 1988.
35. *See* also Lens 2002.
36. Dionne et al. 2003.
37. Lens 2002: 137.

38. The overall cooperation rate was 20.3 percent, which is comparable to similar telephone surveys and is calculated using an AAPOR method.
39. *Contemporary Catholic Trends (CCT) and other National Studies of American Catholics: A Cross-Validation Analysis*, Robert F. Kelly, William C. Rinaman, and William R. Barnett, Co-Principal Investigators, CCT, Departments of Sociology, Mathematics, and Religious Studies (respectively) Le Moyne College, Syracuse, NY. Copies available from the authors upon request.
40. Hasenfeld and Rafferty 1989.
41. Hasenfeld and Rafferty 1989: 1034.
42. Cronbach's alpha = 0.682.
43. Voorhis 2002; Amenta et al. 2001.
44. Hasenfeld and Rafferty 1989.
45. Cronbach's alpha = .475. Despite the well-established nature of the scale used for GOVINT and WRKETH, as reported in Hasenfeld and Rafferty (1989), the low Cronbach's alpha for these scales suggest that perhaps they are not as adept at measuring nuances among Catholics. This variation merits further study, but is not addressed in the present work.
46. Cronbach's alpha = .814.
47. Hasenfeld and Rafferty 1989.
48. Cronbach's alpha = .327.
49. Cronbach's alpha = .762.
50. Manza and Brooks 1996.
51. D'Antonio 2000; Traverso 2003.
52. This is the position of Linda Chavez: see the arguments about this position as explained in the Introduction to this book.

Epilogue: The Growing Influence of the Latino Catholic Vote

Mark M. Gray

In 2008, exit polls[1] indicated that Barack Obama won a significant majority of the Latino vote (66%)—which represented about 1 in 10 voters overall at that time. Winning this subgroup was important to Obama victories in Western states such as Colorado, New Mexico, and Nevada as well as in Florida, all of which carry a significant Latino vote. Obama carried the Latino vote across all religious subgroups that can be measured in exit polls and other surveys. However, Latinos self-identifying as Catholic were his biggest supporters within this group. Nearly three in four Latino Catholics (71%) told exit pollsters that they had voted for Obama (see Table E.1). By comparison, two-thirds of Latino Protestants and other non-Catholic Christians (66%) voted for Obama, and just over 6 in 10 evangelical or born-again Christian Latinos (61%) cast a vote for the Democratic candidate.[2] This result underscores the trend highlighted throughout this volume about the emergence of Latino Catholics as an especially loyal segment of voters for Democratic party candidates. In other words, what was reported for the 2000 through 2006 elections continued and even intensified in the 2008 presidential election. As will be shown, although there are issues to be further explored, the Latino Catholic vote continued to exhibit a special character in the 2010 congressional election.

Yet there was an interesting overlap here, and the groups cited above are not mutually exclusive.[3] About one in four Latino Catholics (24%) surveyed in the 2008 exit polls also self-identified as *a born-again or evangelical Christian*. This is a noteworthy finding. People in general tend to assume that the born-

TABLE E.1   *In today's election for president, did you just vote for*: Hispanic/Latino (a) Respondents by Religion in 2008 Exit Polls (in percentages)

	Obama	McCain	Other/No Vote
All Catholics	71	27	2
Catholic and *not* Born-again/Evangelical Christian	75	24	2
Catholic and Born-again/Evangelical Christian	60	38	2
All Protestants/other Christians	66	32	1
All Born-again or Evangelical Christians	61	38	1
Born-again/Evangelical Christian and *not* Catholic	63	38	0

again experience is largely a non-Catholic Christian experience. However, as Cristina Mora expounded in Chapter 5 of this volume, this is clearly not the case. A sizable segment of the Catholic electorate has also had this experience of spiritual rebirth. Moreover, the findings from these exit polls reveal some important divisions between Latino born-again and Latino Catholics who did not identify as such. For instance, 75 percent of Latino Catholics who do not consider themselves to be born-again voted for Obama, whereas only 60 percent of those Latino Catholics who do consider themselves to be an evangelical voted for the Democratic candidate.

The *born-again or evangelical Catholic* category was not a fluke of the 2008 exit polls, but rather a pattern evident in other public opinion surveys. For example, in the 2008 American National Election Study, 18 percent of all Latino Catholic respondents who were eligible to vote indicated that they are *born-again Christians*.[4] Although this group only makes up about one in five or one in four Latino Catholics, it makes up a sizeable share of all Latinos who self-identify as born-again or evangelical. Moreover, where it is possible to measure, about *half* of all evangelical Latinos (49%) in the 2008 exit polls self-identified their religion as Catholic.[5] As Mora described in this volume, experiences in movements like the Catholic Charismatics may incline some Catholics to embrace the label of *born-again*. Strictly speaking, in Catholic theology the sacrament of baptism suffices for birth into the faith; however, Stevens-Arroyo's review of the PARAL Study (Chapter 2) suggests that movements like the Cursillo and the Charismatic may function like the born-again adult conversion experiences more properly identified with Evangelicals and Pentecostals. This category of "born-again" Catholics certainly deserves continued attention.

Overall, the most recent elections sustain the findings described in this volume for earlier periods: Catholicism appears to pull Latino voters closer to

TABLE E.2 *On most political matters do you consider yourself*: Hispanic/Latino(a) Respondents by Religion in 2008 Exit Polls (in percentages)

	Liberal	Moderate	Conservative
All Catholics	26	41	33
Catholic and *not* Born-again/Evangelical Christian	30	43	27
Catholic and Born-again/Evangelical Christian	15	35	50
All Protestants/other Christians	23	54	23
All Born-again or Evangelical Christians	14	45	40
Born-again/Evangelical Christian and *not* Catholic	13	57	30

Democratic votes and affiliation and issue stances consistent with that party, whereas identifying oneself as an evangelical or born-again Christian appears to exert some force toward Republican affiliation, voting, and issue stances. Which of these opposing forces is winning out among these voters?

Most often, Catholicism seems to outweigh the influence of also considering oneself to be born-again or evangelical. The two strongest exceptions to this are the vote for president, which was already noted above, and political ideology, as shown below.[6] Among Catholics, those self-identifying also as born-again look somewhat similar to non-Catholic evangelical Protestants. Only about 15 percent of either group says they are liberal (see Table E.2). However, Catholics who are born-again are more likely than those of all other Latino Christian subgroups to self-identify as a conservative (50%).

Yet on many other questions where distinctions can be made by ethnicity and religion, Catholics, whether they consider themselves to be born-again or not, tend to cluster together. In 2008, about 8 in 10 Latino Catholics (81%) voted for a Democrat when they cast their ballot for the House of Representatives (see Table E.3). There is only a four-percentage-point difference between Catholics who consider themselves to be born-again and those who do not. Notably, only about 6 in 10 Latino evangelical Protestants (61%) voted for a Democratic member of the House.

A similar rank-order of subgroups is evident in responses to the question regarding general partisan affiliation (see Table E.4). Nearly 6 in 10 Latinos Catholics in 2008 consider themselves to be Democrats (61%), and this is slightly higher among those who do not also self-identify as born-again or evangelical (63%). Yet there was about a 10-percentage-point gap in Democratic affiliation among Latino Catholics who are born-again (53%) and those who are not.[7]

TABLE E.3 *In today's election for the U.S. House, did you just vote for*: Hispanic/
Latino(a) Respondents by Religion in 2008 Exit Polls (in percentages)

	Democrat	Republican	Other/No Vote
All Catholics	81	16	3
Catholic and *not* Born-again/Evangelical Christian	82	14	4
Catholic and Born-again/Evangelical Christian	78	20	2
All Protestants/other Christians	66	29	4
All Born-again or Evangelical Christians	70	27	3
Born-again/Evangelical Christian and *not* Catholic	61	35	4

Given the way in which exit polls are administered, it is not possible to
combine all of the data for ethnicity, religious affiliation, and issue stances.
However, it is possible to examine this in recent General Social Surveys
(GSS).[8] In the tables below, data are pooled for the 2004, 2006, and 2008
surveys to ensure a sufficient number of respondents in subgroups. This pool-
ing also allows for a focus on the state of these groups in the mid- to late
2000s.

Looking at issues and policy questions where the Catholic Church takes a
clear stance, we can see some patterns that are similar to those noted above.
For example, consider the attitudes regarding the death penalty detailed in

TABLE E.4 *No matter how you voted today, do you usually think of yourself as a*:
Hispanic/Latino(a) Respondents by Religion in 2008 Exit Polls (in percentages)

	Democrat	Republican	Indep./Other
All Catholics	61	16	23
Catholic and *not* Born-again/Evangelical Christian	63	13	25
Catholic and Born-again/Evangelical Christian	53	28	19
All Protestants/other Christians	53	23	24
All Born-again or Evangelical Christians	52	27	21
Born-again/Evangelical Christian and *not* Catholic	52	25	23

TABLE E.5 *Do you favor or oppose the death penalty for persons convicted of murder?* Hispanic/Latino(a) Respondents by Religion 2004-08 GSS (in percentages)

	Favor	Oppose
All Catholics	64	36
Catholic and *not* Born-again	66	34
Catholic and Born-again	56	45
All Protestants	73	27
Protestant and Born-again	71	29

Table E.5 All Catholic sub-groups are more likely than Protestant sub-groups to oppose the death penalty for convicted murders. Note that majorities of all groups still support the use of the death penalty. Of course the Catholic Church opposes the death penalty.[9] All those classified as Catholic had higher rates of opposition to the death penalty than did those identifying themselves as Protestant. Importantly, this is one case where Catholics who also consider themselves born-again are *more* consistent with Church teachings than both Catholics in general and also Latino Catholics who do not self-identify as being born-again.

Majorities of all Latino religious subgroups oppose legal access to abortion on demand. Yet, opposition to this is highest among both Protestant and Catholic Latinos who also say they are born-again. As shown in Table E.6, the Catholic cluster is broken on this issue, and evangelical identity pulls Latinos toward stronger opposition to abortion than Catholicism in general. In other words, calling yourself a *born-again Catholic* is more likely to make Latinos agree with the Catholic Church's political stance on this issue.

TABLE E.6 *Please tell me whether or not you think it should be possible for a pregnant woman to obtain legal abortion if the woman wants it for any reason?* Hispanic/Latino(a) Respondents by Religion 2004-08 GSS (in percentages)

	Yes	No
All Catholics	35	65
Catholic and *not* Born-again	38	63
Catholic and Born-again	26	74
All Protestants	33	67
Protestant and Born-again	23	77

TABLE E.7 *We are faced with many problems in this country, none of which can be solved easily or inexpensively. I'm going to name some of these problems, and for each one [WELFARE] I'd like you to tell me whether you think we're spending . . .* Hispanic/Latino(a) Respondents by Religion 2004-08 GSS (in percentages)

	Too Much Money	About the Right Amount	Too Little Money
All Catholics	40	37	23
Catholic and *not* Born-again	43	36	21
Catholic and Born-again	30	42	28
All Protestants	40	35	25
Protestant and Born-again	43	33	24

There is another slight break in the Catholic cluster of subgroups on the issue of welfare spending. However, here the pattern is more complex. Only 3 in 10 Catholics (30%) who say they are born-again think the country is spending too much on welfare, whereas 43 percent of Latino Protestants who are born-again respond similarly (see Table E.7). Catholics who are not born-again respond very similar to evangelical Protestants. The real outlier here is among Catholics who say they are born-again but who adhere still to Catholic Church orthodoxy. This group is *most* likely to say we are spending "about the right amount" on welfare (42%). As Ridzi, Loveland, and Ruhland discussed in Chapter 6 in their analysis of the position of U.S. Catholics on social safety net spending, Latino Catholics are significantly more likely to favor such social spending than any other group of Catholics. The present findings suggest an even more precise distinction: Latino born-again or evangelical Catholics are more supportive of social safety net spending than Catholics who are not born-again or evangelical as well as other Latino Christians.

The overall patterns emerging from these recent data collections confirms the theme in this volume that Catholicism among Latinos is more often associated with issues on the left of the political spectrum that are consistent with the Democratic party and its candidates. Protestant Latinos stand apart—a bit to the right and more often so when they say they are born-again.

Some candidates appear to be trying to capitalize on the overlap of Catholic identify and born-again identify among Latino Catholics. For example, in the 2010 senate races, Tea Party candidate Christine O'Donnell (R-DE) would at times claim both Catholic and evangelical identification. Yet O'Donnell lost whereas fellow Republican Marco Rubio won in Florida using a similar double

TABLE E.8 *In today's election for the U.S. House, did you just vote for*: All Respondents by Race/Ethnicity and Religion in 2010 Exit Polls (in percentages)

	Democrat	Republican	Other/No Vote
All Hispanic/Latino(a)s	60	38	2
Non-White Catholics	58	40	2
All Catholics	44	54	2
White Catholics	39	59	2
All Protestants/other Christians	38	59	3
All Born-again or Evangelical Christians	*nr*	*nr*	*nr*
White Born-again or Evangelical Christians	19	*11*	4

nr = not reported

identity. Although he has listed his religion officially as Catholic and has celebrated Catholic sacraments, it was also widely reported that Rubio more frequently attended and donated to his wife's Southern Baptist church.[10] In the future, we may seem more candidates like Marco Rubio—especially in states with large Latino populations that seek to capitalize on these overlapping religious affiliations. It is important to distinguish among Latino Christians, whether Catholic or evangelical, as potentially half of all self-described born-again Christians are self-described Catholics. Non-Catholic evangelical Christian Latinos may be different from Latinos who are Catholic, as evidence in this Epilogue shows, but unless disaggregated as it is herein, some differences between Catholic and evangelical Latinos may be marked by the born-again experience and not by denominational affiliation.

There are limited data available at the time of publication for 2010 exit poll data. The Table E.8 includes *all* respondents to exit polls for the midterm elections. Here we can see that the strongest supporters of the Democratic party—even in an election where this party lost the House majority—were Latinos. Non-white Catholics similarly more strongly supported Democrats than others. Among all other available groups where race and ethnicity and religion can be isolated, majorities voted Republican.

In the years ahead, the pattern of results seen in the 2008 election and the 2010 midterms will likely grow in strength. Latinos are expected by many demographers and social scientists to become more numerous in the electorate. In recent years, polling has consistently indicated that about 60 percent to 65 percent of Hispanics/Latinos in the United States self-identify as Catholic. Even if this percentage were to fall further—to only about 55 percent of all Latinos—research conducted by the Center for Applied Research in the

Apostolate (CARA) at Georgetown University indicates that that the rapid growth of the Latino Catholic population will likely boost the total Catholic population numbers significantly in the decades ahead. CARA projects an expected growth in the Latino Catholic population to 65 percent between 2010 and 2050. The same study estimates a Catholic population total of 128 million in 40 years, representing 29.2 percent of the total U.S. population.[11] Note that the Census Bureau's 2010 Current Population Survey (CPS) estimates that 16.1 percent of the U.S. population currently self-identifies as Hispanic or Latino, and this percentage is expected to grow to 29.2 percent in 2050. This result would more than double the 12.5 percent of Latinos identified in Census 2000. Based on these numbers, the CARA projection estimates that by 2038 there will be more Catholics who self-identify as Hispanic/Latino than those who do not. As this shift occurs, we can expect that the overall "Catholic vote" will shift toward the Democratic party and perhaps look much more like it did in the 1960s than in the 1990s or 2000s.[12] Thus, the future of the Latino Catholic vote is in fact the future of the U.S. Catholic vote.

Notes

1. Conducted by Edison Media Research and Mitofsky International.
2. 2008 exit poll questions: Are you of Hispanic or Latino descent?; Race: Hispanic/Latino; Would you describe yourself as a Born-Again or evangelical Christian? (ver. 1, 2, 4 questionnaires); Are you: Protestant, Catholic, Mormon/LDS, Other Christian, Jewish, Muslim, Something Else, None (only ver. 4 questionnaires). Non-Catholic Protestant or evangelical subgroups analyzed here are limited to those who self-identify their religion as Protestant or Other Christian.
3. For more on this phenomenon see: Pew Hispanic Center 2007b.
4. 2008 American National Election Study. http://sda.berkeley.edu/cgi-bin/hsda ?harcsda+nes08new.
5. All Catholic evangelicals cannot be selected out specifically, for most exit poll questions as the evangelical question is on three of four exit poll questionnaires while religious affiliation is only on one of four.
6. Unfortunately, due to religious affiliation appearing on only one of four exit poll questionnaires and most of the "issue" questions appearing on the other versions of the questionnaires, the possible scope of any analysis is limited.
7. Some of the difference between partisan affiliation and party of House vote among Catholics who also self-identify as born-again may be related to the local competeveness of those races and the availability of a viable Republican candidate.

Many in this group might wish to vote Republican for a House member but may be unable to do so given the local nature of the election.

8. It is also important to remember that the General Social Survey (GSS) differs substantially from exit polls (voters) and the NES (voting eligible), as its sample includes all adults (including those who would not be eligible to vote). http://sda.berkeley.edu/cgi-bin/hsda?harcsda+gss08.

9. This is the case in the United States generally. However, the death penalty could be supported in areas of the world where it might not be possible to secure a convicted murder and the threat to society of this person escaping and committing more murders is more evident.

10. Oppenheimer 2010.

11. See: Mark M. Gray (2010), "Pies, damned pies, and statistics: Is the Catholic population growing?" http://nineteensixty-four.blogspot.com/2010/11/pies-damned-pies-and-statistics-is.html. Note: Even stronger Catholic and specifically Latino Catholic growth is estimated by Skirbekk et al. (2010). Factoring in immigration and fertility differences, the authors conclude that "Catholics in the youngest age cohorts will outnumber their Protestant counterparts by 2043 and take over some time in the second half of the 21st century" (Skirbekk et al. 2010: 303). They expect Catholics to be 32 percent of the population by 2043 and their upper-range estimate for the Catholic population in this year exceeds 160 million (their lowest estimate tops 100 million).

12. Latino Catholics are expected to continue to be an essential target group for presidential candidates given their current and expected growth in key Electoral College states.

Suggestions for Further Reading on Latinos and Religion

The most available overview of Latino religion and political mobilization is *Recognizing the Latino Religious Resurgence* (1998) by Ana María Díaz-Stevens and Anthony M. Stevens-Arroyo. This book links both secular sociological issues with religious motivations to describe a half-century of social movement. The three volume historical treatment of Hispanics in the United States, co-edited by Jay Dolan with Latino scholars for the University of Notre Dame Press, is divided among the Mexican American history (Volume 1), the Cubans and Puerto Ricans (Volume 2), and a thematic treatment of events since 1964 (Volume 3) that have produced a nationwide Latino identity in both church and society. David Badillo's *Latinos and the New Immigrant Church* (2006) provides a useful update on the issues raised in the Notre Dame series. Of similar usefulness, although not focused exclusively on religion, is *The Columbia History of Latinos in the United States Since 1960* (2004) edited by David G. Gutiérrez. Generic social and cultural themes are treated in the 2004 book *Mexican American Religions: Spirituality, Activism, and Culture*, edited by Gastón Espinosa and Mario T. García although it deals almost exclusively with Mexican Americans. Alyshia Gálvez's 2009 study of Mexicans in New York, *Guadalupe in New York: Devotion and the Struggle for Citizenship Rights among Mexican Immigrants*, adds an East Coast perspective to the usual research efforts focused on the Southwest and California.

The PARAL series published out of the Bildner Center for Western Hemisphere Studies (CUNY) in New York adopts a more inclusive perspective of religion and culture for all the Latino nationalities and their religions. *An Enduring Flame: Studies in Latino Popular Religiosity* (1994) is the first volume, while the second, *Old Masks, New Faces: Religion and Latino Identities* (1995) examines issues specifically related to political science themes. The third volume, *Enigmatic Powers: Syncretism with African and Indigenous Peoples' Religions Among Latinos* (1995) is a cross-cultural examination of the new religious phenomenon that has created spin-offs from traditional institutional religion. Somewhat in the same vein, *La Llorona's Children: Religion, Life and Death in the United States–Mexican Borderlands* (2003), Luis León's study of a Mexican *curandera*, offers participant observer insights into noninstitutionalized religious expression.

For those seeking information on specific locations in political and religious developments, one cannot neglect *Oxcart Catholicism on Fifth Avenue* (1993), a pioneer study by Ana María Díaz-Stevens, which examines Puerto Ricans in New York City; and Thomas Tweed's important contribution to diasporic religion, *Our Lady of the Exile: Diasporic Religion at a Cuban Catholic Shrine in Miami* (1997). Anneris Goris's chapter on Dominicans in *Bridging Boundaries: The Pastoral Care of US Hispanics* (2002) hopefully will open the way to more and different interpretations of these local experiences. In this light, the 1998 book co-edited by Stephen R. Warner *Gatherings in Diaspora: Religious Communities and the New Immigration* merits inclusion for a generic and national analysis of the rising tide of Latino religious awareness. Political science has welcomed David Leal's 2010 chapter "Religion in Latino Political and Civic Lives" in Alan Wolfe and Ira Katznelson (eds.), *Religion and Democracy in the United States: Danger or Opportunity?* (Princeton and New York: Princeton University Press and Russell Sage Foundation).

A valuable overview of colonialism in Latin America and the formation of Latino communities in the United States can be found in Juan Gonzalez's *Harvest of Empire: A History of Latinos in America* (2000). Political science explorations of Mexican Americans, often with the word *Chicano* in the title, are abundant. The classic work by Rudolfo Acuña, *Occupied America* (1972, first edition) is a good place to gain an overview of the internal colonialism dynamic for Texas, California, and the Southwest. No less important is the work on Mexican Americans published by David Gutiérrez in 1995: *Walls and Mirrors: Mexican Americans, Mexican Immigrants and the Politics of Ethnicity*. The most complete of secular histories of the Mexican territories until the twentieth century is David Weber's, *The Spanish Frontier in North America* (2002), which has the virtue of recognizing the important role for religion and its institutions. The forthcoming series from Cambridge University Press on religion in the Americas edited by Stephen Stein will also provide chapters written in English on specifically Latino experiences.

Many of the best works on Puerto Rican history are in Spanish. *Colonial Subjects: Puerto Ricans in a Global Perspective* (2003) addresses the colonialism question and is available in English. *The Puerto Rican Movement: Voices from the Diaspora* (1998) is focused exclusively on Puerto Ricans in the United States, although along with *Puerto Ricans in the United States: A Contemporary Portrait* (2006) by Edna Acosta-Belén and Carlos E. Santiago, it contains little on religion. Finding a link between political movements and religion is easier when analyzing Mexican American communities, especially because of the religious convictions of the United Farm Workers' leader, César Chávez. Together with the outreach around cultural and political issues provided in the works by San Antonio priest and theologian, Virgilio Elizondo, there is much to be gained in reviewing the various roles of the image of Our Lady of Guadalupe as both a religious and political icon. The previously referenced *Recognizing the Latino Religious Resurgence* offers a digest of this process along with a useful bibliography on this topic and for this theology of Mexican American identity.

Other topics worthy of research are those on PADRES, a militant priest organization, and on figures like Pedro Albizu Campos of the Puerto Rican Nationalist Party and Bert Corona, a labor organizer in the Southwest. A great many studies of religious aspects of traditional culture are also useful. New Mexico's *Penitentes*, studies on crypto-Jewish identities, and customs like *compadrazgo* and the role of women in challenging religious barriers all contribute to the theme of political mobilization of religious believers. These might be added as specialized reading beyond the works referenced in other chapters of this book that provide statistics and political science perspectives. Among the most important journals on this topic is the *American Politics Research*, which published key articles in March 2007—one by the team of Jongho Lee and Harry P. Pachon and another by Rodolfo O. de la Garza and Jeronimo Cortina. These and other periodical pieces contribute to a growing literature on Latinos and politics.

A Layperson's Guide to Research on Hispanics/Latinos

Anthony M. Stevens-Arroyo

There is research that is reliable and research that is questionable. The difference between the two often rests upon technical details that are well understood only by experts. This is especially true when the research begins to explore religion and the Latinos and Latinas who are the subjects of this book. Voting patterns for this group and the role of religion in shaping their political mobilization have only recently become the focus of scholarly attention, a circumstance that increases the need for careful understanding of the data. This chapter is intended as an aide to two kinds of readers: first, those who might be acquainted with Latinos and Latinas but not with academic issues of research; and second, experts in the scholarly fields who are new to a focused look at Latinos and Latinas. Responding to what often become the frequently asked questions for these types of readers, we outline here some common premises and a few misconceptions about surveying Latinos and Latinas on issues related to religion. We have attempted to explore the issues in the common sense language of a layperson, that is, a person who is not expert in all the dimensions of the issue at hand.

Which Term Is Correct: *Latino* or *Hispanic*?

Both *Hispanic* and *Latino* are used in research when identifying the target population. Latino is linked to *Latin American,* and there is a political reason that part of America came to be *Latin* during the reign of the Napoleon III in

France. Essentially, the European mind-set wanted to recognize that there was an affinity for the Catholic nations of the Old World with the southern hemisphere of the New World, just as Northern (and Protestant) Europe claimed to have given birth to the Republic of a Protestant United States. Since Mexico and most of the Central American republics lie north of the equator, *South America* did not encompass these important Spanish-speaking republics. Moreover, "South America" is a geographical term for a continent, independent of culture and politics. Hence, *Latin America* was intended to refer to all the non-English-speaking countries. Of course, questions might be asked about where Creole-French-speaking Haiti belongs. And what can be said about Dutch-speaking Curaçao or English-speaking Jamaica and Bermuda? Clearly, the term *Latin American* is not as neat as it might appear at first, although it is vastly superior as a term of cultural reference to *South American*, which is more descriptive of accidental geography than any sociological or political reality.

In the United States, the term Hispanic was used both extraofficially by humanists, and then officially by the Census Bureau. The advantage of this term over Latin American is its purely cultural connotation. There is no *Hispania* anywhere except in dusty history books about the Roman Empire's colonies in today's Spain. But the term Hispanic includes not just people born in this hemisphere as Latin Americans, but also those from Spain. Those born in Brazil can be called "Luso-American" using the Roman term for Portugal, "Lusitania." To refer to both Spain and Portugal, one would use the name "Iberia," and Spanish and Portuguese speakers in the Americas would be "Ibero-Americans."

All of these distinctions can be confusing, largely because such terms are overlapping. A person born, let us say, in Uruguay, but living in New York is a South American by geography, a Latin American by nationality, and a Hispanic by language. That person could be called "Hispano-American" or "Ibero-American" without error.

The U.S. Bureau of the Census makes the important distinction between *foreign born*—in our example from Uruguay—and the child born in New York who is *native born* and Hispanic. Since the term Hispanic is used in official census data, many researchers feel obligated to repeat that term when reporting on demographic and other official reports. The term has encountered disfavor, however, because some people feel that it too rapidly suppresses the unique history of each Latin American nation. Mexicans living in Los Angeles would represent themselves as considerably different in looks, culture, and Spanish accent from our hypothetical Uruguayan in New York City. They would be right.

There was also a political reason that many began to use the term Latino or *Chicano* or *Mexican American* and reject Hispanic. The latter, as explained above, was a term gradually adopted by government during the 1970s to lump together a rapidly growing and increasingly militant segment of the population. While Hispanic was preferable to the term *Spanish-surnamed* persons that had been used previously by the U.S. Bureau of the Census, it emphasized a cultural and linguistic commonality at the expense of a historical and colonial one in which Spain had imposed itself upon indigenous peoples. Readers will observe that Hispanic is repeated often in census data or in publications focused on a shared Spanish civilization while Latino is more current among those concerned with emphasizing the historical and social concerns within in only this hemisphere. Usage of these terms may also indicate political preferences with Latino preferred by liberals and Hispanic by those more conservative.

What are the substitutes? One is *Chicano*, which found its greatest popularity in 1970s California. Based on a conclusion that the Aztecs pronounced the name of their land as something that sounded like *Meh-chée-cah*, the name Chicano was supposed to revert back to that original identity that predated either Spaniards or North Americans. In Texas, however, the label *Mexican American* was found more frequently. In New Mexico, *Hispano* was used to distinguish some of the earliest settlers who came directly from the Spanish Canary Islands under order from the king, and never had set foot in Mexico.

But neither Chicano nor Mexican American nor *Hispano* should be used to describe Puerto Ricans, Cubans, Dominicans, or any Central or South Americans. Not only are these other groups not included in the experience of what is now the Southwest of the United States, each of those groups has its "insider" equivalents. Thus, for instance, Puerto Ricans will call themselves *Boricuas*, based on the name used by the natives who greeted Columbus who described their island as *Boriké* (often written in Spanish orthography as *Borinquen*). Similarly, Dominicans will use *Quisqueyanos* also borrowed from the same natives' language, *Quisqueya*, (although the natives' other name for the island was *Haití*). To distinguish those born in the continental United States from the Puerto Ricans born on the island, the term *Niurican* was coined in the late 1960s by fusing together *New York* and *Puerto Rican*. For much the same reason we have *Dominicanyorks* for Dominicans born in New York.

What Are the Advantages or Disadvantages in Using *Latino* rather than *Hispanic*?

Latino has inherited popularity as the all-inclusive term over the past several decades among academics and political leaders. It is also the term that predominates in this book. However, it is not uniformly used everywhere. Surveys often find that a cross-section of grass-roots respondents prefer *Hispanic* to *Latino*. The PARAL Study (Graphs III.6.4 and III.6.5) reported that among lay leaders, *Hispanic* was preferred (41%) to *Latino* (17%) but that in actual usage, "Hispanic" (44%) was only slightly more common than "Latino" (42%). In other words, people understand both terms even when they prefer one over the other.

Latino is an Anglicization of the adjective in Spanish derived from *latino americano* (Latin American). Since Spanish registers gender by the ending on its adjectives, however, while *Latino* refers to male persons, *Latina* with "a" at the end refers to females. A bilingual speaker using *Latino* encounters such complications of grammatical use and gender meanings, even if others do not. At times the reference is written *Latin@* on the supposition that the ampersand, @, is a feminine "a" inside a masculine "o" and thus is short shrift for *Latino/a* or a longer *Latino and Latina*. So while using *Latino* in surveys and reports has some advantages, it also presents complications that are not linked to simply using the official label of Hispanic.

Latino as a term is often—but not always—preferred to distinguish descendants of Latin Americans who have been born in the United States. Thus, a Latino differs from a Latin American inasmuch as the Latin American may or may not be a U.S. citizen, but surely is an immigrant. On the other hand, as one born in the United States, the Latino is always a citizen. The term, *first-generation* clearly represents the immigrant who has come to the United States from another country while *second generation* has always referred to the children born in the United States to that immigrant. This distinction becomes harder to maintain when the Latin American person has entered the United States as a small child and been socialized in the United States. While in legal terms, such a child immigrant is foreign born, he or she has grown up in the United States, is likely to speak English better than Spanish, and in cultural behavior and preferences to resemble the U.S.-born Latino more than a Latin American immigrant. Now, one can speak of a *one-and-a-half generation* to represent the generation born there but raised here. Such persons have never lived as adults in the Latin American country of their parents and have known little else in life than the U.S. society and culture, so they share unique characteristics of the two different generations in a unique combination. It has not been uncommon to find in a Latino family, parents and grandparents who are first-generation Latin American immigrants, children who are one-and-a-half generation, and children who are from the U.S.-born second generation. Thus, enforcement of immigration laws without consideration of how it affects the family unit is of major concern to many families of this type.

When it comes to taking surveys, the one-and-a-half generation often functions like a *spoiler*. For instance, if a survey asks about which language is preferred, Spanish is more likely to be the choice of those born in a Spanish-speaking country (the first generation) and English the preference for the second generation born in the United States. However, some in the one-and-a-half generation, while technically *first-generation immigrants*, will likely report cultural and linguistic preferences that are closer to the second generation. This might incline those counting the responses to this question to understate the importance that the Spanish language has for those who immigrated as adults.

Distinctions about place of birth implicitly also carry reference to citizenship status. Only those born in the United States are guaranteed citizenship. However, the foreign born may not only be resident aliens, they may also be naturalized citizens. In addition to these two categories, the foreign born may also be undocumented persons whose legal status is irregular. It must be added here that only about 30 percent of those classified as Hispanic in the census are foreign born, including many of the undocumented. This means that ambiguity about citizenship or legal status is an issue for less than a third of the total Hispanic population in the United States, and that the *undocumented* or illegal status is the condition for a still smaller slice. Only citizens can vote in U.S. elections (local school boards may have different rules), so the reliability of a political poll depends upon how results are focused upon the natural-born citizens and the naturalized citizens. In contrast, as this book takes pains to point out, the formation of political attitudes and opinions for these voters can never be totally divorced from the experiences and convictions of the nonvoting immigrants. Thus, research into how Latinos and Latinas vote is only part of the story of political mobilization.

It has always been difficult to estimate the number of undocumented aliens, including Latin Americans. After all, clandestine crossings that break the law would be stopped if they were observed. Precisely because they go undetected, the number of people making illegal border crossings can only be estimated. Experts rely on approximations based on how many people are caught and then, extrapolating from those accurate statistics, make an educated guess about how many persons escaped detection in any given period.

There are problems with estimates, however. A single individual attempting crossings two or three times is included in these statistics, but ought not be considered two or three persons. Thus, an estimate based on the number of attempted crossings may be counting the same individual more than once: one million suspected illegal entries might be only 500,000 persons. These estimates may vary widely, often dependent on political postures that want either to minimize or maximize public fear about the number of illegal immigrants.

Actually, the only certain count about the number of persons illegally resident in the United States is for those who enter legally but whose visa as visitor, student, or temporary resident has lapsed. In fact, it is estimated that only about 1 in 10 of persons from Latin America without proper documents entered the United States illegally across the border. It is far more common for one to enter the United States legally but lose that status. The officials in the formerly-named Naturalization and Immigration Service have actual records for those who entered but lost their legal status for any number of legitimate reasons and remain in the country. For instance, a student visa obliges the foreigner to a certain number of credit hours at university or college. If a course is canceled by the institution on the eve of the first class, a person on a student visa could be in technical violation of the requirements for legal residence. Immigration officers may exercise judgment to waive the literal application of the law in specific cases, or the student may appeal for a hearing to forestall any deportation. Immigration courts are backlogged with such cases about overstaying one's visa or losing the job specified on the visa application. It is important here to note that such issues constitute an offense before civil law, more or less like a parking ticket and are not felonies or other criminal acts.

There is, of course, a significant number of persons who enter the United States illegally, without any attempt to secure proper papers for entry. These are the immigrants slipping through deserts late at night, climbing walls, or tunneling underground to avoid detection. They commit a crime, punishable not only the United States but also in Mexico since that border country ordinarily obliges immigrants to register their intended departure for the United States. The targeting of the Mexican–U.S. border alone to control all undocumented entries does not address the entire population, however. Countries like the Dominican Republic are not on that U.S.–Mexico border. The great majority of the undocumented entered legally but stayed illegally. Often, once present in the United States with a legal visa, they engage in criminal activity to secure a false identity that allows them to function as either legal residents (the green card) or even as natural-born U.S. citizens. Puerto Rican officials have found an extremely high incidence of identity theft. Puerto Ricans named *José Rivera* or *María Rodríguez* living on the island will discover that a copy of their birth certificate has been used by a Mexican national with the same name in order to file a valid Social Security number on a job application in a place as far away as, say, Wisconsin.

These legal issues affect surveys of Latinos. The persons with dubious resident status or with false papers would be inclined not to respond to any strangers calling on the phone or mailing a questionnaire. Given the precariousness of such constructed identities, any verification process might likely destroy a stability built up over the years. Certainly, laws regulating immigration and identity theft need to be enforced, but the person conducting a survey ought not to be expected to simultaneously engage in spying on individuals or reporting on violations to the authorities. In fact, adulterating research with such a law enforcement function may doom the reliability of the research. Even when researchers divorce their science from these legal clouds, respondents with immigration issues may decline to participate, skewing the survey results. There is a scientific procedure used by researchers called *weighting* to overcome such drawbacks, and this is discussed below.

Is It Better to Talk about *Migration* rather than *Immigration*?

The technical literature makes a difference for the *im-migrant* who is moving *into* a new country; simultaneously, he or she is also an *e-migrant* moving away from a country of origin. The important fact stated above should be repeated here, however, that about 70 percent of the persons often called Hispanic in government documents are citizens born in the United States, with about 30 percent as foreign born. Just as we don't often refer to people moving from New York to New Jersey as *immigrants*, it would be imprecise to call immigrants the Puerto Ricans moving from their island to Orlando, Florida. A better term for such movement in residence for citizens is *migration*. The trend is similar to *migration to the suburbs* or *migration to the Sun Belt* for persons already U.S. citizens. Common usage makes migration the experience of persons of the same nationality, while *immigration* is reserved for those who move from one nation to another.

In the example of Puerto Ricans migrating to Orlando, however, we ought to recognize that while legally of the same nationality as the Americans already there, the language and the culture of these migrating Puerto Ricans differ from the other Americans. In fact, despite their long-standing U.S. citizenship, Puerto Ricans in Florida have more in common with Cuban immigrants when it comes to culture and language than they do with non-Hispanic Floridians.

Why Puerto Ricans have been American citizens for nearly a century but are still primarily Spanish-speakers is a conundrum for those who identify citizenship with Americanization. It certainly is true that naturalization for an immigrant requires proficiency in English, but Puerto Ricans were made citizens by congressional fiat in 1917 without being asked to undergo Americanization and learn English as a precondition. Neither can it be said that preference for the Spanish language is the result of ignorance or lack of schooling, since the public schools in Puerto Rico use Spanish and not English as the principal language of instruction.

The reason for this grand exception to the pattern of Americanization lies in history. Puerto Rico was invaded by U.S. troops and the island with its people was annexed as colonial territory at the end of the Spanish–American War in 1898. Similarly, the Southwest from New Mexico to California became territories that were annexed in 1848 as a result of military invasions during the Mexican–American War.[1] These events lend a special dimension to the Latino presence in the United States. Unlike the European groups, such as English, German, Irish, Italian, and Slavic peoples who were immigrants to these shores, Puerto Ricans as well as descendants of the 1848 inhabitants of today's New Mexico, California, and the 1836 Texas Republic were never immigrants. They did not immigrate to the United States: it "migrated" to them at the point of a gun.

While researchers can ignore these historical issues and related ideological undercurrents when conducting research, it is useful for the researcher to understand that the dynamics that shape Latino identity in the United States are different from those that have influenced Euro-Americans, who all have an immigrant past. The Mexican American in Santa Fe is more like the Irish Catholic in Belfast than he or she is to the Irish American in Boston. They have been invaded in their own homeland by outsiders: they are not the outsiders themselves, since they are not immigrants. Thus, the descendants of the conquered peoples in Puerto Rico and parts of the Southwest and California constitute a distinct category of *American*, more like the Native Americans encountered by the Pilgrims than like the Pilgrims themselves. Moreover, as conquered peoples, they have an older ancestral claim to being in America than most of the descendants of the English-speaking Euro-American immigrants.

Surveying Discrimination and Americanization

The salient result for those conducting research today is a significant difference in perception about discrimination. Latinos and Latinas who have been American citizens the longest may be more critical of their experiences in U.S. society than the immigrants from Latin America. While immigrants may consider it unsurprising that as newcomers they receive fewer benefits and consideration than natural-born American citizens, the perspective would be different among the Latinos and Latinas who are Puerto Ricans or descendants of several generations from the original inhabitants of Texas, the Southwest, and California. The researcher may find that those with citizen rights and generations of life under the U.S. flag may perceive themselves to be discriminated against more readily than the immigrants, while others may expect just the reverse: that the immigrants see themselves victim of more discrimination than those with citizenship.

Historical reality serves as basis for such perceptions. In 1848 as in 1898, the U.S. settlers who arrived in the conquered territories were the *minority*, while the Spanish-speaking were the majority of the population. The invading United States erected a series of laws and tolerated a set of institutional procedures in Texas, Puerto Rico, and the Mexican territories to ensure the power of the English-speaking minority. These measures influenced property, banking, loans, investments, and voting rights. In all cases, Washington assumed legal control over all governance while denying the people of the territory political representation in the Congress. Without mincing words, these conquered areas were treated as colonies. Admission into the federal union as states alleviated the most glaring of these constitutional inequalities, although Puerto Rico remains a full-blown colony.

Inside these conquered areas, new institutions fostered assimilation. Education was conducted in English, voting and running for political office required English language proficiency, hiring in public positions or major industries demanded English—even worship in the Churches tended to set up a structure wherein the English-speaking were given more attention than the Spanish-speaking. Life in these Americanizing circumstances fostered abandonment of the pre-invasion cultural patterns.

But access to the Americanizing institutions was unevenly available, with a preference for service to the already English-speaking population. The public schools serving the rural areas or a city's Latino population were often inferior to those found elsewhere. Services like police protection and legal procedures for property transfer and business permits could become stages for unequal and discriminatory treatment. Consider this pattern a Latino equivalent of the Jim Crow policies used against African Americans in the South.

Adopting such a perspective, some academics have introduced the notion of *internal colonialism* as a way of labeling the systematic discrimination against a class of people who were the first inhabitants of the conquered territories. Puerto Ricans, it might be said, continue to suffer from classical colonialism on their island as well as internal colonialism when in any of the 50 states.

However labeled, the discriminatory policies often resulted in the creation of ghettos wherein those who wished to preserve their language and culture were effectively segregated from the rest of the people.

Policies sometimes have unintended consequences, and this is also the case for colonialism directed against Latinos and Latinas. Segregating the people into ethnic ghettos with inferior housing, government services, and public schools may have sustained the hegemonic status for the non-Hispanics, but the concentration of Latinos and Latinas had another consequence. Segregation preserved the previous cultural identity. It also impelled the improvisation of social conventions like obtaining business loans outside the banking system by relying on relatives and mutual associations. These spontaneous innovations allowed cultural distinctiveness to survive and for community pride to flourish.

The Spanish-speaking, finding little fairness in treatment by police or the courts, relied on their own resources, avoiding officialdom whenever possible. Although the process differed from place to place, by the mid-twentieth century there were recognizable traditional enclaves—or barrios—of the Spanish-speaking. Some were in the colonial sectors of sprawling cities like Los Angeles or in historic districts of places like San Antonio and Santa Fe, but most were in rural areas where people were mostly poor and mostly Hispanic. These U.S. citizens of Puerto Rican or Mexican American heritage had developed a set of coping mechanisms to maintain their cultural identities and the Spanish language in the face of discrimination. Moreover, through literature, popular music, and other media, the marginalized enclaves often were celebrated as the fountains for a culture of resistance, somewhat in the way that Harlem served African Americans and the multiple *Little Italies* in U.S. cities served the Italians.

The wars of the twentieth century and industrial needs in large cities, however, stirred a significant population shift in urban centers as Latinos in search of better opportunities began to migrate away from their traditional enclaves. Nowhere was this more evident than in Puerto Rico, where between 1946 and 1964 some 40 percent of the population migrated, virtually emptying the mountainous hill country of its subsistence farmers. This Great Puerto Rican Migration has been described in greater detail elsewhere, but similar if less dramatic migrations of Latinos led up to the 1960s. In most cases, these Spanish-speaking U.S. citizens were perceived as newcomers in the receiving communities, but often, addressing their needs, copied patterns previously employed with noncitizen immigrants from Europe.

This treatment of the already-citizens as if they were immigrants without full rights and in need of Americanization may be considered discrimination, and there have been considerable energies spent in the past half-century to remedy this situation. Treating the Latinos and Latinas differently from the rest of the population, of course, is a two-sided coin. On the one hand, special educational classes for remediation and separate offices for social services can smack of inferior care; on the other, affirmative action, bilingual education, and ballots printed in Spanish for American citizens can be considered benefits. It is not uncommon to find that political ideology of either right or left provide opposite mirror images. Latinos and Latinas may favor affirmative action, but based on the logic that affirmative action is a restoration of legitimate rights, they man not consider this special treatment. On the other hand, there are sectors of the non-Latino population that view affirmative action as *racial discrimination in reverse*, denying equality to non-Hispanics. Conducting research among Latinos and Latinas, therefore, requires the construction of questions that fairly reflect the differing perspectives on what constitutes equal treatment and what is discriminatory.

This perception of a two-sided nature to programs focused upon special groups has an echo in the way some immigrants from Latin America are perceived as *desirable* and others as less so. Thus, for instance, Cuban immigrants leaving Cuba after the 1959 Revolution were given special treatment as immigrants who also were *refugees*. As persons fleeing from anti-American governments, these Cuban refugees were given assistance that was not generally offered to other immigrants from Latin America. In fact, the decision of who is and who is not a refugee is often influenced by political persuasions rather than social needs.

What Are the Racial Components of a Latino or Hispanic Identity?

Another area with differing perceptions among Latinos and non-Latinos is racial identity. In its long history, the Catholic experience of Latin America permitted, and at times even encouraged, the marriage between persons of different races. The term *mestizo* was used for mixtures of white European and Native Americans: *mulato* was used for black African and white European liaison. During Spanish colonial history, elaborate schema for the degree of mixtures emerged in the cultural toolkit. The extent of racial mixture and its social acceptance among Latin Americans contrasted sharply with more rigid racial intermarriage boundaries in the United States, both before and after the American Civil War.

Researchers have found, not surprisingly, that Latinos and Latinas have different perceptions of race from other segments of the U.S. population.

Notably, while North Americans tend to view race in terms of descent from ancestors of one or other race, Latinos and Latinas often look at an individual's color of skin when making a racial classification. Thus, the historic legal phrase "one drop of black blood makes a person black" does not apply among most Latin American cultures. Instead, a family member with mestizo features may be called an *Indio* ("Indian") and another with African like curly black hair the *mulato*. Note that these may be siblings in the same family, so that one sibling may enter adult society as *white* and the other as *African American*.

Adding to these complications is a trend to claim a multiple racial heritage for Latinos and Latinas in the U.S. Census. The Bureau of the Census considers race and ethnicity as separate categories, so marking oneself as black-and-white or black-white-and-Native-American creates some processing problems in reporting results. Readers will note the use in official census publications of the category, *Non-Hispanic Whites* and the omnipresent disclaimer, "Hispanics may be of any race." In fact, in reporting the number of African Americans (i.e., *blacks*), the census will include Latinos and Latinas who identify themselves racially as African American and ethnically as Latino. This means that when calculating whether Latinos and Latinas outnumber African Americans, the African American count may include Latinos and Latinas because the categories are not mutually exclusive. One should recognize, therefore, that *black and brown* used as racial categories for African Americans and Latinos respectively are not generally sustained in the approach employed in official census documents. Nonetheless, the racial stereotyping of Latinos and Latinas influences the perception of discrimination.

How Should One Use the Term *Catholic* in Surveys?

Who is really a Catholic? That question is theological as well as a sociological. The theologian will emphasize acceptance of dogma and correct ethical and ritual behavior as tests for membership as a Catholic. Most social science efforts, on the other hand, rely on self-identification: they ask the person interviewed to indicate their religion. But while social science may avoid entering into the theological thicket, doctrine may enter through the *back door*. Certainly, the self-perception of who is a Catholic is highly influenced by the reigning theology of the moment. This is especially true when theology teaches that particular behavior disqualifies a person from claiming a Catholic identity. This may be done for any of several transgressions, such as not attending Sunday Mass, remarrying after divorce, using birth control pills, or—even in the opinion of some prelates—in voting for a Democrat. Thus, when identifying oneself as *Catholic*, some or none of these theological views may influence the answer of an individual respondent.

In the case of Latinos and Latinas, the Catholic identity question is complicated by a generational experience wherein the Catholic culture of the homeland society was considered an inescapable heritage, not at all dependent on choice or behavior. In other words, one might actively practice the Catholic religion by attending Mass regularly—or reject the Catholic identity by joining a non-Catholic church and participating in its religious activities. But even if you did neither, you were part of a Catholic culture and were automatically Catholic. This experience contrasts with the transactional nature of church membership in much of American Protestantism. For instance, membership in many Protestant churches often bestows rights to vote for or against who is pastor, or obligates the member to a strict patter of donations under the rubric of tithing. As a general trend, Protestant Churches will only count such enrolled members as belonging to the congregation. In contrast, Catholic pastors will count even those who do not attend church regularly to be Catholics under their care.

The cultural Catholic identity is labeled *popular religiosity* in much of the academic literature, *popular* being a direct transliteration from Spanish. This cultural Catholicism is not directly chosen, however, and does not mean that the person has internalized the doctrines and behavioral norms imposed by the institution. In fact, in the case of many from Latin American countries with a history of anticlericalism, the popular character of this cultural Catholicism may be praised as an authentic religion in resistance to institutionalized Catholicism.

To this mix, one must also add the historical lack of clergy for many rural areas in Latino homelands. As part of the need to cope with the dearth of priests, popular religiosity developed an elaborate schema of seasonal celebrations and customs for families undergoing rites of passage. Rosaries, holy water, statues, religious pictures, home *altars*, First Communion dress, burial customs, funeral anniversaries—the list is very long—are all elements of what has been called *material Christianity*.

How Should One Use *Protestant* and *Evangelical* among Latinos?

There are also issues with labels used for non-Catholics. Historically, those who followed Luther in the sixteenth century maintained bishops, sacraments, consecration of the host, and the like but *protested* the abuses of Catholic

Church. These were the *Protestants*. Calvin radically recast the institutions of Christianity, replacing many with egalitarian forms of governance and eliminating much reliance on material aspects of religion and his followers (when not called *Calvinists*) were the *Reformers*. In sixteenth-century Europe, a third group emerged with a message of independence from all religious institutions, contesting Protestants, Reformers and Catholics alike. Beginning with the baptism of infants—which they opposed—they instead relied upon an individual's private interpretation of scriptures and the emotional experience induced by acceptance of Christ's divinity to guide the faith above and beyond any authority of church officials. Many different religious groups, such as Baptists and Quakers, have incorporated this antinomian approach to Christianity. Unfortunately for those seeking theological purity, all three tendencies are usually lumped together when referring to the *Protestant Reformation*, and in the course of American history, there has been a substantial blurring of the original distinctions. Individual believers today or specific congregations may not necessarily accept the original doctrinal statements that created them.

More important to social science than the purity of theological definitions has been a set of larger categories that helps evaluate the influence of such overlapping beliefs. Sociology, for instance, has employed the categories of *Church* and *sect* to selectively analyze organizational dynamics. But more central to contemporary analysis of Latino religion are terms like *Fundamentalist* and *Evangelical*, or *Pentecostal* and *Charismatic*. These have become tools for analysis because they enable researchers to examine differences and similarities that transcend theological idiosyncrasy.

Of the above, the most troublesome are Evangelical and Pentecostal. Evangelical widely applied means *of the Gospel*. Virtually no Christian denies the centrality to the Gospel of Jesus Christ to all belief. But in history, there have been movements and individuals that have refocused faith and the practice religion upon a more purposeful imitation of strictures taken directly from the scriptures. In its history, Christianity has repeatedly experienced calls to return to Gospel roots, and these moments of evangelical witness did not begin with the Protestant Reformation. For instance, one can consider the call to poverty by St. Francis of Assisi in twelfth-century Europe as an evangelical moment. Methodism began in a similar way within the Church of England. Many Lutherans in the United States belong to the *Evangelical Lutheran Church of America* (ECLA) and have adopted that title as a badge of loyalty to Luther's teachings.

Today's research, however, has generally limited the meaning of Evangelical to a type of believer who generally applies the call to Gospel imitation as a restoration of previously uncomplicated application of religious values to daily life. Moreover, rather than emphasize personal practice by individuals of the Gospel values, in the 1980s, Evangelicalism in the United States became associated with the Moral Majority as led by the Reverend Jerry Falwell. In addition to visibility in supporting conservative political issues advocated by the Republican Party, the Evangelicals in Falwell's association made effective use of media, particularly the radio. The success of such organizations in establishing new churches and strengthening the existing ones of similar tendencies created a new transdenominational phenomenon of *the Evangelicals*. To further complicate the issue, in Spanish, *evangélico* is often used for all Protestants, even if they are not included in the English language meaning of Evangelical. The PARAL Study reported a wide divergence between those responding in Spanish, where *protestante* was generally avoided, while in English, *Protestant* was more widely used in self-identification (The PARAL Study: Part I:27, Graph 1.9.2). In sum, Evangelical is an imprecise term, often fuzzy in application, that can refer to Fundamentalists on one side and Lutherans on the other.

A similar ambiguity clouds the easy application of the term *Pentecostal*. Borrowing on the event narrated in the Acts of the Apostles (2:1–15) that took place 50 days after Easter, Pentecostal refers to a repetition among contemporary individuals of the apostolic experience. On the first Pentecost, the previously timid apostles were emboldened by the Holy Spirit manifested in *tongues of fire* to preach the Gospel spontaneously and publicly. Moreover, those hearing them understood the message *each in their own tongue*. This spiritual translation of words of praise and preaching without human intermediaries is called *glossolalia* by the Apostle Paul (1 Corinthians 14:2; 13–18; 27–28), who considered it a gift of the Holy Spirit and a miracle that confirmed the righteousness of Christianity. Accompanying this gift was the ability to heal the sick and infirm by prayer and the laying on of hands. Incorporating these scriptural gifts in the early church to their own practices, Pentecostals in the modern era considered that rededication to Christ in these circumstances made the person a *born-again* Christian, because these experiences reconstituted the effect of Baptism by adding an emotional and adult acceptance of the Christian faith.

Pentecostalism began, as had many evangelical movements before it, as a movement within existing churches at the very beginning of the twentieth century. Its origins among poor working class and generally uneducated believers became a source both of its success and also of its expulsion from most Protestant denominations—even Evangelical ones. Moreover, the emphasis upon the emotional states that produced the miracles of *glossolalia* and the immediate effects of faith healing subjected the movement to accusations of charlatanry.

Rather quickly, Pentecostalism was considered a marginal if not also heretical expression of Christianity. Forced out of other churches, Pentecostals then created their own denominations. By the last quarter of the twentieth century, not only had the Pentecostal Churches survived, they had created their own style of music and worship.

The music and worship styles created by the Pentecostal Churches have been borrowed sometimes by other churches. Thus, alongside the noun *Pentecostalism* (with a capital *P*) which formally belongs to a specific denomination, there is also the adjective *pentecostalistic* (with a small *p*) for a lively style of worship and singing with secular musical forms and hand clapping. This pentecostalistic music style may be performed by churches that do not accept the basic tenets of the Pentecostal Church.

There is also a significant Catholic movement that emerged after the Second Vatican Council that incorporated much of the pentecostalistic form of prayer along with musical style and an open door to faith healing and manifestation of the glossolalia. After clarifying the orthodoxy of its beliefs in communion with the bishops and the pope, this movement took the name of *Catholic Charismatics.*

Today, at 4 million,[2] there are twice as many Latino Catholic Charismatics than all Pentecostals of any nationality in the Assemblies of God, the largest Pentecostal Church that reports 2 million members. A sociological emphasis upon numerical majorities makes it difficult to equate the historical and theological beginnings of Pentecostalism as the measure of what Pentecostalism means today. If the Catholic Charismatics, for instance, reverence Marian devotion to Our Lady of Guadalupe, does their numerical superiority make the refusal of the Assemblies of God to reverence Marian devotion the exception rather than the rule for most Pentecostals? Moreover, it would be a fallacy to suggest that Catholic Charismatics are somehow lesser committed to Catholicism because of their pentecostalistic rituals.

To bridge these issues while respecting such differences, the researchers for the Pew Center's *Changing Faiths* have created a catch-all category of *Renewalist.* To sustain this new category, an effort was made to compare belief and religious experience of Catholic Charismatics and the historical Pentecostals by focusing on healing, exorcism, and speaking in tongues as if these are distinctively Pentecostal experiences. In fact, many Latino Catholics outside of the Charismatic Movement have also recognized these religious events, so that the authors of *Changing Faiths* admit that the tendency seems to be more a question of being Latino than of being Renewalist.[3]

The researcher today ought to recognize that the religious landscape for Latinos and Latinas of all professed denominations is different from the majority of non-Latino believers. The experience of exorcism mentioned above that perplexed the report's authors may well be related to contact with *Santería*, a religion that incorporates elements of African belief in healing and spirit possession. A typical Latino believer might be inclined to accept that there is spiritual power in such religions, perhaps identifying it with the power of Satan. This recognition of religious power outside the Christian experience would not necessarily diminish the orthodoxy of the believer. However, because non-Latinos have little or no contact with *Santería* and its adherents, they might more easily deny any authenticity of religious experiences in cases of spirit possession or miraculous healing. Thus, there are significant differences of perception and experience in Latino religion when contrasted with other American traditions.

Who Is Christian?

It would be an easy presumption to expect that the doctrinal statement of belief for the official congregation determines what each individual member believes. While not denying the usefulness of this definitional approach, researchers have found that the belief professed by local congregations or certain individuals do not always match. Moreover, there has been a rise in the number of churches opting not to link themselves to any specific Protestant denomination. Called *nondenominational* on that account, there sometimes has been an accompanying tendency to organize these churches with multiple clergy and house them in sprawling buildings with myriad activities and services, including private schools. Often labeled *megachurches*, these have become counterparts to the organizational size that Catholics and many Jewish congregations have long embraced.

One important advantage of these megachurches over the traditional 100- to 200-member denominational church is in the economy of size. Caution should be used, however, in mistaking the growth of megachurches as evidence for an increase in the number of Protestants, since their membership is largely drawn from the same pool as belonged to smaller denominational churches. Thus, the significance of the megachurches would seem to lay more in their creation of new styles of organization rather than in representation of new forms of faith.

The megachurches have had a role in promoting the term *Christian* as a surrogate for *Protestant*. Based on the notion that it is no longer accurate to consider these believers as *protesting* Catholicism, proponents have suggested it is simpler to reaffirm their discipleship to Christ with the all-inclusive term, Christian. Non-denominational churches are thus freed of the need to identify as *Lutheran, Baptist,* etc., and can rest simply upon their identity as Christian.

A problem arises when using this term to exclude Roman Catholics. Are we to reformulate *Protestant, Catholic, and Jew* for *Christian, Catholic, and Jew?* The documents of the Second Vatican Council, ironically, use *Christian* more often than *Catholic* when describing the faithful. If Catholicism is included (as it ought to be) as part of Christianity, then the term Christian is not really a substitute for Protestant, Evangelical or the like. Imprecise use of this term can confuse the issue while omitting it from the list of religious affiliations can create headaches for research analysis.

What Is Secularization?

Secularization, the term, was first used in the nineteenth century to describe *the confiscation by state authority of property belonging to churches.* Buildings such as churches, hospitals, and schools as well as convents and monasteries were the first targets of secularization. The properties were transferred from the control of religious authority and given over to secular officials. By analogy, secularization has come to mean *not just the transfer of buildings, but also the functions appropriate to those buildings.* Thus, for instance, not only is the control of the hospital building transferred from church to state, but the church contribution to hospital care is also given over to the state in the act of secularization.

The most devastating forms of secularization came with opposition to *all* religion. Secular liberals promoted nonreligious, even atheistic, social goals. Instead of channeling tax money through the churches for services such as schools and orphanages, governments now held the money themselves and substituted state agencies for religious ones in dispensing charity, education, and healing. In the United States today, most services previously within the direct sphere of religious institutions are commonly considered part of the obligations of the state. Admittedly, there has been a recent effort to enlist faith-based communities in the distribution of social services using religious buildings and institutions in the process, but despite sporadic confusion of what such partnership with religion entails, the separation of church and society has been sustained.

In common usage today, *secularization* refers to the separation of church and state, and does not generally entail European-style anticlericalism. Ironically, secularization often benefits a minority religion by affording it equal claim on public services that otherwise would be linked to membership in a majority religion. Consider the example of prayer in the public schools. Until the middle of the twentieth century, these prayers usually conformed to Protestant practices despite the objections of Jews and Catholics who sometimes found such forms of prayer to be offensive. *No prayer at all* in the public schools was often preferred to the imposition of a formulation particular to

Protestants. Favoring secular schools and services, therefore, does not necessarily imply a loss of faith or opposition to religion.

What Does *No Religion* Mean as a Survey Category?

The American Religious Identification Survey (ARIS) has conducted three major surveys over the decades. By asking the same questions and following more or less the same methodology, this repetition—or replication, if you will—enables researchers to measure change from the way a question is answered at one time and how opinions are altered after another. The 2001 ARIS survey provided special information on Latinos and Latinas in terms of religious identity and was incorporated into the PARAL Study.

But while questions in a survey may be repeated, they may also be improved. In 1990, ARIS asked: *What is your religion?* In 2001, the question was changed by adding a phrase at the end: *What is your religion, if any?* In the opinion of the ARIS Director, Barry Kosmin, that added phrase "... if any?" gave permission for respondents to say, "None." In other words, if a survey seems to presume that every person has a religion, there is a tendency to satisfy the questioner by designating a particular religion as one's own. When *permission* is implicitly given to have no religion, on the other hand, respondents feel free to say they have none. By allowing Latinos and Latinas to say they had *no religion*, the most significant result was a dramatic drop of 9 percent in Hispanics from those identifying as Catholic in 1990 (66%) to those saying the same in 2001 (57%). The loss to Catholicism did not show up as an increase for Protestants, Pentecostals, or the like, however. Instead the *no religion* category went from 6 percent in 1990 to 13 percent in 2001. In light of this evidence, it is a fallacy to suppose that when a Latino Catholic leaves the Church, he or she becomes a Protestant or Pentecostal.

Ariela Keysar, who worked on both the ARIS and the PARAL Study, showed moreover that Latinos saying they had *no religion* did not mean they were atheists or did not believe in miracles. In fact, 85 percent of Hispanics who professed no religion agreed that God exists. Of the respondents without religion, 76 percent said that God performs miracles and 82 percent agreed that "God helps me."[4] There is an apparent contradiction between professing no religion on the one hand and faith in God and miracles on the other. However, given the traditional strength of Catholic culture as a stand-alone component of popular religiosity, the contradiction can be explained as a loosening of traditional adherence to the Catholic Church as institution rather than a loss of belief in God, miracles, and Divine Providence. One might say that the Hispanic *nones* lost faith in the Church but kept faith in God. Somewhat akin to the way that secularization means separation of Church and State rather than rejection of religion, *no religion* may mean *no organized religion*. Whatever the case, there does not appear to be a zero-sum game in which one fewer Latino Catholic means one more Latino Pentecostal or Evangelical.

What Is the Importance of a Random Sample for Surveys?

Surveys may ask the same questions on a subject but come up with very different answers about Latinos if they use divergent methodologies. As contrasted with a census that asks a question of *every* individual, surveys rely on what is called a *sample* to gauge opinions. Traditionally, to reliably generalize the findings of a survey, a sample is chosen to represent the population under study. The manner in which the sample is chosen determines its reliability. Randomization is often the most straightforward, if not necessarily the simplest, form of obtaining a representative sample. The key behind randomization is that one can calculate the probability of choosing any given member of the population under study. Random digit-dialing phone surveys and cluster sampling incorporate this concept of being able to calculate the probability of choosing a given member of a population under study. Sampling often involves sophisticated procedures based on mathematical probabilities. But there are always errors in the process of surveying a population. There may be errors in how a population is sampled, but also in how questions are asked, the number of people who refuse to answer a survey, and how the answers are recorded. All of these errors come to affect the reliability of a survey or poll.

While the mathematical formulae may be logically unassailable, how a survey gets to choose a random *1 out of 10* (or 1 out of 1,000, etc.) is the heart of the matter. Thus, for instance, many researchers rely on a list of phone numbers of everyone in the group to be surveyed and randomly choose a portion of those phone numbers to select the interviews that will stand for the whole group's opinions. But every list is limited and prone to missing key groups of the sample. For instance, if those phone numbers are of *land lines*, the survey runs the risk of ignoring the growing number of persons who own only cellular phones. Selecting only cellular phones, on the other hand, might eliminate many senior citizens who prefer the *old-fashioned* phone lines.

In the case of Latinos and Latinas, telephone interviews require Spanish-language capability, since some persons to be interviewed may not speak English fluently. Twenty years ago, when Latinos and Latinas were 5 percent or less of the country's population, those conducting or funding the research project for all of America may have thought that the extra cost to include the Spanish-speaking was an unnecessary expenditure. But the rapid rise in Latino population as a segment of voters and as the largest group of Catholics has rendered that line of thinking obsolete.

To different degrees, survey authors have come to recognize the need for including in their efforts not just Latinos and Latinas who speak English but also those who speak only Spanish. After all, to ignore Spanish-speaking respondents from a survey would present a false rendering of the total population, since so many persons prefer Spanish to English, particularly in the first generation. Consider, for instance, that those who speak only Spanish are more likely to be Catholic than Latinos who speak only English. Thus, surveys that failed to include a Spanish-speaking component—roughly corresponding to 30 percent of all Hispanics—might seriously underreport Catholics.

The data collection process with bilingual and Spanish-speaking capability is more frequently adopted in surveys as we move past the first decade of the twenty-first century. By utilizing the same methodology and Spanish-language formulation of questions, future research will provide greater insight into whether attitudes have changed and if they have, in what ways. For now, it is admirable that past surveys that lacked this Spanish-speaking capability in data collection have addressed the issue of reliability by recourse to weighting their results so as to compensate.

What Is Weighting?

Put in simplest terms, weighting for surveys may be defined as follows: "Weighting is used by researchers to correct for intentional for over- and under-sampling of particular groups and for departure of respondent characteristics from population characteristics due to non-response or other error."[5] There are more technical and detailed definitions of this procedure,[6] and we encourage readers so inclined to consult specialized literature on weighting.

The issue for the layperson, however, concerns the reason for utilizing weighing. The researchers may come to recognize their errors when comparing their methods and findings with other surveys. For instance, the random process may produce a higher percentage of women respondents—say 62 percent—than is reported by the census (52%). The results of the survey may be weighted so that the overrepresented female opinion is diminished in the final assessment while the underrepresented male opinions are augmented. This is poststratification. It relies on another source to adjust the results of the survey according to a recognized over or under strata of the total population.

It is important to stress that such weighting follows mathematical formulae and that the proper use of weighting generally increases rather than decreases the reliability of the survey. Nonetheless, there are aspects of weighting that need critical review when approaching the relatively new field of research on Latino religion. Suppose the weight itself is based on an inaccurate reading of what was over- or underrepresented? In such a case, instead of equalizing the findings and restoring balance, erroneous weighting would exaggerate the differences providing false information.

Here is an example of just such a problem for accurate weighting. As mentioned above, the one-and-a-half generation is constituted by persons born in a foreign country but socialized since infancy in the United States. When gauging language preferences among immigrants, an unwitting researcher may fail to account for this difference and create a false weight in favor of the English language use that distorts the actual importance of Spanish among the first-generation immigrants. For instance, in the collection of data, the first-generation immigrants most likely to speak in English on the phone had been the one-and-a-half generation, raised in the United States. Based on the collected data, it might be presumed that 70 percent of the immigrants watched English-language TV news and 30 percent did not. In actuality, the Spanish-speaking persons not interviewed might watch English-language TV news only 10 percent of the time. Weighting the final results to correspond with a supposed 70 percent favor for English-language TV news might proceed *by the book* but it would be based on a false conclusion. Thankfully, as the CARA report indicated: "The results are consistent: weighting never makes more than a few percentage points difference." But when there was a difference, it tended to reduce the percentage of Catholics.

It is useful to examine the review for key methodological issues as reflected in major surveys of Latinos and Latinas and about their religious preferences. CARA has included these in the Appendix to its report, and it is reproduced here to provide a handy summary for the similarities and differences among the various surveys.

Details on Surveys

1. National Survey of Religious Identification, 1990

Measure of Hispanic Ethnicity: "Are you of Hispanic origin or background?"
Bilingual Interviewing: English only.
Weighting Used: Yes.
Unweighted Proportion of Entire Sample that is Hispanic: 4 percent.

2. American Religious Identification Survey, 2001

Measure of Hispanic Ethnicity: "Are you of Hispanic origin or background?"
Bilingual Interviewing: English only.
Weighting Used: Yes.
Unweighted Proportion of Entire Sample that is Hispanic: approximately
6 percent
Notes: The exact N for valid responses on religious identification is not
available. There were 2,957 Hispanics in the entire sample, with approximately 3 percent refusing the question. The number of "don't know"s is
unavailable.

3. General Social Survey

Measure of Hispanic Ethnicity: The GSS never directly asked about Hispanic
ethnicity until 2000: "Are you Spanish, Hispanic or Latino/Latina?"
Bilingual Interviewing: English only.
Weighting Used: No.
Proportion of Entire Sample that is Hispanic: 7 percent.

4. National Election Studies

Measure of Hispanic Ethnicity: "Are you of Spanish or Hispanic origin or
descent?"
Bilingual Interviewing: Very small numbers of Spanish interviews were conducted through the early 1990s. In 1990, 16 percent of interviews with Hispanics were conducted in Spanish. In 1992, 14 percent were conducted in
Spanish. In 1994, 3 percent were conducted in Spanish. Since 1994, interviewing has been conducted completely in English.
Weighting Used: Yes. We have generated percentages for Table 1 using the
post-stratification variable vcf0009a in the cumulative dataset.
Unweighted Proportion of Entire Sample that is Hispanic: 8 percent.
Measure of Religious Identification: The NES counts those who attend worship
at a congregation of a particular denomination as being affiliated with that
denomination.
Notes: NES respondents are U.S. citizens, which seems likely to screen out
some Hispanic or Latino immigrants. Responses of "don't know" religious
identification are included with "none," so percentages and Ns in Table 1
include some invalid responses.

5. World Values Study

Measure of Hispanic Ethnicity: Analyses in Table 1 are based on respondents who select "Above all, I am an Hispanic American" in response to "Which of the following best describes you?" In the 1999–2000 wave, interviewers also had the option of "Hispanic" in recording a race or ethnicity based on physical observation.
Bilingual Interviewing: The 1999–2000 wave was conducted entirely in English. A very small number of interviews in the 1995–1997 wave took place in Spanish, including 7 percent of interviews with Hispanics.
Weighting Used: Yes.
Unweighted Proportion of Entire Sample that is Hispanic: 6 percent based on the self-identification question (for both waves combined). 8 percent based on interviewer observation in the 1999–2000 wave.
Measure of Religious Identification: Respondents were asked: "Do you belong to a religious denomination?" (If "Yes:") "Which one?" A precise estimate of Protestant or other Christian is unavailable.

6. Religion and Public Life Survey
(Pew Research Center for the People & the Press)

Measure of Hispanic Ethnicity: "Are you of Hispanic origin or descent?"
Bilingual Interviewing: English only.
Weighting Used: Yes.
Unweighted Proportion of Entire Sample that is Hispanic: 6 percent in 2001, 7 percent in 2002, and 11 percent in 2003.
Notes: Religious identification is missing for a rather high proportion (8 percent) of all Hispanics in the 2003 survey.

7. Latino National Political Survey, 1990

Measure of Hispanic Ethnicity: To qualify, respondents had to have at least one parent or two grandparents solely of Mexican, Puerto Rican, or Cuban origin.
Bilingual Interviewing: 60 percent of interviews were conducted in Spanish.
Weighting Used: Yes.
Sampling: Forty primary sampling units consisted of Standard Metropolitan Statistical Areas and groups of rural counties. High density Latino neighborhoods were over-sampled within these primary sampling units.

8. National Survey on Latinos in America, 1999
(Washington Post, Kaiser Family Foundation, Harvard University)

Measure of Hispanic Ethnicity: "Are you, yourself of Hispanic or Latin origin or descent such as Mexican, Puerto Rican, Cuban, or some other Latin background?"
Bilingual Interviewing: 53 percent of interviews were conducted primarily in Spanish.
Weighting Used: Yes.
Sampling: Most of the Latino sample was drawn from five states and the District of Columbia. Further details on the sampling are not available.

9. Hispanic Churches in American Public Life, 2000

Measure of Hispanic Ethnicity: "Do you consider yourself Hispanic or Latino?"
Bilingual Interviewing: The percentage of interviews conducted in Spanish is not available.
Weighting Used: No information available.
Sampling: The sample was drawn from six metropolitan areas and rural areas of two states. Over-samples from high-density Hispanic areas and directory-listed households with Spanish surnames were used.
Notes: The exact N for valid responses on religious identification is not available. There are 1,709 Hispanics or Latinos in the entire sample.

10. National Survey of Latinos
(Pew Hispanic Center, Kaiser Family Foundation)

Measure of Hispanic Ethnicity: In 2002 and 2003: "Are you, yourself of Hispanic or Latin origin or descent, such as Mexican, Puerto Rican, Cuban, Dominican, Central or South American, Caribbean, or some other Latin background?" In 2004, this was changed to read "some other Latin American background?"
Bilingual Interviewing: 57 percent of interviews in 2002 and 2004 and 49 percent of interviews in 2003 were conducted primarily in Spanish.
Weighting Used: Yes.
Sampling: States with high proportions of Latinos were over-sampled, as were telephone exchanges with high Latino population incidence. The 2002 survey included over-samples of Salvadorans, Dominicans, Colombians, and Cubans.
Notes: The exact Ns for valid responses on religious identification are not available for 2003 and 2004. There are 1,508 Hispanics or Latinos in the entire 2003 sample; and 2,288 in the entire 2004 sample.

11. *National Survey of Hispanic Adults*
(The Latino Coalition)

Measure of Hispanic Ethnicity: "What is your national ancestry? If you are not of Hispanic origin, just say so." To qualify, respondents had to give one of the following responses: Mexican, Puerto Rican, Cuban, Dominican, South American, Central American, or other Hispanic.

Bilingual Interviewing: 56 percent of 2001 interviews, 55 percent of 2002 interviews, and 60 percent of 2003 interviews were conducted in Spanish.

Measure of Religious Identification: The question for religious identification apparently did not offer a "none" response, leading to an inflated number of "don't know"s/ refusals. Thus, invalid responses are included in the percentages and Ns in Table 1. A precise estimate of Protestant or other Christian is unavailable.

Weighting Used: No.

Sampling: Published information states that interview selection was "random within predetermined population units . . . structured to statistically correlate with the nation's adult Hispanic population." Our understanding is that the population units were states and that there was no other stratifying of the samples.

12. 2003 CARA Catholic Poll
(Center for Applied Research in the Apostolate)

Measure of Hispanic Ethnicity: "Are you of Hispanic, Latino, or Spanish descent?"

Bilingual Interviewing: 35 percent of interviews with Hispanics were conducted primarily in Spanish.

Unweighted Proportion of Entire Sample that is Hispanic: 9 percent.

Sampling: An epsem RDD sample was used. It was not stratified to produce a higher incidence of Hispanic respondents.

Notes: "Other Christians" were coded from verbatim responses to a question asking those who initially described their religion as "other" to specify it.

   Used by permission of CARA.

Where Do We Go from Here?

The field of religious examination of Latinos and Latinas is a relatively new one. This summary of existing research and the problems encountered ought not to discourage readers from viewing the inclusion of Hispanics as indispensable in framing the political directions within the United States. As the previous chapters in the book have indicated, some key issues have emerged in defining what should be done and what should be avoided in assessing political mobilization among these peoples in the United States.

Notes

1. Texas was annexed after it had been a republic, so for technical legal reasons its history is different from the Mexican territories annexed in 1848. However, the patterns of discrimination against the Latinos in Texas do not differ notably from those in the other regions.
2. This estimate is based on the report of 54 percent of all Hispanic Catholics who are Charismatics: *Changing Faiths: Latinos and the Transformation of American Religion,* 2007, the Pew Forum on Religion & Public Life and the Pew Hispanic Center: Washington D.C., page 31, Figure 3.4.
3. Op. cit. 27–28.
4. Religious Identification Among Hispanics in the United States, second report of the PARAL Study, 2002, pp. 18–20, Tables 6,7, and 8.
5. CARA: "How Many Hispanics Are Catholic? A Review of Survey Data and Methodology," 2005, p. 11.
6. Weighting is the process by which the responses of a group of people within the sample (i.e., the subsample) are assigned a different value that accounts for the representativeness of that subsample within the larger population. Sometimes members of a given group of people within a population are sampled in greater proportion (i.e., with greater probability) than they appear in the population in order to ensure that the internal variations that may exist within that segment of population are properly incorporated into the survey results. However, in order not to skew the total results of the survey, the responses from that subsample may be added to the total at a different proportion (in keeping with their proportion of the population as a whole) than their numbers in the total survey sample may reflect. Thus if a segment of the population is oversampled in a survey (i.e., chosen with greater probability), then the responses of that representative subsample are incorporated at a lower proportional value than the responses of the rest of the sample that was chosen with equal probability. On the other hand, if a sample includes fewer members of a given segment of the population than it is known to exist in the population, then the responses of that smaller segment are given greater proportional value in order to make them representative.

Bibliography

Acuña, R. 1972. *Occupied America: A History of Chicanos*. San Francisco: Canefield Press.

Alegría, R. 1954. *La fiesta de Santiago Apóstol en Loíza Aldea*. San Juan, Puerto Rico: Colección de Estudios Puertorriqueños.

Amenta, E., Bonastia, C., and Caren, N. 2001. "U.S. Social Policy in Comparative and Historical Perspective: Concepts, Images, Arguments, and Research Strategies." *Annual Reviews of Sociology* 27: 213–234.

Bellah, R. N., Madsen, R., Swidler, A., Sullivan, W., and Tipton, S. 1985. *Habits of the Heart: Individualism and Commitment in American Life*. Berkeley: University of California Press.

Bennett, S. 1993. "Civil Religion in a New Context: The Mexican-American Faith of César Chávez." In *Religion and Political Power*. G. Benavides and M. W. Daly, eds. Albany: State University of New York Press, 151–166.

Berryman, P. 1984. *The Religious Roots of Rebellion: Christians in Central American Revolutions*. Orbis: Maryknoll.

Bevans, S. B. 1992. *Models of Contextual Theology*. Maryknoll: Orbis Books.

Bourdieu, P. 1980/1990. *The Logic of Practice*. Translation of *Le Sens Pratique* (trans. Richard Nice). Cambridge, UK: Polity Press.

Brown, T. A. 1988. *Migration and Politics: The Impact of Population Mobility on American Voting Behavior*. Chapel Hill: University of North Carolina Press.

Browning, R. P., Marshall, D. R., and Tabb, D. H. 1984. *Protest Is Not Enough: The Struggle of Blacks and Hispanics for Equality in Urban Politics*. Berkeley, CA: University of California Press.

Burns, G. 1992. "Commitments and Non-Commitments: The Social Radicalism of U.S. Catholic Bishops." *Theory and Society*, 21: 703–733.

Cadena, G. R. 1989. "Chicano Clergy and the Emergence of Liberation Theology." *Hispanic Journal of Behavioral Sciences*, 11(2): 107–121.

Calvo, M. A., and Rosenstone, S. J. 1989. Hispanic Political Participation. San Antonio, TX: Southwest Voter Research Institute, Inc.

Casanova, J. 1994. *Public Religions in the Modern World*. Chicago: University of Chicago Press.

Centeno, M. 2005. "Who Are You?" *Contexts*, 4(1): 56–57.

Chaves, M. 2004. *Congregations in America*. Cambridge: Harvard University Press.

Chesnut, A. R. 2001. *Competitive Spirits: Latin America's New Religious Economy*. Oxford: Oxford University Press.

Conway, M. M. 1991. *Political Participation in the United States*. Washington, DC: Congressional Quarterly, Inc.

Cox, H. 1965. *The Secular City: Secularization and Urbanization in Theological Perspective*. New York: Collier Books.

Csordas, T. J. 1994. *The Sacred Self: A Cultural Phenomenology of Charismatic Healing* Berkeley: University of California Press.

D' Antonio, W., Davidson, J., Hoge, D., and Wallace, R. 1989. *American Catholic Laity in a Changing Church*. Kansas City: Sheed & Ward.

D'Antonio, W. V., Davidson, J. D., Hoge, D. R., and Meyer, K., eds. 1996. *Laity: American and Catholic: Transforming the Church*. Kansas City: Sheed & Ward.

D'Antonio, W. V., Davidson, J. D., Hoge, D. R., and Meyer, K. 2001. *Gender, Generation, and Commitment*. Walnut Creek, CA: Altamira Press.

Dávila, A. M. 1997. *Sponsored Identities: Cultural Politics in Puerto Rico*. Philadelphia: Temple University Press.

Day, J. C., and Gaither, A. L. 2000. "Voting and Registration in the Election of November 1998." *Current Population Report*, U.S. Census Bureau (P20-523RV).

De la Garza, R. O., and Cortina, J. 2007. "Are Latinos Republicans But Just Don't Know It? The Latino Vote in the 2000 and 2004 Presidential Elections." *American Politics Research*, 35(2): 202–223.

De la Garza, R. O., DeSipio, L. L., Garcia, F. C., Garcia, J., and Falcon, A. 1992. *Latino Voices: Mexican, Puerto Rican and Cuban Perspectives on American Politics*. Boulder, CO: Westview Press.

Deck, A. F., SJ. 1995. "A Pox on Both Your Houses: Liberal-Conservative Polarizations from the Hispanic Margin." In *Being Right: American Catholic Conservatives*. M. J. Weaver and R. S. Appelby, eds. Bloomington: University of Indiana Press, pp. 88–106.

Devroye, D. 2003. "Who Wants to Privatize Social Security? Understanding Why the Poor Are Wary of Private Accounts. *Public Administration Review, 63*(3): 316–29.

Diaz, W. A. 1996. "Latino Participation in America: Associational and Political Roles." *Hispanic Journal of Political Science, 18*(20): 154–174.

Díaz-Stevens, A. M. 1993a. *Oxcart Catholicism: The Impact of Puerto Rican Migration on the Archdiocese of New York.* South Bend: Notre Dame University Press.

Díaz-Stevens, A. M. 1993b. "La misa jíbara como campo de batalla socio-política en Puerto Rico." *Revista de Ciencias Sociales,* 3: 139–62.

Díaz-Stevens, A. M., and Stevens-Arroyo, A. M. 1998. *Recognizing the Latino Resurgence in US Religion: The Emmaus Paradigm.* Boulder, CO: Westview Press.

Dionne, E. J., Haskins, R., Bane. M. J., and Mead, L. M. 2003. "Lifting Up the Poor: A Dialogue on Religion, Poverty, and Welfare Reform. A Pew Forum on Religion and Public Life/Welfare Reform and Beyond Discussion." November 21, 2003, Holeman Lounge, The National Press Club, Washington, DC.

Duany, J. 2002. *Puerto Rican Nation on the Move: Identities on the Island and in the United States.* Chapel Hill and London: University of North Carolina Press.

Duany, J., and Matos-Rodríguez, F. V. 2006. *Puerto Ricans in Orlando and Central Florida, Policy Report, 1*(1). New York: Centro de Estudios Puertorriqueños, Hunter College, CUNY.

Ebaugh, H. R. and Chafetz, J., eds. 2000. *Religion and the New Immigrants.* Walnut Creek, CA.: Altamira Press.

Ecklund, E., and Park, J. 2005. "Asian American Community Participation and Religion: Civic Model Minorities?" *Journal of Asian America Studies, 8*(1): 1–21.

Ellwood, D. T. 1988. *Poor Support.* New York: Basic Books, pp. 14–44.

Espinoza, G., Elizondo, V., and Miranda, J. 2005. "Introduction: US Latino Religion and Faith-Based Political, Civic and Social Action." In *Latino Religions and Civic Activism in the United States.* G. Espinosa, V. Elizondo, and J. Miranda, eds. Oxford: Oxford University Press, pp. 3–19.

Estado Libre Asociado de Puerto Rico, Junta de Planificación. 1968. *Informe del estudio para determinar la viabilidad de crear el municipio de Canóvanas, hoy Loíza y restaurar al mismo tiempo el municipio de Loíza, hoy Aldea.*

Feagin, J. R., and Feagin, C. B. 1999. *Racial and Ethnic Relations.* Englewood Cliffs, NJ: Prentice Hall.

Fitzpatrick, J. P. SJ. 1971. *Puerto Rican Americans: The Meaning of Migration to the Mainland.* Englewood Cliffs: Prentice Hall.

Flores, J. 2000. *From Bomba to Hip-Hop: Puerto Rican Culture and Latino Identity.* New York: Columbia University Press.

Fuchs, E. R., Minnite, L. C., and Shapiro, R. Y. 2000. "Political Capital and Political Participation." Paper presented at the 2000 Annual Meeting of the American Political Science Association, Washington, DC.

Fuchs, Ester. R., Shapiro, R. Y., and Minnite, L. C. 2001. "Social Capital, Political Participation and the Urban Community." In *Social Capital and Poor Communities*. S. Saegert, J. P. Thompson, and M. W. Warren, eds. New York: Russell Sage Foundation, pp. 290–324.

Garcia, J. A. 1997. "Political Participation: Resources and Involvement Among Latinos in the American Political System." In *Pursuing Power: Latinos and the Political System*. F. C. Garcia, ed. Notre Dame: University of Notre Dame Press, pp. 44–71.

Ganz, M. 2009. *Why David Sometimes Wins: Strategy, Leadership and the California Agriculture Movement*. Oxford: Oxford University Press.

Gillian, J. P. 1947. "Modern Latin American Culture." *Social Forces*, 25(3): 243–248.

Gimpel, J. G. 1999. *Separate Destinations: Migration, Immigration, and the Politics of Places*. Ann Arbor: University of Michigan Press.

Giusti Cordero, J. A. 1994. *Labor, Ecology, and History in a Caribbean Sugar Plantation Region: Piñones (Loíza), Puerto Rico 1770–1950*. Ph.D. dissertation, State University of New York.

Glasser, R. 1997. *Aquí me quedo: Puerto Ricans in Connecticut*. Middletown, CT: Connecticut Humanities Council.

Glazer, N. and Moynihan, D.P. eds. 1975. *Ethnicity: Theory and Experience*. Cambridge, MA: Harvard University Press.

Gordon, M. 1963. *Assimilation in American Life*. New York: Oxford University Press.

Grebler, L., Moore, J.W. and Guzmán, R. C. 1970. *The Mexican-American People*. Free Press: New York.

Greeley, A. 1977. *The American Catholic*. New York: Basic Books.

Green, J. C. 2004. "The American Religious Landscape and Politics, 2004." Pew Forum on Religion & Public Life. http://pewforum.org/publications/surveys/green.pdf.

Gutiérrez, D. G. 1995. *Walls and Mirrors: Mexican Americans, Mexican Immigrants and the Politics of Ethnicity*. Berkeley, CA: University of California Press.

Halsey, W. M. 1980. *The Survival of American Innocence: Catholics in an Era of Disillusionment, 1920–1940*. University of Notre Dame Press: Notre Dame.

Hamilton, N., and Stoltz Chinchilla, N. 2001. *Seeking Community in a Global City: Guatemalans and Salvadorans in Los Angeles*. Philadelphia: Temple University Press.

Hammond, P. E. 1989. "Religion and Nationalism in the United States." In Gustavo Benavides and M. W. Daly, eds. *Religion and Political Power*. Albany: State University of New York Press, pp. 167–172.

Hanson, Russell L. 1991. "The Political Acculturation of Migrants in the American States." *The Western Political Quarterly*, 45(2): 355–383.

Harris, M. 2000. *Aztecs, Moors and Christians: Festivals of Reconquest in Mexico and Spain*. Austin: University of Texas Press.

Harris, M. 2001. "Masking the Site: The Fiestas de Santiago Apostol in Loíza, Puerto Rico." *Journal of American Folklore*, 114(453): 358–369.

Harrison, L. E. 1997. *The-Pan American Dream: Do Latin America's Cultural Values Discourage True Partnership with the United States and Canada?* New York: Basic Books.

Harrison, S. J. 1985. "Ritual Hierarchy and Secular Equality in a Sepik River Village." *American Ethnologist*, 14: 413–426.

Hasenfeld, Y., and Rafferty, J. A. 1989. "The Determinants of Public Attitudes Toward the Welfare States." *Social Forces*, 67: 1027–1048.

Herberg, W. 1955. *Protestant, Catholic, Jew*. Garden City, NY: Doubleday

Hernández Hiraldo, S. 2006. *Black Puerto Rican Identity and Religious Experience*. Gainesville: University Press of Florida.

Hervieu-Lever, D. 1997. "What Scripture Tells Me: Spontaneity and Regulation within the Catholic Charismatic Renewal." In *Lived Religion in America: Toward a History of Practice*. D. Hall, ed. Princeton: Princeton University Press.

Hirschman, C. 2004. "The Role of Religion in the Origins and Adaptation of Immigrant Groups in the United States." *International Migration Review*, 38: 1206–1233.

Hondagneu-Sotelo, P. 2008. *God's Heart Has No Borders: Religious Activism for Immigrant Rights*. New Brunswick: Rutgers University Press.

Huntington, S. 2004. *Who Are We? The Challenges to American Cultural Identity*. New York: Simon & Schuster.

Hurbon, L. 2001. "Current Evolution of Relations between Religion and Politics in Haiti." In *Nation Dance: Religion Identity, and Cultural Difference in the Caribbean*, P. Taylor, ed. Bloomington and Indianapolis: Indiana University Press, pp. 118–128.

Ignatiev, N. 1996. *How the Irish Became White*. New York: Routledge.

Jansson, B. S. 2001. *The Reluctant Welfare State: Engaging History to Advance Social Work Practice in Contemporary Society*. Belmont, CA: Wadsworth Press

Jelen, T. G. 2003. "Catholic Priests and the Political Order: The Political Behavior of Catholic Pastors." *Journal for the Scientific Study of Religion*, 42(2): 591–604.

Jones-Correa, M., and Leal, D. L. 2001. "Political Participation: Does Religion Matter?" *Political Research Quarterly*, 54(4): 751–770.

Key, V. O. 1949. *Southern Politics in State and Nation*. New York: A.A. Knopf.

Kurien, P. 2004. "Multiculturalism and Ethnic Nationalism: The Development of an American Hinduism." *Social Problems*, 51(3): 362–385.

Laurentin, R. 1977. *Catholic Pentecostalism*. New York: Double Day Press.

Lawson, M. P. 1996. "The Structure of Charismatic Action." Princeton University, Ph.D. dissertation.

Lee, J., and Pachón, H. P. 2007. "Leading the War: An Analysis of the Effect of Religion on the Latino Vote." *American Politics Research*, 35(2): 252–272.

Leighly, J. E. 2001. *Strength in Numbers? The Political Mobilization of Racial and Ethnic Minorities*. Princeton, NJ: Princeton University Press.

Leighley, J. E., and Vedlitz, A. 1999. "Race, Ethnicity, and Political Participation: Competing Models and Contrasting Explanations."*Journal of Politics*, 61(4): 1092–1114.

Lens, V. 2002. "Public Voices and Public Policy: Changing the Societal Discourse on 'Welfare.'" *Journal of Sociology and Social Welfare*, 29(1): 137–154.

Leon, L. 2005. "César Chávez and Mexican American Civil Religion." In *Latino Religions and Civic Activism in the United States*. G. Espinosa, V. Elizondo, and J. Miranda, eds. Oxford: Oxford University Press, pp. 53–65.

Lint-Sagarena, R. 2009. "Migration and Mexican American Religious Life, 1848–2000." In *Immigration and Religion in America: Comparative and Historical Perspective*. R. Alba, A. Robateau, and J. DeWind, eds. New York: New York University Press, pp. 56–70.

Lipset, S. M. 1959. "Some Social Requisites of Democracy: Economic Development and Political Legitimacy." *American Political Science Review*, 53(1): 69–105.

Lipset, S. M. 1960. *Political Man: The Social Bases of Politics*. Garden City, NY: Doubleday.

Liptak, D. 1989. *Immigrants and Their Church*. New York: Macmillan Publishing Company.

Lloyd-Moffett, Stephen R. 2005. "The Mysticism and Social Action of Cesar Chavez." In *Latino Religions and Civic Activism in the United States*. G. Espinosa, V. Elizondo, and J. Miranda, eds. Oxford: Oxford University Press, pp. 35–52.

Lopez, D. 2009. "Wither the Flock? The Catholic Church and the Success of Mexicans in America." In *Immigration and Religion in America: Comparative and Historical Perspective*. R. Alba, A. Robateau, and J. DeWind, eds. New York: New York University Press, pp. 71–98.

Luhmann, N. 1984. *Religious Dogmatics and the Evolution of Societies*. New York: Edward Mellen Press.

Maduro, O. A. 1982. *Religion and Social Conflicts*. Maryknoll: Orbis Books.

McBrien, Richard P. 1983. "Roman Catholicism: E Pluribus Unum." In *Religion and America: Spiritual Life in a Secular Age*. M. Douglas and S. Tipton, eds. Boston: Beacon Press, pp. 179–189.

McGuire, M. 1982. *Pentecostal Catholics: Power, Charisma and Order in a Religious Movement*. Philadelphia: Temple University Press.

McDannell, C. 1995. *Material Christianity: Religion and Popular Culture in America*. New Haven: Yale University Press.

McNamara, P. H. 1973. "Catholicism, Assimilation and the Chicano Movement: Los Angeles as a Case Study." In Rodolfo de la Garza, Z. Anthony Kruszewski and Tomás A. Arciniega, eds. *Chicanos and Native Americans*. Prentice Hall: Englewood Cliffs, pp. 124–130.

McNamara, P. H. 1995. "Assumptions, Theories and Methods in the Study of Latino Religion After 25 Years." In Anthony M. Stevens-Arroyo and Gilbert R. Cadena, eds. *Old Masks, New Faces: Religion and Latino Identities*. New York: Bildner Center Books, pp. 23–32.

Manza, J., and Brooks, C. 1996. "The Religious Factor in U.S. Presidential Elections, 1960–1992." *American Journal of Sociology, 103*(1): 38–81.

Martin, D. 2001. *Pentecostalism: The World Their Parish*. London: Blackwell.

Massey, D. 2004. "Samuel Huntington: Who Are We? The Challenges to America's National Identity." *Population and Development Review, 30*: 543–548.

Menendez, A. J. 2000. "The Catholic Vote: Key to the 2000 Election." *USA Today Magazine*, September, *129*(2664): 10.

Misra, J., and Hicks, A. 1994. "Catholicism and Unionization in Affluent Postwar Democracies: Catholicism, Culture, Party and Unionization." *American Sociological Review, 59*(2): 304–326.

Nelli, H. 1970. *Italians in Chicago, 1880–1930: A Study in Ethnic Mobility*. Oxford: Oxford University Press.

Nichols, H. S. 2001 (30 July). "Reaching Out." *Insight on the News* (Washington), *17*(28):10.

Nietz, M. J. 1987. *Charisma and Community: A Study of Religious Commitment within the Charismatic Renewal*. New Brunswick: Transaction Books.

Nie, N. H., Junn, J., and Stehlik-Barry, K. 1996. *Education and Democratic Citizenship in America*. Chicago, IL: University of Chicago Press.

Oliver, J. E. 2000. "City Size and Civic Involvement in Metropolitan America." *American Political Science Review, 94*(2): 361–373.

Olson, J. 1987. *Catholic Immigrants in America*. Chicago: Nelson Hall.

Oppenheimer, M. 2010. "Marco Rubio: Catholic or Protestant?" *The New York Times*, Nov. 26 http://www.nytimes.com/2010/11/27/us/27beliefs.html.

Orsi, R. 1985. *The Madonna of 101st Street: Faith and Community in Italian Harlem, 1880–1950*. New Haven: Yale University Press.

Paige, S. 2002 (11 February). "White House Leads Welfare-Reform Retreat." *Insight on the News* (Washington), *18*(5): 8.

Paul, P. 2003. "Religious Identity and Mobility. *American Demographics, 25*(2): 20–22.

Peña, M. 1997. "Crossings: Sociological Analysis and the Latina and Latino Religious Experience." *Journal of Hispanic/Latino Theology, 4*(3): 13–27.

Perl, P., and McClintock. J. S. 2001. "The Catholic 'Consistent Life Ethic' and Attitudes Towards Capital Punishment and Welfare Reform." *Sociology of Religion, 62*: 275–299.

The Pew Forum on Religion & Public Life, 2004.

Pew Research Center. 2007. *Changing Faiths: Latinos and the Transformation of American Religion.* Washington, DC: Pew Hispanic Center and Pew Forum on Religion & Public Life.

Pew Research Center. 2007b. "The Renewalist Movement and Hispanic Christianity" in *Changing Faiths: Latinos and the Transformation of American Religion.* Washington, DC: Pew Hispanic Center and Pew Forum on Religion and Public Life. http://pewhispanic.org/files/reports/75.3.pdf

Putnam. R. D. 2000. *Bowling Alone: The Collapse and Revival of American Community.* New York: Simon & Schuster.

Quadagno, J. 1999. "Creating a Capital Investment Welfare State: The New American Exceptionalism (1998 Presidential Address)." *American Sociological Review, 64*(1): 1–11.

Regnerus, M. D., Smith, C., and Sikkink, D. 1998. "Who Gives to the Poor? The Influence of Religious Tradition and Political Location on the Personal Generosity on Americans Towards the Poor." *Journal for the Scientific Study of Religion, 37*(3): 481–493.

Romberg, R. 2003. *Witchcraft and Welfare: Spiritual Capital and the Business of Magic in Modern Puerto Rico.* Austin: University of Texas Press.

Roof, W. C. 1998. "Religious Borderlands: Challenge for Future Study." *Journal for the Scientific Study of Religion* 37(1): 1–14.

Rosenstone, S. J., and Hansen, J. M. 1993. *Mobilization, Participation and Democracy in America.* New York: MacMillan Publishing Company.

Said, E. W. 1979. *Orientalism.* New York: Vintage.

Sandoval, M. 1990. *On the Move: A History of the Hispanic Church in the United States.* New York: Orbis Books.

Scarano, F. A. 1993. *Puerto Rico: Cinco siglos de historia.* Santafe de Bogotá, Colombia: McGraw-Hill Interamericana.

Schaefer, R. T. 2004. *Sociology: A Brief Introduction.* New York: McGraw-Hill.

Schreiter, R. J. 1985. *Constructing Local Theologies.* Maryknoll: Orbis Books.

Scherer, F. F. 2001. "Sanfancón: Orientalism, Self-Orientalization, and 'Chinese Religion' in Cuba." In *Nation Dance: Religion Identity, and Cultural Difference in the Caribbean*. P. Taylor, ed. Bloomington and Indianapolis: Indiana University Press, pp. 153–170.

Shaw, D., de la Garza, R., and Lee, J. 2000. "Examining Latino Turnout in 1996: A Three-State, Validated Survey Approach."*American Journal of Political Science*, 44(2): 332–340.

Skirbekk, V., Kaufmann, E, and Goujon, A. 2010. "Secularism, Fundamentalism, or Catholicism? The Religious Composition of the United States to 2043." *The Journal for the Scientific Study of Religion* 49(2): 293–310.

Starobin, P. 1998 (28 March). "The Daddy State." *National Journal*: 678–683.

Stephens, J. D. 1979. *The Transition from Capitalism to Socialism*. Urbana: University of Illinois Press.

Stevens-Arroyo, A. M. 1995. "Latino Catholicism and the Eye of the Beholder: Notes Towards a New Sociological Paradigm" *Latino Studies Journal* 6(2): 22–55.

Stevens-Arroyo, A. M. 1980. *Prophets Denied Honor*. Maryknoll: Orbis Books.

Stevens-Arroyo, A. M., and Díaz-Stevens, A. M. 1994. *An Enduring Flame: Studies in Latino Popular Religiosity*. PARAL Series, vol. 1. New York: Bildner Center Books.

Stevens-Arroyo, A., Goris, A., and Keysar, A. 2002/2003. "National Survey of Leadership in Latino Parishes and Congregations" (NSLLPC). (Parts I, II and III of the PARAL Study). New York: RISC, Brooklyn College.

Stevenson, R. W. 2004 (20 January). "Bush's Address Will Put Focus on Health Care Proposals." *New York Times*, p. A17.

Taves, A. 1986. *The Household of Faith: Roman Catholic Devotions in Mid-Nineteenth Century America*. Notre Dame: University of Notre Dame Press.

Therrien, M., and Ramirez, R. 2001 (March). "The Hispanic Population in the United States." U.S. Census Bureau. *Current Population Report* (P20–535).

Traverso, S. 2003. *Welfare Politics in Boston, 1910–1940*. Amherst: University of Massachusetts Press.

Tweed, T. A. 1999. "Diasporic Nationalism and Urban Landscape: Cuban Immigrants at a Catholic Shrine in Miami." In *Gods of the City: Religion and the American Urban Landscape*. R. A. Orsi, ed. Indiana: Indiana University Press, pp. 131–154.

Vargas-Ramos, C. 2003. "The Political Participation of Puerto Ricans in New York City." *CENTRO: The Journal of the Center for Puerto Ricans Studies*, 15(1): 40–71.

Verba, S., and Nie, N. H. 1972. *Participation in America*. Chicago: University of Chicago Press.

Verba, S., Schlozman, K. L., and Brady, H. 1995. *Voice and Equality: Civic Voluntarism in American Politics*. Cambridge: Harvard University Press.

Verba, S., Schlozman, K. L., Brady, H., and Nie, N. H. 1993. "Race, Ethnicity and Political Resources: Participation in the United States." *British Journal of Political Science*, 23(4): 453–497.

Voorhis, R. A. 2002. "Different Types of Welfare States? A Methodological Deconstruction of Comparative Research." *Journal of Sociology & Social Welfare*, 29(4): 3–19.

Wallace, R. A. 1992. *They Call Her Pastor: A New Role for Catholic Women*. Albany: State University of New York.

Warner, S. J. 1993. "Work in Progress toward a New Paradigm for the Sociological Study of Religion in the United States." *American Journal of Sociology*. 93(5): 1044–93.

Warner, S. J. 1997. "Religion, Boundaries and Bridges." The 1996 Paul Hanly Furfey Lecture. *Sociology of Religion*. 58(3): 217–238.

Warner, R. S. and Wittner, J.G., eds. 1998. *Gatherings in diaspora: Religious communities and the new immigration*. Philadelphia: Temple University Press.

The Washington Post, Kaiser Family Foundation, and Harvard University. 2000. *National Survey on Latinos* (conducted June 30–August 30, 1999). Menlo Park, CA.

Weber, P. J. 2000. "Catholics and the 2000 Election." *America*, 183(13): 19.

Wiarda, H. J. 1989. *The Transition to Democracy in Spain and Portugal*. Washington, DC: American Enterprise Institute for Public Policy Research.

Wuthnow, R. 1988. *The Restructuring of American Religion: Society and Faith since World War II*. Princeton: Princeton University Press.

Wuthnow, R. 1989. *Communities of Discourse: Ideology And Social Structure in the Reformation, the Enlightenment, and European Socialism*. Cambridge, MA: Harvard University Press.

Wuthnow, R. 1996. "Restructuring of American Religion: Further Evidence." *Sociological Inquiry*, 66(3): 303.

Wuthnow, R. 1998. *After Heaven: Spirituality in America Since the 1950s*. Berkeley: University of California Press.

Wuthnow, R. 2005. *America and the Challenge of Religious Diversity*. Princeton: Princeton University Press.

Zaragoza, E. C. 1995. *St. James in the Streets: The Religious Processions of Loíza Aldea, Puerto Rico*. Drew Studies in Liturgy, no. 2. Lanham, MD, and London: Scarecrow Press.

About the Editors and Contributors

Carlos Vargas-Ramos

Carlos Vargas-Ramos is a research associate at the Center for Puerto Rican Studies (Hunter College-CUNY), where he works on the impact of migration on Puerto Rican political behavior, political attitudes, and orientations. A political scientist by training, his most recent peer-reviewed articles include, "La migración y la resocialización política de los puertorriqueños," which was published in *La Revista de Ciencias Sociales* (summer 2010), and "Migration and Political Resocialization: The Impact of Political Environmental Change on Political Orientations among Puerto Rican Return Migrants" which was published in *CENTRO Journal* (Spring 2011).

Anthony M. Stevens-Arroyo

Professor Emeritus of Puerto Rican and Latino Studies
Brooklyn College and Distinguished Scholar
City University of New York
Widely published both in English and Spanish, he has written more than 50 scholarly articles and authored 10 books. His 1980 book *Prophets Denied Honor* has been called a "landmark of Catholic literature." With his spouse, Ana María Díaz-Stevens, he authored the award-winning *Recognizing the Latino Religious Resurgence*. Topics of his scholarly publications range from contemporary issues such as contemporary religious movements among Latinos to historical perspectives on baroque Catholicism. He has testified before the U.S. Congress and the United Nations and was appointed on three

occasions to state advisory boards for the U.S. Commission on Civil Rights. He was the first director of the Center for Study of Religion in Society and Culture (RISC). In 2008, he was given the Luzbetak Award for Exemplar Church Research by the Center for Applied Research in the Apostolate (CARA) at Georgetown University.

Mark M. Gray

Mark M. Gray is a research associate professor at Georgetown University and the director of CARA Catholic Polls at the university's Center for Applied Research in the Apostolate (CARA). Dr. Gray has a PhD in political science from the University of California, Irvine. His research focuses on culture and politics, political participation, democratization, and religion and politics. Methodologically, he specializes in survey research, trend analysis, and cross-sectional time-series studies. Among the courses he teaches are Introduction to the Social Sciences, Latino/a Culture, and American Cultural Experience.

Samiri Hernández Hiraldo

Samiri Hernández Hiraldo is currently an independent researcher in Puerto Rican and Latino religion, popular culture, and racial identity. She received her doctoral degree in anthropology from the University of Michigan. Author of the well-received *Black Puerto Rican Identity and Religious Experience* (Florida University Press, 2006), she has contributed various articles about Puerto Rican religion to peer review journals in both Spanish and English. She has taught at the University of Puerto Rico, the University of Michigan, and Florida State University. Her next research project is about race and gender in the Puerto Rican popular culture and media.

Matthew T. Loveland

Matthew T. Loveland is assistant professor of sociology at Le Moyne College, where he is director of the Sanzone Center for Catholic Studies and Theological Reflection. His interests are in American religion, Catholic identity and organizations, and civil society. His published work has appeared in *Social Forces, Journal for the Scientific Study of Religion, Sociology of Religion, Review of Religious Research, Interdisciplinary Journal of Research on Religion,* and *Information, Communication, and Society.*

G. Cristina Mora

G. Cristina Mora is originally from Los Angeles and is currently a provost postdoctoral scholar in sociology at the University of Chicago. She earned her BA at UC Berkeley in 2003 and her doctorate degree in sociology at Princeton University in 2009. Her work mainly uses the case of Latin American migration to examine questions of racial and ethnic categorization. She is currently working on a book manuscript concerning the institutionalization of Hispanic panethnicity in the United States. She has also published works on Latino immigrant religious organizations and civic engagement.

Frank Ridzi

Frank Ridzi is associate professor of sociology and director of urban studies at Le Moyne College in Syracuse, New York.

Jillian Ruhland

Jillian Ruhland collaborated in this research while completing her BA in criminology at Le Moyne College in Syracuse, New York. She is also a graduate of the Greater Rochester Collaborative Master of Social Work Program of SUNY Brockport and Nazareth College in Rochester, New York.

Index